To Bertha and Alex

COURTS, LAWYERS AND TRIALS

UNDER THE LAST THREE TSARS

by

SAMUEL KUCHEROV

Foreword
by
MICHAEL KARPOVICH

FREDERICK A. PRAEGER
New York

BOOKS THAT MATTER

Number 7 of PRAEGER PUBLICATIONS IN RUSSIAN HISTORY
AND WORLD COMMUNISM

Published in the United States of America
in 1953 by Frederick A. Praeger, Inc.,
Publishers, 105 West 40th Street,
New York 18, N. Y.

Library of Congress Catalog Card Number 53-6441

Printed in the United States of America

FOREWORD

With the exception of the revolutionary movement, the internal history of Russia during the last half century of the imperial regime has attracted relatively little attention on the part of Western scholars. In the light of the momentous events which began to unfold with the fall of the monarchy in 1917, these decades, with their intermittent attempts at reform, have assumed in the eyes of many foreign observers the character of a brief historical interlude, a mere passing phase in Russia's transition from one form of authoritarianism to another.

Understandable as such an attitude may be, it still must be viewed as a distortion of the historical perspective. In reality, the period in question was one of the most significant in the evolution of modern Russia. It saw far-reaching and substantial changes in Russia's economic, social and even political structure. Without analyzing the tendencies of this evolutionary process and studying its positive achievements, one cannot reach a proper understanding of the Russian Revolution nor can one evaluate the Revolution's effect on Russia's national welfare and progress.

Mr. Kucherov's study deals with one of the most important aspects of this evolution—the changes that took place in the Russian judicial system from the 1860's to the end of the imperial regime. As far as I know, this is the first comprehensive treatment of the subject in any western language. The author begins with a discussion of the great judicial reform of 1864 which he properly treats with reference to its native background as well as in comparison with West European practices and institutions. In the subsequent chapters, he traces the working of the system in the course of the decades that followed, pointing out both its merits and its defects as they were revealed by experience.

While Mr. Kucherov's book contains a wealth of factual information on the Russian courts, judicial procedure and organization of the Bar, it is by no means a specialized technical study. Throughout, the subject is treated within the framework of contemporary political and social developments within the country. The author stresses in particular the important part played by Russian lawyers in the struggle for the rule of law and the protection of the rights of the individual. In this part of the story the reader will find many pages of human, and at times dramatic, interest.

To the fulfilment of this task, Mr. Kucherov has brought not only a thorough theoretical preparation but also an equally thorough practical training. Formerly a lawyer in pre-Revolutionary Russia, he writes of his subject with that intimate knowledge which only personal experience can provide.

Michael Karpovich

Harvard University

AUTHOR'S PREFACE

It seems to me that I owe the reader an explanation as to why I attempt to attract his attention, by this book, to the structure and functioning of institutions which belong to the past and, almost certainly, will never be revived in their previous form.

These are the reasons.

It would not be an exaggeration to assert that Russia has been the object of the greatest attention in the world since 1917, and especially after 1945. All aspects of the Soviet State and the life of its people are being intensively studied. It is, however, impossible to correctly evaluate the contemporary life of a state or of its people without knowing their past. The lack of adequate knowledge of prerevolutionary Russian law and administration of justice has led to erroneous conclusions which can be found in present-day American literature on Soviet Russia.

In 1864, an enlightened Russian Tsar enacted a Judicial Reform which was a masterpiece of legislation in its field and which introduced into autocratic Russia modern judicial institutions and a system of administration of justice based on democratic principles. As a matter of fact, the Laws of 1864 may serve as an example of the possibility of producing radical, almost miraculous changes for the better in the administration of justice—even by establishing institutions which are a complete *novum* for the country.

The son and grandson of this Tsar, in their fight against the drive for freedom in a large section of the prerevolutionary Russian society, distorted the Reform of 1864. But never, even in the darkest years of reaction, did the Russian courts sink to the level of Soviet justice. The unbiased reader must come to the conclusion that the political trials described in this book have nothing in common with the Star Chamber procedure in trials, based on extorted "confessions," which were staged in the Soviet Union. If representatives of the prerevolutionary judiciary, yielding to strong administrative pressure, sometimes deviated from the usual path of integrity and equity, these

vii

cases were exceptions which only confirmed the general rule that the judiciary as a whole stood on a very high moral level.

As for the free Russian lawyer, he retained his right of free speech in tsarist courts throughout the fifty years of his existence, and could and did utter some bitter words of truth to the administration which no modern totalitarian government would tolerate and which certainly are not heard in Soviet courts. The Russian prerevolutionary intelligentsia considered service to the public as its first duty. This recognition was one of the most characteristic features of the Russian intelligentsia. The Russian bar as one of the foremost representatives of the intelligentsia thus served the Russian people with the greatest devotion and selflessness.

I also thought appropriate to express appreciation for the institution of the jury in general and particularly for the Russian jury, which conscientiously performed a difficult task and successfully resisted every attempt to influence its decisions. The jury has been the object of vicious attacks and was abolished in some European countries. In my opinion it is still the best judicial body ever devised by men.

My most cherished desire is to transmit to the reader at least a part of the admiration I feel for the Russian judiciary, lawyers and jury of the 1864-1917 period. If I succeed in this, I shall be greatly rewarded.

I would like to express profound gratitude to the Committee for the Promotion of Advanced Slavic Cultural Studies, which made the publication of this book possible by a generous grant.

I am deeply indebted to V. A. Maklakov for permission to quote from his book *Rechi* and from his speeches in the Duma, and to Mrs. Hélène Krivitsky for authorization to cite passages from books by her grandfather, O. O. Gruzenberg, *Vchera* and *Ocherki i rechi*.

My thanks are extended to the editors and publishers of *The American Slavic and East European Review* for permission to reprint my articles "Administration of Justice Under Nicholas I of Russia" and "The Jury as a Part of the Judicial Reform of 1864 in Russia," and the editors and publishers of *The Russian Review* for authorization to reproduce my article "The Case of Vera Zasulich," as well as to E. P. Dutton and Co., Inc., Publishers, who kindly allowed me to quote from the book *Under Three Tsars* by Elisabeth Naryshkin-Kurakin.

My indebtedness is acknowledged to Dr. V. V. Gsovsky and to Dr. Sergius Yakobson for their valuable suggestions.

Colonel W. Webb of the Library of Congress greatly facilitated my work by putting a study room to my disposal. Mr. Nicholas R. Rodionoff, Mr. and Mrs. John Th. Dorosh, Mrs. Ilze Smits and Mr. N. J. Gregg of the same Library were very helpful in providing me with necessary literature. Mr. Edmund Jahn read the entire manuscript. In the New York Public Library, the staff of the Slavonic Division, especially Mrs. R. Yakhnin and Mrs. A. Heifetz, assisted me very efficiently in the task of collecting literary material.

Samuel Kucherov

Washington, D. C.
Spring, 1953.

TABLE OF CONTENTS

INTRODUCTION

A real understanding and correct appreciation of the magnitude and importance of the Russian Judicial Reform of November 20, 1864, which, among other institutions, brought about the existence of the Russian lawyer, the Russian bar and the jury, requires a consideration of what the administration of justice in Russia was before the Reform.[1]

The system of courts in operation in the period preceding the Reform had developed throughout Russian history. Its immediate background was provided by the judicial reforms of Peter the Great and Catherine II.

The variety of courts was extravagant.[2] Special courts functioned for every class of society. The village and village district administration for peasants, called *volostnye sudy*, also had judicial functions. In some civil suits court jurisdiction was shared by the *gubernskoye pravleniye* (an administrative provincial board). The police was given the right to exact dues in civil cases and carry out inquiries in criminal cases.

The members of all these courts were nearly always elected. The *uyezdny sud* (district court) consisted of an appointed president, two assessors elected by the nobility, and two assessors elected by the peasants. The municipal courts and aulic courts were composed of a burgomaster and two elders, respectively.

The second instance was represented by the civil and criminal tribunals called *Palaty*, which in small towns were combined into one court. In this appellate instance all the members were elected, with the one exception of the president's deputy, who was appointed by the government. The president and two assessors were elected by the nobility, while two assessors were elected by the merchants.

The third instance was the Ruling Senate, consisting of senators appointed by the government.

The procedure was just as complicated and varied as the courts.

---

[1] See S. Kucherov, "Administration of Justice under Nicholas I of Russia," The American Slavic and East European Review, VII (1948), No. 2, pp. 125-138.

[2] District courts, municipal courts, guildhalls, aulic courts, boundary offices, commercial courts and a kind of arbitration court called *sovestnye sudy*, were courts of first instance and of original jurisdiction.

1

It was based on the inquisitorial principle, which itself rested upon the doctrine of "formal evidence." This means that all evidence was strictly evaluated. Thus "the best evidence in the whole world" was considered by the law to be the confession of the accused.[3] Evidence was considered perfect when the statements of two witnesses agreed. If their testimony differed, the law prescribed that preference should be given: (1) to the testimony of a man over that of a woman; (2) to the testimony of a nobleman over that of a non-nobleman; (3) to the testimony of an educated man over that of an uneducated man; (4) to the testimony of a clergyman over that of a layman.[4] If the submitted evidence was insufficient for either a conviction or an acquittal, the accused was left "under suspicion." [5]

The preliminary investigation was entrusted to the police, organized into the *zemsky sud*. This institution consisted of a *zemsky ispravnik, i.e.,* a local police officer; a chief permanent assessor, elected by the nobility; two assessors, elected by the peasants who belonged to the state; and several *stanovye pristava, i.e.,* police officers appointed by the government, who functioned also as assessors. In important cases the preliminary investigation was conducted by a division of the *zemsky sud;* in unimportant ones, by a *stanovoi pristav.*

In towns the *uprava blagochiniya*—a police office—was responsible for the preliminary investigation. It consisted of several *politsmeistery* (chiefs of police), *chastnye pristava* (police officers), and other officials.

The system of judicial administration, with its extravagant diversity of courts and complexity of procedure, made rapid and equitable functioning of justice almost impossible. A. F. Koni[6] gives an idea of the degree of complexity of procedure in which a case could be involved under the old order. A suit or a criminal case which started in a district or aulic court could be submitted to the appellate instance of the civil or criminal *Palata;* then to the corresponding department of the Senate; further, in case of divergence of opinions among the senators, to the General Assembly of the Senate; from the General Assembly, in case a majority of two thirds had not been reached, to the Advisory Board of the Ministry of Justice. From there, the case or the suit had to be sent back to the General Assembly of the Senate together with a conciliatory order from the Minister of Justice to the Chief Prosecutor. If again the majority of two thirds

---

3 *Svod zakonov Rossiiskoi Imperii, Izd. 1857g.,* Vol. XV, Section IV, Art. 316.
4 *Ibid.,* Art. 333.
5 *Ibid.,* Art. 313.
6 A. F. Koni, *Na zhiznennom puti,* II, 268-78, *passim.*

required for a decision was not obtained in the General Assembly of
the Senate, the proceedings were taken over by the Department of
Clerical and Civil Affairs of the State Council. Furthermore, if a
decision could not be reached in the Department, it was the General
Assembly of the State Council which was competent as the next instance. Finally, the decision of the General Assembly of the State
Council had to be confirmed by the Emperor.

No wonder that with such a system or procedure the dilatoriness
in obtaining judgment was extreme. Koni relates, for instance, that
in 1906 he had to take part as senator in a decision of the General
Assembly of the First Department of the Senate in a suit which had
begun in 1869 in a place where the Reform of 1864 had not yet been
introduced.[7] Thus the parties of the suit had awaited the final decision
for thirty-seven years.[8]

At the beginning of the reign of Nicholas I there were 2,000,000
cases awaiting decision, and 127,000 persons were in jail, expecting a
sentence. In 1842, the Minister of Justice submitted to the Tsar a
report, in which it was shown that the number of undecided cases in
all the courts of the empire had increased to 3,300,000.[9]

Elected by the population, the judges were completely unprepared for their profession. N. I. Stoyanovsky asserts that the majority
of judges were illiterate or almost illiterate, not only in magistrate
courts and aulic courts, but also in district courts.[10] Another account
on this subject comes from the pen of A. F. Koni, who began his eminent judicial and scholarly career at the time of the Reform. He writes:

> Law itself sanctioned the composition of courts (magis-
> trate and aulic) in which all the judges were illiterate, prescrib-
> ing that in these cases the decision of the judges must be written
> down by the secretary. In district courts, in which the majority
> of the justices were also illiterate or almost illiterate, the cases
> were almost never reported to the bench. In the second instance
> the decisions were usually made without report by the presi-
> dent's deputy—the only member appointed by the government;
> the other members—perhaps with the only exception of the presi-
> dent—just signed the sentence prepared in advance, which de-
> cided upon the fate of the accused, whom they had never seen.
> . . . In the early forties, among all the members of the seven De-
> partments of the Senate in Petersburg, only six senators had re-
> ceived a university education.[11]

---

[7] *Ibid.*

[8] This reminds one of the story told by Charles Dickens in *Bleak House.*

[9] V. O. Klyuchevsky, *Lektsii,* III, 189-94, *passim.*

[10] Quoted by A. F. Koni, "Pamyati Nikolaya Ivanovicha Stoyanovskago,"
Pravo, 1901, No. 2, p. 54-55.

[11] A. F. Koni, *Na zhiznennom puti,* II, 168-69.

Professor Chubinsky asserts that it is not an invention but a historical truth that sometimes persons were appointed senators who were almost illiterate.[12]

A curious episode is related in the highly interesting memoirs of N. M. Kolmakov, who was for a long time in high positions in courts and in the Ministry of Justice before the Reform:

> Once Count V. N. Panin, Minister of Justice, came into the court in St. Petersburg. Entering the courtroom, he found there only a man in underwear with a broom in his hands. To the Minister's question of where the judge was, he answered that the judge was absent, and to the question: "Where is the assessor?" he replied: "I am the assessor." The Count looked at him, gasped in amazement: "You? . . . Thou? . . . " and without uttering another word, left the room.[13]

The secretary, although not a member of the bench, was the most important person in the court. Upon him depended the issue of the suit in the majority of cases.

A pathetic account of the old courts before the Reform, their justices and procedure, is given by the writer I. S. Aksakov, who was himself in his youth a member of those law courts. He writes:

> Reminiscences, one more revolting than the other, appear before us in spite of ourselves. Through what torments, what anguish our soul had to pass, realizing the impossibility to help justice because of the fetters and nets of the judicial procedure of that time! There, at the bottom, the old chicaner charged with the preliminary investigation is preparing the false basis for the future sentence according to all the formal rules of the law. Then, in the district instance, a bribe-taking secretary, with the venal corroboration of judges elected from among the nobility, or with the help of their no less criminal indifference, manufactures a "memorandum" prompting the judges to pronounce a sentence which is hideous not in its form but in its meaning. Thus, after a delay lasting sometimes many years, the case is, finally, reported to the criminal court, the *Palata,* where a similar fate awaits it. In this higher instance there sit this time jurists, also noblemen, but appointed by the crown. They will not, of course, content themselves with a report, but will examine the authentic documents. But in vain does the member of the appellate court read the records from beginning to end, examining the handwriting, questioning the paper persistently, searching for a vivid indication, "vivid" in a human sense. The paper is silent, soulless, and dead is the official record of the testimony of the accused. It is necessary to hear him, to enter into all the

---

[12] M. P. Chubinsky, "Sudebnaya Reforma," in *Istoriya Rossii v* XIX v. III, 245.
[13] N. M. Kolmakov, "Stary sud," *Russkaya Starina,* LII (1886), p. 533.

psychological aspects and details of the crime. Yes, this is necessary! But the old courts did not give either the right or the possibility to do so. If all the evidence required by the law at that time was presented, and the compliance with the form was unimpeachable, in spite of the reproaches of your conscience, nothing remains except to pronounce a sentence which is an iniquity.[14]

Another aspect of the old judicial administration was the venality of its personnel,[15] beginning with the lowest clerks and extending to the holders of the highest positions. Bribery was widespread among the officials. It was an indefeasible feature of Russian life, a habit, something almost natural. The future Decembrist Ryleyev wrote, in 1821, from the province to his friend Bulgarin in St. Petersburg: "In the capital bribes are exacted only from those who ask for something, here —from everyone . . . Marshals of nobility, judges, assessors, secretaries, and even copyists have permanent income from their robberies." [16]

I. S. Aksakov, in his letters from the province, gives a vivid account of the mores of officialdom there. On May 30, 1850, he wrote from Mologa to K. Sergiyevich:

> My God, how much dullness, triviality, and vileness there is in the life of the society of a small district town. . . .The *gorodnichy* [provost] is a thief and bribetaker. His wife also takes bribes but, nevertheless, is a very attractive woman. The *ispravnik* [chief of the district police] is a still greater thief; his wife, a charming lady, manages the district as if it were her own village. The district inspector, the forester, the commander of the invalids, the official pleader, the secretary, and their wives— are all thieves, superthieves. The whole society of officials lives with pretension in a great style, gives balls and parties with money acquired through bribes.[17]

"No greasing—no motion," says the Russian proverb. Similar proverbs reflecting Russian habits of that time can be quoted by the dozen. N. M. Kolmakov relates in his memoirs that the Minister of Justice, Count Panin, himself had to give a bribe of 100 rubles to an unimportant official in order to accelerate the delivery of a deed which he had executed to the benefit of his daughter.[18]

---

[14] I. S. Aksakov, *Sochineniya*, 1860-1886, IV, 656-657.

[15] On the influence of the court secretaries upon the issue of the case, see the very interesting memoirs of D. N. Bantysh-Kamensky, "Shemyakin sud v XIX stoletii," *Russkaya Starina*, VII (1873), 735-84.

[16] Quoted by N. Dubrovin, "Russkaya zhizn' v nachale XIX veka," *Russkaya Starina*, XCVIII (1899), 71.

[17] I. S. *Aksakov v ego pis'makh*, II, 321.

[18] Kolmakov, *op. cit.*, p. 533

Russian officials found encouragement for their listless attitude in some provisions of the law itself. According to the *Russkaya Pravda,* for instance, if a murderer remained at large, they were allowed to fine to their own benefit the whole community on whose territory the victim's corpse had been found.[19]

Perhaps bribery in Russia was a remainder of the old system of *kormleniye* (feeding), which made the Russian people conscious that the official had to live at the citizens' expense. These officials were called *kormlenshchiki* (the fed). They were not remunerated by the government but lived at the expense of the population which was obliged to pay them dues on various occasions, mostly in kind. Klyuchevsky emphasizes that for the *kormlenshchiki,* their administrative activities was just a source of income, which was the real aim of the "feeding." [20] It is peculiar that the government resorted to the "feeding" of its officials even in the eighteenth century. Empress Cathrine I decreed that in the future some officials of the *prikazy* [21] would be deprived of their salary and should accept from the population the so-called *aktsidentsii* (perquisites). She ordered them to "satisfy themselves by taking from the petitioners for every case as much as they consent to give, in accordance with the old order." [22]

Unquestionably, one of the reasons for this widespread bribery was the miserably low salaries of Russian officials. Whatever the causes of bribery in Russia might have been, it is a fact that bribery assumed monstrous dimensions also among the judicial personnel, at the time preceding the Reform. In his famous "Memorandum" on Ancient and Modern Russia" Karamzin wrote that the officials rob everywhere; fingers are pointed at them, but they receive ranks, ribbons and acquire in two or three years several hundred thousand rubbles and buy land although they had nothing before.[23]

According to the witty statement of a contemporary, bribes raged in Russia "epidemically, sporadically and endemically." [24]

Bribe-taking was not only widespread, but also well organized. A. M. Unkovsky, another high official of the period, relates that bribes were paid by subordinate officials to their superiors. The bribe was a

---

[19] See *Russkaya Pravda, Sinodal'ny spisok:* On homicide.
[20] V. O. Klyuchevsky, *Kurs russkoi istorii,* Part II, p. 437-38.
[21] Government agencies.
[22] *Polnoye sobraniye zakonov Rossiiskoi Imperii, Sobraniye pervoye,* nos. 3231, 4917, 9228.
[23] N. Karamzin, "Zapiska o drevnei i novoi Rossii," *Russky arkhiv,* 1870, p. 2230.
[24] Quoted by I. Blinov, "Sudebny stroi i sudebnye poryadki pered reformoi," in *Sudebnye Ustavy 20 noyabrya 1864 g. za pyat'desyat let* [Hereinafter referred to as *S. U.*], I, 34-35.

kind of contribution imposed on the lower officials by the higher ones, upon whom they depended. If an official refused to submit to this "established order, he had to expect every kind of chicanery, administrative punishment, and even an indictment at the first proper occasion." [25]

The corruption of the old Russian officialdom is masterfully depicted in Russian literature. Justice Lyapkin-Tyapkin, in Gogol's play *The Inspector General*, who boasts that he accepts bribes only in the form of borzoi puppies, and all his bribe-taking and bribe-giving colleagues are literary types familiar to all educated Russians. Also unforgettable are the types afflicted with the same moral disease in the novel *Dead Souls* by the same author. The great Russian satirist Saltykov-Shchedrin has a whole collection of them in his gallery of portraits. The hero of the well-known comedy *Krechinsky's Wedding* by Sukhovo-Kobylin gives an original definition of the bribe which is worth quoting *in extenso:*

> There is a rural bribe, a pastoral one, so to speak. It takes the form of natural products, a fixed quantity per snout. This is not yet a real bribe. There is an industrial bribe, which is taken from profits, contracting projects, inheritance, in one word, from acquisitions. It is based on the axiom: "Love they neighbor as thyself": you acquired something? Share it. Well, this isn't a bribe either. But there is also a criminal bribe, a bribe for being caught in a trap. It is exacted to the point of exhaustion, of nakedness. *It is exacted in the shade of the dense forest of the laws with the help and assistance of the traps, wolves' ditches, and fishing rods of justice disposed in the field of human activity.*[26] And into these ditches one falls, without distinction as to sex, age, rank, intelligence or stupidity, old age or youth, wealth or poverty.[27]

The disorder, the brutality, the arbitrariness, and the corruption of justice and police under Nicholas I were so terrible that, as Herzen correctly remarks: "A common man who is brought to trial fears not the punishment, but the trial. He looks forward with impatience to be sent to Siberia. His martyrdom ends when he begins to serve his sentence." [28]

The doctrine of formal evidence was responsible for another

---

[25] A. Unkovsky, "Novye osnovaniya sudoproizvodstva," *Sovremennik,* 1863, No. 1, p. 403.

[26] Italics mine.—s. k.

[27] Quoted by V. Bochkarev, "Doreformenny sud," in Sudebnaya Reforma [Hereinafter referred to as *S. R.*], I, 215.

[28] A. I. Herzen, *Byloye i dumy,* p. 102.

phenomenon which had unfavorable consequences for the accused: in the majority of cases they were neither condemned nor acquitted, but left "under suspicion," because the formal evidence presented was insufficient, either to pronounce them guilty or to set them free.[29] An average of over twelve percent of all the cases ended in conviction. The percentage of acquittals was correspondingly low, and thus the majority of accused fell under the provision of Article 313.[30]

One of the main defects of the old administration of justice was its complete dependency upon the executive power. This dependency was so strong that courts were considered, according to the expression of Katkov the famous reactionary, "as appendices of the administration." [31]

The famous Third Division of His Majesty's Own Chancellery, which played, under Nicholas I, the role reserved later to the *Okhranka*, exercised a special control over the courts. The chief of staff of the gendarmery,[32] Dubbelt, considered himself free to "restore rights transgressed by the courts." When courts, especially in the provinces, were too slow in rendering their sentences, officers of the gendarmery were sent to them with the order not to leave the town before all delayed sentences were pronounced. Kolmakov relates that once a gendarme arrived at a provincial town with such an order for the president of the *Palata,* which functioned as the court of the second instance; the president thought for a moment, then ordered the files of all pending cases to be brought from his office. Taking the first file, he pronounced the sentence: "The decision of the first instance is upheld," and put the file to the right side of the desk. Then he took the next file and announced: "The decision of the first instance is reversed," and put the file on the left side of his desk. Then he grasped quickly the remaining files one after the other, exclaiming "Upheld," "Reversed," "Upheld," "Reversed," and so on until all the cases were decided in this manner. After this "procedure" was finished, the gendarme left with the report that all the pending sentences in the *Palata* had been pronounced.[33]

The secret inquisitorial procedure, with its soulless records, with its formal evidence evaluated in advance and prescribing the judge's decision, could be nothing else but a source of cruelty and iniquity. The judge was deprived of liberty of decision, and bound by the

---

29 *Svod zakonov, Izd. 1857 goda.* Vol. XV, Section IV, Art. 313.
30 Chubinsky, *op. cit.,* p. 247.
31 Quoted by Kolmakov, *op. cit.,* p. 530.
32 Special police employed by the Third Division.
33 Kolmakov, *op. cit.,* pp. 533-34.

rule of formal evidence. He could not acquit or condemn according to his conviction, but only act in conformity with the scale of value of evidence set forth by law. His sentence, though formally correct, was very often nothing but a flagrant injustice.[34]

As an example of "justice", Aksakov cites the case of landowner X, who raped all his female serfs for fifteen years, proceeding systematically from one family to the other according to the official register. His victims, finally, conspired against him and choked him to death in the field when he came to choose a new victim. Because of the gravity of the crime (serfs killed a nobleman), the women were sentenced to 100 strokes of the whip and forced labor in Siberia. During the preliminary investigation, the noblemen of the district where X's estate was located certified that "the murdered X behaved as it is fitting for a well-born Russian nobleman." [35]

Such was the administration of justice in Russia before the Reform of 1864. The secret and inquisitorial proceedings with their doctrine of formal evidence, the complexity of courts and procedure, the venality and corruption of judges, the complete dependence of the judiciary upon the executive—all these factors combined to reduce the administration of justice to a mere parody of equity.

Speaking in April, 1876, at an anniversary dinner of the St. Petersburg Bar, the famous lawyer and professor V. D. Spasovich said of the law courts of the time preceding the Reform of 1864:

> If one had asked us at that time: what is a court? where is it? we would have been put into an embarrassing position and would not have known what to say. A real law court did not exist, but only an almighty and all-powerful police. . . .The settlement of the case of the accused began and ended with the police. In the meantime, something resembling court proceedings took place only *pro forma,* which consisted in the police records concerning the accused being put on the court table covered with a red or green cloth around which men in gold-embroidered uniforms were seated. These men, without having questioned or seen the accused, would deliberate among themselves about something, decide something, and then send the records back to the police again. It was a court only in name. . .[36]

De Cardonne summarized his impression of the administration of

---

[34] The memoirs of the time are full of examples of such iniquities. Zakhar'in for instance, relates that a manifest murderer was not sentenced because the testimony of the girl who was present during the murder was not perfect evidence according to law. The man confessed to his act later. I. N. Zakhar'in, "Razskazy iz prezhnei sudebnoi praktiki," *Russkaya Starina,* IX (1874), 780.

[35] Aksakov, *op. cit.,* p. 657.

[36] V. D. Spasovich, *Zastol'nye rechi,* p. 12.

justice in Russia as follows: "When Alexander II ascended the throne, the courts were in a most sad condition. The judges sold their decisions shamelessly, trading with property, honor and liberty of the people. In the presence of general corruption of the judiciary, the law often remained on paper, iniquity reigned supreme. Even the name of justice was vilified. Such a situation was at the same time a danger and a scandal in a great empire and was prejudicial to public morality and the national conscience." [37]

Was this lamentable state of things known to the government? Of course; the government was not blind and deaf.

The general dissatisfaction with the administration of justice was clearly expressed in the letters, memoirs, and other writings of the Decembrists which were brought to the knowledge of Nicholas I. In the report of the Commission of Inquiry on the Decembrists which was submitted to the Emperor it is stated that in 1823, in the first deliberation of the secret society in the apartment of Pushchin, special assignments were given to the members. Thus Nikolai Turgenev took upon himself the task of writing on criminal procedure.[38] The Decembrist A. N. Murav'yov notes in his diary (*Mon journal*) that "*publicité dans la procédure judiciaire*" [39] will be introduced after the *coup d'état*, among other liberties and reforms.[40] In the draft of the Manifesto found in the papers of the "Dictator" of the Decembrists' upheaval, Prince S. P. Trubetskoi, publicity of judicial proceedings and the use of the jury in criminal courts were provided for in Articles 14 and 15, respectively.[41] The Manifesto was to be published after the successful seizure of power.

In his ardent letter to Nicholas I from the Fortress of Peter and Paul, the Decembrist Kakhovskoi (one of the five who were executed later) wrote on March 19, 1826: "The safety of the individual and his property are in no way protected. Complete absence of legality and justice prevails in the country. . ." [42]

And in his letter of February 24, 1826, he writes: "I do not know what hinders the government from introducing criminal chambers like those in France and England. . .Why not introduce the jury and base court decisions on conscience and punishment on law?" He

---

[37] C. de Cardonne, *L'Empereur Alexandre II. Vingt-six ans de règne* (1855-1881), p. 512.
[38] M. K. Schilder, *Imperator Nikolai I*, 650.
[39] Publicity in court proceedings.
[40] Quoted by I. V. Hessen, *Sudebnaya Reforma*, pp. 32-33.
[41] M. V. Dovnar-Zapol'sky, *Memuary dekabristov*, pp. 94-95.
[42] P. E. Shchegolev, *Dekabristy*, p. 208.

called the attention of the Tsar to the fact that laws are not clear and incomplete, that one ukase contradicts another and the officials are corrupt.[43]

Furthermore, after the trial of the Decembrists, Nicholas I ordered all the expressions of opinions made by the Decembrists on the internal situation of the empire to be delivered to Borovkov, the secretary of the Commission of Inquiry, who was entrusted by the Emperor with the preparation of a report on the subject. In the concluding words of his report to Nicholas, Borovkov says: "It is necessary to enact clear, positive laws, to establish justice by means of the speediest judicial procedure." [44] According to Count Kochubei, the Tsar often consulted the report and was well acquainted with its contents.[45]

But Nicholas was warned not only by the representatives of the progressive part of Russian society but by men from his own surroundings as well.

In 1828, when Nicholas left for the army which waged the first Turkish war during his reign, a special commission of three persons[46] was created in order to rule the empire in his absence. After the Emperor returned, a report of the Commission was submitted to him on October 16, 1828 in which the Commission stressed the people's expectations of "general and substantial measures." [47] Count Nicholas S. Mordvinov, President of the Department of the State Council, frequently expressed to the Tsar opinions which very often did not agree with the decisions of the government. Mordvinov complained to the Tsar that "the Minister of Public Education says 'it is dangerous to teach peasants to read and write; the Minister of Finance cannot think of anything other than increasing taxes and borrowing money; the members of the State Council are of the opinion that the Russian peasants know how to till the soil better than any learned agriculturist," [48] etc.

Of course, public opinion did not reach the Tsar since public opinion was not allowed to form and publicity was suppressed under the iron heel of censorship.

However, there was an institution which, according to Nicholas' desire, had to replace publicity: it was the Third Division of His Majesty's Own Chancellery! Indeed, the scope of duties of this famous

---

[43] A. K. Borozdin, *Iz pisem i pokazany dekabristov*, pp. 8-9 and 20.
[44] Schilder, *op. cit.*, II, 31.
[45] A. M. Zaionchkovsky, *Vostochnaya voina*, I, 58.
[46] Count Tolstoi, Count Kochubei, and Prince Golitsyn.
[47] Zaionchkovsky, *op. cit.*, I, 66.
[48] *Ibid.*, p. 61.

agency included not only the supervision of the behavior of individual persons, but also of the administration of affairs by other state agencies. In other words, the Third Division had to procure for the government the information which under other circumstances and in other countries is supplied by the press.[49] An example of such supervision in the case of the law courts was given above.[50]

In 1832, Benckendorff, chief of the Third Division, called the attention of the Emperor to the fact that the majority of officials in province agencies did not behave well and were extremely negligent. "Fear of being brought to trial does not affect them," he wrote, "because the courts always let them free—if not in criminal chambers, then in the Senate, in the chancelleries, among which they find powerful sponsors in the person of their colleagues, especially since criminal proceedings are *very long and the sentences do not reach their goals.*"[51]

Thus Nicholas knew that administration of justice in his empire was very deficient. Schilder, in his monumental history of Nicholas' reign, has reproduced his speech in the State Council in 1833. The Emperor said:

> As soon as I ascended the throne, I considered it my duty to direct my attention to various branches of administration, of which I knew almost nothing. Naturally, the main problem which occupied me was the administration of justic. Already in my youth I heard about the lack of adequate laws, or confusion resulting from an exaggerated number of ukases, often contradictory ones. That induced me in the first days of my reign to investigate the work of the Commission for the Formulation of Laws. Unfortunately, the report I received convinced me that its work remained almost completely unproductive. It was not difficult, indeed, to discover the cause which produced this effect: *the lack of results was due mainly to the fact that the administration always resorted to the writing of new laws, whereas it was necessary to set the old ones on a solid foundation.*[52] This induced me to begin with the definition of the aims which must direct the government's activity in the field of legislation. Among the methods proposed to me I chose one, which was directly opposed to the previous ones. Instead of preparing new laws, I gave the order to collect and systematize the existing laws, took the whole matter into my own hands—in accordance with its importance—and discontinued the previous Commission.[53]

---

49 See S. M. Seredonin, *Istorichesky obzor deyatel'nosti Komiteta ministrov,* I, 70.

50 See p. 8.

51 *Ibid.,* p. 71. Italics mine. s. к.

52 Italics mine. s. к.

53 Schilder, *op. cit.,* I, 459-460.

This speech gives a most edifying picture of Nicholas' policy in the matter of reforms. As a typical reactionary, he was afraid of everything new and radical. To retain the old structure as long as possible and to the greatest possible extent, to suppress every attempt to bring fresh air into the musty atmosphere of Russian government administration and public life remained the aim of his entire reign. Its unfortunate beginning, marked by the sound of guns on the Senate Square, the overthrow of the legal dynasty in France, the Polish insurrection of 1830, the political earthquake of 1848 in Western Europe, inspired him to a deep hatred of everything which as much as appeared like a progressive innovation—to say nothing of radical measures.

Nicholas was completely unprepared for the job of autocratic ruler of a tremendous empire. This position came to him unexpectedly, since the renunciation to the throne of his older brother Constantine and the testament of Emperor Alexander I, which proclaimed him heir, were held in secret and were unknown to him. Educated for a military career, without any knowledge of state affairs and of statesmanship, he was aware of his unpreparedness and acknowledged it in a pathetic letter to his brother Constantine, dated November 29, 1827: "Nobody has a greater need for being judged indulgently than I do. Those who may judge me must take into consideration by what unusual circumstances I was raised to the place I occupy now from the position of a newly appointed commander of a division. . ." [54]

In his conversation with the French Ambassador, Count de Laferroné, at the first audience the Emperor gave him on December 20, 1825, Nicholas said: "When one is twenty-nine, dear Count, and under such circumstances as those in which We act, it is permissible to be afraid of the task for which We, consequently, never prepared Ourselves." [55]

However, while claiming indulgence for himself, he made the following promise in the same conversation with de Laferroné: "I will be inexorable. I am obliged to give Russia and Europe a lesson." [56]

This lesson lasted for the thirty years of his reign, and he succeeded in silencing Russia to such an extent that at that time, according to the witty remark of Aksakov, "only silence could be heard in Russia."

As an illustration of how strictly silence had to be kept, the case

---

[54] Zaionchkovsky, *op. cit.*, I, 55.
[55] Schilder, *op. cit.*, I, 346-47.
[56] *Ibid.*

of the famous poem *To Russia* by the Slavophile A. K. Khomyakov, may be cited. This poem was written in March, 1854, on the occasion of the breaking of diplomatic relations with England. Although inspired by high patriotism and Slavophile feelings, it contains violent criticism of the internal conditions of the country in the following lines addressed to Russia:

> Your courts are black with black untruth;
> You are branded with the yoke of slavery,
> Filled with godless flattery, putrefying lies,
> With dead and shameful laziness
> And lowly filth of every kind.

For this poem, which was widely circulated in handwriting, Khomyakov was almost banished from Moscow. The poem was mentioned openly for the first time by Pogodin in his speech on Khomyakov, delivered on November 6, 1860.[57] It was published with other poems by Khomyakov in 1861.

After the death of Nicholas I, the silence was broken. In 1884, describing law courts before the Reform of November 20, 1864, I. S. Aksakov wrote: "The mere reminiscence of them makes one's hair stand on end and one's flesh creep. We have the right to speak thus. The writer of these lines has devoted the best years of his youth to service in the law courts before the Reform. . . .He witnessed the administration of justice at that time on a wide scale in the provinces and the capital. . . .It was, indeed, the abomination of desolation in the holy place." [58]

Aksakov relates how he threw himself with the whole ardor of youthful indignation into the fight against judicial injustice, but in vain.

Certainly Nicholas could have counterbalanced his unpreparedness by the knowledge and experience of people he employed. But such was not his desire. He surrounded himself with servile nonentities whose only aim was to act in the sense of, and in accordance with, the desire of their master. Arakcheyev, Benckendorff, Panin, Dibbich, Lanskoi and hundreds of others were a living confirmation of the truth of the French proverb: "Tel maître, tel valet."

As far as Count Panin, Minister of Justice for thirty years, was concerned, the following episodes sufficiently characterize the whole man. Count Panin introduced the rule of punishing the censors when

---

[57] I. Pogodin in *Russkaya beseda*, II (1860), 15-16.
[58] Aksakov, *op. cit.*, IV, 656.

they occasionally let through an article which he found inadmissible. Once Panin decided to punish a censor. The District Education Curator objected, saying that, first, explanation should be asked from the censor. But the Minister of Justice exercised justice in a simplified manner, by ordering: "First punish and then ask for an explanation." [59] Another example is a case which occurred in the reign of Alexander II. A fourteen-year old boy tried to pay for a loaf of bread in a bakery with a crudely counterfeited coin. The boy was sentenced to 100 strokes of the whip, according to the law. The Senate commuted the punishment to 100 strokes of the rod. However, considering also this punishment to be too severe and not having the power to commute it further, the Senate asked Count Panin to submit, in his capacity of Minister of Justice, a petition to the Tsar, asking him to reduce the penalty to 50 strokes of the rod. Count Panin rejected the request of the Senate because in his opinion the granted commutation was already an abundance of clemency. Alexander II, who happened by chance to be informed about the case, ordered the release of the boy from any punishment.

Dzhanshiyev gives the following characteristics of Count Panin: "A slave at heart, he was at the same time a despot who put the fancies of his extravagant arbitrariness and wicked phantasy higher than law and justice. He was a vehement defender of serfdom, the whip, the branding iron, censorship—in one word, an inveterate conservative, a typical representative of the stupid stagnation which lasted thirty years. . ." [60] According to Hessen, Count Panin was rated as follows by public opinion: "Justice is entrusted to the power of a man whom one half of Russia considers as enemy No. 1 of the fatherland and of every kind of justice, and the other half—as being obviously insane." [61] Nikitenko, Panin's contemporary and a high official himself, who knew the Count intimately, wrote in his diary on February 15, 1860: "The frame of mind of Count Panin is well known. He was constantly opposed to any progress whatsoever. He has the reputation of being first with regard to obscurantism, muteness, lawlessness, and the like." [62]

Another example of Nicholas' official family was Count P. K. Essen, Governor-General of St. Petersburg, about whom Baron Korf wrote in his memoirs: "The complete incapacity and narrow-mindedness of a man who was absolutely uneducated and knew nothing, ex-

---

[59] Nikitenko, *Zapiski i dnevnik*, I, 534-35.
[60] G. Dzhanshiyev, *Epokha velikikh reform*, p. 372.
[61] I. V. Hessen, *Sudebnaya Reforma*, p. 48.
[62] Nikitenko, *op. cit.*, I, 582.

cept writing and reading German and Russian with difficulty, could not have escaped the notice of the clever Emperor. . . .This man. . . was completely in the hands of his . . . secretary of the chancellery, a man without an education but a cold-hearted scoundrel. Personally Essen did not perform any work, not because of lack of diligence but because of complete inability to work. He did not read any papers, and if he did, he did not understand their contents." [63]

In 1843, at a time when Essen was in office, an inspection of the aulic court[64] took place in St. Petersburg. The state of affairs disclosed on this occasion was such that even for that period of general maladministration, the scandal was unusual. The picture of abuses in court drawn by the inspection was so ugly that, as Baron Korf writes, "the members of the State Council. . .were deeply shocked and, so to speak, beside themselves with indignation, although the aged members of the State Council were hardened enough against any kind of administrative horrors by their experience. During the session, the heir to the throne [the future Alexander II], who listened to the report with strained attention, constantly changed his facial expression." [65] Nicholas himself wrote on the memorandum concerning the case: "What an awful shame! The carelessness of the immediate supervisor is incredible and cannot be excused. I am ashamed and afflicted that such disorder could exist almost before my eyes and remain unknown to me." [66]

And what was the result? The small officials were dismissed and replaced by others who stood on the same moral level as their predecessors. And Count Essen? He defended himself with the argument that in other courts which were not under his control, the state of affairs was even worse, and four days after he had been removed from his position he was granted, by Nicholas, the right to wear the emperor's initials on his epaulettes and his salary was restored to him for life.

Nicholas' able officials acted completely in his spirit. Count D. N. Bludov, one of the outstanding jurists of that time, head of the Second Division of His Majesty's Own Chancellery[67] since 1839, to whom the

---

[63] M. A. Korf, "Memuary," *Russkaya Starina*, X (1899), p. 38-39.

[64] The aulic courts were reestablished in 1802 in St. Petersburg and Moscow. Their competence included criminal and civil cases, the latter between non-residents of the capitals and commoners without real estate in the capitals or in the provinces of the capitals, when the cases concerned their personal obligations. The aulic courts were definitely abolished in 1866.

[65] Korf, *op. cit.*, p. 42.

[66] *Ibid.*, p. 43.

[67] The Second Division of His Majesty's Own Chancellery was created on

task of drafting laws was assigned, thoroughly adapted his work to Nicholas' desires, and the laws prepared under his direction were nothing but poor attempts to improve the existing criminal laws and procedure without eliminating the revolting state of affairs in the administration of justice. Under Nicholas I, he completely forgot the time when he had been a founder of the liberal society *Arsamas* and an enthusiastic partisan of Alexander I's liberalism, according to which "only liberal principles can serve as cornerstones of the happiness of peoples." That same Count Bludov, in the beginning of Alexander II's reign, when the wind blowing from the Winter Palace again changed direction, came forward with plans which revealed a complete change in the spirit of their author. Bludov became a propagandist of radical reforms and repudiated the "law of historical development" which was the basis of all the reform measures during the reign of Nicholas I. In his report of 1857, Bludov wrote:

> At first glance one would think that it suffices to limit oneself to some specific corrections in the civil procedure. . .But the more carefully I investigate the problem of the defects of the existing order, the reasons for these defects and—if I may use the word—their sources. . .the more clearly and strongly does the truth appear to me,. . .*i.e.* that we shall not reach the desired and projected goal by specific corrections. . .In order to improve the existing state of affairs adequately, it is necessary to. . .eliminate the causes of the evil, *i.e.*, the roots of the disorders. For this purpose it is indispensable to adopt another system, completely different from the present one, based on those general, immutable principles without which correct civil procedure in the strict sense of the word is impossible. . .To improve this part of our legislation without changing its basic ideas, without accepting principles not only different from those ideas but to some extent even opposed to them, is out of the question. . .[68]

What kind of changes and improvements in the field of legislation were introduced during the reign of Nicholas I? As a consequence of his desire to "set the old laws on a solid foundation," Nicholas ordered Count M. M. Speransky to collect and classify the existing laws. It is only reluctantly that he entrusted that task to Count Speransky. Speransky was the author of the draft of the Code of 1809, and

---

April 26, 1926, in accordance with Nicholas' desire to take the drafting of laws into his own hands.

[68] Quoted by Dzhanshiyev, *Epokha velikikh reform*, p. 369-70. It may be remarked that, in spite of the evolution of his views, Bludov in 1857 was still against the accusatory system, publicity of court proceedings and the jury, the inconvenience of the latter being felt, according to him, "everywhere, with the possible exception of England."

the ideas which inspired him at that time—the time when Alexander I's changeable frame of mind inclined him toward liberalism—made him suspicious to Nicholas. Speaking about Speransky with the first chief of the Second Division of his Own Chancellery, M. A. Balug'yansky, Nicholas said: "See to it that he [Speransky] does not play the same tricks as in 1810; you will be responsible for him." [69]

The work of codification entrusted to M. M. Speransky did not change anything in the court system and its functioning. Speransky collected all the legislation beginning with the *Ulozheniye* of Tsar Aleksei Mikhailovich (1649) and arranged it chronologically in forty-six huge volumes, which were published in 1830 under the title *Polnoye sobraniye zakonov Rossiiskoi Imperii* (Complete Collection of Laws of the Russian Empire). From this material Speransky extracted those laws which were still in force and classified them in fifteen volumes as the *Svod zakonov Rossiiskoi Imperii* (Code of Laws of the Russian Empire), published in 1833. "It is enough," writes Klyuchevsky, "to cast a glance upon the Code of Laws to be aware of its defects. The material extracted from the huge store of Russian legislation is too raw. It is too tremendous to serve as a convenient handbook for individuals and institutions. Speransky himself looked upon it only as a foundation for the future legislative structure." [70]

Nicholas I was greatly interested in the creation of the *Svod zakonov*. Speransky had to report to him every month on the work. The act of confirmation of the *Svod* was very dramatic. In a solemn session of the State Council, Nicholas I held his hand over the fifteen volumes of the *Svod* and pronounced the words: "I confirm."

However, the laws were not observed. So detailed were the provisions of law that it was impossible to abide by them. The *Svod* was based on the system of unlimited tutelage by the state over the individual. All the efforts of the Tsar to create real order were frustrated by the dark injustice of the courts. The laws were violated constantly because of the venal interests of bribers who crowded the judicial institutions.[71]

It is evident that not the improvement of the old system—as Nicholas I desired it—was necessary, but the creation of a completely new judicial system based on new principles, and of a new judiciary—things to which Nicholas did not agree. As a matter of fact, the *Svod*

---

[69] Schilder, *op. cit.*, I, 461.

[70] V. O. Klyuchevsky, *Kurs russkoi istorii*, V, 219-220.

[71] M. I. Sveshnikov, "Gosudarstvennoe znachenie sudebnykh ustavov," *Pravo*, 1899, p. 2293-2296, *passim*.

contained many humane provisions, such as, for instance, the provision that "no one should be deprived of class rights, or restricted in them, without a court sentence for a crime," [72] or the provision concerning the principle of the election of judges. But provisions on individual rights and the people's participation in the administration of justice had no value under a regime based on serfdom.

When Speransky in 1828 tried to have his draft of separation of powers, which he had unsuccessfully proposed to Alexander I in 1809, accepted by the Secret Committee, the draft was rejected by Nicholas I.

In 1839, Count Bludnov succeeded Balug'yansky as Chief of the Second Division. He began to work on the draft of a criminal code. At the same time, work was begun on the draft of a code of civil procedure. In 1843, Bludov requested the members of the judiciary to submit to him considerations on the defects of the laws in operation which revealed themselves in practice. On the ground of those considerations Bludov prepared "suggestions concerning improvement of the Criminal Code." These suggestions, pertaining to minor technical improvements, could not bring about any change in the general character of the criminal laws, but only attenuate their extreme cruelty in some cases. The Criminal Code in the revised edition appeared in 1845. However, even in the case of these very modest improvements, Bludov still had to argue constantly with the Minister of Justice, V. N. Panin, to whom the slightest changes appeared as dangerous innovations. In order to keep Panin out, Bludov asked the Emperor to establish a special committee for drafting codes of criminal and civil procedure. Two such committees were established in 1850 and 1852, respectively. S. I. Zarudny acted as secretary to the committee for civil procedure. He was an astronomer by education and a self-taught jurist, but was destined to become the Minister of Justice of Alexander II and one of the main supporters of the 1864 Reform.

The work of the committees had not yet been completed when Nicholas I died in 1855.

---

[72] *Svod zakonov. Izd. 1857 goda.* Vol. 9, Art. 14.

CHAPTER I

THE JUDICIAL REFORM OF NOVEMBER 20, 1864

A. ENACTMENT OF THE REFORM

With Alexander II on the throne, the way was clear for liberal reforms and reorganizations in Russia. As mentioned above, Bludov did not keep aloof from the requirements of the changed era. In the period 1858-1860, he submitted to the State Council four drafts: a code of civil procedure, statutes concerning lawyers, a code of criminal procedure, and statutes governing the court system.

However, it is only with the liberation of the serfs in 1861 that the period which is called the epoch of the great reforms begins.

All the reforms of the reign of Alexander II, and especially the liberation of the serfs in 1861 and the Judicial Reform of 1864, are undoubtedly interrelated. The Judicial Reform would have been impossible without the liberation of the serfs, and an emancipated people could not have lived under the old administration of justice. The proper functioning of the judicial system is impossible where the majority of the people are deprived of liberty and are merely the object of rights of other people, degraded almost to the level of things. On the other hand, free people need an adequate judicial system. The old courts and their representatives were typical features of the epoch of serfdom. They developed under its shelter to exercise a monstrous abuse of justice and they had to go out of existence with it.

The peasants were liberated from serfdom and consequently from the jurisdiction of their owners. For millions of people new courts had to be created. Thus the necessity for a sweeping reform became evident. The Minister of the Interior wrote in his report to the Tsar in September, 1861: "In order to facilitate the economic revolution which is taking place in European Russia, it is necessary to strengthen economic activity and to foster initiative in various sectors of industry.

It has been acknowledged for a long time that the essential obstacles to this are the defects in our judicial institutions and practice." [1]

S. I. Zarudny, one of the prominent fathers of the Judicial Reform, wrote: "It is difficult to understand why certain opinions develop and are considered not only correct, but even indispensable for the structure of the state, whereas the same ideas, only some days ago, were considered pernicious and destructive for the state order." [2] Certainly Zarudny's remark is very profound. Sudden changes of ideas were not rare in high places in Russia. As a matter of fact, both Bludov—and also Panin, of course—were opposed to the jury system and the accusatory principle up to 1860; furthermore—and this is much more important—their viewpoint was shared by Emperor Alexander II himself. This is stated by Bludov in his letter to Panin dated July 21, 1859.[3] Let us recall, further, that as late as 1858 Alexander wrote the following in the margin of a report of the Minister of the Interior, E. P. Kovalevsky, on the abolition of some restrictions which appeared to the Minister incompatible with progress: "What does 'progress' mean? I demand that this word be not used in official papers." Nikitenko states that the use of this word was prohibited in the press also.[4] On May 31, 1858, Nikitenko notes in his diary: "Here in our country, the movement of regression is becoming evident. . ." [5]

According to Zarudny, "if, in 1861, the peasants had not been liberated with an allotment of land, the Judicial Institutions of November 20, 1864, would never have been confirmed." [6] Dzhanshiyev emphasizes that as long as a single Russian was subject to serfdom, there could be no mention of the "rights" of the Russian citizen. Only at the beginning of 1861 were the first elements of a "legal" order introduced, whereupon an independent court—the main support and safeguard of legality—became the first problem on the agenda of the day.[7]

The definite impulse for the Judicial Reform was given in the fall of 1861, eight months after the Liberation Act. Emperor Alexander returned from the Crimea in September in a very good mood. A

---

1 Pletnev, "Raboty po sostavleniyu proyektov sudebnykh preobrazovany do 1861 g.," in *S. R.*, p. 302.

2 Quoted by Dzhanshiyev, "Sergei Ivanovich Zarudny," *Russkaya Starina* LVII (1888), No. 9, p. 613.

3 See Pletnev, *op. cit.*, p. 301.

4 Nikitenko, *op. cit.*, I, 520 and footnote. According to Alexander's order, the word "progress" was banished from the official vocabulary by a circular of Count Bludov, dated May 15, 1858. See also Dzhanshiyev, *Epokha*, pp. 325-26, footnote.

5 Nikitenko, *op. cit.*, I, 520.

6 Quoted by Dzhanshiyev, "Sergei Ivanovich Zarudny," *Russkaya Starina*, LVII (1888), No. 9, p. 614.

7 Dzhanshiyev, *Epokha*. . ., p. 378.

change in his frame of mind concerning "progress" (compared with his viewpoint expressed in official documents mentioned above and in the press in 1858) now became evident. "The Tsar was happy, with that particular and great happiness which the consciousness of a fulfilled duty and the accomplishment of a difficult but noble mission bequeathed by history, gives to persons ruling over the fate of peoples. The spirit of liberty and humanity. . .in spite of the 'fluctuations' of Russian progress, soared at that time over Russia," [8] wrote Dzhanshiyev.

The Emperor ordered at once that a report on the progress of work on the judicial reform be submitted to him. The report was prepared by the Secretary of State, V. P. Butkov. After having approved it, Alexander ordered Butkov to prepare, together with Count Bludov, a new, more detailed report concerning the sequence in which the various projects were to be examined by the State Council. The new report was approved by the Emperor as early as in October 1861. The Emperor ordered that the State Chancellery, in collaboration with the jurists attached to it, extract the basic principles from this report. At the time, this work was nominally headed by Butkov (Bludov, 77 years old, was relegated to the sidelines), and it was actually conducted by Butkov's deputy, S. I. Zarudny. Furthermore, the following distinguished jurists took part in the project as experts: N. A. Butskovsky, N. I. Stoyanovsky, D. A. Rovinsky, K. P. Pobedonostsev, A. M. Plavsky, P. N. Danevsky, S. I. Shubin and A. P. Velibakhov.

The extracted Basic Principles were ready on January 22, 1862, and they were sent, in the form of a report, to all the members of the State Council. In this report it was made clear that the "Basic Principles" must be examined in the light of "modern science." [9] In the beginning of 1862, Count Bludov was replaced as President of the State Council by Prince P. P. Gagarin, who asked the permission of the Emperor to examine the Basic Principles in the proposed manner.

In January 1862, the Emperor ordered a statement, in general terms, of the deliberations of the State Chancellery, and of the jurists attached to it, on those Basic Principles, "the incontestable qualities of which are now recognized by science and in the practice of the European countries, and in accordance with which the judicial institutions should be reorganized in Russia." [10]

The importance of this order by Alexander II cannot be over-

---

8 *Ibid.*, p. 378.
9 Dzhanshiyev, *Osnovy sudebnoi reformy*, p. 46, and V. D. Nabokov, "Obshchaya kharakteristika sudebnoi reformy," in *S. R.*, I, 306-307.
10 Dzhanshiyev, *Osnovy*. . .p. 47.

estimated. After the dark years of Nicholas' reign, after the fluctuations of the political barometer in the beginning of the new reign, Alexander opened widely the doors to the most liberal principles in the field of the administration of justice, to the utilization of West European experience, which until very recently had still been a scarecrow to his predecessors and collaborators. Indeed, how long ago was it that works of a philosophical nature by West European scholars, and discussions of these works, were forbidden in Russia? Let us remember that in the Code of Laws of 1857, Art. 12 of the Statutes of Censorship prohibited every discussion on the needs and methods of improvement of any sector of the state economy and, in general, on any measure in the field of government action.

In April 1862 the Basic Principles, reworked by the jurists according to the ukase of the Emperor, were discussed in the Departments of the State Council and, on August 27 and September 3 and 4, in the General Assembly of the State Council. The Emperor approved the Basic Principles on September 29, 1862, and then, on the suggestion of S. I. Zarudny, who was the soul of the Judicial Reform, the Basic Principles were published in the Collection of Ordinances and Decrees of the Government, so that the Judicial Reform might be openly and thoroughly discussed by the public.

This measure was without precedent in modern Russian history. Indeed, only ten years had passed since the time when the critical analysis of any law in operation, even in scientific dissertations, was forbidden by the Law of November 2, 1852. This unique appeal to public opinion by Alexander II was a kind of consultative referendum in which everyone could take part, without any distinction as to class or property.

It is self-evident that a few persons only were actually able to participate in such discussions, because the overwhelming majority of the Russian people lacked the special education necessary for this purpose. And still the bare fact of such an appeal directed to the people, including millions of yesterday's serfs, was a phenomenon of extreme significance.

The public was given one month and a half in which to present its suggestions. Suggestions were received from all parts of Russia. They were collected—466 in all—and published in six volumes (about 3,500 pages in folio). A detailed analysis of the suggestions is given by Hessen in his book on the Judicial Reform.[11]

It is peculiar that among the professors only two offered suggestions.

---

[11] Hessen, Sudebnaya Reforma. . .,pp. 79 ff.

One of them was A. M. Bogdanovsky, professor at the Richelieu College. The other was a well-known legal scholar, Chebyshev-Dimitriyev, who began his paper with the folowing words: "The Russian professors of law are hardly capable of giving a weighty opinion on this subject. Indeed, the requirements of science are more or less known to all of us, but the conditions and requirements of Russian life are as obscure to us as the activities of our law courts." The Basic Principles were also widely commented upon in the entire Russian press—in newspapers and periodicals.[12]

However, the six volumes of public suggestions were left almost unused, and public opinion remained without effect upon the shaping of the reform. Hessen writes that in the numerous explanatory notes of the Commission, the Ministry and the State Council, it is difficult to find six to ten quotations from, or references to, the suggestions.[13]

The complicated and difficult task of preparing the drafts of the various codes according to the Basic Principles approved by the Emperor was entrusted to a special commission attached to the State Chancellery. The most outstanding minds in the judicial field were members of the Commission or experts on special topics. The Commission, under the presidency of V. P. Butkov, with S. I. Zarudny as his deputy and *spiritus rector* of the entire work, was divided into three sections: civil, criminal, and judicial. It took only eleven months to complete the work. In the fall of 1863 the Commission submitted the drafts of the Judicial Institutions and the Codes of Civil and Criminal Procedures to the Second Division of his Majesty's Own Chancellery and to the Minister of Justice, D. N. Zamyatin, with explanatory notes on 1,758 pages in folio which, according to Dzhanshiyev, were a chef-d'oeuvre of legislative creation.[14]

The drafts now had to undergo fresh examination. Zamayatin added his own remarks (which fill a book of 500 pages) and collected remarks and suggestions from all the senators and chief prosecutors of the Senate. All this material and the drafts reached the State Council which, as the legislative body, had to decide upon their approval or rejection, in December 1863. The State Council acted upon the drafts with great speed. The drafts passed the Divisions of the State Council and, after a detailed discussion, were finally adopted (with some changes) by the General Assembly of the State Council and confirmed by the Tsar, as the following codes: *Ustav grazhdanskago sudoproizvodstva* (Code of Civil Procedure); *Ustav ugolovnago sudoproizvodstva*

12 *Ibid.*, p. 79.
13 *Ibid.*, p. 108.
14 Dzhanshiyev, *Epokha. . .*, p. 387.

(Code of Criminal Procedure); *Uchrezhdeniye sudebnykh ustanovleny* (Statutes of Judicial Institutions); *Ustav o nakazaniyakh, nalagayemykh mirovymi sud'yami* (Code of Laws on Punishments to be Inflicted by Justices of the Peace).

On November 20, 1864, an Imperial ukase announced the Reform to the Russian people:

> One of Our first desires, expressed publicly in the Manifesto of March 19, 1856, upon Our accession to the throne of Our ancestors, was: 'Let truth and mercy reign in the law courts.'
>
> From that time onward, among other reforms called forth by the needs of the people, We did not cease to be concerned over the achievement of this goal by means of a better organization of the judicial activities . . .
>
> Drafts of Statutes completed in pursuance of . . . Basic Principles by a special Committee established by Us, have now been considered in all details and corrected by the State Council.
>
> After having examined these drafts, We find that they correspond entirely to Our desire to establish in Russia fast, just and merciful courts, equal for all Our subjects; to increase judicial power, to give it the necessary independence and, in general, to strengthen in Our people the respect for law without which public prosperity is impossible, and which must serve as a permanent guide for the actions of all and everybody, from the person of the highest to that of the lowest rank . . .[15]

Concerning this ukase Dzhanshieyev wrote: "Those flaming words deserve to be learned by heart by young people, as the *'carmina'* of the XII Tables were memorized in old Rome." [16]

Thus, the aims of the reform were defined in the ukase of the Emperor. Let us see now to what extent this goal was achieved.

B. FUNDAMENTAL PRINCIPLES

1. *Separation of Powers*

Scholarly tradition considers Montesquieu as the father of the doctrine of separation of powers, although the practical development of the doctrine took place in the American colonies long before *"L'Esprit des lois"* was published in 1746—a fact which induces J. R. Pennock to call this principle "peculiarly American." [17] Whatever the

---

15 *Polnoye sobraniye zakonov. Sobraniye vtoroye,* No. 41473.
16 Dzhanshiyev, *Osnovy. . .,*p. 56.
17 J. R. Pennock, *Administration and the Rule of Law,* p. 11.

case may be, the doctrine as formulated by Montesquieu remains until our days one of the fundamental pillars of a democratic government. He wrote:

> When the legislative and executive powers are united in the same person, or in the same body of magistrates, there can be no liberty, because apprehensions may arise, lest the same monarch or senate should enact tyrannical laws, to execute them in a tyrannical manner.
>
> Again, there is no liberty, if the judiciary power be not separated from the legislative and executive. Were it joined with the legislative, the life and liberty of the subject would be exposed to arbitrary control; for the judge would be then the legislator. Were it joined to the executive power, the judge might behave with violence and oppression.[18]

Thus, according to Montesquieu, the legslative power should be separated from the executive on the one hand, and the judicial power from both legislative and executive, on the other.

The concentration of all three powers in one hand is the characteristic feature of every state in the primitive stage of its development. However, it is also a pertinent feature of the "police state," [19] the state which intrudes in the most complete manner into the life of the individual, and of the autocratic or totalitarian state of our days.[20]

The doctrine of separation of powers was introduced in Russia for the first time by the Reform of November 20, 1864, and dropped again by the Soviet Government.

In the ninth century, the Slavic population of Russia, which was at that time organized in rural cells or united in small town communities, fell under the control of Scandinavian vikings. Thus the origin of the Russian State somewhat reminds one of the founding of the Norman Duchy, the County of Holland or the English kingdoms of Canute the Great and of William the Conqueror.

As the Scandinavian princes and their *druzhiny*[21] gradually adopted the Slavic culture, the state became more unified. However, in the unified State of Holy Vladimir, Yaroslav the Wise and Vladimir Monomakh of the Kievan Period, every prince retained in his hands the

---

[18] Charles de Montesquieu, *The Spirit of Laws*, I, 222.

[19] The German *Polizeistaat*.

[20] The fact that in theory the separation of powers existed in Nazi Germany is irrelevant. In reality the courts and the whole judicial apparatus were under the influence of the ruling party. The Soviet ideology conceives the state as an apparatus of class domination and believes that all branches of government receive their authority from the same source and have the same ultimate aim, differing only in the functions they perform.

[21] Bodyguards.

whole power over his principality. The prince of Old Russia was ruler and judge at the same time, and there was no institution whatever in possession of any power independent of that of the prince. All the officials derived their power from the prince, who, as holder of all powers, could naturally delegate them to various persons.

When in the thirteenth and fourteenth centuries the center of the Russian State was transferred from Kiev to the North and the process of consolidating the Russian lands started around Vladimir and Moscow, the prince, as head of his *votchina*,[22] retained his functions of universal administrator, tax collector and judge. His officials—*boyare, namestniki, tiuny* and *volosteli*—possessed unlimited administrative and judicial powers, which were delegated to them by the prince. These officials were inclined to look after their own interests much more than after the interests of the prince, and looked still less after those of the population. They administered justice accordingly.

It should be emphasized that separation of powers was unknown also to the Russian "republics" of Novgorod and Pskov. There the prince retained his functions as head of the administration, commander-in-chief of the army and judge, even in the period of the worst quarrels with the "free" people of the "republics." Other members of the judiciary were: the *posadnik*, who, apart from his administrative functions (similar to those of a mayor), administered justice together with the prince in important matters; the *tysyatsky*, who commanded the troops, was responsible for the police and dealt, as a justice, with all commercial suits except those which were left to the richer merchants themselves; and the Archbishop, who, in addition to his administrative functions as head of the Church, had jurisdiction over all cases involving the clergy and the duty to comment upon and explain laws in the so-called *doklady* (reports).

In Muscovy, the functions of the highest central law court in civil and criminal affairs were fulfilled by the *Boyarskaya Duma*, which was presided over by the Tsar himself. At the time of Ivan III, the *Duma* was exclusively composed of the highest nobility. Only *Boyare* and *Okol'nichiye* had the right to sit there. But under Ivan IV a new element was introduced into the *Duma*, which received the name of *Dumskiye dvoryane* (Nobility of the Duma).[23] Under the same Tsar, a new system was also inaugurated in the field of local government: he ceased to send officials into the provinces to be remunerated, not by the government, but by the local population. The *kormlenshchiki*

---

22 Patrimonial principality.
23 S. P. Shipov, "Kratkoye obozreniye istorii sudoustroistva i sudoproizvodstva v Rossii," *Vremennik Obshchestva istorii drevnostei rossiiskikh*, XXII (1885) - 6-7.

were abolished, but not the principle of feeding itself, as we have seen above.[24]

Already in the fifteenth century and then in the sixteenth century, steps were taken to protect the local population from the maladministration of the governors. Charters of Regulations, called *Ustavnye gramoty,* and the two codes of laws, *Sudebniki,*[25] give an account of this concern of the government for its subjects. The local population was permitted to take part in the administration of justice provided by the *namestniki* (governors). First in certain districts, and then everywhere, the election of *gubnye starosty* (elders) by all classes of the population was organized. They participated in the administration of justice in criminal cases.[26] The police work was also entrusted to elected officials—*sotniki, pyatidesyatniki, desyatniki* (100th, 50th, and 10th men).

However, even when in some districts almost the whole local administration was transferred into the hands of elected representatives of the population, the administration and judicial powers remained united in the same hands.

In places where the entire local administration was in the hands of representatives of the population, *zemskiye starosty* (local elders), *izlyublennye* (the desired), and *tseloval'niki* (sworn men) were elected, in addition to the *gubnye starosty.* They fulfilled judicial, fiscal and police duties. Where governors or other appointed officials were retained, elected assessors had the duty of countersigning the judgments pronounced by the officials.

The absence of separation of powers prevailed also in the system of the *prikazy* in the period when Muscovy reached the peak of its development. Many territorial *prikazy,* as, for instance, the *Prikaz Kazanskago dvortsa* (*Prikaz* of the Kazan Palace), which managed the affairs of the Tsardoms of Kazan and Astrakhan, and of the towns of the lower reaches of the Volga,[27] had to fulfill judicial functions as well. Further, the *Posolsky prikaz,* in addition to its main function in foreign affairs, also handled disputes between Muscovites and foreigners from all countries—merchants and all kinds of people.[28] The several existing judicial *prikazy* dealt only with a part of the cases, and their jurisdiction was not extended over all Russia.

According to the *Ulozheniye* of Tsar Aleksei Mikhailovich, 1649,

---

[24] See p. 6.
[25] *Sudebnik* of Ivan III, 1497, and that of Ivan IV, 1550.
[26] Klyuchevsky, *op. cit.,* p. 467.
[27]Grigory Kotoshikhin gives a description of all the *prikazy* at the time of Aleksei Mikhailovich in his book, *O Rossii v tsarstvovaniye Alekseya Mikhailovicha,* p. 85-117.
[28] *Ibid.*

the *Boyarskaya Duma* and the Tsar had to decide upon the cases "which for some reasons could not be solved in the *prikazy.*"[29] The majority of cases submitted to the *Duma* were not decided at plenary sessions, but by a special department of the *Duma* called *Raspravnaya zolotaya palata.*[30]

In the seventeenth century, the agent of local administration was the *voyevoda.*[31] In 1606, Pseudo-Dimitry sent *voyevodas* not only to border towns, as usual, but also to almost all the interior towns. Since the *voyevodas* were primarily in charge of the military command, the civil and judicial affairs came under the rule of the military administration. In the same way the *gubnye starosty,* who were elected from the gentry and had to deal with criminal justice, were subordinated to the *voyevodas.* Moreover, the *gubnye starosty,* in addition to their judicial functions, at that time also had to fulfill administrative ones—collecting special duties and serving as deputies of the *voyevoda* in his absence.

The ingenious reformer of the eighteenth century, Peter the Great, could not remain insensible to the needs for a judicial reform. The rationalistic way of thinking was dominant in the West at that time. The ideas of Pufendorf, Hugo Grotius and Hobbes were also penetrating into Russia through the window which Peter opened so widely on Europe.

Peter had at his service two "Europeans" whose function it was to draw up drafts of laws at the request of their master. Fick, one of these writers of drafts, and Count A. A. Matveyev, completed drafts of a judicial reform to create an independent judicial administration in the state, according to the postulates of the new ideas.

This judicial reform was introduced in 1719, then revised in 1722.

The court system was patterned closely after the Swedish model, with the addition of a Senate, which was unknown in Sweden. The courts of first instance consisted of collegiate or provincial courts and courts with a single judge. Over the courts of first instance stood the courts of second instance, consisting of aulic courts with a president and several members. The court of the highest instance was the *Yustits Kollegiya* (Board of Justice), functioning as an appellate court and a court of cassation. This edifice was crowned by the Senate, which in some cases functioned as a court of first instance and in other cases

---

[29] *Ulozheniye Tsarya Alekseya Mikhailovicha 1649* g. Chap. X, Art. 2. *Polnoye sobraniye zakonov. Sobraniye pervoye,* Vol. I.

[30] The Golden Chamber of Justice.

[31] Military Governor.

as a court of the highest instance. To the jurisdiction of the Senate belonged also the general control of the administration of justice.

However, separation of powers was not achieved, because on the one hand the *voyevoda* remained a member of the court, and, on the other, the Senate had both judicial and administrative functions. Nevertheless, some authors consider this reform as an act of separation of powers. Thus Shipov wrote in 1855 about the Reform of 1719 that "this separation of the judicial power from the executive power was a tremendous improvement." [32]

Dzhanshiyev apparently shared Count Bludov's opinion on this reform by Peter I, expressed by Bludov in his report of 1860 to Alexander II, in which he wrote that the reform introduced "a more rational organization of state agencies in general and of the courts in particular." Bludov thought that "Peter strove for the complete separation of the judicial power from the executive power." [33]

Actually, Peter recognized the necessity for separation of powers, but did not achieve it in his reform.

Even this incomplete reform became the victim of the reaction against the innovations of Peter which set in after his death. In 1728, all the judicial cases and investigations were again transferred to the competence of the administrative agents—the *voyevodas* and governors.[34]

The separation of powers remained a vain dream also under the reign of Catherine II, although her *Nakaz* (Instruction), published in 1766, was written under the influence of Montesquieu (half of the five hundred paragraphs are directly borrowed from the French philosopher). The Law of 1775 concerning the administration of the provinces affected the judicial administration also. It was worked out by Semyon Desnitsky, who was co-author of the *Nakaz*. This law introduced class courts for every class of society. According to it, the head of every province, considered as its "boss," had the right to intrude into every sphere of judicial administration. Criminal sentences were submitted for his approval, and it was his duty to supervise the administration of justice in his province.[35]

"The court system of Catherine II," writes Gautier, "is a compromise between the desire to separate the administration of justice from

---

[32] Shipov, *op. cit.*, p. 10.

[33] *Ibid.*, pp. 63, 64.

[34] On the judicial reform of Peter the Great and on the following one of Catherine I, *see* Yu. Gautier, "Otdeleniye vlasti sudebnoi ot administrativnoi," in *S. R.*, I. 188-204, and especially Dmitriyev, *op. cit.*, pp. 440-586.

[35] Shipov is wrong in his opinion that the law of 1775 brought about separation of powers in the provinces. Shipov, *op. cit.*, p. 12.

the executive power, to create a separate court for every class of the population, and to turn the chief of the province into the ear and eye of the sovereign." [36]

In the reign of Alexander I, M. M. Speransky made an attempt to introduce separation of powers into the draft for a new code. In his introduction to the Code of 1809, he wrote:

> The general purpose of this reform is to base and establish the government, which was until now autocratic, upon the rule of law. It is impossible to base a government on the rule of law if the same supreme power formulates the law and carries it out. That is why it is necessary to have institutions which make laws and institutions which execute them. The three divisions of these institutions derive from the threefold character of public power. The first of the divisions must act as a legislative, the second as an executive and the third as a judicial one. [37]

However, Speransky was not allowed to carry out his project. In 1826, under Nicholas I, he tried once more to have his draft accepted by the Secret Committee, but again without success. [38]

Admiral Mordvinov, whose liberal ideas were already mentioned above, wrote in one of his reports to Nicholas I: "The fact that separation of powers represents perfection in government was accepted as an unalterable truth always and everywhere. Legislative, judicial and executive powers have to be separated with regard to their competence and activity . . . The degree and completeness of separation of these three main state powers defines the quality of the government." [39] The attention of Nicholas I was also called to this matter by Secretary of State Balug'yansky in his views on the establishment of provinces, which he submitted to the Secret Committee on December 6, 1826. In these remarks he wrote: "There is no justice under the law without independence of the judicial power from the administrative power. The necessity of separation of judicial affairs from those of the administration cannot be subjected to any doubt in our country. Everyone feels that where the government has the right to order judges to judge this or that case, to review or to suspend the execution of their decisions, there reigns not law but arbitrariness . . ." [40]

The *Nakaz* of 1837 left to the *gubernator* (head of the province) the same rights with regard to the judicial administration as he had according to the Law of 1775. The *gubernator* retained the rights to

---

36 Gautier, *op. cit.*, I. 199.
37 M. M. Speransky, *Vvedeniye k Ulozheniyu 1809 goda*, pp. 30-31.
38 Syromyatnikov, *op. cit.*, p. 179.
39 Blinov, *op. cit.*, p. 54.
40 Quoted by Blinov, *Ibid.*, p. 55.

initiate criminal proceedings, to supervise the preliminary investigation and the procedure in all the courts, and to suspend proceedings. Finally, he had to approve (or reverse) the decisions of the criminal *Palaty* and the lower courts.

In the draft of the reform of civil procedure submitted by Count Panin to the State Council in 1857, and in the 1858 draft of Count Bludov concerning the reform of criminal procedure, there was not a word about separation of powers. On the contrary, the *gubernatory* were invested with the right to approve judicial decisions as before.

There is no doubt that Alexander II and the State Council, as the legislative power of the country, had the desire to separate the administration of justice from the executive and the legislative powers. This clearly appears in the Ukase of the Tsar quoted above and in the minutes of the session of the State Council in 1862, in which the Basic Principles of the Code of Criminal Procedure were examined. When the provision of Art. 5 was discussed in which it was stated that "the judicial power belongs to the court . . . without any participation whatsoever by the administration," [41] only two members of the Council opposed this text. They were Prince Oldenburg and, of course, Count Panin. All other members remained firm, asserting that if the administrative and judicial powers are concentrated in one hand, there is no guarantee that either the administrative or the judicial power will remain within its natural limits, that decisions of the administrative power in judicial cases always inspire distrust on the part of the population, and that every punishment inflicted without judicial decision is considered as abitrariness on the part of the government and provokes grumbling.[42]

The principle of separation of the judicial power from the other powers was proclaimed in Art. 1 of the Basic Principles of the Statutes of Judicial Institutions: "The judicial power is separated from the executive, administrative and legislative powers." [43]

This principle found expression in the provision of Art. 1 of the Statutes of Judicial Institutions, in which all institutions invested with judicial power are listed exhaustively.[44]

Thus, with the exception of the military, clerical and peasant courts, which were regulated by special laws, no institution in the

---

41 *Sudebnye Ustavy 20 noyabrya 1864 goda, s izlozheniyem razsuzhdeny, na koikh oni osnovany, izdannye Gosudarstvennoi kantselyarieyu.* 2. dop. izd. (St. Petersburg, 1867) (hereinafter referred to as *Sudebnye Ustavy.* . .) , Part II: *Ustav ugolovnago sudoproizvodstva,* p. vii.
42 *Ibid.,* p. 24.
43 *Sudebnye Ustavy.* . .Part III: Uchrezhdeniye sudebnykh ustanovleny, p. XLII.
44 *Ibid.,* p. 13.

Empire other than those listed in Art. 1 had the right to exercise judicial power.

The same principle is embodied in some provisions of the Codes of Criminal and Civil Procedure. According to the Code of Criminal Procedure, nobody may be punished for a felony or misdemeanor without a definite judgment of the competent court. Furthermore, Articles 12 and 13 of the Code of Criminal Procedure prohibited the court from suspending criminal proceedings on the ground of incompleteness of the law. Such action of the court was considered similar to "unlawful inactivity of the judicial power." In the Code of Civil Procedure, Articles 9 and 10 prescribed that the court must decide cases according to the strict meaning of the law. However, in cases when the law seemed incomplete, unclear or contradictory, the court was obliged to base its decision upon "the general sense of the law." Thus, the courts received the right to comment on, and supplement, the law. Discussing the provision mentioned above, Shcheglovitov comes to the conclusion that "the statutes adopted the viewpoint that not legislation alone but legislation and the judge together create law for people." [45]

The doctrine of separation of the judicial power was invariably upheld by the decisions of the Senate. As an example, we may refer to Decision No. 606 of the Criminal Department of Cassation of the Senate, in 1869, in the case of Ikonnikov. Upholding the right of the court to review a decision of the police, the Senate ruled that if this right were denied, the court would be obliged to inflict punishment only because it was imposed by the police and required by the prosecutor, and continued in the following words: "Such decisions would not correspond to the substance of judicial power and to the basic principle of separation of the judicial power from administrative power."

How deeply the old conception of the dependence of the judiciary on the administration was rooted in the minds of the bureaucracy and even of the Tsar himself is illustrated by the following episode related by Prince Meshchersky in his memoirs. One year after the Reform, it happened that a very liberal speech was delivered by a Senator at a meeting of the Zemstvo. When the Emperor heard of the speech, he ordered the Minister of Justice, Zamyatin, to remove the

---

[45] Shcheglovitov, "Vliyaniye inostrannykh zakonodatel'stv na sostavleniye Sudebnykh Ustavov 20 noyabrya 1864 g." in *S. U.*, I, 264-265.

This function of the court cannot be compared with the unique right of the American Supreme Courts to nullify legislation on constitutional grounds.

[46] V. P. Meshchersky, *Moi vospominaniya*, I, 429-30.

Senator from his office. Zamyatin had no objections. However, when he gave the order to prepare an ukase to that effect, his attention was called by his subordinates to the fact that the removal of the Senator, as an irremovable judge, was inadmissible according to the new laws. Zamyatin had the unpleasant duty to report to the Tsar that his order could not be carried out. Listening to his Minister's report on the provision dealing with the irremovability of judges, the Tsar exclaimed: "Did I really sign such nonsense?"

The incident is very significant. Perhaps for the first time in Russian history the law conflicted with the will of the autocrat, and the law prevailed.[47]

"In order that the decisions and verdicts of the judges inspire confidence and do not lead to suspect influence on the judge's conscience and particularly pressure from the state power—the same state power of which the judicial power is a branch—and in order that the public be convinced that the court really is the personification of legality and the judge a living expression of justice, it is necessary to separate judicial power and to make it independent, not only of the parties involved in the proceedings, but also of the administration," writes Lazarenko.[48]

Was independence of judicial power achieved by the Reform? This question may be answered affirmatively, but with some reservations. Some gaps were left open in the legislation through which the reaction could—and did—infiltrate. Those gaps were, first of all, the existence of special courts, such as ecclesiastical and military courts and, above all, peasant courts in village districts, called *volostnye sudy*. Of course, the *volostnye sudy* were not very important as far as their competence was concerned, since they tried suits involving not more than fifteen rubles and criminal cases in which punishment could not exceed a fine of five rubles or a confinement of six days. The *volostnye sudy* were introduced by the Reform of 1861 for the liberated peasants and consisted of three judges elected by the population. It is easily understood why these courts could not be included in the new judicial system of 1864,[49] the main reasons being the considerable distance between villages and towns and the poor transportation facilities which made it impracticable for the peasant to make the trip to the justice of the peace for every petty quarrel or case of drunkenness.

---

[47] This is a counterpart to the story told about Frederick II and the miller of Sans-Souci, ending with: "There are judges in Berlin", and to the words of Lord Coke to James I that the King "is under God and law."

[48] Lazarenko, "Ocherk osnovnykh nachal sudoustroistv Rossii i glavneishikh zap. yevropeiskikh gosudarstv," in *S. U.* I, 405.

[49] That was achieved later by the Law of July 15, 1912.

Ecclesiastical courts also had to be retained, since the clergy had its own special rights and privileges which could not be changed by the Judicial Reform. In particular, divorce remained under the jurisdiction of these courts because Russia knew, till 1917, no kinds of marriage and divorce other than those performed by the Church.

Military courts functioned at that time only for persons belonging to the armed forces.

Another gap was the note to Article I of the Code of Criminal Procedure. The provision of this article was duly inspired by the principle "nullum crimen, nulla poena sine lege," but the note reads: "The administrative power takes measures, in the form prescribed by law, in order to prevent and limit the commitment of felonies and misdemeanors." The "preventing" and "limiting" of crimes was interpreted by the administration as a very extensive police power applicable first of all to political matters.

Furthermore, according to the new laws, officials could be indicted, for offenses committed in their official capacity, only with the consent of their superiors. Thus the way to protection and unlawful sheltering was open.

A further reproach which can be addressed to the Reform in matters of separation of power is the fact that the Senate retained three administrative departments along with the two judicial ones.

Complete separation of the judicial power from the executive is achieved only when the field of activity reserved to the judicial power is not defined arbitrarily and when this field covers all the cases which are judicable, without any exception whatsoever. Mere abstention on the part of the administration from interference with the field of activity of the judicial institutions is insufficient, by itself, for realizing definitely the principle of independence of the judicial power.

The defects mentioned above are not important enough to warrant a denial of the fact that separation of judicial power from the two others was achieved in a very high degree by the Reform of 1864.

2. Oral Proceedings

Briefs and other papers were the basis of the inquisitorial procedure. As we know, the judges had to decide on the basis of written material presented by the parties in civil proceedings and by the defendant in criminal proceedings, as well as material gathered by the court *ex officio*. The characteristic feature of the written procedure is the fact that papers play a decisive role in the proceedings.[50] The

---

[50] *Quod non est in actis, non est in mundo.*

judges do not see and hear the parties involved, or the accused. There is no pleading before the court. In place of a living man fighting for his fate or his rights there is a pile of mute, lifeless papers.

Oral proceedings in essence are just the opposite of the principle of written procedure: only that which is orally reported to the court is taken into consideration. For instance, according to the German Code of Civil Procedure of 1877, the parties were obliged to formulate their *Antraege* (motions) orally, and if the *Antraege* were not repeated by the lawyer before the court, they were not taken into consideration. The amendment to the German Code of Civil Procedure, introduced in 1909, attenuated the rigidity of the oral principle inasmuch as the parties (or the lawyers) were permitted to confine themselves to oral references to their written *Antraege*, without repeating their content as was required before 1909.

The new Russian Code of Civil Procedure, dated 1864, introduced a mixed principle: oral proceedings with the taking into consideration of briefs and other papers.[51] The parties were free to appear at the session or to give written explanations; both were permitted. If a party did not appear in court and was not represented at the session of the court, there was no judgment by default to threaten the absent party (as is the case in Germany). The judge, in making the decision, had to consider every previous motion or explanation of the absent party, written or oral.

In criminal cases, the principle of oral procedure found strict application: the testimony of the witnesses and the depositions of the experts, as well as the presentation of all evidence, had to take place orally in open court. The court had to check every fact, and the testimony and evidence collected in the preliminary investigation had to be repeated before the court. The law prohibited the reading of the testimony of a witness who did not appear in court, with the following exceptions only: if the witness did not appear in court because of death, illness, complete senility, remoteness of residence or because of his right to be interrogated at his domicile.[52] In case the witness did appear in court, the testimony he gave in the preliminary investigation could be read only to establish a discrepancy between his testimony in the preliminary investigation and in open court.[53]

---

[51] *Ustav grazhdanskago sudoproizvodstva,* Art. 331.
[52] *Ustav ugolovnago sudoproizvodstva,* Art. 626.
[53] *Ibid.,* Art. 627.

3. Publicity

Publicity of procedure means, first, the extent to which the accused in criminal proceedings is permitted to participate in various phases of the proceedings, and, secondly, the extent to which the public has access to the proceedings. Furthermore, publicity during the preliminary investigation and during the trial must be differentiated.

Only the Anglo-American procedure admits publicity during the preliminary inquiry. All the continental codes exclude the public from attending steps pertinent to the preliminary investigation and more or less exclude the presence of the accused himself.

In Russia the new Laws of 1864 opened wide the doors of the courts to the public, but excluded the public completely from the preliminary investigation and gave to the accused very restricted rights of participation in it. His presence during the hearing of the witnesses and other similar actions in the preliminary investigation was admitted only with the permission of the magistrate in charge of this investigation.[54] The presence of defense counsel was excluded.

And this limitation was adopted against the desire of the fathers of the Reform. Indeed, according to the draft of the Code of Criminal Procedure, the accused and his attorney had the right to be present during all the acts of the preliminary investigation.[55] The State Council excluded the participation of the attorney in the preliminary investigation and limited the rights of the accused.

The trials were open to the public and conducted in the presence of the prosecutor, the accused and his attorney in criminal proceedings, and, in civil suits, of the public, the parties involved, and their lawyers.[56]

The elimination of secret procedure and its replacement by publicity were expressed in Art. 153 of the Statutes of Judicial Institutions, and in Art. 324 of the Code of Civil Procedure which reads: "The report on the case and the oral pleadings of the litigants shall take place in open court."

Provisions which excluded publicity in civil procedure were exhaustively formulated in Articles 325 and 326 of the Code of Civil Procedure. Article 325 reads that publicity may be excluded "if, ac-

---

[54] Special magistrates called *sudebnye sledovateli* (judicial investigators) were in charge of the preliminary investigation under the supervision of the prosecutor. For details see Brazol', "Sledstvennaya chast'," in *S. U.*, Vol. II.

[55] *Sudebnye Ustavy.* . .Part II, p. 128.

[56] *Ustav ugolovnago sudoproizvodstva*, Art. 620; *Ustav grazhdanskago sudoproizvodstva*, Art. 13.

cording to the special features of the case, it might prove to be prejudicial to religion, morals or public order."

Publicity could also be excluded at the desire of both parties.[57]
Further, the Law prescribed the absence of the public in cases when
a challenged judge gives his explanations to the court.[58] Finally, the
public was not admitted in cases when judicial magistrates were sued
for damages due to wrongs committed in their official capacity.[59]

Article 620 of the Code of Criminal Procedure enumerates the
cases to be tried without admission of the public as follows: 1. Blas-
phemy, offenses against sanctity and religion. 2. Crimes against morality. 3. Crimes against the honor and chastity of a female person. 4.
Cases of immoral behavior, unnatural vices, and pandering.

The State Council expressed the opinion that publicity in criminal proceedings in the manner and to the extent provided for in the
Basic Principles contributes to the finding of truth and to the security
of the apprehended; that it leads judges to a careful consideration and
just solution of cases, and that there is no possible doubt as to its
advantages. "Publicity of court sessions is one of the best guarantees
of just actions on the part of the court and one of the main prerequi-
sites for society's confidence in the court," [60] the State Council declared.

According to some authors—A. Karabegov, for instance—publicity
in court is incomplete if the judges do not give reasons for their
opinions publicly, as is the case in England. The duty to give reasons
therefor would, according to these authors, highly increase the sense
of responsibility of the judges and make evident to the public their
ability and conscientiousness.[61] With regard to this question, Odilon
Barrot writes: "It would, no doubt, be possible to compel each judge
to state verbally his reasons for voting the way he did; this rule is
actually applied in some countries [Great Britain and the USA]. This
would make each judge responsible for his vote, but would entail
the serious disadvantage of reducing the weight of the decision by
revealing to the public the diversity of opinions which went to make
up that decision." [62] Jhering is of the opinion that "secrecy of deliberation is one of the most important guarantees of the judges' independence." [63]

The reasons which induced the State Council to prescribe secrecy

57 *Ustav grazhdanskago sudoproizvodstva*, Art. 326.
58 *Ibid.*, Art. 672.
59 *Ibid.*, Art. 1334.
60 *Sudebnye Ustavy*. . .Part II, p. 229-230.
61 Karabegov, *Reforma sudebnykh ustavov*, p. 79.
62 Odilon Barrot, *De l'organisation judiciaire en France*, p. 69.
63 Rudolf von Jhering, *Der Zweck im Recht*, p. 294.

in the balloting of the jury are given in the official message to accompany Art. 677 of the Code of Criminal Procedure. The Council was of the opinion that jurors who voted against the accused must be preserved from his or his kin's vengeance. Jurors should not vote under the fear of such vengeance. "The necessity of keeping secret how each of the jurors voted cannot be denied in Russia, where so many examples exist of the most thorough scoundrels escaping justice because of the fear of their vengeance." [64]

Publicity was highly appreciated by the people. Even the reactionary press considered at the time of the Reform that publicity was one of the most valuable changes brought about by the Reform. In 1876, when rumors concerning possible restrictions in the innovations introduced in 1864 spread among the public, Katkov's *Russkiye Vedomosti* said of publicity in court that it is a principle "which sheds light on everything and which appeals to everyone to participate consciously in the interest of the fatherland and to cooperate in bringing it benefit; a principle without which nothing can develop evenly and fruitfully, nothing can be preserved from decay and rotting, nothing can be protected against abuse and treachery," and concluded by asking whether this principle has entered Russian life, or whether it is only "a spark deprived of reality, a ghost about to disappear?"[65]

On the other hand, there were also fanatic defenders of the old order, who completely denied the value of publicity. S. Barshev, for instance, asserted in his article on the advantages of the inquisitorial procedure over the accusatorial procedure that publicity in court has no sense at all, since the majority of the public present at the trial has not the necessary education to understand what is going on and to exercise control over the judges.[66]

During the debates on the principle of publicity in the State Council, Count Panin dissented. He made a last attempt to exclude publicity at least from the sessions of the Senate, but his efforts remained fruitless.

4. Controversial and Accusatory Principles in
Civil and Criminal Procedures

The *sostyazatel'ny* (controversial) principle in civil procedure, which was adopted by the Code of Civil Procedure, is based on con-

---

[64] *Sudebnye Ustavy.* . ., Part II, p. 246.
[65] Blinov, *op. cit.*, p. 227-8.
[66] S. I. Barshev, "Ob ustnosti i glasnosti v ugolovnom protsesse," *Yuridicheskiye zapiski, izd. Petrom Redkinym*, II (1842).

troversy between two opposing parties. The parties compete before
the bench in order to prove the soundness of their case. The right to
initiate the presentation of evidence, to insist that lawful claims be met
and to give up claims already made, belongs only to the parties. By
virtue of this principle, a civil suit can be started only by having an
interested party bring an action (*nemo judex sine auctore*). The court
may proceed only if asked to do so by a party involved.[67] The court,
again according to this principle, must base its decision only upon evidence presented by the parties involved. Article 367 of the Code of Civil
Procedure reads: "The court itself shall not collect evidence in any
case, but base its decision exclusively upon evidence presented by the
competing parties." Furthermore, the court may not decide matters
regarding which no claim was presented, pass sentence in excess of the
claimant's demands, or raise the question of prescription if such a question has not been raised by the parties.[68] Still, the court is not deprived
of all initiative: for instance, the presiding judge may put questions to
the parties in order to bring about a complete clarification of the case,
and he is obliged to try to bring about a settlement during the whole
proceedings.[69]

The court had the right to initiate local visitations with or without experts,[70] to order an investigation by experts[71] and to ask the
parties to produce further evidence if in its opinion no substantial
evidence had yet been produced.[72] Another exception to the principle
of passiveness of the civil court was the right of the Senate, in civil
cases, not only to reverse the decision, but to quash the proceedings
when it was of the opinion that the courts were not competent to
decide the case, i.e., that the litigation was not subject to civil law.[73]
In such cases, the Senate was obliged to act *ex officio*.[74]

Parallel to the adversary principle in civil procedure is the accusatory principle in criminal procedure. Here, likewise, two parties
confront each other: the prosecutor and the accused. The producing
of evidence and its interpretation is the business of the prosecutor and
the defense counsel, who have, in principle, equal rights, and not that
of the bench, which must restrict itself to the role of an impartial
umpire between prosecution and defense.

---

[67] *Ustav grazhdanskago sudoproizvodstva*, Art. 4.
[68] *Ibid.* Art. 706.
[69] *Ibid.*, Art. 361.
[70] *Ibid.*, Art. 507.
[71] *Ibid.*, Art. 515.
[72] *Ibid.*, Art. 368.
[73] See *Ibid.*, Art. 1.
[74] *Resheniya Grazhdanskago kassatsionnago departamenta Pravitel'stvuyushchago Senata*, 1913, Nos. 10 and 54.

However, these features of the accusatory procedure in their pure form, as they existed in Rome at the time of the Republic, are no longer to be found in the modern codes. The Anglo-Saxon courts approach this ideal to a higher degree than courts of other countries.

The fathers of the Reform of 1864 thought it impossible to entrust the outcome of a criminal case entirely to the parties, to let it depend upon their ability and resourcefulness or mistakes and carelessness. A strictly passive role could not be assigned to the bench in criminal courts, since the aim of criminal proceedings affects public interest and consists in finding the truth and not in the satisfaction of private interests. Striving for this goal, the court cannot take into consideration the desires of the parties, even when the accused does not want to prove his innocence or the prosecutor is lenient toward the accused.

Therefore, the Code of Criminal Procedure did not strictly follow the accusatory (or adversary) principle. The prosecutor was given more rights than the accused, and the court a greater right of initiative than in civil proceedings. With regard to this question, Shirkov thinks that while the independence of the criminal court does not mean a complete return to the inquisitorial system, it is the expression of an "investigational principle" justified by the necessity of finding the material truth in every criminal case.[75] It may be argued, however, that, whereas the inquisitorial principle was retained in the preliminary investigation—which was a great defect of the Reform—the court in criminal cases was *de facto* neither more nor less active or passive than in civil cases. Indeed, the Code of Civil Procedure gave the court the right to ask experts for advice or opinions and to order local investigations on its own initiative (Articles 515 and 507). The criminal court had precisely the same right (Articles 690, 692 and 688 and 689 of the Code of Criminal Procedure).

True, the prosecutor had more rights in the proceedings than the accused or his attorney. The prosecutor was not bound by the deadline prescribed for the accused by Article 557; whereas the accused had the right to summon witnesses at public expense after the expiration of the deadline only in case new circumstances became known,[76] the prosecutor could summon new witnesses at any stage of the proceedings. But this disadvantage of the accused was compensated to a great extent by his right to summon witnesses *at his own expense* at any stage of the proceedings, including those witnesses whose examin-

---

75 Shirkov, *op. cit.*, p. 626-627.
76 *Ustav ugolovnago sudoproizvodstva*, Art. 577.

ation was previously refused by the court,[77] and to demand the hearing in court of all the witnesses who testified in the preliminary investigation.[78]

As far as pleadings were concerned, the rights of the accused and his counsel were in no respect curtailed as compared to those of the prosecutor. The defendant even had a privilege: the "last word" in the pleading always belonged to him.

Thus, it can be asserted that, with the exception of the preliminary investigation, the accusatory principle had been safeguarded to a great extent.

In his pleading before the Criminal Department of Cassation of the Senate in the Case of Olga Palem, N. P. Karabchevsky, one of the most famous Russian trial lawyers, said: "It is known that our criminal procedure has a secret, one-sided, so-called inquisitorial character with regard to the preliminary investigation and up to the time of the opening of the public court session. The defendant, deprived of defense and very often also of liberty,[79] is merely an object of examination and experimentation for the investigating magistrate and the prosecution, and not an individual with all the attributes of a person, with rights of self-defense and self-vindication . . . With the opening of the public session, the picture changes at once . . . The stuffy vaults of the inquisitorial procedure collapse of themselves, as if by a stroke of the magic wand of an invisible, beneficial fairy. Light, publicity and various means of justification for the accused appear at once."[80]

C. JUDICIAL INSTITUTIONS

1. Structure

The Reform of 1864 brought about a salutary simplification of the court system. The former district courts were unified into circuit courts which formed the first instance in civil and criminal cases, with the exception of petty cases which were transferred to the newly created justices of the peace. In the same way, the former *Palaty* were replaced by *Sudebnye Palaty* with civil and criminal divisions, which acted as the second (appellate) instance for civil cases decided by the circuit courts and for criminal cases judged by the same courts without the participation of the jury. The *Sudebnye Palaty* also served as courts

---

[77] *Ibid.*, Art. 576.
[78] *Ibid.*, Art. 574.
[79] The Anglo-Saxon system of bails was not liberally applied in Russia.
[80] N. P. Karabchevsky, *Rechi, 1882-1902*, pp. 293-294, passim.

of first instance in some criminal cases, especially with the participation of class representatives.[81]

The Civil and Criminal Departments of Cassation of the Ruling Senate and their General Assemblies and Joint General Assemblies, were set up as the third highest instance.

The basic function of the Senate was that of a court of cassation. This means that it was concerned with those procedural actions of the courts, and opinions formulated in court decisions, against which complaints in cassation were directed. Unlike the Supreme Court of the United States, it did not decide upon the essence of the case. Hence, if a decision of the *Palata* or of a circuit court in criminal cases with the participation of a jury was reversed by the Senate, the case was remanded to the same or to another court for a new trial, in accordance with the ruling of the Senate.[82]

The Law of June 10, 1877,[83] divided the Departments of Cassation of the Senate into Divisional Benches, composed of three Senators, and Departmental Benches, occupied by seven Senators each.[84] Previous to the enactment of this law, cases submitted to a Department of Cassation were examined by all the members of the Department,[85] and all the decisions were published. According to the Law of June 10, 1877, an appeal in cassation was examined by a Divisional Bench of one of the Departments of Cassation if all that was involved was the application of an existing law in compliance with an already adopted practice of the Senate. When a new interpretation of the law or a deviation from the existing opinion of the Senate became necessary, or if one of the Senators so demanded, the case was referred to a Departmental Bench.

General Assemblies and Joint General Assemblies of both Departments of Cassation functioned as cassation instances (the latter for cases decided by the Special Bench of the Senate, according to Article 1061¹ of the Code of Criminal Procedure),[86] and as appellate (second) instances for cases judged by the Criminal Department of Cassation as a court of first instance without class representatives (cases

---

81 See below, p. 49

82 *Ustav grazhdanskago sudoproizvodstva*, Art. 809 and *Ustav ugolovnago sudoproizvodstva*, Art. 928.

83 *Polnoe sobranie zakonov. Sobraniye Vtoroye*, No. 54471.

84 *Uchrezhdeniye sudebnykh ustanovleny*, Art. 140.

85 The law of June 10, 1877 increased the number of Senators in both Departments of Cassation from 30 to 50. This number was brought to 76 by the Law of June 30, 1913 (49 in the Civil and 27 in the Criminal Departments).

86 The Special Bench of the Senate, created by the Laws of 1872 and 1904, consisted of a President and five Senators selected by the Tsar from among members of any Department of the Senate for a period of one year. The Special Bench had to decide on political cases assigned to it as a court of first instance.

of crimes committed by high officials). Furthermore, the Joint General Assemblies had to rule on differences in questions of competence which arose between civil, military and clerical courts.

The Joint General Assembly of the First Department and of one of the Departments of Cassation formed a Bench to deal with differences in questions of jurisdiction between courts and administrative bodies.[87] The same Bench of the Senate had to answer questions put to it by the Minister of Justice.[88]

Joint Benches of the Senate were created by the Law of June 10, 1877. They consisted of six Senators (two from the First Department and two from each of the Departments of Cassation) and a President, all of them appointed by the Tsar for one year. The Joint Benches had the power to supervise all the judicial institutions in the country, to indict members of the judiciary (with the exception of prosecutors), to transfer cases from one judicial district to another, etc.

The Highest Disciplinary Bench of the Senate was organized in accordance with the Law of May 20, 1885. To it belonged the Presidents of both Departments of Cassation, the Senators of the Joint Bench and four Senators of the Departments of Cassation appointed by the Tsar for one year. One of the Senators of this Bench was designated by the Tsar to be President of this Bench. It functioned as highest disciplinary court for the members of the judiciary.

The Senate also acted *ex officio* in criminal and in civil cases on the basis of its right of general supervision.[89] This right was commented upon by the Senate very extensively. For instance, in its decision in the Case of Olga Palem (1895, No. 15) the Senate deemed it within its competence to check the entire complex of judicial actions and circumstances established by these actions in order to evaluate them from the viewpoint of the "basic purpose of the administration of justice, which is to protect public order and peace and the interests of citizens." In accordance with this viewpoint, the Senate analyzed not only the questions of the proceedings submitted to it in the action for cassation, but took up all the judicial actions in the preliminary investigation, the indictment and the pleadings. It decided that the court had extended its findings to circumstances which had no connection with the offense of the accused, and not only reversed the verdict of the jury and the sentence of the court, but even quashed the indictment.

An analogous attitude was taken by the Senate in its decision con-

---

87 *Uchrezhdeniye sudebnykh ustanovleny*, Arts. 117, 117[1] and 117[2].
88 *Ibid.*, Art. 259[1]. See below, p. 48, Footnote 99.
89 *Uchrezhdeniye sudebnykh ustanovleny*, Art. 249, 250.

cerning the case of B. Prasolov (1913, No. 9).[90] The Civil Department of Cassation of the Senate was similarly entitled to quash the whole proceedings, as we have mentioned above.

It is certain that in such cases the Senate went beyond the limits of "pure cassation" activity. However, it can be argued that the Senate acted in such cases in accordance with its general right of supervision of the administration of justice, which had been conferred upon it separately and apart from its cassation functions by Article 249, §1, of the Statutes of Judicial Institutions.

In the field of cassation, only the decisions of the Departmental Benches of the Departments of Cassation and of the General Assemblies were printed in the Collection of Rulings of the Senate, according to the Law of June 10, 1877, and provided guidance for a consistent interpretation and application of the law. Thus, decisions of the Divisional Benches of the Departments of Cassation were binding only for the case involved and on the court to which the case was remanded, whereas Departmental and General Assembly decisions were applicable to all analogous cases in the future, according to the opinion of the Senate. This opinion of the Senate was especially clearly expressed in the Joint Decision No. 25 of both Departments of Cassation and of the First Department, dated 1903. The Senate ruled: "A clarification [of a law] . . . given by a Departmental Bench of the Civil Department of Cassation and published for the knowledge of everyone . . . must . . . serve . . . as guidance for a consistent interpretation and application of the law . . . up to the time when cases placed before the Senate for its decision . . . will make it necessary to bring new clarification into the same topic. It is evident that such a new clarification must also issue from a Departmental Bench of the Civil Department of Cassation, and not from a Divisional one, in order to have guiding value."

However, the legislative, universally binding character of the Senate's rulings was denied by a number of prominent Russian scholars.[91] Thus, according to Prof. G. F. Shershenevich,[92] decisions of judicial institutions do not have a universally binding character, and therefore cannot be regarded as law sources comparable to legislation and custom. A similar opinion was expressed by Prof. K. Annenkov.[93] Prof. Vas'kovsky wrote that "the Senate has steadily proclaimed the obliga-

---

[90] See N. M. Reinke, "Kassatsionnaya instantsiya" in *S. U.*, II, 316-317.

[91] For pro and con, see P. Orlovsky, "Znacheniye sudebnoi praktiki v razvitii sovetskogo grazhdanskogo prava," *Sovetskoye gosudarstvo i pravo*, 1940, No. 8-9, pp. 91-97.

[92] G. F. Shershenevich, "Primeneniye norm prava," *Zhurnal ministerstva yustitsii*, 1903, No. 1, pp. 63 ff., and *Uchebnik russkago grazhdanskago prava*, I, 42.

[93] K. Annenkov *Sistema russkago grazhdanskago prava*, I, 36.

tion to follow its interpretations in all analogous cases, but the Senate itself fails to observe these interpretations, making completely different comments on the same subject or returning again to viewpoints previously abandoned; it is displaying an instability of opinions which only embarrasses the courts by arousing doubts as to which opinion of the Senate they should adhere to." [94]

On the other hand, some other eminent Russian jurists supported the opinion of the Senate, as, for instance, Prof. D. D. Grimm [95] and especially Prof. S. A. Muromtsev.[96] Both were of the opinion that court practice serves as a source of law together with legislation and custom.

It seems that the truth lies, as is often the case, midway between the opposing opinions. Thus, Prof. N. M. Korkunov, assigning to judicial practice a place among other sources of law, thinks that this place is not of the same importance as those of legislation and custom. He writes: "Admitting judicial practice as an independent source of law, we must make a reservation to the extent that this [assertion] must not be understood in the sense that a decision once taken by a court in a controversial question unconditionally binds the court in the future." [97] Prof. Yu. S. Gambarov's opinion is that judicial practice, although having a great influence on the development of law, differs from legislation and custom as a source of law, because it has no "formal binding character." [98]

It seems evident that if the rulings of the Senate had binding power for the case at hand, they had only "guiding value" for decisions in similar cases in the future. The guiding character of the decisions of the Senate did not prevent the courts from deviating from the opinion of the Senate. If such a deviating decision reached the Senate, it could uphold its previous ruling, reprimand the court for not having observed it, and remand the case; but it also often happened that the Senate reversed its previous opinion on the question involved and upheld the decision of the court. Hence, rulings by the Senate, and judicial practice, cannot be regarded as a full-fledged source of pre-revolutionary Russian law, similar to legislation and custom. The Senate was only interpreting and clarifying the existing laws. Certainly, as has already been emphasized, every Russian court

---

94 E. V. Vas'kovsky, Kurs grazhdanskago protsessa, I, 216. For an example of fluctuation in the decision of the Senate, see below, pp. 66 ff.

59 Grimm, "K voprosu o ponyatii i istochnike obyazatel'nosti juridicheskikh norm," Zhurnal ministerstva yustitsii, 1896, No. 6.

96 S. A. Muromtsev, "Sud i zakon v grazhdanskom prave," Yuridichesky Vestnik, 1880, No. 11.

97 N. M. Korkunov, Lektsii po obshchei teorii prava, p. 298.

98 Yu. S. Gambarov, Kurs grazhdanskago prava, I, 340.

had a kind of law-making capacity, since it was obliged, according to Art. 12 of the Code of Criminal Procedure and Art. 9 of the Code of Civil Procedure, to decide every case submitted to it which fell under its jurisdiction, including those cases to which it could not apply an appropriate legal provision. But it is not correct to describe such decisions as a source of law, since nothing prevented another court from deciding differently in an analogous case.

It must be remarked that the Senate itself was very cautious not to interfere in the domain of legislation or engage in law-making activity. This is evident from the fact that the Senate declined to answer "questions" by the Minister of Justice when it did not find an appropriate basis for an answer in the provisions of existing laws or in the general spirit of those laws.[99]

Thus, V. Gsovski is exaggerating somewhat when he writes: "As a result [of the rulings of the Senate], the private law applied by the Russian courts on the eve of the Revolution was to a large extent judge-made law, a law of judicial precedent. Hence it may be argued that in this respect the imperial Russian private law is comparable to the Anglo-American law, in spite of the civil law background."[100] Gsovski attributes to the rulings of the Senate a greater law-making importance than they actually had;[101] there is not enough reason to compare in this respect the sources of Anglo-American private law, which is almost exclusively judge-made law, with Russian imperial private law, which is almost exclusively code law.

In addition to the Departments of Cassation, the Senate had three other separate Departments: the First Department, which was competent in cases arising in provinces of the Empire where the Reform of 1864 had not yet been introduced; the Second Department of Boundaries; and the Department of Heraldry.

The circuit courts, the *Palaty* and the Senate were provided with prosecutors[102] (called Chief Prosecutor in the Senate). The prosecutors were subordinate to the Minister of Justice, who had the title of General Prosecutor.

Bars of lawyers were established for civil and criminal cases. They

---

99 According to Art. 259¹ of the Statutes of Judicial Institutions the Minister of Justice had the right to ask the Senate for clarification of legal questions which aroused doubts in the practice of the courts and were differently resolved by them. For a list of refusals of the Senate to answer questions see Reinke, *op. cit.*, p. 306. An answer to such a question is quoted below, p. 276.
100 V. V. Gsovski, *Soviet Civil Law*, I, 258-259.
101 Gsovski does not mention the difference between Divisional decisions, on the one hand, and Departmental and General Assembly decisions, on the other, with respect to their binding character.
102 Known also as procurators.

were attached to the *Sudebnye Palaty* and functioned under their supervision.

The court system after the Reform of 1864 and up to the October Revolution is shown in the following table.

GENERAL COURTS

First Instance	Second Instance	Third Instance
Justice of the Peace	Conference of the Justices of the Peace (appellate instance)	Senate (cassation instance)
Circuit Court (civil cases, and criminal cases without jury)	*Sudebnaya Palata* (appellate instance)	Senate (cassation instance)
Circuit Court (criminal cases, with jury)	None (no appeal)	Senate: Criminal Department of Cassation; its General Assembly; or Joint General Assembly of both Departments of Cassation (cassation instance)
Sudebnaya Palata (criminal cases, without class representatives)	Senate, Criminal Department of Cassation (appellate instance)	Senate: Joint General Assembly of Departments of Cassation (cassation instance)
Sudebnaya Palata (criminal cases, with class representatives)	None (no appeal)	Senate: Criminal Department of Cassation; Joint General Assembly of Departments of Cassation (cassation instance)
Senate, Criminal Department of Cassation (cases of crimes committed by high officials)	Senate, Joint General Assembly of Departments of Cassation (appellate instance)	None (no cassation)
Senate, Special Bench (criminal cases against the state, with class representatives)	None (no appeal)	Senate; Joint General Assembly of Departments of Cassation (cassation instance)

Thus, the variety of courts which existed before was abolished. All cases, civil and criminal, were decided essentially in only two instances (or in only one instance if the jury or class representatives participated).

The report on the case to the bench in civil cases was prepared by one of the three justices of the bench in the circuit court or the

Palata, not by the secretary, as before the Reform. A single judge functioned only in the capacity of justice of peace. The principle of collegiate courts was strictly upheld in Russia as in France, Germany and other continental countries.[103]

The following courts were not affected by the Reform of 1864:

SPECIAL COURTS

First Instance	Second Instance	Third Instance
	a. *Military Courts*	
Regiment Court	Circuit Court-Martial (appellate instance)	Main Court-Martial (cassation instance)
Circuit Court-Martial	None (no appeal)	Main Court-Martial (cassation instance)
	b. *Ecclesiastic Courts*	
Bishop's Court	Ecclesiastic Consistory	Most Holy Synod (cassation instance)
Ecclesiastic Consistory	None (no appeal)	Most Holy Synod (cassation instance)
	c. *Peasant Courts* (*Volostnoi Sud*)	

The courts-martial were courts the jurisdiction of which was extended, under special conditions and by special laws, to civilians. Introduced by Peter the Great in 1716, the courts-martial were subjected to a sweeping reform in 1867. The basic principles of the Reform of 1864—the accusatory principle, equality of rights of the prosecution and defense, pleading and publicity—were also observed as far as possible under conditions of military service. These courts consisted of regimental courts for petty offenses committed by members of the military forces, circuit courts-martial which had to judge important military and general criminal offenses, and the Main Court-Martial in St. Petersburg, which was a court of cassation. The members of the Main Court-Martial and circuit courts-martial were military jurists, usually graduates of the Military Academy. The preliminary investigation was entrusted to military judicial investigators, and the prosecution was represented by the military prosecutor. The defense of military personnel was in the hands of military men, and the defense of civilians was in the hands of lawyers.

---

[103] The French proverb says: "Juge unique—juge inique."

2. Jury[104]

a. Historical Development

The introduction of the institution of the jury was one of the most outstanding features of the Reform of 1864. England is usually considered the birthplace of the jury. However, the question of when and whether trial by jury originated in England is still a matter of discussion, even with regard to the existence of the jury in the Anglo-Saxon period.

It is peculiar that the origin of the jury has not yet been definitively established. Many nations claim the honor of having originated this institution. In Germany the opinion exists that the roots of the jury are to be found in the German forests. This opinion was supported by such authorities as Savigny and Gneist.[105] A legend has it that Odin, who led the Germans to Europe, created the court with jury. In the north of Europe, the opinion is widespread that the jury was established by Scandinavians: Danes, Swedes and Norwegians.[106] Maciejowski brought forward the hypothesis that the court with jury is a product of Slavic national genius.[107] It has also been asserted that the jurors are related to the *judices jurati* of the Old Rome, and some have claimed the privilege of priority for the Jerusalem Kingdom, founded by the crusaders.[108]

Although such authorities as Coke, Spelman, Nicholson, Blackstone and Turner assert that the jury existed in England before William the Conqueror, other jurists, as for instance Hickes and Reeves, contend that this form of trial was derived from Norman law and was not of Anglo-Saxon origin.[109] Proffatt comes to the conclusion that "the principle of trial by jury was not unknown to the Anglo-Saxons . . . among them we still find a system of trial that afterwards gave the jury its popular character, its vitality and its utility." [110]

When under Henry II national unity between the English and Normans was achieved, trial by jury became general. In the beginning the jury functioned in civil cases. Questions relating to property were

---

104 *See* S. Kucherov, "The Jury as Part of the Russian Judicial Reform of 1864," *The American Slavic and East European Review*, IX (1950), No. 2.
105 Rudolf von Gneist, *Die Bildung der Geschworenengerichte*, pp. 29-30.
106 N. N. Rozin, *O sude prisyazhnykh*, pp. 6-7.
107 Waclaw Maciejowski, *Slavische Rechtsgeschichte*.
108 Rozin, *op. cit.*,
109 John Proffatt, *A Treatise on Trial by Jury*, p. 14, Footnote 1.
110 *Ibid.*, p. 15.

submitted to *duodecim liberos et legalis homines juratos veritatem dicere.*[111] This tribunal was called *assisa.*[112] Later the functions of the civil jury were gradually extended to cases other than those involving property rights.

"In the reign of Henry VI . . . the jury system [in civil cases] had become in all its essential features similar to what now exists," Lesser writes. [113]

The direct application of the assize to criminal jurisdiction also began in the reign of Henry II, in the assize of Clarendon in 1166. At first the jury in criminal cases fulfilled only the functions of a grand jury, *i.e.*, formulated the indictment. The case in substance was decided by ordeal, according to the criminal laws of that time.

When the Fourth Lateran Council in 1215 forbade clergy participation in the ceremonial of the ordeal, a substitute for it became necessary. This substitute was found in the *verdictum patriae* of the twelve jurors. Lesser, quoting Bracton and Fleta, asserts that at the end of the thirteenth century trial by jury in criminal cases had become usual in England.[114] However, the grand jury, in addition to its functions of indictment, also fulfilled those of the future petit jury. The separation of the grand and petit jury had been already achieved in the fourteenth century and was an established factor in English criminal jurisprudence in the reign of Edward III.[115] The grand jury, which retained its functions of returning indictments, was abolished in Great Britain by Parliament in 1933. In place of the grand jury, indictments are now prepared by prosecutors' clerks. The grand jury functions at the present time only in the United States.

The institution of the jury was fully developed in England long before her colonies were established in the New World. The English settlers brought with them the common law and the institution of the jury in both its forms. Already in 1787, the Superior Court of North Carolina declared, in the decision Bayard & wife v. Singleton, I Mart. (N.C.) 48, that it is the right of every citizen to have "a decision of his property by a trial by jury." However, the original Constitution of the United States did not foresee the civil jury. This was rectified by the Seventh Amendment to the Constitution with regard to controversies exceeding twenty dollars and subject to common law.

---

111 Instead of a decision by duel as before.
112 In France the court to which the jury is attached is called *cour d'assises.*
113 M. A. Lesser, *The Historical Development of the Jury System*, p. 124.
114 *Ibid.*, p. 143. See also Bluntschli in *Staatswörterbuch*, IX, 349, and Brunner, *Die Entstehung der Schwurgerichte*, pp. 469-477.
115 Lesser, *op. cit.*, p. 148. See also Mittermaier in *Zhurnal ministerstva yustitsii*, 1865, No. 9.

The Constitution of the United States provides that "the trial of all crimes, except in cases of impeachment, shall be by the jury." [116] In the Sixth Amendment, as a part of the Bill of Rights, it is provided that "in all criminal prosecutions, the accused shall enjoy the right to a speedy and public trial by an impartial jury . . . " Similar provisions concerning the jury in criminal and civil cases were enacted by the individual constitutions of the states.[117]

The jury was first adopted in continental Europe in France by the Constituante in August, 1790. The great discontent with the administration of justice in the period preceding the French Revolution —it was subjected to such vigorous attacks as, for instance, those by Voltaire (in the Calas Case), and by d'Alembert—led to the search for new institutions and new methods. It is quite natural that the English institution of the jury found ardent adherents among the Encyclopedists and particularly in the person of Montesquieu. The Constitution of September 3, 1791, accepted the English system of the grand jury (eight members) [118] and the trial jury (twelve members).

The grand jury and the competence of the jury in civil cases did not meet with appreciation in Europe. They disappeared in France with the introduction of the new *Code d'instruction criminelle* of 1811, which gave to the French jury the structure it still has in essence.

The participation of the jury in criminal cases spread from France gradually over all Europe. About 1848, it was put into practice virtually in all the German states with the exception of Austria and Saxony.

The institution of the jury was a complete innovation for Russia. It is true that the custom of admitting popular participation in the decision in criminal cases was known in Russia from the oldest time of Russian history. However, neither the officials elected by the people before or after the *Sudebniki,* nor the assessors of the time after Peter the Great, were judges in the sense of jury members. The *tseloval'niki* and *sudebnye muzhi* were not real judges, since the judicial power was in the hands of the appointed officials (*tiuny, voyevody,* or *namestniki*), who pronounced the sentences. The duty of the elected *tseloval'niki* and other elected officials was only to supervise the lawfulness of the decision and its correct recording.

---

116 Art. III, par. 2, 3.

117 Trial with jury can be waived by the accused in some States, as for instance, in Massachusetts.

118 In the National Assembly Du Port, Barnave and Robespierre voted for the competence of the jury in civil cases. Such eminent jurists as DuPort and Tronchet were against the irremovability of judges.

The assessors, in their capacity as class representatives, did not represent the whole people, as it is the case with the jury. But what is most important, both elected and appointed judges were tied up by the doctrine of formal evidence and deprived of the right to judge according to their conscience.

D. A. Rovinsky, the Moscow Province Procurator attached to the State Chancellery, was first to suggest officially the adoption of the institution of the jury in criminal cases. He did so in his report dated February 1862. This report is dedicated in its first part to a refutation of the objections against the timeliness of the introduction of this institution presented by Count Bludov, who wrote:

> The expediency of creating juries at the present time is very doubtful. It is not easy to imagine the functioning of such a court when the majority of our people are not only deprived of juridical knowledge, but lack the most elementary education; when the notions of right, duty and law are so undeveloped and unclear that the violation of the rights of others—especially of property rights—is considered by many as a most normal act, other crimes are considered as expressions of boldness, and criminals are regarded as nothing but unlucky persons. The admission of such people to pronounce judgment on an important, sometimes very complicated, question of the guilt or innocence of an accused involves the risk, not only of inconvenience, but almost of direct unlawfulness. . . . Without contesting the advantages of the court with a jury, especially in criminal cases, we are, however, of the opinion that decisions in cases involving crimes and misdemeanors have to rest, for the time being, with the judges.[119]

Thus Bludov did not object to the institution of the jury itself and even not to its introduction in Russia, but only considered that the time for this measure had not yet come.

Rovinsky refuted Bludov's arguments one after the other. According to Rovinsky, the assertion that the Russian people see in criminals nothing but "unlucky people" is wrong. If they get hold of a criminal on the spot, they beat and often even kill him. They do so because they have no confidence either in the conscientiousness of the police, which may hush up the case, or in the fairness of the judges. The fact that the people look with compassion upon criminals already condemned, whipped and sent to Siberia as a result of proceedings based on rules of formal evidence is a sign of deep moral qualities rather than backwardness. Rovinsky agreed with Bludov that

---

[119] Quoted by Dzhanshiyev, *Epokha. . .* , p. 81-82.

theft had become a most usual phenomenon in the private and public life of their time. But he did not see the cause of it in the lack of juridical or general education—since educated people also are often involved in this crime—but in the lack of public control and public opinion. Once the people participate in judgments over crimes, they will learn to discern and to condemn criminal actions. Hence, concluded Rovinsky, a court with a jury must precede the development of the juridical sense in society, for with its help the people will cease to consider theft as a most normal act.

In the discussion of the Reform in the State Council, the question of the jury was thoroughly re-examined, and we find in the minutes of the session of the State Council reasons expressed for the necessity for the introduction of the jury which are profoundly and wisely thought out.[120] The State Council was perfectly aware of the fact that the main objection against the introduction of the jury in Russia was the assertion that the people were not sufficiently educated for entering into the consideration of questions demanding logical thinking and adequate education. However, it considered this objection as unconvincing. Of course, educated people have a beneficial influence upon the quality of institutions in which they participate, but on the other hand people are developed and perfected by good institutions, the State Council argued, and in this respect a well-organized court is more important than any other institution, because it teaches the people the notion of justice and lawfulness without which no order or prosperity is possible; the insufficient education of the people not only is a poor argument for the inopportuneness of establishing jury courts, but, on the contrary, leads to the opposite conclusion: such people must be particularly defended in court; they need judges from their own milieu who would fully understand their frame of mind and mode of action; the degree of punishment should be determined exclusively by judges enjoying juridical education, but no special juridical knowledge nor juridical experience is needed for a conscientious answer to the question whether the accused is guilty or innocent in a crime; a person with sound comprehension, even if poorly educated, may give a correct answer to this question. Moreover, the State Council considered the introduction of the court with jury in Russia even more necessary than in other countries, since the historical life of the people had nowhere created such a sharp difference between various strata of the population as in Russia. The morals, the conception and mode of life of professional judges, belonging generally to

---

120 *Sudebnye Ustavy*. . .,III, 95-99, *passim*.

higher classes of society, differed considerably from those of an accused from a lower class; the law requires from a person who has to decide upon the question of guilt or innocence an answer based only on complete internal conviction, unconstrained by any formal evidence, and it is clear that the jury, elected usually from the same class of the population to which the accused belongs, may better evaluate the fact than a judge who is alien to the milieu in which the crime has been committed; special knowledge of local morals, customs and mode of life sometimes throw light on circumstances which may seem to à scholar unclear and without connection with the crime.

It is peculiar that almost the same objections which were so convincingly refuted by the State Council were brought forward not only by reactionaries but by progressive elements as well. Even a man like V. D. Spasovich, professor of law at the time of the Reform and later one of the most outstanding attorneys-at-law, in 1861 declared in a lecture on the theory of criminal evidence:

> Where the people are so simple morally that the great majority of them do not even understand the criminal nature of most of the crimes; where they are so unaccustomed to judging and thinking that the legislator refuses to rely on the convictions, not only of the masses of the people, but also of his specialized judges; where the people are so primitive politically that, pitying the convicted and considering them miserable, they view the court as a fearful thing to run away from; where blind fear of the authorities replaces respect for the law, and the law itself is respected, not as an expression of a moral idea, but as an order from the authorities,—there the establishment of the jury is an entirely impossible affair, and there is no use even mentioning it.[121]

Later, however, Spasovich changed his viewpoint completely. In the Introduction to the third volume of his *Works* he wrote in 1890: "In 1861 . . . I did not foresee the possibility of introducing the jury into Russia. Of course, I am glad more than anyone else that I was wrong, and that the daring experiment was carried out and was crowned with success." [122]

As far as juridical science in Russia was concerned, the opposition came from K. P. Pobedonostsev, who was an enemy of the institution of the jury in general. Whereas, in his opinion, in England the evil consequences of this institution were attenuated by the influence of

---

121 V. D. Spasovich, *Sochineniya*, III, 269.
122 *Ibid.*, Introduction, p. i.

the judiciary, which had behind it centuries of experience and education, that was not the case in Russia. Pobedonostsev wrote:

> One can imagine what aspect the administration of justice will assume in a land where this directing power [the judicary in England mentioned above] is not exercised, and in place of which there exists a hastily formed crowd of lawyers who are helped by interests of self-love and covetousness in reaching speedily considerable skill in the art of sophistry and logomachy in order to influence the masses; where there is in action a herd of jurors, selected either haphazardly or by skillful means from among the masses, which possesses neither a conception of the duty of a judge, nor the capacity to master the complexity of facts requiring analysis and logical examination; and, finally, where there is a mixed crowd which attends the courts as though it were a show in the midst of a lazy and empty life. And this mass of people, according to the idealists, represents the *people*.[123]

The plan to introduce the jury into Russian jurisprudence was criticised not only in Russia, but in Western Europe as well. Herbert Spencer, for instance, wrote in 1850:

> That justice can be well administered only in proportion as man become just, is a fact too generally overlooked. 'If they had but trial by jury' says some one moralizing on Russians. But they can't have it. It would not exist among them. Even if established it would not work. They lack that substratum of honesty and truthfulness on which alone it can stand. To be of use this, like any other institution, must be born of the popular character. It is not trial by jury that produces justice, but it is sentiment of justice that produces trial by jury, the organ through which it is to act; and the organ will be inert unless the sentiment is there.[124]

b. *Structure and Functioning*

The Russian law of 1864 did not copy the foreign legislation of the time. Also in the case of the jury, neither the Anglo-Saxon nor the French system were fully adopted.[125] The Russian system differed in many essential ways from both these systems.

---

123 K. P. Pobedonostsev, *Moskovsky sbornik,* p. 56.
124 Herbert Spencer, *Social Statics,* p. 289.
125 It is incomprehensible that the translator of the *Modern Russian History* by Kornilov introduced into the text the following sentence: "The jury system was copied from the English courts." A. Kornilov, *Modern Russian History,* trans. by A. S. Kaun, Part II, p. 102. The Russian original does not contain such an assertion (See Kornilov, *Kurs istorii Rossii XIX veka,* Part II, pp. 259-63).

The structure of the jury is outlined in the provisions of the Statutes of Judicial Institutions.[126]

To the duty of serving as members of the jury[127] were subject the district inhabitants of all classes, provided they were: (1) Russian citizens; (2) between 25 and 70 years of age; (3) residents of the district for not less than two years.[128] Excluded from election to the jury were: (1) those under investigation or indictment for felony or misdemeanor, or condemned to prison or heavier punishment; (2) those expelled from official positions by virtue of a judgment, or from the clergy as a consequence of vice, or from communities and class organizations; (3) those declared to be insolvent debtors; (4) those under guardianship because of extravagance; (5) blind, dumb, deaf and insane persons; and (6) persons not knowing the Russian language.[129]

There were general and alternate lists of members of the jury. In the general lists were entered: (1) honorary justices of the peace; (2) all civil service officials having the rank of fifth class and below, with the exception of (a) members of the judiciary, district justices of the peace, chief secretaries and secretaries of law courts, marshals of the court and notaries-public; (b) prosecutors; (c) lieutenant-governors; (d) treasurers and foresters of state forests; and (e) members of the police; (3) all persons elected to positions in organizations of the nobility and municipalities, with the exception of mayors; (4) peasants holding any elective position in the field of peasant affairs; (5) all other persons having landed property extending over no less than 100 dessiatines (270 acres) or other immovable property worth 2,000 rubles in the capitals, 1,000 rubles in province centers and 500 rubles in other towns, or those having an income of 500 rubles per annum in the capitals and 200 rubles in other places.[130]

Excluded from the lists were: (1) members of the clergy and monks; (2) members of the armed forces of all ranks, and civilian officials attached to the armed forces; (3) teachers at public schools;[131] and (4) servants of private persons.[132]

The general lists were prepared by a commission elected by district assemblies of the zemstvos and by a mixed assembly of the

---

126 *Uchrezhdeniye sudebnykh ustanovleny*, Arts. 81-109.

127 To be a member of the jury is considered in England and the United States as a political right and a public duty. In Germany it was an honorary function; in France and Russia—a duty.

128 *Uchrezhdeniye sudebnykh ustanovleny*, Art. 81.

129 *Ibid.*, Art. 82.

130 *Ibid.*, Art. 84.

131 *Ibid.*, Art. 85.

132 *Ibid.*, Art. 86.

municipality and the district *zemstvo* in capitals.[133] The lists had to be presented to the governor for confirmation.[134]

Among persons who had the right to be members of the jury, those who were to be called upon to participate in sessions of the courts during the following year were entered on the alternate lists for the coming year.[135]

The participation of the jury in the trial was regulated by the Code of Criminal Procedure of 1864.[136] A list of thirty members of the jury was prepared for every session. The right of peremptory challenge was limited, for the prosecutor, to six members of the jury.[137] The accused and his attorney also had the right to challenge, without explanation, as many members of the jury as was possible without reducing the list to less than eighteen members.[138] From the remaining eighteen members, twelve were elected acting jurors and two—alternate jurors, in the following manner: the president put folded pieces of paper with the names of the jurors into a vase and took them out one by one; the first twelve were acting members of the jury and the following two were alternate members.[139]

According to Art. 670, the jury had to elect a foreman from among its literate members. All the members were obliged to keep secret their deliberation as well as the numbers of votes given for or against the accused.[140]

The Anglo-American practice is to challenge the whole list of the jury in cases where the composition of the list is criticized. And individual members of the jury may be challenged before they have taken the oath, because of assumed partiality or certain other reasons, such as their prejudice against capital punishment and the like. That form of challenge, with indication of causes, was unknown to the Russian law and equally unknown to it was the cross-examination of the members of the jury, so frequently employed in the United States. Also in all other European countries (with the exception of Austria), only the peremptory challenge was practiced.

The right and duties of the jury are similar in all countries. The jurors have the right to participate in every action of the court in the same manner as judges, and to ask for any explanation they desire.

---

133 *Ibid.*, Art. 89.
134 *Ibid.*, Art. 94.
135 *Ibid.*, Art. 98.
136 *Ustav ugolovnago sudoproizvodstva*, Arts. 646-677.
137 *Ibid.*, Art. 656.
138 *Ibid.*, Art. 656.
139 *Ibid.*, Arts. 658, 659.
140 *Ibid.*, Art. 677.

Their main duty is to pronounce a verdict. In Germany and Russia the members of the jury had the right to make observations concerning the questions the jury had to answer. Strict rules are enforced especially in England and the United States, to protect the jury from every outside influence.

Everywhere on the European continent, the jury has to decide on each case subjected to its jurisdiction. That is not the case in Anglo-Saxon law, which does not resort to the jury if the accused pleads guilty.[141]

In order to facilitate the pronouncement of the verdict, written questions were submitted to the Russian jury by the bench. Those questions referred to the guilt and imputability of the accused and to the happening of the criminal act. In England and the United States the jury does not answer those specific questions but expresses its opinion on the whole content of the indictment with the words "guilty" or "not guilty." [142]

In Russia, France, Italy, Germany, Gr. Britain and the United States the president, before sending the jury out for deliberation on the questions put to it, summed up the results of the trial in a speech.

The summing up by the Anglo-Saxon judge has the purpose of making the jury acquainted with the rules of evidence, i.e., to explain to it the force, meaning and character of the submitted evidence. In Germany, only the legal side of the case was explained; in Italy— only the factual side. The Russian president of the bench, who led the trial, had to make clear to the jury both the factual and the legal aspects of the case and to give general instructions about the rules of evidence. However, he was explicitly forbidden by law either to express his own opinion concerning the guilt or innocence of the accused or to introduce facts which had not been the object of examination during the trial.[143] On the other hand, he was ordered by law to remind the jury that it had the right to declare the accused to be deserving of indulgence.[144]

---

141 I. Ya. Foinitsky is of the opinion that, according to the Anglo-Saxon conception of criminal procedure, the accused who pleads guilty renounces the producing of evidence against accusation; this renouncement is binding for the court. (Foinitsky, *Na dosuge*, II, p. 357). He strongly opposed the introduction of such a provision into the Russian Code of Criminal Procedure.

142 In Scotland: "not proved."

143 Arts. 801 and 802. It is inconceivable that Kovalevsky could write: "Instead of supporting the prosecutor, as it is usual in France, the presiding judge has to express his opinion." The last words are in flagrant contradiction with the provision of Art. 802. (M. Kovalevsky, *Russian Political Institutions*, p. 234).

144 Art. 804.

The decision of the jury concerning every question put to it requires unanimity in England and the United States and necessitated a two-thirds majority in Germany and only an absolute plurality in Russia and other European countries. The Russian Code only recommended to the jury the achievement of unanimity and prescribed that in case of equal division of votes, the verdict should be to the benefit of the accused.

The question of unanimity of the jury was discussed in the State Council in all its details, and it is of interest to recapitulate the arguments *pro* and *con* on this principle. It was asserted that only unanimity of the jurors eliminates every doubt of the fairness of the verdict and that a verdict thus arrived at enjoys confidence, as it is considered the product of the whole society. Centuries of English experience show that unanimity of jurors is not an impossible requirement. Further, the defenders of the principle of unanimity argued as follows: the goal of the jurors is to reach a just decision based on the complete certainty of the event; complete certainty is expressed by a unanimous decision only; two correct decisions on one and the same event are impossible, since the essence of a moral verdict—the testimony of unconditional truth—does not stand contradicting opinions; although doubts are possible when moral questions are involved, they easily yield to argument if a sincere wish to recognize the truth exists; absence of unanimity is always a sign of immaturity of conviction and superficiality of discussions; a definitive stubbornness of opinion can only be the consequence of extreme torpidity or complete indifference to the most important question in the world, and in both cases a sign of incompetence to judge; to recognize a non-unanimous verdict is to base the verdict on casual opinion; to admit the possibility of such verdicts is to doubt the competence of the jurors, or, even more, to encourage them in a shameful indifference with regard to the fate of their fellow men; to base the verdict on the majority of votes is to forget the moral character of the institution of the jury, to definitely renounce the concept of inner truth, to sacrifice it to pure arbitrariness under the cover of majority vote, and to make of the court a lottery where questions of life or death are resolved by a simple mathematical equation. It was emphasized that the requirement of unanimity prompts the jurors to a thorough examination of the case, since they know that by no means will they get rid of the case by a bare expression of opinion, but that they will have to sustain their opinion in the discussion with their colleagues. Finally, it was stressed that unanimity of decision corresponds to the character of the Russian people, who for ages have followed the principle of unanimity in the administration of the *mir*.[145]

The arguments against unanimity were that often it is reached by compulsion and is based not on conviction but on the necessity of coming to a conclusion, to a unanimous verdict—thus, it is forced upon the jurors; that sometimes the minority has to yield to the majority, and sometimes, on the contrary, a stubborn and persistent minority may force the majority to submit to an unjust sentence; and—the main argument—that the requirement of unanimity gives to every single juror the possibility of cancelling the decision of his eleven colleagues. Such a juror may be a person whose insistence is based, not on his deep inner conviction, but on some external influence.[146]

After having examined these contradictory viewpoints, the State Council came to the conclusion that an absolute majority of votes is a better system than unanimity.

The prevailing influence on the decision of the State Council was the experience of France in this matter.[147] In France, where all the possible systems were tried out, the requirement of unanimity was rejected and the absolute majority of votes was definitively adopted. Indeed, the fluctuations of French legislation on this question are a good illustration of the difference of opinion on the subject and are worth quoting *in extenso*.

According to the Law of September 16-29, 1791, a majority of ten votes of jurors against two was required for the validity of the verdict. This rule was taken over by the Code of the Third Brumaire, Year IV of the Republic. The Law of 19 Fructidor, Year V, introduced the requirement of unanimity. If unanimity could not be achieved, however, within twenty-four hours, a simple majority decided. The Law of the 8th Brumaire, Year VI, retained the principle of unanimity, but if the jurors could not arrive at a unanimous verdict within twenty-four hours, the accused was acquitted. The Code of 1808 reverted to the principle of a simple majority, but the verdict was

---

145 Village community.

146 It cannot be denied that the requirement of unanimity often leads to an undue lengthening of criminal procedure: if the jury is not capable of reaching unanimity, it must be dismissed and another jury elected for a retrial. If the second trial is also fruitless because of lack of unanimity among the jurors, a third, a fourth, etc., must take place (let us recall, for instance, the trial of Sacco and Vanzetti, which lasted about two years). In the Middle Ages, jurors were subjected to every kind of mistreatment in order to force them to reach unanimity. As late as the end of the 18th century, coercion against jurors in England was carried to the point of requiring them "after the judge's charge to be kept without meat, drink, fire or candle, till they are unanimous agreed." (Lesser, *op. cit.*, p. 189).

147 *Sudebnye Ustavy. . .* ,Part II, 299-301, *passim*.

referred to the bench if seven votes of the jurors were for conviction; the bench had to confirm it if two of the five judges were for conviction. The Decree of May 24, 1821, altered this rule, prescribing that conviction could take place only if voted by at least ten judges and jurors (*i.e.*, seven jurors and three judges) against seven (*i.e.*, five jurors and two judges). The Law of May 4, 1831 required a majority of two-thirds of the jurors (*i.e.*, eight out of twelve). The Decree of September 9, 1835 restored the simple majority (*i.e.*, seven out of twelve). But the Law of March 6-8, 1848, shifted to a three-fourths' majority (*i.e.*, nine out of twelve). The Law of October 18, 1848, again returned to a two-thirds' majority. Finally, the Decree of June 9, 1853 restored simple majority, which has remained in effect up to the present time.

But let us return to Russia. Every answer of the jury had to be preceded by the words "yes" or "no", namely, "yes, guilty" or "no, not guilty," or "yes, but deserves indulgence." The right of indulgence toward the accused is a very important one. In Anglo-Saxon countries the jury is deprived of this right, but uses in place of it the right to recommend the pardoning of the accused.

In France the verdict of the jury is pronounced in the absence of the accused, and this was also the case in Germany. In Russia it was pronounced in his presence. A remarkable provision of Art. 818 of the Code of Criminal Procedure gave to the bench the right to transfer the case to another jury, the decision of which was final, if the three judges were of the unanimous opinion that the jury had condemned an innocent person.[148]

After the verdict of the jury, the bench decided upon the measure of punishment or upon acquittal.

In Russia there was no appeal against the decision of the court with jury.[149] However, both parties—the prosecutor and the accused—had the right to apply for cassation of the sentence to the Criminal Department of Cassation of the Senate, whereas in England and the U.S. a review of an acquitting verdict and sentence is not admitted.

In France, the jury functions with the appellate instance, the *cour d'assises*. In Russia, according to the Code of Criminal Procedure, it could be attached to all the three instances.[150] Ordinarily it acted with the circuit courts of first instance.

Clearly there was no direct borrowing, except of the general idea,

---

148 A parallel to the mistrial provision in the United States.
149 In England the Criminal Appeal Act of 1907 introduced appeal against the accusatory verdict of the trial jury and decision of the court.
150 *Ustav ugolovnago sudoproizvodstva*, Art. 201 and 1106.

in the institution of the jury as it was transplanted to Russia by the Reform of 1864. As Professor Foinitsky puts it: "None of the institutions [introduced by the Reform of 1864] can be called English or French; on all of them there is a seal of originality and all of them fulfill an independent Russian function." [151]

The institution of the jury was limited "to cases of crimes or misdemeanors for which the law prescribed punishment involving deprivation of, or restriction in, civil rights." [152] Thus only major offenses had to be judged with jurors.

Political crimes were excluded from the jurisdiction of the jury. The State Council refused to refer them to the competence of the jury in spite of the recommendation of the State Chancellery to extend the jurisdiction of the jury to these cases also. The viewpoint of the State Chancellery on this subject, written by jurists especially attached to it for this purpose, is of great interest. It is beyond any doubt, argued the Chancellery, that the discussion of the factual part of criminal cases by representatives of the people—called jurors— and not by regular judges, is a real guarantee of equity for the accused. On the other hand, the gravest accusations require the greatest guarantee of equity. Therefore, it is impossible to deprive the accused of this guarantee in cases of crimes against the state without committing an injustice. The guarantee provided by trial with jury has an especially great importance precisely in cases of criminal offenses against the state, because in these cases the state, which prosecutes the crime, is at the same time the legal entity offended or harmed by the crime. That is why no matter how impartial or independent the judges appointed by the state may be, their decision in cases of offenses against the state will never enjoy the confidence of society. Men with an enthusiastic mind are not subject to fear of punishment if society sympathizes with them. But it is possible to deprive the punished of this sympathy only if he is condemned by society itself in the person of its representatives. Although the harmony between the aims of the government and those of society, which is necessary for an energetic prosecution of state crimes by the court with jurors, does not exist in Russia, still these crimes should be referred to the jury because convictions pronounced by a jury would have such a moral power that the influence of law on society would increase, even if convictions by jury prove to be less frequent than convictions by regular judges.[153]

---

[151] I. Ya. Foinitsky, *Kurs ugolovnago sudoproizvodstva*, I, 43.
[152] *Ustav ugolovnago sudoproizvodstva*, Art. 201.
[153] *Zhurnal grazhdanskago i ugolovnago prava*, 1890, No. 8, pp. 235-36.

In introducing the jury into the Russian criminal court, the legislator did not specify which system he wanted to adopt—the Anglo-Saxon system, according to which the jury is bound to pronounce a verdict of guilty if it comes to the conclusion that the defendant did commit the action of which he is accused, or the continental European system, which does not bind the jury with definite rules. In continental Europe, the jury is free to render an acquitting verdict in spite of the confession of the defendant and of the fact that no legal reasons exist to exempt him from punishment; the jury may also acquit the defendant even if it is convinced that the latter is the perpetrator of the act of which he is accused.

In the absence of clear provisions of the law on this question, and faced with the duty to judge according to conscience only, the Russian jury followed the continental system from the very beginning.

Of the right of the jury to decide according to its conscience only, independently of the pleading of the accused, S. A. Andreyevsky said in a lecture delivered to lawyers-in-training in St. Petersburg: "The judicial institutions of Emperor Alexander II have produced a tremendous change. They have conferred to the jurors the right to pronounce their verdicts (accusatory or exculpatory) without being hindered by any evidence, according to their conscience only. The recent ruling of the Senate,[154] which was of an incidental and not a binding[155] nature, and which caused a sensation, cannot change the established practice, because it would mean the abrogation of the Reform itself. The clear and exact law is above all fleeting comments which undermine its foundation. The law remains unshaken." [156]

With regard to the acquittal of Vera Zasulich, Koni wrote: " . . . Many were shocked by the denial of the guilt of the defendant by the jury, since the crime was evident and had been confessed by her. When there is a complete absence of understanding of court regulations and means of administration of justice, as it is the case in our society, the question 'Is he guilty?' is equivalent, almost for everyone, to the question 'Did he do it?' And when the words 'not guilty' are addressed to a person who has confessed that he 'did it,' clamors arise in society in which the frankness of discontent is equal to the depth of ignorance." [157]

---

154 *Resheniya ugolovnago kassatsionnago departamenta Pravitel'stvuyushchago Senata*, 1884, No. 13. See below, pp. 66 ff.
155 Andreyevsky was of the opinion that a decision of the Senate was binding only for the case in connection with which it was made.
156 S. A. Andreyevsky, *Dramy zhizni*, p. 7.
157 Koni, *Vospominaniya o dele Very Zasulich*, p. 230.

The opinion of the Senate with regard to this question was unsteady and fluctuating. In a decision dated 1870, the Senate expressed the opinion that the jury may deny the guilt of the defendant for reasons other than those listed in the Criminal Code,[158] even if there is no doubt about the perpetration of the imputed act.[159] During the fourteen years which followed, no one questioned the right of the jury to acquit a defendant who confessed his crime, nor the right of his counsel to plead for such an acquittal. In 1884, however, the Senate denied the right of the jurors not to impute an act which, according to their own opinion, had been committed by the accused, for reasons other than those defined by law.[160] Further, in a decision of 1894, the Senate imposed upon the presiding judge of the trial court the duty to explain to the jury that if it comes to the conclusion that the accused is the perpetrator of the crime, it has no right to answer negatively to the question of guilt according to the duty imposed on it by law.[161] That viewpoint was confirmed in 1895.[162]

In accordance with the last decision, some of the presiding judges of the trial courts started to instruct the jurors in the sense of this decision, which, however, did not prevent the jurors from acquitting defendants who confessed their guilt when they considered it equitable to do so.

It is peculiar that on another occasion the Senate acknowledged this fact and defended the right of the jury to do so. In 1890 a commission for the reform of the administration of justice was created by the Minister of Justice, Manasein. The Minister intended to include in the new law a provision that the Senate should have the right to transfer a case to a new jury for decision if, according to the unanimous opinion of the bench, the jurors had acquitted a guilty person. The Senate opposed this suggestion vigorously and emphasized in its report to the Commission that the reasons which caused not less than one half of the 19,000 acquittals of accused persons in courts with jurors in 1887 were based on the fact that the jury had taken into consideration circumstances pertaining to the personality of the ac-

---

[158] The *Ulozheniye o nakazaniyakh*, Art. 92, listed six reasons: (1) complete inoffensiveness of the action which unexpectedly and unforeseeably resulted in evil; (2) minority, the defendant not being of an age at which he could have had a real notion of the nature of his action; (3) insanity, or attack of a disease which led to delirium or complete loss of the senses; (4) accidental error, or error resulting from fraud; (5) compulsion by a superior and irresistible force; and (6) self-defense.

[159] *Resheniya ugolovnago kassatsionnago departamenta Pravitel'stvuyushchago Senata*, 1870, No. 354 (in the Subbotin Case) and No. 488 (in the Vachentsev Case).

[160] *Ibid.*, 1884 Nos. 13 and 14.

[161] *Ibid.*, 1894, No. 7.

[162] *Ibid.*, 1895, No. 17 (in the Olga Palem Case).

cused, to the nature and consequences of their acts, to conditions under which these acts were committed—in short, all the circumstances which create the difference between the concepts of "perpetration" and "guilt".[163]

Nevertheless, in the decisions of 1894 and 1895 the Senate took the opposite viewpoint and reached the climax in this respect in 1903, in a decision in the following case. The lawyer K. submitted to the Criminal Department of Cassation of the Senate an appeal in cassation against the decision of a court with jury, in which he wrote that the presiding judge, in his summing up, had explained to the jurors that they have no right to acquit a defendant whose guilt has been proved, whereas he, the attorney, had asserted to the jurors that they have such a right, notwithstanding the confession of the accused, since the jurors have to decide upon the question of guilt or innocence of the defendant according to their inner convictions only. The Senate ruled that since (1) the lawyer K. had acknowledged himself that he had tried to persuade the jurors that they have the right to acquit a defendant who had confessed and whose perpetration of the imputed act was not questioned, and since (2) such an assertion by the lawyer is in contradiction to the evident sense of the law as commented upon in Decisions Nos. 13 and 14, 1884, and No. 7, 1894, of the Senate, which must have been known to K. in his capacity as lawyer, and since (3) K. had thus expressed contempt of the law and attempted to mislead the jurors with regard to their legal rights and in this respect not only failed to cooperate toward a just solution of the case but, on the contrary, hindered the correct administration of justice, the Senate, therefore, decides to order the St. Petersburg *Sudebnaya Palata* to submit the acts of the lawyer K. to the examination of the Council of the Bar attached to that *Palata*.[164]

However, the next year the Senate again completely reversed its viewpoint on the subject in its Decision of Feb. 17, 1904, in the Semyonov Case. The lawyer Petrov had submitted an appeal in cassation to the Senate against the sentence of a circuit court with jurors, in which he asserted that the presiding judge of the trial court had had him removed from the session hall because in his pleading he had called the attention of the jurors to their right to acquit the defendant even without legal reasons for considering him not responsible for his action. The Chief Prosecutor of the Senate, who had to present his "conclusions" on the appeal, was at that time I. G.

---

[163] Quoted by N. Shatrov, "K voprosu o zashchite, soznavshikhsya podsudimykh," *Pravo*, 1903, p. 2333.

[164] *Pravo*, 1903, p. 2330.

Shcheglovitov, the future Minister of Justice and pillar of reaction. He had been newly appointed to this position, and these were the first "conclusions" he delivered to the Senate. After a brilliant analysis of the provisions of the law and the previous decisions of the Senate, Shcheglovitov concluded as follows: "Even where there are no reasons for absolving the defendant from responsibility under Art. 92 of the Code of Criminal Procedure,[165] the jury has the right to acquit a defendant who pleads guilty, since the jury is free to base its sentence upon other reasons than those listed in Art. 92."[166] He also acknowledged that the right of the lawyer to ask the jury for the acquittal of the defendant extends to such cases also.

The Senate decided in accordance with the conclusion of the Chief Prosecutor and reversed the decision of the circuit court. Thus, the question was definitely solved.

Shcheglovitov's conclusion in the Semyonov Case was, of course, strongly commended by lawyers, especially since they had deeply resented the previous decision of the Senate in Case K.: the Moscow Bar in its General Assembly of December 14, 1903, and the Petersburg Bar in the General Assembly of January 18, 1904, had condemned that previous decision of the Senate and carried resolutions asserting the right of the lawyer to ask the jury for acquittal of the defendant in any case. Now the Petersburg Bar wired to Shcheglovitov: "Our congratulations to the successful defender of the rights of the defense." Another Bar wired: "We greet in your person the embodiment of judicial solidarity with us."[167]

The question of the acquittal by jury of a defendant who has confessed his guilt cannot be abandoned without some remarks on the dismissal of the jury in Anglo-Saxon countries when the defendant pleads guilty. There are several reasons why preference should be given to the system which submits such cases also to the jurisdiction of the jury. A long time has passed since the confession of the accused was considered the best evidence of all, as it was the case under the inquisitorial procedure in Russia.[168] It cannot be denied that cases when the defendant takes upon himself the guilt of another person are not rare. He may be moved by the desire to shield a person who is dear to him, or by some other, more complicated psychological motives which cannot be easily determined.[169] The subtlety and the

---

165 See above, Footnote 158 on p. 66.
166 *Pravo*, 1904, pp. 511-526.
167 Hessen, *Advokatura. . .*, pp. 406-407 and Footnote 2.
168 The importance of "confessions" has been revived in the famous trials of the thirties in the Soviet Union and, after World War II, in the satellite states.
169 Let us recall Mikolka, the painter in Dostoyevsky's *Crime and Punishment*,

sense of justice of the jury are never more needed than in such cases. But even in cases when there is no doubt that the crime was perpetrated by the accused, the jurors must have the possibility of acquitting him if they think that for some exceptional reasons the accused should not be punished. In the case of the Anglo-Saxon countries, the required unanimity of the jurors would be a good guarantee that such a decision would not be made lightly by the jury.

In Anglo-Saxon countries it is considered, however, that the jury might safely render a verdict of guilty in such cases and leave the judge to take into consideration all the extenuating circumstances so as to mitigate the punishment. An example of such a case is quoted by Dzhanshiyev. A certain Mrs. Riley was accused of bigamy in England in 1887. The fact was evident, but the accused had been very unhappy with both her husbands, who were scoundrels and conspired against her in order to get her money. Since the fact of bigamy had been proved, the jury pronounced her guilty. The judge declared that he had always sentenced bigamists to forced labor, but that in the present case the court had to deal with a woman already sufficiently punished for her mistake. The law which punishes bigamy severely apparently did not foresee marriages contracted under such sad conditions. And he sentenced Mrs. Riley to five minutes of imprisonment.[170]

Another similar case is related by Count A. A. de Franqueville when he describes the courts in Great Britain. A woman whose husband had converted life into hell for her, killed him in despair. The jurors found her guilty, but the judge declared that he would pronounce no sentence, which was tantamount to an acquittal, since without a sentence the woman could not be punished.[171, 172]

Is it not better, however, to give to the jury the right to decide on the fate of the accused in every case than to have recourse to such stratagems in order to achieve a just sentence? In Russia the jury would have simply acquitted the accused in both cases.

Beside the acquittal of defendants who had confessed their crimes, there was still another kind of verdict by jury which was often criticized. I am speaking of verdicts containing the denial of indisputable,

---

who confessed to a crime he had never committed, the perpetrator of which was Raskol'nikov.

170 Dzhanshiyev, *Osnovy*. . ., p. 297-298.

171 A. C. de Franqueville, *Système judiciaire de la Grande Bretagne*, II, 459.

172 The following case is reported in the *Zhurnal grazhdanskago i ugolovnago prava* (1880, No. 2, p. 113) : In England, a justice refused to accept the plea of guilty of a girl of 14, because of her youth. She had confessed to arson, although it was obvious that she was not the perpetrator. The justice ordered it to be recorded that she pleaded not guilty. The jury acquitted her without leaving their seats.

obvious facts with the purpose of reducing the punishment of the accused. Suppose, for instance, that a man is accused of having stolen a wallet containing 500 rubles. The amount of money contained in the wallet—500 rubles—is beyond any doubt. The subject of the discussion in court is only the fact as to whether the accused did, or did not, steal the wallet. The jurors are asked whether or not he stole the wallet, and reply: "Yes, but it contained less than 300 rubles"—an answer which seems nonsensical. If, however, we take into consideration the fact that punishment for a theft of over 300 rubles was much more severe than for a theft of less than 300 rubles, it becomes clear that the jury, although finding the accused guilty, considered the punishment which threatened him to be too severe and wanted to mitigate it. People who were shocked by such verdicts did not understand the reason for decisions which at first glance seemed senseless. They simply represented rejection by the jury of the severity of the punishment, which could not be mitigated otherwise. According to Russian criminal law, the punishment for each category of crimes was exactly prescribed, and the bench had the right to reduce it within very restricted limits only. The Reform of 1864, while bringing a change into the system of administration of justice, left untouched the penal laws as they appeared in the Code of 1845. Obviously, the provisions of this code often did not correspond any longer to the sense of justice and concepts of guilt and punishment of the subsequent generations. In such cases the jury corrected the law by rendering verdicts which appeared to be in disaccord with logic and evident facts.

The necessity to mitigate the penal severity of a great number of provisions of the Criminal Code was evident to the government itself. On April 22, 1881, a report of the Chief of His Majesty's Own Chancellery, Prince S. N. Urusov, and the former Minister of Justice, D. N. Nabokov, on the formation of a commission for the creation of a new criminal code, was approved by the Tsar. In this report it was pointed out that it became evident from judicial experience that the criminal code in force does not correspond to the requirements of the new judicial statutes and that its structure is an impediment to the sound administration of justice, especially in courts with jury.[173]

The same views were expressed in a report by the Minister of Justice, N. V. Murav'yov, in 1896. Murav'yov attributed the high percentage of acquittals by jury "to the cruel provisions of the Criminal

---

[173] *Ugolovnoye ulozheniye 22 marta 1903 g.* Published and commented upon, by N. S. Tagantsev, p. xviii.

Code, which no longer meet the requirements of life." [174] Almost all representatives of Russian juridical thought were of a similar opinion.[175] The draft of a new criminal code was adopted by the State Council and approved by an ukase of the Tsar on March 22, 1903.[176] However, not the entire code, but only some parts of it, were introduced in 1906, 1909 and 1911.

It is interesting to note how well a foreigner—Sir Donald Mackenzie Wallace—who was in Russia during the first years of the functioning of the jury and was present at the trial of Vera Zasulich, understood the situation created by the discrepancy between an obsolete code of criminal laws and the requirements of life. He writes:

> . . . the juries often gave a verdict of 'not guilty' when the accused made a full and formal confession to the court. . . . In England the Bench is allowed very great latitude in fixing the amount of punishment. The jury can therefore confine themselves to the question of fact and leave to the judge the appreciation of extenuating circumstances. In Russia the position of the jury is different. The Russian criminal law fixes minutely the punishment for each category of crimes, and leaves almost no latitude to the judge. The jury knows that if they give a verdict of guilty, the prisoner will inevitably be punished according to the Code. Now the Code . . . is founded on conceptions very different from those of the Russian people, and in many cases it attaches heavy penalties to acts which the ordinary Russian is wont to regard as mere peccadilloes, or positively justifiable. Even in those matters in which the Code is in harmony with the popular morality, there are many exceptional cases in which *summum jus* is really *summa injuria*. In such cases what is the jury to do? . . . There remains but one issue out of the difficulty— a verdict of acquittal; and Russian juries—to their honour be it said—generally adopt this alternative. Thus the jury in those cases in which it is most severely condemned, provides a corrective for the injustice of the criminal legislation.[177]

c. *The Jury as a Political Institution*

The question of whether trial by jury has a political role may be approached from different viewpoints. On one hand there are

---

[174] *Sudebnaya gazeta*, 1896, No. 29. This is the reason for frequent acquittals and H. Berman is wrong when he explains alleged leniency of the Russian jury by religious concepts of crime and the criminal (See H. Berman, *Justice in Russia*).

[175] Professor N. S. Tagantsev, one of the foremost Russian criminologists, compared the Criminal Code to "threadbare, holey, patched tatters in which, figuratively speaking it is unseemingly to appear even at the Vyaz'ma Monastery [a place always crowded with beggars in rags]."

[176] *Sobraniye uzakoneny i rasporyazheny pravitel'stva*, 1903, No. 38 (416).

[177] Sir Donald Mackenzie Wallace, *Russia*, II, pp. 403-404, *passim*.

strong voices asserting the general political importance of courts with jury. With regard to the English jury, Forsyth wrote:

> It has been strongly said that the whole establishment of King, Lords and Commons, and all the laws and Statutes of the realm, have only one great object and that is to bring twelve men into a jury box. This is hardly an exaggeration. For to what end is the machinery of the constitution employed but to give every man his due and protect all in the enjoyment of their property, liberty and rights? And the twelve men in the jury box are in this country [Great Britain] the great Court of appeal, when in the case of the humble as well as the most exalted citizen, these are or any of these are attacked.[178]

Another great apologist of the political role of the jury is Tocqueville. In his considerations on American democracy, he assigned an important part to the jury. "The jury is above all a political institution," Tocqueville wrote. "He who punishes infractions of the law is therefore the real master of society. Now, the institution of the jury raises the people itself, or at least a class of citizens, to the bench of juridical authority. The institution of the jury consequently invests the people or that class of citizens, with the direction of society." [179] And he continues: "The jury is pre-eminently a political institution; it must be regarded as one form of the sovereignty of the people. . . Thus the jury, which is the most energetic means of making the people rule, is also the most efficacious means of teaching it to rule well." [180]

The political significance which the jury had in Russia is evident. The people of Russia received in the institution of the jury in 1864 full right of participation in the administration of the State in its judicial branch, a right which in the case of the other branches of state power was partially granted to them only in 1905 and to a full extent only by the February Revolution of 1917. The "slave of yesterday" was called to the use of full civil rights in the field of the administration of justice. The measure was, as Spasovich puts it, "a bold experiment," but the experiment testified to the confidence which the government had in this "slave of yesterday," in his ability to solve often very complicated questions and situations involved in criminal cases solely with the help of his common sense and the right approach to the

---

[178] W. Forsyth, *History of Trial by Jury*, p. 499. Sieyès wrote: "The court with jury is the real guarantor of personal freedom in England and in all the countries of the world where people will strive for liberty. This method of rendering justice is the only one which protects from abuses by the judicial power." E. Sieyès, *Qu'est-ce que le tiers état?* p. 67.
[179] Tocqueville, *Democracy in America*, I, 309.
[180] *Ibid.*, p. 310 and 314.

problems of life. With regard to the "slave of yesterday" Gruzenberg wrote: "The Judicial Reform of 1864 is a brilliant example of generous confidence in the masses of the people. Only the authors of the Reform could have dared to take such a step, to turn over the administration of justice to what was literally the slave of yesterday, who was entirely illiterate, more dark than a dark night; to entrust to their reason and conscience that which is the most valuable thing for a human being—liberty and honor. And they were not deceived in their *élan;* the Russian court with jury justified the expectations, and the conscientious work of the ignorant peasant more than once undid a knot tied by bureaucratic contrivances, administering a lesson to the representatives of power and Law. . ." [181]

It is this political significance of trial by jury which made this institution, as Nabokov asserts,[182] a constant target for violent attacks by the reaction. But while enjoying great political importance, the jury remained, in Russia, far above politics and free from any political bias in its functioning.

The State Council flatly contradicted the opinion that the jury is a political institution: "The opinion of some theorists[183] that trial by jury has a political character could be an obstacle to the introduction of this institution in some countries. Not to mention the fact that such an opinion is poorly founded, it should be noted that it is within the legislator's power to create conditions under which this institution could be deprived of any political character." [184] The State Council considered it sufficient to eliminate political cases from the competence of the jury in order to deprive it of any political character. This opinion was shared by some distinguished jurists. Mokrinsky, for instance, writes: "Trial by jury never had a political character in Russia. Criminal cases against the State were excluded from its jurisdiction from the very beginning of the Judicial Institutions." [185] It is evident that the State Council and Mokrinsky, in denying political importance to the jury, kept in mind only its functioning and not its character as an institution.

---

[181] Gruzenberg, *Vchera,* p. 197.
[182] Nabokov, *op. cit.,* p. 350.
[183] Feuerbach, for instance, thought that the jury is "the expression of democratic principles, the nucleus of revolution, a result of rule by the people and constant opposition to the government." (Quoted by Rozin, *op. cit.,* p. 14.)
[184] *Sudebnye Ustavy. . . ,*III, 96.
[185] Mokrinsky, *op. cit.,* p. 116-117.

d. *The Jury Attacked and Defended*

A campaign against the jury began to develop in Europe in about the fourth quarter of the nineteenth century. Especially strong was the propaganda against the jury and for the *Schöffen* in Germany. The institution of *Schöffen* functioned in Germany before the introduction of the jury. The *Schöffen* were judges who, similarly to the jurors, were elected from among the entire population for a definite, short period of time, but who differed from the jurors in that they sat together with the bench and discussed and decided the questions of fact and punishment together with the appointed professional judges. The *Schöffen* were reintroduced into German criminal proceedings with the Reich Criminal Procedure of 1877. The jurisdiction of the *Schöffengericht* was limited to petty criminal cases.

Jhering, in his *Der Zweck im Recht,* had already asserted that the jury was a revolutionary product foreign to the new unified Germany. According to him, it had played its role and could go. Such an authority as Binding was of the opinion that the jury as a juridical institution had no sense. The German victory of 1870-71 gave birth to strong patriotic feelings not only in politics but also in other fields. An institution which came from France provoked suspicion from the very outset. In addition to that, the rise of Prussian nationalism in the midst of the *Kulturkampf* led to the idealization of an old German institution like the *Schöffen*. These ideas were reflected in the attacks against the jury and appreciation of the *Schöffen*.

The battle against the jury and for the *Schöffen* raged in Germany throughout the last quarter of the nineteenth century and the first decades of the twentieth. Beside Jhering and Binding, Schwarze, who is considered the father of the movement against the jury in Germany, Zachariä and some others were also for the *Schöffen*.

At the International Criminal Congress in Vienna in 1912, the jury was subjected to sharp attacks and its abolition was demanded. It found a defender in the person of Lenin, who wrote: "The participation of the people's representatives in trials is a democratic principle. A very reactionary petty bourgeoisie is not seldom predominant in the jury at the present time, because workers are excluded from the jury. This evil must be cured by the development of democracy . . . and not at all by a mean abdication of democracy." [186]

The jury was defended by several prominent German jurists such as Mittermaier, Gneist, Glaser and Kohler. Mittermaier in his treatise

---

[186] Lenin, *Sochineniya,* 2d ed., XXX, 194.

on the functions of the jury in Europe and America comes to the conclusion that "the result of the experience with the jury in Germany ...
shows that Germany possesses the elements necessary for the development of the institution of the jury in the sense of improvement of
criminal procedure." [187] Kohler refutes the main accusations against the
jury and writes that "the desire has been expressed to replace the court
with jury by a special kind of court with *Schöffen*, the structure of
which is very indefinite and completely impractical." [188]

Writing about the abrogation of the court with jury in Germany
and its replacement by *Schöffen*, A. Ya. Vyshinsky remarks that it is
easier for the professional judges to influence and subjugate *Schöffen*
than jurors.[189] Was this one of the reasons which prompted the Soviets
to abrogate the jury and to introduce the People's Court with its professional judge and two assessors—a court which has many more features in common with the *Schöffengericht* than with the court with
jury?

The jury was eliminated in Germany by the Weimar Republic
in 1924 and replaced by *Schöffen*, who were in turn abolished by Hitler
in 1939 as the last remainder of public participation in the administration of justice.

The major defect of the system of *Schöffen* consists in the complete subjugation of the elected *Schöffen* by the professional judges
together with whom they discuss and decide the case. It is quite natural
that the *Schöffen*, who very often belong to uneducated strata of the
population, submit completely to the influence of the professional
jurists whose experience and high position enjoy prestige with people
from the rural or working classes as well as the small bourgeoisie.[190]

The German attitude against the jury was sharply criticized in
Russian juridical literature. Professor Duvernois asserted that Jhering
did not want citizen judges but citizen soldiers; instead of people
consciously loving their fatherland, he admired the type of the over-
drilled Prussian *Grenadier*. Duvernois called Jhering's doctrine *Sturm
Jurisprudenz*.[191] Professor Vladimirov wrote: "Germany desires the re-

---

[187] Carl Mittermaier, *Erfahrungen über die Wirksamkeit der Schwurgerichte
in Europa und Amerika, über ihre Vorzüge, Mängel und Abhülfe*, p. 490.
[188] Josef Kohler, *Moderne Rechtsprobleme*, pp. 70-74.
[189] A. Ya. Vyshinsky, *Sovetskoye gosudarstvennoye pravo*, p. 458.
[190] The present writer had the opportunity, during his time of probation at
the law courts in Berlin, 1929-33, to take part as an acting judge in deliberations
of courts with *Schöffen* and gained the firm conviction that in at least 90% of the
cases verdicts were based on the opinion of the professional judges, whereas the
great majority of the *Schöffen* remained passive and agreed with the opinion of
the judges.
[191] N. L. Duvernois, *Kurs lektsy grazhdanskago prava*, p. 25-28 *passim*.

storation of the old institution of *Schöffen*, forgetting that the dead
are not to be resurrected. Let Germany revive a corpse, let her writers
assert in the most obscure manner that the dead are more useful in
life than the living ones. . . Russia does not need to live according to
borrowed ideas, and she, a young country, which has not to support
on her shoulders the historical weight of archaeological *Schöffen*, has
no reason to imitate Germany's patriotic experiments." [192]

The anthropological or positive school in Italy also led the attacks
on the jury. It was based on the principle that a criminal is born as
such and belongs to one of the categories of criminals established by
this school. The anthropologists wanted the criminals to be judged
by specialists, who would be able to decide to what category the accused
belonged. It is natural that jurors did not meet this demand. In his
Sociologia criminale, Ferri suggested the abolition of the jury system
in the trial of ordinary crimes. He wrote: "Thus, sociology shows that,
whereas in former days a person could be found who knew physics,
theology, mathematics, metaphysics, politics, etc., and whereas there
were among savages men who were at the same time warriors, hunters,
fishermen, architects etc., among civilized persons . . . the physiologist
is never an astronomer, the chemist is never a jurist, etc.; everyone has
his own specialty. However, the institution of the jury is a violation
of this [sociological] law, since it imposes upon the same individual
various functions which are far removed from his usual function." [193]
Ferri denounced the jury because of its lack of ability. One cannot be
certain, he thought, that people who are individually gifted and intel-
ligent will necessarily display the same aptitude as a group. Psychology
teaches, he maintained, that the aptitude of a group is never equal to
the sum of the aptitudes of its members. He wrote: "A number of
persons endowed with common sense may form a group which lacks
common sense completely, as in chemistry the mixture of two gases
may produce a liquid." [194] Ferri quotes in support of his assertion the
Roman maxim: *Senatores boni viri, senatus autem mala bestia.* He
comes to the conclusion that practice results in so many striking
examples of the inability of the jury to understand correctly facts submitted to their judgment in criminal cases that it seems useless to
dwell on this subject any longer. [195]

---

[192] L. E. Vladimirov, *Sud prisyazhnykh*, III-IV.
[193] Enrico Ferri, *Sociologia criminale*, p. 672.
[194] *Ibid.*, p. 662.
[195] Ibid., p. 665. Mentioning the Russian jury, Ferri wrongly asserts in the
4th Italian edition of his book, p. 819, Footnote 1, that in Russia the crimes of
murder and bigamy were excluded from the competence of the jury and transferred to the jurisdiction of the court with class representatives. In the English

Ferri's colleague of the positive school, Garofalo, opposed the jury from the standpoint of practical utility, asserting that this kind of court does not fit Italy; justice there is undermined because of the jury, and one never knows whether an evidently guilty person will be condemned or an innocent one acquitted. In his diatribe against the jury Garofalo wrote in 1891:

> A mighty effort of imagination is necessary in order to assume that a minister of justice would be strongly inclined to prosecute honest citizens, . . . corrupting officials in order to shield the real perpetrators of theft, arson and murder and to sentence in their place honest persons completely innocent of any of these crimes. Never has a government used such weapons, even against its worst foes. It did happen under despotic governments that non-existent conspiracies forged by a too eager police have been prosecuted, but the practice of jailing citizens on the false accusations of vile crimes is something that has never been seen. What contemporary state would avail itself of such infamous means, which . . . could be so easily uncovered? But let us admit for a moment that this is possible. How could one assume that the twelve humble citizens of the jury would be less susceptible to corruption by the government than professional judges? [196]

The Italian attack against the jury was joined by Gabriel de Tarde in France. First of all, Tarde reproached the jury for its English origin. He wrote that it was imported from England by the French Revolution "to the detriment of some of the best creations of the French genius. . . How strange indeed is this enthusiasm suggested to our French eighteenth century, the most refined and artificial century, the century most enamored of the rational and factitious in everything, for the English criminal procedure, i.e., the most archaic and uncultured." [197] Tarde heaped accusations upon the jury: "The ignorance, fear, naivety, fickleness, inconsistency of the jury, and its partiality,

---

translation by Joseph I. Kelly and John Lisle, published in Boston 1917, p. 493, Footnote 1, rape is added to the crimes allegedly withheld from the competence of the jury.

[196] R. Garofalo, *Criminologia*, p. 447. The eminent Italian jurist wrote these lines prior to the Beilis trial in Russia. This case (see below pp. 243-264) made it evident that a government is well able to exercise repression and exert pressures considered impossible by Garofalo, and that the "twelve humble citizens" may offer more resistance to pressure than the permanent judges.

For a reasoned refutation of the arguments of the anthropological school against the jury, see M. P. Chubinsky, *Sovremennaya bor'ba vzglyadov za i protiv suda prisyazhnykh*, where he comes to the conclusion that "the court with jury is the best form of court experienced up to the present time." p. 31. See also N. N. Rozin, *O sude prisyazhnykh*.

[197] Gabriel de Tarde, *La philosophie pénale*, p. 434 and footnote.

which takes sometimes a servile and sometimes a rebellious form, have been sufficiently proved." [198]

With regard to Russia, Tarde asserted that there, as in other countries, the jurors are careful not to condemn persons of high rank.[199] This obviously false assertion may be refuted by many examples.

Tarde recommended the substitution of professional judges for jurors. In this respect he did not follow the anthropological school (especially its left wing, represented by Lombroso) in its desire to replace all judges—jurors and professional ones—by commissions of psychiatrists.

In France the laws concerning the jury were amended in 1932 in the sense that the jury was to participate together with the bench in the determination of the punishment. But the major change came during World War II. The Vichy Government of Maréchal Pétain decreed on Nov. 25, 1941 that the number of jurors shall be reduced to six and that they shall decide questions of fact and punishment together with the professional judges. Thus, without changing their name, the jurors were virtually transformed into *Schöffen*.

The government of the Fourth Republic upheld this decision, but increased the number of jurors from six to seven (Decree of April 20, 1945). The bench thus consists at the present time of seven jurors and three professional judges who decide questions of guilt and punishment. An accusatory verdict requires at least six votes of guilty out of a total of ten votes.

In the camp of the Marxists, the attitude toward the jury was not quite uniform. Marx himself characterized the jury as "a class court of privileged classes, created with the purpose of filling the gaps of law with the width of bourgeois conscience." [200] The same problem occupied Marx in the article on the trial of Gottschalk in 1848. He wrote that the jury cannot insure a just decision in this case and continued: " 'But what about the conscience of the jurors!' some will reply to us. '*Conscience*—is there a better guarantee necessary?' Ah, *mon Dieu*, conscience depends upon consciousness, upon the whole way of life of a person. The republican has a conscience different from that of the royalist, the wealthy person—one different from that of the indigent, the thinker—a conscience difffferent from that of one who never thinks. A man who is required to be a juror only because of his property qualification has, accordingly, a conscience qualified by

[198] *Ibid.*, p. 435.
[199] *Ibid.*, p. 436.
[200] K. Marx i F. Engels, *Sochineniya*, VIII, 558.

property. The point is that the conscience of the privileged is a privileged conscience." [201]

However, Lenin, as mentioned above, had a good word for the institution of the jury, considering it as a democratic principle. A consistent application of this principle according to him requires the abrogation of qualifications for the selection of jurors, *i.e.*, eligibility not restricted by requirements of education, property, residence and the like.[202]

In the years of political reaction, the Russian jury became the subject of the most vigorous attacks. These attacks were conducted by the rightist press under the leadership of Katkov's influential newspaper *Moskovskiye Vedomosti*. The famous reactionary who during the reform period of the sixties was a devoted partisan of these reforms, especially of the judicial reform and the jury, changed his mind radically as soon as the reactionary wave of the seventies began to grow.

Professor Nolde gives a survey of articles which appeared in the seventies in *Moskovskiye Vedomosti* as part of a regular campaign against the jury. The arguments against the jury may be summarized as follows: The jury reflects the judgment of the street; it is a toy in the hands of the prosecutor and, especially, in those of the defense attorney. Is it a matter of conscience when among 36 persons taken from the street the prosecutor and the defense attorney pick the twelve jurors in the same way as a dexterous card player deals out cards?[203]

Other attacks on the jury emanated from the government itself. After the trial of Vera Zasulich,[204] which became the main argument in the campaign against the jury, the attacks against this institution gained new impetus. In his report to the Tsar on February 11, 1887, Minister of Justice N. A. Manasein asserted that the jurors "elected from the local population are far from being impartial and are not responsive to those interests which lead to conflict between private persons and representatives of government power." [205]

The Law of July 7, 1889, performed a major cut in the compe-

---

201 *Ibid.*, VII, 495-496.
202 Lenin, *Sochineniya*, 2d. ed., XXX, 194. When the time came for Lenin to put into practice his theoretical ideas, he chose a form of people's representatives in court which resembles the *Schöffen* system much more than that of the jury. In the People's Courts of the USSR, the two assessors decide, together with the professional judges, both questions of guilt and questions of punishment.
203 Nolde, "Otnosheniya mezhdu sudebnoi i administrativnoi vlastyami," in *S. U.*, II, 609.
204 See below, pp. 214-225.
205 Quoted by S. P. Mokrinsky, "Sud prisyazhnykh," in *S.U.*, II, 155.

tence of the jury in favor of the court with class representatives, to the jurisdiction of which offences against officials and official agencies were transferred.[206] In addition to these cases, breaches of trust committed by officials were also exempted from the competence of the jury. This was explained as follows: it is often difficult for jurors to gain a clear understanding of the public danger of infringements, abuses of power and negligence by officials they have to judge; the jurors have an insufficient notion of public interest, and the rules governing state service are not known to them.

The Law of July 7, 1889, was the expression of a definite course adopted by the government with regard to the jury. It is significant that one of the government's reasons given in the official message to accompany the law was the high percentage of acquittals pronounced by the jury.

While the institution of the jury was severely criticized, it found even more numerous ardent adherents.

In the beginning, the activities of the jury were highly commended by the government itself. In his report to the Tsar on the activities of the new law courts from May 17 to November 17, 1866, the Minister of Justice, D. N. Zamyatin, gave the following characterization of the work of the jury: "The jurors, who very often belonged mostly to the peasantry, fully met the expectations set in them. They had to solve difficult problems, which would embarrass even experienced people accustomed to the correct handling of criminal cases. All these problems were solved by the jury, in most cases correctly and adequately, thanks to the amazing attention with which the jurors considered the cases submitted to them." [207]

After fourteen years of functioning of the jury,[208] on the occasion of the celebration of the twenty-fifth anniversary of Alexander II's reign, the Senate also expressed high appreciation on the activities of the jury: "The masses of the people, who in the past had a very obscure notion of the significance of law courts and their functioning, very often were unable even to distinguish the punishable from the permissible, as a consequence of their ignorance. . . The jurors who were called from these masses . . . very soon became familiar with the

---

206 *I.e.*, all the offences of Chapter 1, Division 4 of the Criminal Code. The majority of the cases of violence against officials were exempted from the jurisdiction of the jury already by the Law of May 9, 1878. The most important of these crimes were transferred to the courts-martial by the Law of August 9, 1878. The Law of May 11, 1882 returned to the competence of the jury some of the minor offences of this kind. The Law of July 7, 1889 dealt another blow to the jury.
207 *Zhurnal ministerstva yustitsii*, 1867, no. 2, p. 144.
208 The court with jury began to function in 1866.

moral concepts and ideas which are inherent in every developed society. By listening to the speeches of the prosecution and the defense, they learned to discern white from black in the usual conditions of their everyday life. They became conscious of the ideal interests pursued by the criminal court. They learned to respect the personality of their fellowmen, and, thanks to the acquired knowledge and experience, they brought light into the darkness of their environment which did not know till then any other elements of right except force and wealth." [209]

It is remarkable that these lines were written by the Senate two years after the trial of Vera Zasulich.

In 1894, the government decided to examine the question of the jury once more. On the initiative of the Minister of Justice, N. V. Murav'yov, a commission consisting of all the chief presidents of the *Sudebnye Palaty* and all the prosecutors attached to these *Palaty* was formed under the chairmanship of Senator A. F. Koni, with the purpose of studying the problem of the jury in Russia. The commission pronounced as incorrect the widespread opinion that the jury handed down an exaggerated number of acquittals. It found that courts with jury in Russia are even more repressive and more unvarying in their verdicts than those without jury and that "the activities of the jury correspond perfectly to its aims and that it has an ennobling influence on the people's sense of equity." [210,211]

Concerning the question of the activities of the jury, the majority of the commission (8) came to the conclusion that "not only does the

[209] Quoted by N. P. Timofeyev, *Sud prisyazhnykh v Rossii*, p. 11-12.
[210] Koni, "Sud prisyazhnykh," in *Entsiklopedichesky slovar' Brokgauza i Efrona*, Vol. 63.
[211] Statistics concerning a later period seem not to confirm the opinion of the Commission that the jury is even more severe in its verdicts than the professional judges in trials without jury. Figures given by Mokrinsky (*op. cit.*, p. 150) for the period 1901-1912 show a lower percentage of verdicts of guilty in courts with jury than in courts without jury.

Year	Percentage of verdicts of guilty in courts with jury	Percentage of sentences of guilty in courts without jury
1901	63	71
02	63	71
04	63	70
05	61	68
06	63	70
07	60	69
08	60	72
09	57	71
10	60	73
11	60	74
12	60	75

work of this kind of court correspond to its aims, but it is the most
perfect form of court which may be imagined for the trial of the
major share of important cases." [212] The majority of the commission
(14) expressed themselves against any further restrictions of the competence of the jury. Five members of the commission emphasized the
necessity for an extension of the jurisdiction of the jury.

The year 1894 certainly marks a turning point in the views of the
government on the jury.

After a recess of fourteen years, new courts with jury were opened
in Astrakhan, Olonets, Orenburg and Ufa Provinces by the Law of
February 2, 1898. According to the Law of May 10, 1909, two districts
of Vologda Province, as well as Archangel, Tomsk and Tobolsk Provinces and Akmolinsk, Semipalatinsk and Ural Territories, were provided with courts with jury. Finally, the Law of June 3, 1914, introduced the jury into the courts of the newly formed Kholm Province.

The Third Duma in 1912, and the Fourth Duma on June 3, 1914,
emphasized the necessity for introducing the jury in the remaining
parts of the empire.

The fifty years in which trials with jury existed in Russia have
brilliantly proved all the futility of the objections presented against
this institution in Russia and of the criticism formulated against its
functioning after it had been introduced. The bold experiment of turning over jurisdiction concerning the most important and complicated
criminal cases to a people emancipated from serfdom "almost yesterday" proved a success. This was a fact which the government had to
acknowledge after several decades of the most furious attacks against
the jury on the part of the rightist press, which, of course, in that case
as in all others, expressed views completely or almost completely inspired by the government.

Soon after the court with jury began to function in Russia, it
became obvious that all the apprehensions based on a supposed lack
of sense of justice (Spencer), absence of education (Spasovich), and
judicial traditions (Pobedonostsev) were unfounded. That this "court
of the street" [213] had a conscience free from social, religious, racial
and other prejudices, was proved frequently. The cases of Vera Zasulich and of Mendel Beilis may serve as striking examples of how the

---

[212] A. F. Koni, "Sudebnye Ustavy 1864-1914," *Zhurnal ministerstva yustitsii*,
1914, No. 9.

[213] The jury was called thus in one of Katkov's vicious articles in *Moskovskiye
Vedomosti* (1883, n. 39). On the morning in which this article appeared, S. A.
Andreyevsky, the famous lawyer, orator and poet, addressed the jury in court
with the following words: "Accept this name, do not be ashamed of the street.
In the street all men are equal—rich and poor, noblemen and commoners. The

"court of the street" could resist the greatest pressure exercised by the ⎯ government of an autocratic state. Vera Zasulich was tried in 1878 and Beilis thirty-five years later, in 1913. One case was tried in the beginning of the existence of the jury in Russia, and the other shortly before its end. Zasulich fired a shot at a high official, avenging an offense committed by him against a revolutionary. She was acquitted. Beilis, a Jew, was accused of ritual murder. The case was instigated by the "Black Hundreders" of the reaction. The Minister of Justice, Shcheglovitov, used all his influence, exercised all kinds of pressure. But as a result of the trial, which lasted over 30 days, the twelve men of the jury—seven of them simple peasants—acquitted Beilis.[214]

Lenin wrote in defense of the "court of the street" in 1901:

> The reactionary press called the jury court a 'street court' and started persecuting it. . .
> The government . . . told the representatives of society that it considers them to be '[people from the] street,' from the populace, who have no right to take part in . . . legislation and in government, who must be expelled from the sanctuary where trial and justice are meted out to Russian citizens. . .
> The court of the street is valuable precisely because it breathes life into the bureaucratic formalism which saturates our government institutions through and through. . .
> Aided by its flair, under the pressure of practical experience in social life and of the growth of political consciousness, the street [is able to] grasp the truth toward which our official, academic judiciary, shackled by pedantry, is so laboriously and timidly groping: [namely], the fact that the alteration of [existing] social and political institutions is an infinitely more important weapon, in the struggle against crime, than individual punishments. That is why the reactionary publicist and the reactionary government hate—and cannot help hating—the court of the street.[215]

Supporters of the jury may be found even among violently reactionary circles. Thus, for instance, the Minister of Justice, I. G. Shcheglovitov, one of the most outstanding figures of tsarist reaction, who could not be suspected of leniency toward any liberal institution, wrote in 1914: "Yes: now, after fifty years of its existence, one may say that the jury in Russia has justified itself, in spite of some dark

---

street is the last refuge in disaster. In case of fire or assault you run into the street, you call for aid, you revert to it." Quoted by Goldstein, *Rechi i stat'i,* p. 26.

[214] On the trials of Zasulich and Beilis, see below pp. 214-225 and 243-264, respectively.

[215] Lenin, *Sochineniya,* 2d ed., IV, 83-84, *passim.*

sides. . . The dark sides notwithstanding, the jury has won the general esteem and confidence of the wide masses of the people. That is why we must defend this institution from changes which could injure its substance." [216]

Among the overwhelming number of opinions favorable to the institution of the jury in Russia, A. F. Koni's deserves first place. As a distinguished judge for many years and as an outstanding scholar of jurisprudence, he may be considered one of the greatest authorities in this field. Koni was of the opinion that the court with jury is the form of tribunal which combines the greatest independence and impartiality with the greatest profoundness and many-sidedness. In his opinion, the jurors evaluate the criminal act in vivid connection with the personality of the criminal, whom they consider, not as an abstraction, but with reference to the features given to him by the environment, by social conditions and by unhappy events in his personal life. From that viewpoint, Koni held, the court with jury is the most perfect court for a society which wishes to combine, in the administration of justice, the principles of equity with Christian clemency. Koni emphasized that the twelve members of the jury, foreign to the routine and bluntness of professional judges, are the best tool for fully clarifying the actual nature of a case, not according to books or class opinion, but according to human comprehension dictated by life. [217]

Professor I. Ya. Foinitsky, one of the most eminent teachers of law in Russia, was also of the opinion that the court with jury is "the form of court which comes closest to the ideal." [218] Professor L. E. Vladimirov, who studied trial with jury in Western Europe and Russia and published a book on this subject in 1873, at the time when opposition against this institution, led by Schwarze and Jhering in Germany, was at its height, wrote: "Whoever studies the problem of the jury in the West inevitably comes to the conclusion that it is the best form of court which history knows. The significance of this institution for Russia is enormous. Our present society can scarcely realize what a step forward it took on the road of progress from the moment that it was called upon to participate in the administration of justice. . . Only to the future historian of our epoch will it become apparent that the period of real public life began in Russia at the time when the jury was introduced into her courts." [219]

---

216 I. G. Shcheglovitov, "Novye popytki izmenit' postanovku suda prisyazhnykh v Zapadnoi Evrope," in *S.U.*, II, 163-64.

217 A. F. Koni, "Sud prisyazhnykh," in *Entsiklopedichesky slovar' Brokgauza i Efrona*. Vol. 63.

218 I. Ya. Foinitsky, *Kurs ugolovnago sudoproizvodstva*, I, 43.

219 Vladimorov, *op. cit.*, pp. ii-iii.

Indeed, the power vested in the jurors was tremendous. They did not follow strictly the letter of the law, but acted according to their conscience only, and were the most independent of all judges. If a law seemed to them obsolete or unjust, they *de facto* abrogated it by not applying it, as shown above. Thus to these twelve men of the people was granted the power to correct legislation, *i.e.,* a certain portion of that legislative power of which the people as a whole were deprived at that time. This is, undoubtedly, one of the features of the political nature of trial by jury in Russia.

A. M. Bobrishchev-Pushkin, a distinguished lawyer, wrote a voluminous treatise on the jury in Russia. On the basis of 716 cases and 1,508 verdicts rendered by juries, he tried to establish the empirical laws which govern their activity. He came to the following conclusion: "Thus, a fruitful meeting of the written criminal law with practical views on life of members of society takes place in the court with jury. . . The product of this lawful collision between them is concrete justice, *i.e.,* living justice. This [kind of] law, which corresponds not only to the ideas of equity but also to the sense of justice, determines how and to what extent the interests violated in an individual case can be defended by the court, which acts independently of any influence foreign to the substance of the court. The necessity for judicial impartiality is an axiom similar to the necessity for the juridical and moral independence of the judge. . . However high the ordinary Russian court might stand, these two necessary conditions are realized in the jury much more completeley; being selected by lot from all classes for a definite time, standing aside from the conventions of judicial life, free, therefore, from any class, caste, official and personal influences, the Russian juror is not only juridically, but also *de facto* in an exceptionally good position to act justly . . . and humanely." [220]

The educational importance of this institution also cannot be disputed. The jurors are taught the practice of equitable dealing. Put in a position to judge another man, the juror cannot avoid the feeling that he might be judged in his turn. Tocqueville called the jury a school of life into which admission is free and always open, which each juror enters to be instructed in his legal rights, where he engages in daily communication with the most accomplished and enlightened people of the upper classes, where the laws are taught to him in a practical manner and are brought to the level of his apprehension by the efforts of the attorneys, instruction by the judges and the very

---

[220] A. M. Bobrishchev-Pushkin, *Empiricheskiye zakony deyatel'nosti Russkago suda prisyazhnykh,* pp. 614-615.

passions of the parties concerned. The institution of the jury spreads, among all classes, respect for the decisions of the court.

The introduction of the institution of the jury in Russia opened the way for a creative sense of equity on the part of the people. The court with jury is first of all a court of the people's conscience. Its verdict reflects the characteristic features of the people's sense of justice. At the same time it has, in its turn, an educational influence on the people, showing to them what is prohibited, directing and shaping their sense of justice.

An especially precious attribute of the jury is the freedom from every kind of routine and stagnation. Also foreign to the jury is the conservatism and adherence to established patterns typical of professional judges—factors which often influence their reaction to evidence presented.

Professor Talberg was right when he wrote: "Of all forms of people's administration of justice in past history and in our time, trial by jury is the most perfect." [221]

3. Courts with Class Representatives

A peculiar form of popular representation was chosen by the legislator of 1864 for dealing with crimes against the State: courts with participation of class representatives, which were attached to the *Sudebnye Palaty*. They consisted of the bench of the *Palata* (five judges) and four class representatives, namely, the province and district marshals of the nobility, a mayor, and a *volostnoi starshina*. The Law of July 7, 1889, reduced the number of judges from five to four and the number of class representatives from four to three, discarding one member of the *Palata* and the district marshal of the nobility. The representatives, together with the professional judges, decided both questions of guilt and punishment.

These courts were neither a revival of the old class courts of Catherine II nor a copy of the German *Schöffengerichte*. Created by provisions of the Code of Criminal Procedure, Arts. 1032 and 1051, they differed from class courts of the time of Catherine II because the latter were competent in cases of one class of the population alone, and from the *Schöffengerichte* because the German *Schöffen* were not elected from individual classes of the population.

The point of similarity between the Russian courts with participation of class representatives and the *Schöffengerichte* was the sub-

---

[221] D. G. Talberg, *Russkoye ugolovnoye sudoproizvodstvo*, p. 65.

jugation of the representatives by the professional judges, and the total passiveness of the former in the presence of the latter.

The Law of July 7, 1889, expanded the jurisdiction of these courts. As a general rule, all cases of murder of officials and violence against them when performing their official duties, as well as contempt of official agencies and officials, were submitted to the jurisdiction of the *Sudebnaya Palata* with class representatives.

4. *Justices of the Peace*

The institution of the justice of the peace was borrowed from England and France, but also in this case it was not just slavish copying. The institution was remodeled in accordance with Russian conditions and needs. The name chosen for these justices signified, in Russian as well, that their primary aim was to seek a "peaceful," voluntary agreement between the parties. However, their activity also had to be influential in matters of preservation and consolidation of general order and peace in districts assigned to their activity. Thus the formulation of their duties much resembles that used in Great Britain, where the King appoints a justice of the peace of a county with the following words: "Know ye that we have assigned you . . . to keep our peace in the said county of . . . ." [222]

The institution itself created a special body of justices, separated from the general judiciary of the country, as it is the case in England. However, the unity of administration of justice was not affected by this fact, because of the justices of the peace and their functions were also put under the general supervision of the Senate, through Department of Cassation. An appeal against the decision of justices of the peace could be submitted to the conference of justices of the peace in criminal cases according to Articles 145 and 149 of the Code of Criminal Procedure and in civil cases if the controversy involved more than 30 rubles, according to Art. 162 of the Code of Civil Procedure.

Similarity to the Western European system consisted in the fact that the justice of the peace acted as a single judge, whereas in other courts in Russia the bench consisted of three judges. [223]

The difference between the English and French institutions, on the one side, and the Russian on the other, consisted in the manner of selecting the justices of the peace. In the first two countries they were appointed, in Russia—elected. [224] The duty of electing the justices

---

[222] N. Polyansky, "Mirovoi sud," in *S.R.*, II, 193.
[223] *Uchrezhdeniye sudebnykh ustanovleny*, Art 3.
[224] *Ibid.*, Arts. 23 and 24.

was entrusted to the newly created *Zemstvo*, as representative of all classes of the population. The honorary and the district justices were elected for the districts and towns for a period of three years. Only in St. Petersburg and Moscow were these justices elected by the Town *Dumas*.[225]

"Of all the European States," writes de Cardonne, "Russia was first in daring to introduce, for a part of the judiciary, the elective system. . . The Imperial Government could not have been unaware of the fact that such an elective judiciary has brought most detestable results in the United States of America, where judges too often become servile instruments of political passions. That is why the Government endeavored to make the justices of the peace independent of the administration as well as of the people under their jurisdiction . . . and has conferred upon the *Zemstvo* the right to elect these magistrates." [226]

The jurisdiction of the justices of the peace in criminal cases extended to misdemeanors, punishable by: (1) reprimand, rebuke, or slight reprimand; (2) fine not exceeding 300 rubles; (3) arrest for a period of not more than three months or imprisonment up to one year.[227]

Within the competence of the justices of the peace in civil cases came (1) claims based on personal obligations and on property not exceeding 500 rubles in value; (2) claims for damages not exceeding 500 rubles in value; (3) actions for insults and outrages; (4) suits for transgression of rights of possession, if the transgression occurred not more than six months before the case is brought to court.[228]

The introduction of this institution in Russia was a success from the very beginning. The Minister of Justice, Zamyatin, emphasized in his report to the Emperor in September, 1866, that "the new activity of the justices of the peace has won general confidence due to the simplicity of procedure, full publicity and the absence of burdening formalities." [229]

There is no doubt that a great, salutary impression was made on the people by the justices of the peace, who received the nickname *mirovye*.[230] People looked with amazement at these new judges, accessible, deprived of formalism, equally friendly with everyone. The first decisions of these justices of the peace were a sensation, and began to

---

225 *Ibid.*, Art. 40.
226 C. de Cardonne, *op. cit.*, p. 515.
227 *Ustav ugolovnago sudoproizvodstva*, Art. 33.
228 *Ustav grazhdanskago sudoproizvodstva*, Art. 29.
229 *Zhurnal ministerstva yustitsii*, 1867, No. 2.
230 *Mirovye*—Peace-makers.

destroy the traditional distrust of the people for the courts—the belief ✓
that the privileged man may wrong the underprivileged one with impunity, that the rich man may always buy himself free, regardless of
what he had done. Soon justices of the peace achieved enormous popu-
larity. "The people crowded the courts of the justices of the peace,
and new words were heard among them: Now all are equal. Now
beating is forbidden. Now the *mirovoi* will show you yet, . . ." writes
Chubinsky.[231]

This opinion is not shared by Soviet writers. "Bourgeois histor-
ians" writes A. Ya. Vyshinsky, "represent the institution of justices of
the peace as having stirred the sympathy and love of the population,
without distinction of classes. All the hypocrisy and falsity of such an
assertion hardly needs to be proved." [232]

The aims of the legislator in creating the institution of the justices
of the peace is clearly shown in the minutes of the State Council:
"The duty of the justice of the peace is the examination of petty cases
occurring almost daily among the majority of the population, a considerable part of which has no knowledge of laws, cannot endure formalism, respects natural equity only, has no time to lose and seeks,
first of all, a rapid decision in accordance with its notion of justice.
The main goal of the justice of the peace is to satisfy this elementary
need of administration of justice according to conscience." [233]

The strong desire of the State Council to free the justice of the
peace of every formalism and let him decide according to conscience
and sound equity (just as the jurors were bound to do) is manifested
in the State Council's official message to accompany the provision
conferring the jurisdiction of an appellate court over decisions of
the justice of the peace on a conference of the justices of the peace,
and not on an ordinary court (the circuit court, for instance), as had
been advocated by many jurists. In this statement, the State Council
emphasizes that ". . . the examination of one and the same case by
the justice of the peace and the ordinary court is inconvenient because
the first is subordinated to conscience and the second to law, and thus
a decision of a justice of the peace could be overruled by a sentence
of an ordinary court which is bound by the formalism of the statutory
law." [234]

However, the institution of the justices of the peace itself, in the

---

[231] M. P. Chubinsky, "Sudebnaya reforma," in *Istoriya Rossii v XIX veke*, III.
260.
[232] A. Ya. Vyshinsky, *Sud i prokuratura*, pp. 16-18, *passim*.
[233] *Zhurnal Soyedinennago Departamenta Gosudarstvennago Soveta*, No. 65
(1864), p. 300.
[234] *Ibid*.

form in which it had been primarily conceived, did not last long; it was struck dead in 1889. As a matter of fact, in the eyes of those people for whom the reforms of Alexander II, and especially the Judicial Reform, became a target of steady and vicious attacks, the justice of the peace, this genuine symbol of people's administration of justice, was as odious—if not more so—than the other elected judges—the jurors. In the press, the campaign against the Judicial Reform, and the justices of the peace in particular, was led by V. Fuks, a contributor to Katkov's *Moskovskiye Vedomosti* and *Russkiye Vedomosti*. In his book *Court and Police*, which appeared in 1889, the crucial year for the justices of the peace, Fuks summed up all the fault-finding against them. He wrote that the institution of the justice of the peace was "the most artificial, perhaps the most original, but at the same time the most worthless accomplishment of the Judicial Reform." [235]

A series of laws of minor importance restricted the jurisdiction of the justices of the peace as well as of the jury. The government did not dare to administer a final blow to the institution of the jury, but the justices of the peace were abolished in their primary form by the Law of July 12, 1889, which referred some of the cases belonging to their jurisdiction to the newly created institution of *zemskiye nachal'-niki*.[236] It is significant that the blow came from the highest place itself. It was Alexander III who personally ordered the transfer of the functions of the justices of the peace to the *zemskiye nachal'niki*.

The original bill concerning the *zemskiye nachal'niki*, which was introduced into the State Council by the Minister of the Interior, did not provide for the abolition of the institution of the justices of the peace, and envisaged the assignment of very restricted juridical functions to the *zemskiye nachal'niki*— an organ of peasant administration. These juridical functions were supposed to be limited to petty cases directly related to agricultural activities, such as the hiring of agricultural workers, lease of land, wood cutting, vindication of rights of possession, etc. The State Council presented a memorandum to the Tsar to this effect, and asked for directives on the question as to whether the planned institution of *zemskiye nachal'niki* should have the character of a special organ of peasant administration or be made more expedient and more adaptable to needs manifested by practice, and whether to give to the new institution the importance of an organ included in the general system of local administration. On January 23, 1889, Alexander III resolved as follows: ". . . I wish that the justices

---

235 Fuks, *Sud i politsiya,* p. 237.
236 Land captains.

of the peace be abolished in the districts in order to secure the necessary number of reliable *zemskiye nachal'niki* in the districts and to relieve the districts of economic burdens. A part of the jurisdiction of the justices of the peace may be transferred to the *zemskiye nachal'niki and volostnye sudy,* and the rest to the circuit courts." [237]

Thus the issue was decided beforehand by the Tsar. The principle of separation of judicial power from executive power, so jealously guarded by the legislator of 1864, was ignored in 1889.

The Law of July 12, 1889 transferred the functions of the justices of the peace in districts to the *zemskiye nachal'niki,* who became judges, administrators and trustees in peasant affairs at the same time. In the cities, the jurisdiction of the elected justices of the peace was transferred to borough justices of the peace appointed by the government. The honorary justices of the peace, who had no actual importance, were retained. Exception was made for large cities such as St. Petersburg, Moscow, Kharkov, Odessa, Kishinev, Saratov, Kazan, and Nizhny-Novgorod, as well as for the Territory of the Don Army, where justices of the peace were retained.

The poor results produced by the new measure could not be denied by the government. The Third Duma passed a bill restoring the institution of justices of the peace and abolished the *zemskiye nachal'niki* and the peasant courts, but the State Council opposed such radical changes. Finally, the Law on Local Courts, dated June 15, 1912, stripped the *zemskiye nachal'niki* of judicial functions and returned these functions to elected justices of the peace. In its main features, the situation of 1864 was restored with respect to the justices of the peace (with the exception of minor changes concerning the degree of education required and the like).

It is interesting to note one of the changes which is characteristic for the epoch of 1912 as compared with 1864: the State Council added to the four grounds preventing a candidate from being elected justice of the peace, which were mentioned in Art. 21 of the Statutes of Judicial Institutions, a fifth one barring Jews from the candidacy. Whereas the Judicial Reform of 1864 was filled with the idea of equality of all citizens before the law, the legislation of 1912 did not observe this principle any more and introduced into the great work of 1864 a provision discriminating against a part of the population because of its religion.

---

[237] *Otchet o deyatel'nosti Gosudarstvennago Soveta za 1889 g.,* p. 7-36, *passim.*

5. Judiciary

The Reform of 1864 produced the effect of a miracle with regard to bribery in the courts. "The places of the former bribees, venal and unjust, deprived of conscience and shame, dishonored by the people's voice and public opinion—people who were a disgrace to the very idea of jurisprudence—were occupied by men who considered their judicial profession as a great and honorable vocation. . . These men rose to the level of the expectations set for them. They created high traditions. . ." writes Nabokov.[238] And as a matter of fact bribery disappeared from the field of administration of justice. During the fifty years that the new courts existed in Russia, there was not one important case, not one scandal related to a venal action of a judicial magistrate.

Furthermore, the illiterate and uneducated judges of old times were eliminated. Higher legal education (graduation from a law school or faculty of law of a university) became the prerequisite for an appointment to a judicial position. Only persons with three years of experience in legal work at court could be appointed regular members of the court. Lawyers could be appointed to the position of judges only after ten years of practice. I. S. Aksakov asks the following question: "How did it happen that the most essential evil of the old courts, bribery, which existed for many hundred years, of which the country could not be freed by any measure and punishment by the government, suddenly ceased after the introduction of the new court, and at once, as if cut off with a knife? . . . There was even no gradual development: one day—indifference, ignorance and the most shameless bribery, which provoked the indignant verse of the poet,[239] 'Your courts are black with black untruth,' and, lo, the next day, not later than the next day—no indifference and no ignorance, the whole 'black untruth' is washed away, as if it had never existed before! How can this be explained?" He gives the following answer to this question: "It is evident that the reason for such a sudden, unusual, miraculous change, is to be found in the forms of the new procedure in court—in its publicity, its popular character, in court investigation and in the jury." [240]

It was clear to the authors of the new Statutes that in order to put judges in an independent position, it was necessary to shelter them

---

238 Nabokov, op. cit., p. 351.
239 A. K. Khomyakov. See above, p. 14.
240 I. S. Aksakov, Sochineniya 1860-1886, IV, 672-673.

from any influence exercised by superiors other than judicial ones. That is why supervision over courts and their members was entrusted to courts of higher instance. Supervision over the courts by the presidents, prosecutors and the Minister of Justice himself should be, according to the fathers of the Reform, very restricted, namely, limited to a report of the Minister or prosecutor to the higher court concerning unlawful actions or transgressions of existing rules which came to the knowledge of those officials.[241]

Thus, according to the provisions of Articles 249 and 250 of the Statutes of Judicial Institutions, the Departments of Cassation of the Senate were to exercise supervision over all judicial institutions of the Empire, and the *Sudebnye Palaty*—over the circuit courts and all their members, as well as over the lawyers of the district.

As mentioned above, the judges were appointed—judges of the circuit courts and *Sudebnye Palaty* by the Emperor on recommendation of the Minister of Justice, and Senators by individual ukases of the Emperor.[242] The bureau officials were appointed by the president of the court.

In order to exclude protectionism and interference with judicial affairs by the administration, the candidates to be appointed by the Emperor were designated by the general assembly of the members of the court in which a vacancy opened.

Comparatively high salaries were granted to members of the judiciary, in order to make them materially independent. Lazarenko prepared a survey of salaries paid to the judiciary in Russia, Germany, Italy and Austria, and came to the conclusion that "comparing the salary of our judges with the highest salaries paid abroad, . . . we must acknowledge that our magistrates occupy first place as far as salary is concerned." [243]

But the greatest guarantee of the independence of the judiciary, as well as the realization of the principle of separation of powers, is to be seen in the fact that the judges were appointed for life, irremovably. The provision of Art. 243 of the Statutes of Judicial Institutions precribed that presidents of the court and their deputies and members of all judicial institutions should not be either discharged or transferred to another place without their consent. A temporary removal was permitted only in case of indictment, and a definitive dismissal—only pursuant to a sentence of the criminal court.

---

241 *Sudebnye Ustavy* . . . , Part III: *Uchrezhdeniye sudebnykh ustanovleny*, pp. 177-178.
242 *Uchrezhdeniye sudebnykh ustanovleny*, Art. 216.
243 Lazarenko, *op. cit.*, p. 450.

The irremovability of the judges was a fact to which the reactionaries could never reconcile themselves. Thus, *Moskovskiye Vedomosti* wrote in an editorial on this subject in 1882: "It seems that the Tsar has relinquished his rights in favor of the pupils of the law schools and law faculties, who have been permitted to organize into an independent corporation in the activities of which no mortal is allowed to interfere." [244]

Neither did the irremovability of the judges find appreciation in the opposite, radical camp. Thus, Lenin wrote on this question that "the irremovability of the judges, which seems so important to the liberal bourgeois in general and to the Russian liberal bourgeois in particular, is merely a partitioning of the remains of the Middle Ages . . . between proponents of serfdom and the bourgeoisie." [245]

The independence of the judicial power is an indispensable basis of justice. The mere separation of powers is insufficient to guarantee this independence. The judiciary should be put in a position which attenuates, in the highest possible degree, the danger of pressure or interference from outside. The measures described above were in our opinion adequate to reach this goal. If complete independence of the judiciary from the administration was not achieved in reality, this was not the fault of the legislators of 1864, but of the subsequent regime which ruled Russia till 1917.

Lazarenko, who compared the provisions of the Laws of 1864 concerning the irremovability of the Russian judge with those of other European countries, came to the conclusion that the Statutes of Judicial Institutions of 1864 guaranteed to the judge a more independent position than that of his colleagues abroad (except in England). This opinion is corroborated by Professor A. V. Zavadsky, who in his work "The Irremovability of the Judge and his Independence" asserts that the Statutes of Judicial Institutions created for the Russian judge "a position unique in Europe." [246,247]

As an illustration of the feeling with which the new judiciary began its task, let us again quote A. F. Koni, who was at that time a member of it. "Those who lived through that time . . . cannot forget it. The first officials of the new courts were inspired with confidence in their strength. They had a clear view of the future, and the conviction that the newly introduced order was a masterpiece in every

---

[244] Quoted by A. E. Nolde, *op. cit.*, p. 615.
[245] Lenin, *Sochineniya*, 2d ed., XXX, 195.
[246] Lazarenko, *op. cit.*, Footnote 1 on p. 410.
[247] A. V. Zavadsky, *Nesmenyaemost' sud'i i ego nezavisimost'*, p. 47.

sense. All energies were dedicated to the new activity, unselfishly, and not without sacrifices." [248]

6. Prosecutors

In 1711 Peter the Great created the office of *fiscals*,[249] whose main duties consisted in exposing violation of ukases, bribery and actions against the financial interests of the state, as well as the prosecution of cases in which no applicants took part. The *fiscals* had also to report on the sluggishness of procedure of official agencies. Considering, however, that the *fiscals* were unable to secure a smooth functioning of administrative affairs, Peter the Great also created the office of prosecutors at all the *Kollegii*,[250] by the Ukase of January 12, 1722.[251] The prosecutors had the task of supervising the course of affairs in the *Kollegii* and the activity of the *fiscals*. Fiscals and prosecutors were attached to every kind of administration, even to the army and fleet.

After Peter's death, the *fiscals* and the prosecutors experienced the fate of many of his reforms: they were abolished. In 1730, however, the prosecutors were re-established.

The *Uchrezhdeniye o guberniyakh* of 1775 expanded the functions of the prosecutors to a very great extent. They were entrusted with the general supervision of the activity of all the government agencies and their officials.

The aims of the legislator of 1864 with regard to the prosecution and its representatives were clear. Article 135 of the Statutes of Judicial Institutions reads: "The activity of persons entrusted with prosecutor's supervision is limited to judicial affairs." This intention, however, was not carried out; according to subsequent legislation, the prosecutor retained his capacity of custodian of legality in every branch of administration, beside his accusatory functions in criminal procedure.[252] Prosecutors were officials of the Ministry of Justice, subordinated to the Minister of Justice, who himself had the title of General Prosecutor. A prosecutor was attached to every circuit court and *Sudebnaya Palata,* as well as to the Senate and the Synod, where they had the title of *Ober-Prokuror* (Chief Prosecutor). The prosecutors of the circuit courts and *Sudebnye Palaty* had a number of assistant prosecutors who usually pleaded in court.

The assistant prosecutor had to prepare the indictment brief on

---

[248] A. F. Koni, *Za poledniye gody,* p. 483.
[249] *Polnoye sobraniye zakonov Rossiiskoi Imperii, Sobraniye pervoye,* Nos. 2336 and 2331.
[250] A kind of ministry with collegiate administration.
[251] *Ibid.,* . . . , No. 3877.
[252] See Gredinger, "Prokurorsky nadzor," in *S.U.*, II, 197-249.

the basis of the preliminary investigation, which took place under his supervision, in cases of major offenses—including all cases subject to the jurisdiction of the jury. The indictment was formulated by a special division of the *Sudebnaya Palata,* called *Obvinitel'naya kamera* (Indictment Chamber).

The role of the prosecutor in the trial is a major one. He is the natural opponent of the lawyer. The lawyer must vanquish him. Victory over the prosecutor is the goal of the lawyer in court.

With regard to the accusatorial functions of the prosecutor, the motives of the State Council contain remarkable words of wisdom.

In the official message to accompany Article 573 of the Code of Criminal Procedure, which orders the bench to hear *every* witness summoned by the prosecutor, we read: "A complete equalization of rights of the prosecutor and the defendant concerning the summoning of persons whose testimony at court is demanded by the parties is impossible, because their attitude in the case is not similar in every respect. The prosecutor exposes the crime in the name of the law, to which the conviction of an innocent person is even more contrary than the acquittal of a guilty person. Therefore, all the actions of the prosecutor should aim, not towards conviction, *but exclusively towards the disclosure of truth* regardless of whether it shows the guilt or innocence of the defendant. It is true that the prosecutor appears before the court as an accuser, but he must support the accusation during the court proceedings not for the sake of bringing about a conviction of the defendant *at any price,* but only to bring to light all the grounds and reasons for the accusation and thereby give the defense an opportunity to interpret them from its standpoint and even to eliminate them completely if they can be rebutted. The more vague the accusation, the more difficult the defense . . . The prosecutor is obliged to summon all the witnesses whose testimony may serve to disclose the truth—not exclusively those whose evidence confirms the accusation." [253]

Guided by the same spirit of justice and humaneness, the legislator included in the Code of Criminal Procedure the following provision (Art. 740): "If the prosecutor considers the defendant's excuses valid, he must declare so to the court according to his conscience and decline to uphold the accusation refuted by the proceedings in the court."

In the official message to accompany Article 740 it is said: "The

---

[253] *Sudebnye Ustavy* . . . , Part III: *Ustav ugolovnago sudoproizvodstva,* pp. 218-219.

prosecutor must not . . . uphold the accusation . . . if he is not convinced of the guilt of the accused." [254]

D. THE REFORM ATTACKED AND DEFENDED

We have seen that the introduction of the jury in Russia met with scepticism on the part of people who, one would think, ought not to have been its opponents *a priori,* and who in fact later became its fervent supporters. The judicial reform *in toto* also became the object of bitter attacks, even by some liberals. For instance, N. A. Ogarev, a poet and famous friend of Alexander Herzen, wrote in 1862 an article in Herzen's *Kolokol* in which he criticized the Basic Principles of the Reform, which had just been published in Russia, pointing out that it was a slavish copy of French and, to a certain extent, English institutions, entirely foreign to the Russian spirit.[255] And Koshelev, who participated in the Emancipation Reform of 1861, wrote as follows to M.P. Pogodin, distinguished historian and publicist: "I read the opinion of the State Council on the Basic Principles of our future judicial procedures and institutions. Indeed, they are very good. But would it not also be opportune to publish a law which obliges everyone in Russia to till exclusively with ploughs? Such a law would certainly be very useful for agriculture. The only question is, where to take the ploughs from and where to find a sufficient number of people who are able to handle ploughs? It is really magnificent! Decrees provide for lawyers and court presidents able to deal with litigation and pleading according to the requirements of legal science. You know, one cannot read this remarkable work without laughing: good, very good, but completely useless." [256]

And Shevyrev, a professor of the University of Moscow, voiced the following objections: "Peculiar are the discussions about the Judicial Reform. I do not think that such a judicial comedy, played by the representative of the state and the counsel adorned with omni-pardoning eloquence, could take hold in Russia. I think that the Russian is capable of saying in public to his defender: 'You are lying all the time: in fact I am the killer!' " [257]

During the first years of its functioning, the Reform was praised by official places and by the Katkov press. "It is really difficult to believe," wrote Katkov's paper, "that in such a short time things of

254 *Ibid.,* p. 263.
255 *Kolokol,* Nov. 15, 1862, p. 1237.
256 N. Barsukov, *Zhizn' i trudy M. P. Pogodina,* XIX, 475.
257 *Ibid.,* p. 476.

such tremendous importance and so unlike our previous order in everything from fundamental ideas to individual details could occur in Russia. That which only a couple of years ago seemed to be a dream and provoked so many seemingly justified objections is now in full operation." [258]

In the late seventies, and then after the assassination of Alexander II, when the tide of reaction began to rise in Russia, attacks against the individual principles and institutions of the Reform, such as publicity, irremovability of judges, the jury, the bar, etc., were resumed with particular force. Some of these attacks were already discussed above.

In the eighties, when charges against the Reform and its individual institutions became violent, the Slavophile writer Ivan Aksakov, whose political views can by no means be described as liberal in the modern sense of the word, published, in defense of the Reform, an article in the newspaper *Rus'*, on February 1884, which produced a sensation at that time. Aksakov wrote:

> Our Russian public has a strikingly short memory . . . Are we really so forgetful that we completely lost the memory of what the old court was, less than a quarter of a century ago? . . . There was no light in the darkness of injustice! . . . Court and injustice were synonyms in the mind of the people . . . Injustice was a kind of inescapable feature of life . . . Our boldest dreams did not go so far as to assume that a court completely without bribes—ah, but for a court without bribes!—could exist in our fatherland.
>
> And such a court became possible. What a miracle! . . . And not only possible—it exists in reality! This is not an assumption, not a dream. It is our reality, which is understood by the *entire* people!
>
> The fact that the contemporary judges do not accept bribes, that one can approach them without presents, that poverty is not a vice in the eyes of the court, that there is equal justice for the poor and oppressed and for the rich and noble—this fact at the present time is known in all corners of Russia, to every peasant on the immeasurable expanse of our country. The young generations of a hundred million people are now being brought up in this spirit. And we, we ourselves, are suddenly shouting at, spitting on, abusing and trampling upon the tool of our resurrection —as though we were possessed—the very institution which dragged us out of the malodorous mire where we were stuck almost up to our heads, . . . this 'new court' which in only twenty years has already succeeded in pushing the old, godless iniquity

---

[258] *Moskovskiye Vedomosti*, 1867, no. 69.

into the background of our memory and even in knocking it out of there. . . . Yes, our memory is short!"[259]

Indeed, a series of laws was published which constituted a flagrant violation of the principles promulgated in 1864. But the Reform as a whole was not shaken.

The most serious attempt at a general reform of the Reform was made by the Commission for the Revision of the Laws Concerning Judicial Administration, appointed by the Tsar in 1894—the so-called Murav'yov Commission. In his speech on the occasion of his appointment as Minister of Justice, N. V. Murav'yov said: "Judicial power is a branch of government activity and judicial institutions are organs of the government. It is evident that . . . our activity must be always strictly coordinated with the intentions and views of the government."[260] Murav'yov developed the same ideas in his April 9, 1894 report to the Tsar, in which he asked for the appointment of the Commission: "The principle, always true, of the state character, and of the subjection to governmental direction, of the courts and judicial institutions, must be established as a basis for the projected reform. The conception of such a court did not find a sufficiently clear and definitive expression in the Laws of 1864. This fact, together with the principle of a sharp separation of the court from the administration carried out in the Statutes of Judicial Institutions, as well as the inadequate formulation of the principle of the irremovability of the judges, could be interpreted, and indeed were interpreted, as an intention, on the legislator's part, to put the representatives of the judicial power in an exclusive position among other governmental organs."[261]

Clear enough. This was an attempt to break with the principle of separation of the judicial power from the administrative power and the irremovability of judges as a guarantee of their independence. The reaction could never digest what Alexander II, in an adverse mood, had called "a piece of nonsense," i.e., the fact that the administration of justice was no longer an adjunct to internal affairs under the direction of the government. It was intended definitively to deprive the courts of the independent position assigned to them by the Laws of 1864.

But in case these words were not clear enough, the Minister did not hesitate to be even more specific: ". . . The government must have

---

259 I. S. Aksakov, *Sochineniya 1860-1886*, IV, 652-659, *passim*.
260 Nolde, *op. cit.*, p. 627-628.
261 Vysochaishe uchrezhdennaya komissiya dlya peresmotra zakonopolozheny po sudebnoi chasti. *Ob"yasnitel'naya zapiska*, I, 70.

the opportunity of exercising influence over the composition of the personnel entrusted with judicial powers and to direct the activities of that personnel according to the interests of the entire state."[262]

The Commission shared the opinion of the Minister that the abolition of the elective principle for the appointment of local judges would be the best method of making the administration of justice dependent on the internal policy of the government.

However, the drafts worked out by the Commission were not passed by the legislator.

It is peculiar that in a speech delivered three years later Minister Murav'yov said, on the occasion of the introduction of the Statutes of Judicial Institutions (without jury) in the Siberian provinces: "The Laws which were granted to Russia in 1864 are the summing up of what has been thought by mankind in the matter of justice for many centuries," and he added: ". . . it is regrettable that this judicial system has been shaken by subsequent amendments and practice."[263] Was it not Murav'yov himself who shook, with all his strength, the system he later praised so highly?

Another Minister of Justice of Tsarist Russia, the last Minister of Justice of Nicholas II, I. G. Shcheglovitov, who did not take any notice of the independence of judges or the freedom of conscience of the jury whenever his political designs were involved, wrote in 1914: "The importance of the Judicial Reform of November 1864 for our state and public life is tremendous. It is one of the greatest legislative monuments in our history, one which characterizes our epoch."[264] On paper Shcheglovitov was a supporter of the independence of the court. "A dependent administration of justice will never produce justice. The judge must consider only: (1) the case, (2) the law and (3) his conscience."[265] However, he writes further: "The judges are first of all servants of the state. They are a very important part of the tremendous state apparatus and have to reckon with the general interests of the state."[266]

That is where the crux of the matter lies. According to the ideology of Murav'yov and Shcheglovitov, the judge is independent on the one hand, but on the other he is an official like all other servants of the state, who first of all has to consider, not the requirements of jus-

---

262 Quoted by Nolde, *op. cit.*, p. 628-629.
263 See *Zhurnal ministerstva yustitsii*, 1897, No. 7.
264 I. G. Schcheglovitov, "Vliyaniye inostrannykh zakonodatel'stv na sostavleniye Sudebnykh Ustavov 20 noyabrya 1864 g.," in *S.U.* I, 233.
265 *Ibid.*, p. 284.
266 *Ibid.*

tice, but the interests of the state—in the sense, of course, in which these interests are understood by the government. This meant that when Shcheglovitov thought that the interests of the state demanded the conviction of Beilis, for instance, he did not hesitate to make use of every kind of pressure upon the court to bring about a conviction. But on paper Shcheglovitov maintained that *"jus dicendi officium* requires that the actions of the court be subordinated to law only, be free from any influence of the administration, even of the highest places of the government, which, although they appoint judges, must not prescribe their decisions."[267]

As for Katkov and his disciples, every occasion was good enough for the most vicious attacks upon the Reform and its institutions as soon as the political wind turned against it. The criticism of individual institutions by the Katkov press has been given above. Among assertions of a general character, let us quote the following: "An independent court is a judicial republic." "In a state which is to live, there cannot exist two autocracies."[268]

All the attacks of the Katkov newspapers were repeated by V. Ya. Fuks in his pamphlet, *Court and Police,* mentioned above. Fuks asserted that the Statutes of Judicial Institutions were the result of evil and foreign influences which distorted, in 1861-1864, the drafts of judiciary acts of 1857-1861.[269] "The institutions created by the Laws of 1864 did not meet the expectations of either the public or the government and, to a certain extent, not even those of the authors of the Statutes themselves. Emancipated from the general state discipline, unrestrained by law, infatuated with a mania of independence, these institutions, which had an inadequate personnel, put forward aims, and were imbued by ideas, which were incompatible with the tasks of justice. As a result, they brought into the administration of justice discord which does not make for the correct adjudication of civil and criminal cases, introduces disorder in our state organism and in the moral foundations of our social development as well."[270] Fuks was of the opinion that by the introduction of the electoral system for the justices of the peace the legislator of 1864 adhered to a radical theory "reminding one of the wrong views of J. J. Rousseau on the social con-

---

[267] *Ibid.*
[268] *Moskovskiye Vedomosti,* 1884, no. 316. In 1866, the same Katkov wrote: "The difference between the old and the new courts lies in the fact that the old courts corrupted people, whereas the new ones improve and educate them." (*Moskovskiye Vedomosti,* 1866, No. 263).
[269] Fuks, *op. cit.,* p. 146.
[270] *Ibid.,* p. 135.

tract."[271] The same legislator, according to Fuks, changed "the declaration of principles à la J. J. Rousseau into a bill of rights."[272]

With regard to Fuks, Shcheglovitov rightly declares that "such grave and highly unjust accusations against our Laws of 1864 . . . do not deserve to be answered."[273]

"The reformed [civil and criminal] procedures have remained exotic plants in Russia: they suit the general structure of the state as a silk top hat suits an Eskimo clothed in animal skins," Plekhanov wrote in 1890.[274]

Let us see now what a prominent Soviet jurist and a no less prominent Soviet historian have to say about the Reform.

In his book, *The Marxist-Leninist Doctrine of the Court and the Soviet Court System*, A. Ya. Vyshinsky writes: "The representatives of the bourgeoisie and liberals of the type of Nabokov, Milyukov and Hessen used much paper to extol this Judicial Reform, describing it as the greatest achievement of human culture and civilization. In reality the Judicial Reform of 1864 was nothing more than a rather poor bourgeois reform."[275] According to Vyshinsky, the purpose behind the new judicial system was "to serve more effectively the cause of exploitation and oppression of the working population, insuring better than did the old court the defense and protection of the nobility and of the young bourgeoisie, which gained, through the Reform, institutions beneficial to them—such as the jury, lawyers, justices of the peace, judicial investigators and others—and formed according to European patterns." [276,277]

Vyshinsky thinks that the attitude of the Russian people toward the Reform was a negative one. He undertakes to present evidence for his point of view and thinks that exhaustive proof can be found in the text of an address presented by the Town Duma of Petersburg to Alexander II. This is what the Duma wrote with regard to the Reform and the new court: "The opening of the new court fills the hearts of all loyal subjects with the kind of joy which Russia experiences in the greatest moments of her historical life." The way in which this Reform

---

271 *Ibid.*, p. 73.

272 *Ibid.*, pp. 74-75.

273 I. G. Shcheglovitov, "Vliyaniye inostrannykh zakonodatel'stv na sostavleniye Sudebnykh Ustavov 20 noyabrya 1864 goda," in *S.U.*, I. 240.

274 G. V. Plekhanov, *Sochineniya*, V, 10.

275 A. Ya. Vyshinsky, *Marksistsko-leninskoye ucheniye o sude i sovetskaya sudebnaya sistema*, p. 16.

276 *Ibid.*, p. 18.

277 This statement by the leading Soviet jurist contradicts the assertion of H. J. Berman that the Soviets praise the Judical Reform of 1864. (Harold J. Berman, *Justice in Russia*, p. 147).

was met by the bourgeoisie and nobility as shown in this address constitutes by itself, according to Vyshinsky, a sufficient answer to the
question of "what the attitude of the working population of our
country was to this 'notorious' juridical reform."[278]

The opinion of M. Pokrovsky is more moderate than that of Mr.
Vyshinsky. He writes in his *Brief History of Russia* that in lauding the
Judicial Reform, bourgeois writers were perhaps a step nearer the
truth than in lauding the allegedly disinterested character of the
Emancipation Reform, because the Judicial Reform was unquestionably the most effective reform of the sixties, especially since it was
accompanied by the abolition of corporal punishment.[279] However, the
Soviet historian also comes to the conclusion that the only class whose
interests were effectively safeguarded by the Reform was the bourgeoisie. With regard to the question of the attitude of the Russian
people towards the Reform, Pokrovsky remarks: "The real attitude of
the masses of the people of the sixties towards the new court is, for
the time being, unknown to us, and will possibly remain unknown for
a long time."[280]

These are the main unfavorable judgments on the Reform. It
would be impossible to give a more or less exhaustive account of the
favorable appraisals; this alone would require a whole book, since the
entire Russian juridical literature dealing with the Reform has only
words of appreciation and admiration for it. Opinions concerning individual institutions introduced by the Reform were already mentioned above. At this point I would like to cite the opinion of two
foreigners who lived in Russia shortly after the Reform. C. de Cardonne gives the following veracious account of what he had the
opportunity to observe in Russia: "Broad in spirit, liberal in its application, based on the principles of modern jurisprudence, the Judicial
Reform of 1864 is one of the most fecund reforms of the reign of
Alexander II. It has given to Russia courts which are worthy of this
name, and has inaugurated an honest and independent administration
of justice. It has proclaimed the separation of judicial and administrative powers and the equality of all Russians before the law. By institut-
ing an elected judiciary and the jury, it has brought important innovations and has associated the citizens with the administration of justice.
It has dispersed the clouds which during many centuries obscured the

---

[278] A. Ya. Vyshinsky, *Sud i prokuratura,* p. 16-18.
[279] M. N. Pokrovsky, *Brief History of Russia.* In reality, the abolition of corporal punishment preceded the Judicial Reform by more than one year. See The
Imperial Ukases of April 17, 1863.*Polnoye sobraniye zakonov Rossiiskoi Imperii,*
Nos. 39504, 39506.
[280] M. N. Pokrovsky, *Russkaya istoriya s drevneishikh vremen,* IV, 131.

notion of rights, revived respect for the law and the sense of legality which the former prevarications had weakened. It has thus raised public dignity and reinforced public consciousness. In matters of morality as well as in the material field, the Judicial Reform has already exercised and will continue to exercise in the future the most salutary influence upon the whole Slavic world."[281]

Another witness is Leroy-Beaulieu. He writes: "Of all the reforms of Alexander II, the Judicial Reform is . . . the most important one, the one which was to have the greatest influence on the mores and on social life, on the country and the government." And he explains his assertion in the following words: "Emperor Alexander gave Russia tribunals charged with the mission of substituting the rule of law for the rule of arbitrariness and corruption."[282]

The thoughts and feelings of a Russian, a contemporary of the Reform, are conveyed to the reader by the diary of Nikitenko. Under the date of October 10, 1862, Nikitenko entered into the diary the following lines: "I have read the drafts for the new judicial procedures and of the judicial system approved by the Tsar. What incredible progress Russia made under this reign! If somebody had dared to dream about such things at the time of Nicholas and his dream had slipped from his lips, he would have been regarded as either crazy or a state criminal. And here you have open proceedings in courts, publicity, a jury, the bar, emancipation of the court from administrative power. . ."[283] "What did the Laws of 1864 give to Russia?" writes A. N. Lazarenko years after Nikitenko: "They gave to our fatherland what did not exist before—justice; they created courts, not only in name—courts existed also before the Reform—but courts powerful because of their independence, with the means for the realization of legality, this main basis of culture. . . The Laws of 1864 may justly be regarded as the pride of Russian juridical thought, as one of the best monuments of our legislation which even in the remote future will serve as the highest glorification of the epoch which produced them and of the unforgettable fathers of the Reform who gave their entire soul to the task of the establishment of an impartial court on their native soil."[284]

The Laws of November 20, 1864 occupy an exceptional place in the Russian legislation of the pre-revolutionary period. Never before

---

281 C. de Cardonne, op. cit., p. 527.
282 A. Leroy-Beaulieu, L'Empire des tsars et les Russes, II, 278, 277.
283 Nikitenko, op. cit., II, 103.
284 Lazarenko, op. cit., p. 488-489.

were Russian codes the object of such vicious attacks on the one hand and such fervent veneration on the other.

The new laws opened the way in Russia to equity, which hitherto was not to be found there. Law courts were created in place of institutions which had only the name of "courts" in common with the new ones—tribunals powerful because of their independence and ability to serve real enforcement of law. Lazarenko writes: "The necessary guarantees of justice were provided by the Reform with such perfection that almost every institution of the new judicial system proved to be far better than the foreign models. As a whole, the Laws of November 20, 1864, rank higher than the judicial organization of other contemporary European countries on the continent." [285] As Gruzenberg put it in one of his brilliant speeches in 1909: "Due to the same energy, passion and persistance with which they fought and are still fighting for participation in legislation, the people obtained predominance in the administration of justice. They control the activity of the court by means of publicity and oral proceedings; they resolve the question of guilt through their representatives. They oppose the accusation formulated by the state with a defense endowed with equal rights and powerful in its knowledge and independence."[286]

Professor Chubinsky, summarizing the consequences of the Reform, comes to the conclusion that "the creation and realization of the Reform belong to the best and most important moments of our history." [287]

The lasting enthusiasm created by the Reform may be explained only by the fact that it was more than a piece of legislation on judicial matters, with more or less substantial technical advantages or defects. It was its ideological and political importance which gave the Reform the unique place it occupies in Russian history and explains why it was so cherished by many, and so cursed by some. In the ideological sense, the Reform was an expression of the victory of humanitarian and cultural principles, admitted to Russia after many years of persecution and negation and embodied in the controversial procedure, publicity, jury, pleading in court and admission of a free defense. Another humanitarian aspect of the Reform was the emancipation of the individual from the yoke of the State in judicial matters. To this aspect of the Reform we shall return later.

On September 22, 1866, Katkov's *Moskovskiye Vedomosti* wrote:

---

285 *Ibid.,* p. 415.
286 O. O. Gruzenberg, *Ocherki i rechi,* p. 66.
287 M. P. Chubinsky, "Sudebnaya reforma," in *Istoriya Rossii, v XIX veke,* III, 251.

"Judicial power is not a power which is given to a limited number of persons or to one class of the population. It is a privilege which is granted to the whole people; it is a right which is awarded to the Russian citizen. With the creation of an independent and uncoerced judicial power, the entire society is raised. Where a well-organized court exists, there is justice. Where justice exists, there the individual is defended and there is legal freedom. With the consolidation of the new order and the introduction of it into all parts of Russia it becomes possible to live there as in a civilized country." And then comes a sentence which is pure prophecy. "As long as Russia flourishes, as long as her affairs improve rather than deteriorate the principles embodied in the Judicial Reform will remain in force." [288]

---

[288] *Moskovskiye Vedomosti*, 1866, No. 198.

CHAPTER II

THE EMERGENCE OF THE RUSSIAN LAWYER

A. His Predecessors

The institution of representation in court was unknown to the oldest Russian law codes and sources. The *Russkaya Pravda* and the treaties between the Slavs and the Greeks do not mention it at all. This may be explained by the fact that personal appearance in court was obligatory at that time. Actions in court such as ordeal, oath-taking and combat, had to be performed by the parties themselves, sometimes with the help of their family members or kin.

But already in the 15th century, the law codes record a considerable development of this institution.[1] The *Novgorodskaya Sudebnaya Gramota* gave everyone the right to have a representative in court (Arts. 15, 19 and 32). The *Pskovskaya Sudebnaya Gramota* gave this right only to women, children, monks, nuns, senile men and deaf persons (Arts. 68 and 69). These representatives were generally chosen from among the nearest relatives and were "natural" representatives, like a son acting for his mother or a husband for his wife. But any other person, even if not a "natural" representative, was allowed to assume the representation of a defendant in court, with one exception only: an official had no right to represent private interests, so as not to be able to exert influence upon the court. Vladimirsky-Budanov is of the opinion that paid representatives were admitted to the representation of other people's interests only reluctantly.[2] He sees confirmation of his opinion in the provision of Art. 71 of the *Pskovskaya Sudebnaya Gramota,* which prohibited a person from representing two different parties on the same day.[3]

Subsequent codes—the *Sudebniki* of Ivan III and Ivan IV, as well as the *Ulozheniye Tsarya Alekseya Mikhailovicha*—speak of hired rep-

---

[1] See M. F. Vladimirsky-Budanov, *Obzor istorii russkago prava,* p. 516, and the texts of the *Gramoty* referred to by Vladimirsky-Budanov.

[2] Vladimirsky-Budanov, *op. cit.,* p. 5.

[3] This opinion is shared by E. V. Vas'kovsky, *Organizatsiya advokatury,* I, 308.

resentatives in court as of a well-established institution.[4] But none of these codes provides for a definite organization of this institution, and neither did later decrees, which merely forbade active and former officials to represent others in court or required a written power of attorney for this purpose.[5]

The *Svod zakonov Rossiiskoi Imperii* contained, for the first time, a regulation stating that "every person who according to the law can be a plaintiff or defendant has the right to carry on a suit through a representative" who acting in court "in his place, represents his person."[6] These representatives were called *stryapchiye*.[7] The *Svod* enumerates the persons disqualified as representatives in court.[8] These are: (1) underage persons; (2) peasants belonging to the *Udely* (properties of the imperial family) when litigation concerned peasants of those *Udely*; in other cases, they were allowed to be representatives in court with the permission of their superiors; (3) members of the clergy; (4) monks and nuns; (5) officials; (6) persons of all classes who, having been indicted for crimes punishable by deprivation of rights, conscription, or exile to Siberia and forced labor, were freed from those punishments pursuant to an imperial manifesto or remained unacquitted because their cases were dropped pursuant to a manifesto; (7) persons declared infamous by decision of a court, although not deprived of all rights; (8) persons who were subjected to corporal punishment for criminal offenses pursuant to a court decision, although they were not excluded from urban or rural communities; (9) former officials and employees of chancelleries dismissed for criminal offenses or bad behavior; (10) those under police supervision and those to whom representation is prohibited as a consequence of illegal acts committed by them. Article 185 gave the right to anyone, except those listed above, to be a representative in court. Thus, until the Reform of 1864, the profession of a representative in court, i.e., the profession of a counsel or lawyer, remained open to anyone with the few exceptions mentioned above.

Whereas the doors of the profession of lawyer were thrown wide open to anyone, the criminal and civil procedures preceding the Reform of 1864 reduced the functions of a representative to the writing

---

[4] See *Sudebnik* of 1497, Art. 36; *Sudebnik* of 1550, Art. 13, and *Ulozheniye* of 1649, X, 108; XIV, 5.

[5] *Polnoye sobraniye zakonov, Sobraniye pervoye,* No. 3282.

[6] *Svod zakonov, Izd.* 1857g., Vol. X, Part 2, Art. 184.

[7] The *Uchrezhdeniye o guberniiakh* of 1775 introduced another kind of *Stryapchiye,* called *sudebnye stryapchiye* who were officials,—assistants of the prosecutors and defenders of state interests.

[8] *Ibid.,* Art. 191.

of controversial papers, presentation of evidence and the like. These functions Vas'kovsky compares with those of a French *avoué* or an English *solicitor*.[9]

Indeed, we have already seen above[10] that the inquisitorial and secret procedure in criminal cases completely excluded judicial inquiry in open court with witnesses' testimony in the presence of the accused. Instead, a member of the court examined the records of the preliminary investigation and prepared an excerpt from them which served as the only basis for the decision of the court.[11] Civil procedure was founded on the same principle. First of all, the parties exchanged briefs four times. This usually took about four months but could be dragged out for two years. Then, an abstract was prepared from the records and was communicated to the parties in order that they should approve and sign it. The parties had the right to ask for supplements to, and changes in, the abstract. During the reporting of the abstract to the court, the parties or their representatives had the right to be present. But the discussion of the litigation, and the decision, took place in the absence of the parties.[12]

The low moral and educational level of the pre-Reform judiciary have already been depicted. Let us say that the reputation of the representatives in court at that time was even worse. Peter the Great in a decree accused them of unduly dragging out lawsuits and impeding the task of the judges rather than facilitating it. He called them *"yabedniki"* (chicaners, slanderers), "accomplices of thieves" and "seducers".[13] The name of *yabedniki* stuck to them for a long time.[14]

The true value of these private solicitors was well known also to the subsequent governments. Thus, the Commission for the Suggestion of Laws, set up by Alexander I in 1820, wrote in its report: "Those who are called *stryapchiye* are as little respected in Russia as most of them actually deserve according to examples of how they fulfill their obligations toward their clients. This can be confirmed by the courts themselves. Who can in all confidence entrust them with his interests and rely upon them? It has happened that the same solicitor helped the one and the other party at the same time and that solicitors dragged out and embroiled lawsuits and, instead of con-

---

9 Vas'kovsky writes "attorney" but evidently means "solicitor." Vas'kovsky, *op. cit.*, p. 311.
10 p. 8.
11 *Svod zakonov, Izd., 1857g.*, Vol. XV, Part 2, Arts. 279, 287, 349.
12 *Ibid.*, Vol X, Part 2, Arts. 443-447, 463. Vas'kovsky, *op. cit.*, p. 311.
13 *Polnoye sobraniye zakonov, Sobraniye pervoye*, Nos. 3006, 1572.
14 The *yabedniki* are satirized in V. V. Kapnist's famous comedy *Yabeda*, written in 1798.

ciliating the litigants, irritated them still more; they did it as a consequence of their ignorance, or purposely, and almost always it was they who were the main cause of chicaneous, unjust and unclear sentences in the lower instances, which are so difficult and sometimes even impossible to change in the higher instances." [15] They were correctly characterized by Leroy-Beaulieu, who wrote: "Formerly, there were no people who could be called anything like lawyers. There were only ignorant individuals who were provided with power of attorney, who composed or presented briefs on behalf of the parties and followed the cases in court. They were known as *stryapchiye* (*stryapchiye* derives from the verb *stryapat'*, which means to prepare meals, to cook and, in a figurative sense, to whip up a case)." [16]

The Russian memoirs and literature of the 19th century give a distressing picture of the activity of the judicial representative of the time before the Reform of 1864. A. V. Lokhvitsky wrote in 1860 that Russia has no legal profession in the West-European sense of the word, and that Russia's court representatives may be divided into two categories. Those belonging to the first one are direct descendants of the *pod'yachiye* of the old times. They take 20 kopecks and a *shtof*[17] of vodka for preparing a petition, 5 or 10 rubles for a forged passport. They also have a fixed price for a forged certificate or signature, etc. Anything which legislation undertook against them, beginning with the time of Peter the Great, was in vain, because they are the natural result of the secret and written judicial procedure, administration of justice according to the letter (and not the spirit) of the law, complete absence of publicity in court procedure and absence of a well-organized legal profession. The second category of representatives is an aristocratic one. It comprises people with decent manners, well clad, who ask several hundred rubles for the preparation of papers. In the majority of cases, they graduated from a higher educational institution. They despise the cheap *pod'yachiye*, although they often revert to them for the performance of some tricks. They adorn themselves with the impressive name of "advocates"—nobody knows by what right and on what grounds. Among them there are persons who acquired great notoriety and a considerable fortune and whose smallest fault is that they write briefs for the plaintiff and the defendant in the same case, taking money from both of them.[18]

---

[15] I. V. Hessen, *Advokatura, obshchestvo i gosudarstvo*, Vol. I of *Istoriia russkoi advokatury 1864-1914*, pp. 9-10.

[16] Leroy-Beaulieu, *op. cit.*, II, 360.

[17] About 2 liters.

[18] A. V. Lokhvitsky, 'O nashikh khodatayakh po delam," *Russkoe Slovo*, Febr. 1860, pp. 43-46, *passim*.

Another testimony belongs to the pen of N. A. Potekhin, a distinguished lawyer, who joined the bar after the Reform of 1864. He divided the pre-Reform advocates into three categories: "To the first group belonged advocates who were at the same time court officials, i.e. secretaries, chief clerks, assistants to the sheriff, registrars and other employees of the courts. They were not bribees in the direct sense of the word; they merely assumed the carrying on of lawsuits in the courts where they were employed, and directed these suits toward a just decision according to their understanding. . . The second group of advocates, a very numerous one, included the professionals . . . It consisted of retired officials who in the majority of cases had retired because of some 'troubles in the service'. . . Their juridical knowledge, acquired mainly during their service, was very poor. . . The third group cannot be generally defined: it was merely a mixed crowd, such a mish-mash of positions, qualities and conditions that it is impossible to find common traits, to give a general description. . . There were noblemen, ruined landowners and merchants, clerks who formerly conducted suits of their masters, retired military men, even bartenders from houses of prostitution and beer houses, officials expelled from the service, etc. . ." "Such advocates," continues Potekhin, "were called *yabedniki*, blood-suckers and ink-souls. But the best name for them was *krapivnoye semya* (nettle seed). . . . Indeed, nettle grows on every rubbish, close to hedges; it does not need fertile soil; it is very branchy; it has a rather nice greenness but contact with it is dangerous. It burns so strongly, and causes such pricks, that the comparison of 'advocates' of old times with nettle seed is quite correct." [19]

The Russian literature of the 19th century gives a vivid description of the activities of the "advocates" before the Reform. Gogol' in his *Dead Souls* has left us a striking portrait of one such "lawyer."

This lawyer was a man of extraodinary experience. He had fallen under the jurisdiction of the court fifteen years before this date, but he had so managed that it had been utterly impossible to interdict him in his profession. Everybody was perfectly well aware of the fact that he had deserved transportation half a dozen times. He was suspected to the last degree in every quarter, but it was impossible to produce plain and convincing proofs. There really was something uncanny about him, and he might have been boldly proclaimed as a wizard if the history which we are transcribing referred to an uncivilized epoch. [20]

[19] P. A. Potekhin, "Otryvki iz vospominany advokata," *Pravo*, 1900, No. 47, pp. 2213 ff, *passim*.
[20] N. V. Gogol, *Tchitchikoff's Journeys; or Dead Souls*, II, 148.

Gogol also describes the means employed by the lawyer to defend his client:

> . . .The lawyer was working wonders in civil circles: the governor was given to understand indirectly, that the procurator was preparing a complaint about him; the commandant of the gendarmes was informed that an official who had been living privately in town, was writing a denunciation about him; the official who had been living privately was told that there was another and still more mysterious official personage, who was lodging information against him: and all of them were led into such a position that they were forced to resort to him for advice. This was the utter nonsense which resulted: denunciation was mounted upon denunciation, and things were on the point of being divulged, such as no one had ever heard of, and which had never had any existence in reality. . . . The exceedingly clever and sensible official to whom the preparation of the abstract was intrusted came near losing his mind. It was absolutely impossible, by any means whatever, to grasp the thread of the transaction.[21]

There was another type of advocate, described by Saltykov-Shchedrin in his *Poshekhonskaya starina*. Pyotr Dormidontovich Mogil'tsev was appointed directly from school as clerk at the district court. After fourteen years of service he was still a simple clerk, cherishing the vague hope of becoming chief clerk one day, "although his talents in matters" of chicane did not leave much to be desired. He valued his office, not because of the beggarly salary, but because it gave him a position in society and the possibility to come into contact with clients. His main source of income was not his office, but his private activity, of which everyone made use. All the landowners, not only of his district, but also of the neighboring ones, knew him as an ingenious scribbler and entrusted him with soliciting in their affairs, so that his home was a kind of office in which two clerks worked under his direction." Saltykov cites an example of a consultation given by this "advocate" to the author's mother:[22]

> It happened that my mother asked:
> 'Tell me, how is it according to law. . .'
> 'According to law, it is thus and so. . .'
> 'Yes, but "they" (i.e. the opposite party) also reason "according to law," and in their opinion the law is not on our side.'

---

21 *Ibid.*, p. 185.
22 M. E. Saltykov (N. Shchedrin), *Poshekhonskaya starina* in his *Sochineniya*, v. 12, p. 148.

'In such a case we may apply another law. If one law does not suit us—another one will. We can rummage in the Complete Collection of Laws and find an appropriate ukase of the Senate...'

'All right, you will find a second law, but "they" will dig out a third one...'

'Well, concerning this third law, we can write an explanation or arrange it so that the brief with the third law will be returned to the party. One only needs an appropriate mind and a pen and ink; the rest will come by itself. The main thing is not to hurry, to proceed slowly, without letting the prescribed dates expire. When the opponent sees that the suit is being dragged out endlessly, and, as time goes on, becomes unworthy of the expenses involved, he will be confused. Then he can be twisted round one's little finger: he will allow a deadline to lapse or will agree to a compromise...'

Mother kept her eyes on him carefully, because he had the reputation of a 'double bag'[23] and, even more than that, of a man well versed in the law.[24]

From another part of the story we learn that one of Mogil'tsev's main activities was advice on where, how, and to whom bribes should be given.[25]

B. Reluctance to Introduce the Institution of Lawyers

The necessity of creating a guild of juridically educated lawyers, bound by professional ethics, was realized by the first reformers already at the time of Nicholas I. Afterward, in 1858, in his draft of the reform of the criminal procedure, submitted to the State Council, Count Bludov wrote that it is insufficient to introduce prosecutors in courts without "providing the accused with similarly reliable counsels." "As long as we do not have good counsels," concluded Bludov, "the introduction of the accusatorial procedure is impossible."[26] Count Bludov warned, however, against calling these counsels "advocates," and suggested the name of *poverennye* or *stryapchiye*. This he did because the *avocats* were odious to the Russian rulers since the French Revolution. But hatred of the representatives of this profession reached even further back than the French Revolution. Thus the aversion of Peter the Great toward lawyers was clearly expressed by him during his visit to London in 1698. The following incident is

---

23 Figuratively, a man apt to change.
24 Saltykov, *op. cit.*, p. 149-150.
25 *Ibid.*, p. 50.
26 Quoted by V. Pletnev, *op. cit.*, I, 291.

related in *The Book of Days:* "It being term-time while the Czar was in London, he was taken into Westminster Hall; he inquired who all those busy people in black gowns and flowing wigs were and what they were about? Being answered 'They are lawyers, Sir', 'Lawyers!' said he, much astonished. 'Why, I have but two in my whole dominions, and I believe I shall hang one of them the moment I get home.' " [27]

Peter's daughter, Empress Elisabeth, wrote in an ukase of 1752: "To our greatest discontent we learn of corruption and oppression of our subjects by *yabedniki.*"[28]

Catherine the Great did not have a better opinion of the advocates or *yabedniki.* In her letter of June 25, 1790, to Grimm, which was directed against the French National Assembly, she wrote that first of all the deputies should be deprived of their allowances of 18 pounds and then "those poor people would return to their occupations in order to win their bread, and they would pass a law that no lawyer should be admitted as deputy, since they are a mass of chicaners, against whom laws, even very strict ones, are made in every country, but in France these 'pug dogs' are raised to the dignity of legislators. These canailles are like the 'Marquis' Pugachev, of whom I always said that nobody is more than he himself persuaded that he is a scoundrel. These lawyers support now truth, now lies, now justice and now injustice according to what they are paid for, and where; I would chase these people away. . ." [29] And in another letter, on Sept. 15, 1790, she wrote: ". . .the lawyers. . .are not, and will never be, legislators in my country as long as I live, and after me my principles will be followed." [30]

Catherine's prediction was right in one sense: aversion to lawyers was inherited by her descendants. I. G. Kolmakov relates in his memoirs that Prince D. V. Golitsyn, in his capacity of governor-general of Moscow, had to confirm the sentences of the Criminal *Palata.* He refused to fulfill this duty, being of the opinion that administrative power should not interfere with the activity of the judiciary. Questioned by Nicholas I, the Prince replied that since the accused had no advocates, he could not be sure that the sentences of the *Palata* were just and begged the Tsar to free him from the duty of confirming sentences. "Nicholas frowned at the word 'advocate,' " Golitsyn related to Kolmakov, "and said: 'I see you lived a long time in France, and ap-

---

[27] "Peter the Great in England", *The Book of Days* (London, 1863,) I, 175.
[28] *Polnoye sobraniye zakonov, Sobraniye pervoye,* No. 9989.
[29] *Sbornik Imperatorskago Istoricheskago Obshchestva,* XXIII, 489.
[30] *Ibid.,* p. 497.

parently during the Revolution; no wonder that you had time enough to adopt their view on the order of things. But who' continued the Tsar, speaking very loudly, 'ruined France if not the advocates? Don't you understand that? Who was Mirabeau, Marat, Robespierre, and others?! Russia does not need advocates; we will live without them. Do what the law requires of you; I do not want anything else.' " [31]

Nicholas' aversion to lawyers may be illustrated by the following episode. When Pushkin completed his *History of Pugachev's Rebellion* he sent to Nicholas some notes on it, which he did not dare to publish but considered might be of interest to the Tsar. Nicholas himself passed on these notes, whereupon they were published. Note 19 to the *History* reads as follows: "In accordance with privileges granted by an ukase, the death penalty was not applicable under any circumstances to Padurov,[32] who was a deputy. I do not know whether he resorted to the protection of this ukase; maybe he was not aware of it; maybe the judges did not think about it. Anyhow, the execution of the criminal was against the law. *This is one of thousands of examples showing the necessity for a bar.*" (Italics mine. S. K.)[33] The last sentence, concerning the bar, was crossed out by Nicholas and did not appear in the note to page 164 of the first edition of the *History*.

Catherine II and Nicholas I were afraid of the political activities of lawyers as evidenced in the French Revolution and considered the institution of the bar and the corporation of lawyers as a source of faction and rebellion. It is noteworthy that the corporation of lawyers, together with other privileged organizations and class institutions, was abolished in France on Aug. 16 and Sept. 2, 1790, by the *Constituante*, which wanted to free the lawyer from the ties of the bar organization and the parties to a suit, as well as the accused in criminal proceedings, from the obligation to be represented in court by a lawyer. This measure was taken as a part of the general reorganization of the system of the administration of justice, which was carried out by the *Constituante*. As far as privileges are concerned, the lawyers of prerevolutionary days in France were free from some taxes and duties, had the right to require the removal from the vicinity of their houses handicraftsmen who disturbed them in their activity by noise made in working, could not be arrested on the way to or from court when dressed in their professional attire, etc.[34] The reaction of the lawyers

31 Kolmakov, *op. cit.*, p. 535-536.
32 One of Pugachev's lieutenants, executed in Moscow on the same day as Pugachev.
33 A. S. Pushkin, *Polnoye sobraniye sochineny*, V, 427.
34 Vas'kovsky, *Organizatsiya advokatury*, p. 119-120.

among the members of the *Constituante* to the bill changing the system of administration of justice was quite remarkable: they decided not only to abolish the bar, but to extirpate the very name of *avocat* from the legal language and to destroy the whole profession of lawyers, in order to avoid its invasion by people unworthy to carry the name of *avocat*, i.e., people lacking the customs, traditions, discipline and moral standards of the old days. It was said: "Better to destroy the subject of our love with our own hands than to let it be exposed to injury and insult." [35] When the bill was discussed only one of many spoke against it and in defense of the old organization of lawyers: it was Robespierre.

The French bar was re-established under Napoleon I, but with major changes in its form of organization, since Napoleon shared the viewpoint of Catherine and Nicholas on this organization. The eminent French lawyer M. Dupin, in his book *Profession d'avocat*, quotes a note made by Napoleon on a project submitted by Treilhard to Chancellor Cambacérès in 1810 concerning the introduction of the bar in its pre-revolutionary form. Napoleon wrote: "The [projected] decree is stupid; it does not permit any measures against the advocates. They are rioters, instigators of crimes and treasons. As long as I shall carry a sword at my side, I shall never sign such a decree. I wish that the tongue of every advocate who uses it against the government should be cut out." [36] Napoleon did not permit the existence of a free and self-governing body of lawyers. Under Louis XVIII, in 1822, the Law of 1810 was partly changed, and only the Laws of 1830, 1852 and 1870 gave to the bar the organization it retained up to our time.

Thus, in France, the bar was eliminated by the Revolution as a privileged and reactionary institution, whereas the same organization was feared in reactionary France after the revolution, and in Russia, as a source of faction and revolution.

Alexander II was not quite immune to the aversion to lawyers which his father had to such a large degree. In the beginning of his reign he was not inclined to introduce the profession of lawyers into Russia. When in 1857 the Second Division of His Majesty's Personal Chancellery submitted to the State Council the project of a judicial reform, the debates in the Council were preceded by the reading of an Imperial Order forbidding the discussion of the problems of jury and bar.[37] Only later, when the Tsar conceived a broad judicial reform

---

[35] *Ibid.*, p. 122. Vas'kovsky calls this action worthy of old Rome.
[36] A. Dupin, aîné, *Profession d'avocat*, I, 132-133.
[37] Hessen, *Advocatura. . . .*, p. 31.

which appeared impossible without the creation of a bar, were debates on the question permitted.

The question of the necessity of having lawyers and a bar was discussed also in the press. There were people who denied this necessity. A certain P. S-ov wrote an article for the *Russky Vestnik* in 1859, in which he expressed the peculiar opinion that lawyers, although necessary in criminal trials, should be eliminated from civil procedures. In civil suits, he argued, there are two parties with contrary interests, and one of these parties must be wrong so that one of the two opposing lawyers must be immoral. "Strict consistency would require the indictment of the losing party's lawyer for an immoral and premeditated attempt to violate the right of the winning party." [38]

A brilliant article was written by K. P. Pobedonostsev in the same periodical some months later. Pobedonostsev served at that time in the Ministry of Justice. The future pillar and one of the chief inspirers of the reaction of 1880-1900 was in the middle of the century an advocate of liberal reforms. He wrote: "Only with the help of lawyers can you have pleading in court of such plenitude and liveliness as to enable the judge to consider the case from all sides, to penetrate into its essence and form a definite opinion. . .When the vivid speech of the lawyer is heard in court. . .when the court and all the participants are not confined behind closed doors, when the public is present and taking a lively part in all events in court, the procedure will take the shape of a real, vivid and rational fight. Then no judge will be able to remain inattentive and indifferent. Only under such conditions, *i.e.,* with the participation of the lawyer and in public session, will the court become the best school of education for judges and lawyers. . .The struggle of the poor against the rich, of the weak against the strong, of the dependent against the one upon whom he depends, is difficult and dangerous everywhere and at all times. In some cases a struggle is impossible without a lawyer. If a lawyer is in a position independent of the government and court, as he ought to be; if he relies on the moral force of the case which he defends and, at the same time, upon the moral force of a whole corporation to which he belongs and also upon the consciousness of the public present at the fight, then the lawyer—and, let us add, the lawyer only—is able to enter the fight against the personal interest of material force and to oppose to it the weapon of spiritual force. . .The lawyers' guild. . .can reach its goal only if it is a closed guild placed beside the judiciary and independ-

---

[38] P. S-ov, "Ob advokature v grazhdanskom protsesse," *Russky Vestnik,* March 1859, Book 2, p. *149.*

ent of it. . .As soon as the guild is organized, it will become necessary to grant to it permission for a free and independent activity." [39] Indeed, *tempora mutantur nos et mutamur in illis.*

The State Council in its minutes of 1861 acknowledges the necessity for a guild of educated and honest attorneys, "since without them it would be impossible to introduce the controversial principle in civil procedure and pleading in court in criminal procedure with the purpose of finding the truth and supplying the parties and the accused with full defense in court. . .One of the causes of the disastrous situation of the judicial procedures is the fact that persons who solicit for others have in the majority of cases a very dubious morality and are completely deprived of any juridical knowledge, either theoretical or practical." [40]

Finally, the Tsar was won to the idea of creating officially accredited lawyers and made the following remark on the report of Count Bludov: "If you consider this idea really useful, it might be suggested at the next discussion of the code of procedure in the State Council."[41]

The draft of Count Bludov and that of the Second Division of His Majesty's Own Chancellery, in which the work was concentrated since 1848, were transferred to the State Chancellery according to the Tsar's ukase of October 23, 1861, as described above.

Provisions concerning lawyers occupied 16 articles of the Basic Principles (Nos. 80-95). The final draft of the Basic Principles was discussed in the General Assembly of the State Council on September 4, 1862, and adopted without important opposition, except on the question of the monopoly of the lawyers, i.e., the exclusive right of the lawyers to represent parties in court. The Basic Principles were confirmed by the Tsar on September 29, 1862. The controversy in the State Council was decided by the Tsar in favor of the monopoly. In the final wording of the Basic Principles, 15 articles are devoted to the question of lawyers—one less than in the draft of the State Chancellery.

The General Assembly of the State Council passed the bill concerning the lawyers on October 2, 1864, and the entire Reform was confirmed by the Tsar and published on November 20, 1864, together with the famous Manifesto of Alexander II. The Russian lawyer was born.

This was a peculiar birth. The Russian lawyer and the organization of the bar had no roots in the preceding history of Russian legal

[39] K. P. Pobedonostsev, "O reformakh v grazdanskom sudoproizvodstve", *Russky Vestnik,* (July 1859) , Book 1, pp. 162-166, *passim.*
[40] *Zhurnal Gosudarstvennago Soveta,* 1862, No. 65, p. 339.
[41] Hessen, *Advocatura. . . .,* p. 43.

institutions. The Russian lawyer's predecessors were not his ancestors. The institution created by the Laws of Nov. 20, 1864 was a complete innovation for Russia.

In one of his after-dinner speeches,[42] V. D. Spasovich a distinguished Russian lawyer, said: "Zoologists search in vain for a [case of] spontaneous generation of an organism and believe in such a phenomenon. We gave precisely such an example of spontaneous generation. Nothing similar ever existed in Russia. We are not hatched *ex ovo*. We are without kith or kin." [43]

C. West European Systems of Organization of Lawyers and Their Influence on the Organization Adopted in Russia

Indeed, the legislators of 1864 had to resort to foreign samples in order to create this new institution. There were two different systems of representation in court in Western Europe at that time: one was adopted in England, France, and Belgium, and the other in Prussia, the other German States and Austria-Hungary. According to the first system, the representation of the client is divided between two jurists: the solicitor and the barrister in England, and the *avoué* and *avocat* in France and Belgium. The first type of jurist is entrusted with the preparation of the civil cases. The second is the pleader properly speaking who has to present the civil or criminal case to the court. The *avoué* in France is an official of the Ministry of Justice, although he is remunerated by the client.

The profession of *avocat* has preserved, outwardly at least, some of the old ideas of disinterestedness. For instance, the *avocat* (like the barrister in Gr. Britain) has no legal claim in court for his fees, and is supposed to act merely as a "knight of justice and equity." [44]

The system of two representatives has the great disadvantage of separating the *avocat* from his client, whom he sometimes sees for the first time in court; of making the procedure more expensive, since two jurists must be paid; and of depriving the *avocat* of the possibility of acquiring a better knowledge of the case by working on it in all the phases of the procedure, in and out of court.

---

[42] Every year, on April 17, the St. Petersburg Bar celebrated with a banquet the anniversary of the opening of the newly organized courts in St. Petersburg, which took place on April 17, 1866. On this occasion, eminent members of the guild usually delivered speeches.

[43] V. D. Spasovich, *Zastol'nye rechi*, p. 85.

[44] That is why fees of the *avocat* and barrister are usually paid in advance.

The German *Rechtsanwalt*[45] retains in his hands both the functions of preparing the case and of pleading in court. However, his professional training makes him more similar to an *avoué* than to an *avocat*. Until 1878, when the new regulations for the German Reich were adopted, the *Rechtsanwalt* was an official in the service of the *Justizministerium*, and the number of *Rechtsanwälte* was limited (*numerus clausus*) for every court. Their activity became a free profession with the regulations of 1878, which also abolished the *numerus clausus*.

Nevertheless, German law placed the *Rechtsanwalt* in an official position, requiring his participation in all civil cases before the *Landgericht, Oberlandesgericht (Kammergericht* in Prussia) and *Reichsgericht*, as well as in important criminal cases. The so-called *Anwaltszwang* excludes other persons than *Rechtsanwälte* from representation in the above-mentioned courts. Also, the fees of the *Rechtsanwalt* are fixed by law.[46]

The question of the pattern according to which the Russian lawyer was created is a controversial one. Thus, Vas'kovsky writes: "It is clear at first glance that the organization of the Russian bar adheres to the Austro-German system. In consequence of a strange misunderstanding, however, which is caused by an insufficient knowledge of the West European bar, the opinion that our bar is organized according to the French sample prevails in our literature. In reality, if there is anything in common between the French *avocat* and the Russian *prisyazhny poverenny*, it is only the freedom of the profession and the corporate organization. . .In every other respect our organization of the bar not only does not resemble the French one, but is the exact opposite to it." [47] However, G. B. Sliozberg is of quite a different opinion. "The institution of the bar," he says, "was created by the laws of 1864 according to the French pattern, with changes to suit the difference in political conditions in the two countries: a most disadvantageous imitation which, in my opinion, gave unfavorable results. The German organization is more practical and expedient, at least with regard to the training during the period of probation." [48]

It is true that the fathers of the Judicial Reform in Russia repudiated both the dualism of the English-French system and the

---

45 This name was adopted in Prussia in 1849 in place of *Justiz-Kommissar*.

46 The *Rechtsanwalt* has not the right to charge more or less than the official rates prescribe. Especially prohibited is the arrangement providing increased fees in case of success, or the *pacta de quota litis*. Such agreements were permitted in Russia. In the U. S., contingent fees, if unconscionable, are set aside: U. S. Supreme Court (Wright v. Tebbels, 91 U. S. 252; Taylor v. Benis, 110 U. S. 42.)

47 Vas'kovsky, *Organizatsiya advokatury*, I, 333-334.

48 G. B. Sliozberg, *Dela minuvshikh dnei*, I. 191.

German semi-official position of the *Rechtsanwalt*. The Russian lawyer prepared the case and pleaded in court, but he was not bureaucratically influenced by his training; his profession was a free one, and he had no semi-official position.

CHAPTER III

THE BAR

A. Admission to the Bar

1. *Rules of Admission*

The Statutes of Judicial Institutions of November 20, 1864 determined the functions of the lawyer,[1] gave the requirements for admission to this profession, and regulated the structure, the functioning of, and the admission to the bar.[2]

Upon graduation from a law school or a faculty of law of a university, the candidate had to be registered with a lawyer in the capacity of a lawyer-in-training[4] in order to begin a five-year period of probation. The probation period under the patronage of a lawyer could be replaced by five years' service with the Ministry of Justice in a position which gave the opportunity to acquire experience in judicial affairs, or in the capacity of a candidate for a judicial position at a law court. The position and functions of a lawyer-in-training correspond to those of an *avocat stagiaire* in France. It is peculiar that in the entire Statutes of the Judicial Institutions the lawyer-in-training is mentioned only in one sentence, in Art. 354. His position and duties during the time of probation remained undefined by the laws of 1864. This gap should have been filled by subsequent legislation.

The Laws of 1864 deliberately omitted to regulate the status of the lawyer-in-training. In the explanatory note submitted to the State Council in 1863, it was suggested that the lawyers-in-training should be entitled to carry on lawsuits with the permission of the Council of the Bar.[5] The State Council rejected this suggestion, explaining its decision as follows: since the requirements for admission to the bar are juridical education and five years of practical work, a

---

[1] Called *prisyazhny poverenny*.
[2] *Uchrezhdeniye sudebnykh ustanovleny*, Art. 353-406.
[4] The lawyer-in-training was called *pomoshchnik prisyazhnago poverennago*.
[5] *Sudebnye Ustavy. . .*, Part III: *Uchrezhdeniye sudebnykh ustanovleny*, p. 220.

122

person who lacks the required experience cannot be admitted to act as a lawyer. "If a lawyer-in-training meets both the requirements," the State Council argued, "he can join the bar and become a lawyer; if he fails to meet one of the requirements, he cannot substitute for a lawyer and, consequently, the right to carry on lawsuits on the same level as a lawyer cannot be given to him." Thus it was decided not to introduce a provision into the Statutes permitting lawyers-in-training to carry on lawsuits.[6]

It was also planned to admit to the bar professors and instructors of law in universities, in spite of the fact that these persons had not served in the Ministry of Justice. In this case the State Council also decided that these persons, "lacking practical experience in carrying on lawsuits, fail to meet one of the requirements which lawyers must meet under the Basic Principles and thus cannot be admitted to the guild of the bar." [7]

Professor Foinitsky disapproves of this decision, feeling that professors of law would acquire, in practicing law, important experience which would supplement their theoretical knowledge and contribute to the rapprochement of school and life.[8] On the other hand, Vas'kovsky is of the opinion that admission of professors to argue civil cases is inexpedient.[9]

In order to be admitted to the bar as a lawyer, the candidate after the probation period had to file an application with the council of the bar, in which he had to indicate the city of his residence and declare that in his case there were none of the obstacles listed in Art. 355.[10] The council of the bar had to consider the application and decide on the admission of the candidate to the bar. A certificate of admission was handed to the candidate, which he had to file with the *Sudebnaya Palata* with which he was registered. The *Palata* made him take the following oath, which is characteristic of old Russia and the views of the legislator on the future duties of the candidate:

"I promise and swear by God the Almighty, before His holy Gospel and His vivifying cross, to remain faithful to His Imperial Majesty the Emperor and Autocrat of All-Russia, to fulfill exactly the laws of the Empire according to my best knowledge, not to write or say any-

---

6 *Ibid.*
7 *Ibid.*
8 Foinitsky, *Zashchita v ugolovnom protesse kak sluzheniye obshchestvennoye*, p. 38.
9 Vas'skovsky, *Organizatsiya advokatury*, p. 324.
10 See p. 124. In case of a false declaration, the lawyer was not only excluded from the bar but had to face criminal prosecution. *Uchrezhdeniye sudebnykh ustanovleny*, Art. 379.

thing tending to weaken the Orthodox Church, the state, society, family and morality, but honestly and conscientiously to fulfill the duties of the position which I accept, to respect the courts and the authorities and to defend the interests of my clients or persons whose affairs I shall have to direct, keeping in mind that for all that I shall have to give account before the law and before God on doomsday; in witness whereof I kiss the cross and the words of my Savior. Amen." [11]

After having taken the oath, the candidate was entered by the *Sudebnaya Palata* into the register of lawyers of its district and by this act he became a lawyer and a member of the bar.

2. Exclusion from Admission

The following persons were not admitted to the profession of lawyers: 1. Those under twenty-five of age, 2. Non-Russian citizens, 3. Those who were declared insolvent debtors, 4. Persons in government service or elected officials, with the exception of those who occupy honorary or public positions without remuneration, 5. Those condemned to deprivation or restriction of rights, as well as priests unfrocked by sentence of an ecclesiastic court, 6. Those who are under preliminary investigation for crimes involving deprivation or restriction of rights. 7. Those dismissed from state service by a court sentence, or from ecclesiastic service for vices, or from community and nobility assemblies in virtue of sentences of the class to which they belong. 8. Those whom a court decision prohibits from soliciting for other persons, or those already excluded from the bar.[12]

Women were also excluded from the profession of lawyers, although the Statutes of Judicial Institutions contained no direct provisions to that effect. In 1910 the Senate ruled that "women. . .according to law have no right to be admitted to the bar and to receive the position of a lawyer or lawyer-in-training." [13] This right was not conferred upon them until after the February Revolution of 1917.

"In order that the bar present the most definite guarantees of morality, erudition and honest conviction, it is necessary, at the very time of the creation of this new guild, to select most carefully the persons admitted thereto. For this new institution of lawyers to bring all the expected benefits, careful selection for the profession of lawyers

---

11 *Ibid.*, Supplement to Art. 381.
12 *Ibid.*, Art. 355.
13 *Zhurnal ministerstva yustitsii*, Sept. 1912, p. 242.

must be practiced and such supervision established over them which, on the one hand, does not deprive them of the independence necessary for the defense of their clients and [at the same time] provides fast and effective protection of private persons against constraint on the part of lawyers, and on the other serves the establishment and support of a sense of truth and honor and a consciousness of moral responsibility before the government and the people among the lawyers." [14] This was, in the words of the State Council, what was expected of the new guild of lawyers by the legislator who called it into being.

A lawyer had to register with a *Sudebnaya Palata* and take residence in a city within the district of the *Palata* with which he had registered.[15] The duties of lawyers were to carry on lawsuits entrusted to them by a party, by an accused and by other persons involved, or turned over to them in certain cases by councils of the bar or by presidents of the courts, by appointment.[16] Article 390 provided in more exact terms that the lawyers carry on civil cases by virtue of a power of attorney conferred by a party, or in consequence of a declaration made by a party to the court, or pursuant to an appointment by a council of the bar according to the demand of a party, or, finally, pursuant to an appointment by the president of a court. In criminal cases, according to Art. 393, the lawyers took over the defense of the accused by virtue of agreements with them, or were appointed by presidents of the courts. The power of attorney could be extended to all actions pertinent to a given case or be limited to specific actions.[17] A lawyer appointed by a council of the bar or the president of a court had no right to decline the appointment without adequate reasons.[18]

B. Forbidden Activities

The law introduced the following restrictions for lawyers: According to Arts. 400-403, lawyers were not allowed: (1) to acquire claims under litigation of their clients either under their proper name or under the disguise of acquiring them for other persons; all such transactions were declared void and lawyers made to answer before the council of the bar, (2) to sue their parents, children, brothers, sisters, uncles and cousins, (3) to serve as counsel for both parties and to go over to the opposite party during a suit, (4) to divulge secrets of their

---

[14] *Sudebnye Ustavy...*, Part III: *Uchrezhdeniye sudebnykh ustanovleny*, p. 219.
[15] *Ibid.*, Art. 356.
[16] *Ibid.*, Art. 353.
[17] *Ibid.*, Art. 391.
[18] *Ibid.*, Art. 394.

clients, not only during the lawsuit, but also in case of dismissal by the client, or even after the termination of the lawsuit.

The lawyer was held responsible if he allowed a legal deadline to lapse or did not observe other prescribed forms or rules. In such a case, the client had the right to sue him for damages.[19] For premeditated actions to the detriment of his client, a lawyer was not only liable for the damage inflicted but was also responsible to a criminal court in case his client complained.[20]

C. REMUNERATION

The remuneration of the lawyer in civil cases depended upon the agreement between him and his client. This agreement required written form.[21] *Pacta de quota litis* were allowed.

In the absence of an agreement, the remuneration had to be calculated according to legal rates in a schedule which was to be worked out by the Minister of Justice in accordance with suggestions of the *Sudebnaya Palata* and the councils of the bar approved for three years by the legislative body. The schedule served also for calculating the amount of costs which the winning party was entitled to recover from the losing one.[22] According to the schedule, the remuneration of the lawyer was calculated as a percentage of the value of the suit carried on in two instances. If, for instance, the claim of the suit was 500-2000 rubles, the remuneration was 10%. As the value of the suit increased, the percentage of remuneration went down: in a 2000-5000 ruble suit the remuneration was 10% of the first 2000 rubles and 8% of the rest, ec. If the value of the suit could not be determined from the claim, the remuneration was fixed by the court in accordance with the importance of the suit for the party, financial conditions of the latter and the time and amount of work spent by the lawyer. In such cases, the remuneration set by the court varied from 50 to 1200 rubles. If the lawyer carried on the suit in the first instance only, his remuneration was $2/3$ of the usual one; if in the second instance only—$1/3$, and if in the Department of Cassation only—$1/4$. It is noteworthy that the remuneration of the losing lawyer, according to the schedule, was curtailed: if the plaintiff lost, the legal remuneration of his lawyer was reduced to $1/4$, and if the respondent was the loser, his lawyer had to be satisfied with $1/3$ of his legal remuneration.

---

19 *Ibid.*, Art. 404.
20 *Ibid.*, Art. 405.
21 *Ibid.*, Art. 395.
22 *Ibid.*, Art. 396.

In criminal cases there were no established rates.

If the remuneration of the lawyer was based on agreement in both cases, civil and criminal, the amount of the remuneration was not limited and the lawyer could stipulate a higher remuneration in case of a favorable outcome of the litigation.

A certain percentage of the legal remuneration of the lawyer was retained and paid into a special fund. This fund served for the remuneration of lawyers appointed as counsels by presidents of law courts throughout the country. The distribution of this fund among the judicial districts was done by the Minister of Justice, according to the number of lawyers appointed to such duties by presidents of courts in every district. The apportionment of the remuneration between the lawyers involved was carried out by the council of the bar in every district.[23]

D. STRUCTURE OF THE BAR

1. *General Assembly*

The Laws of 1864 organized the lawyers into a guild, or bar. The bar consisted of all the lawyers entered in the lists of a *Sudebnaya Palata*. If the number of registered lawyers reached twenty, they could request the permission of the *Palata* for electing a council, a president of the council and an assistant president in a general assembly.[24] The assistant president had to act as the president's deputy in case of his illness or absence. The *Palata,* having received such a request, designated one of its members to act as chairman of the general assembly in which the election of the council took place. The designated member of the *Palata* summoned all the lawyers of the district to the *Palata.* If not less than one half of all the lawyers were present, he called the general assembly to order which elected the president, the assistant president and the members of the council, voting for each office separately.[25] A simple majority of votes was sufficient for the election. If two or more candidates received the same number of votes, the candidate who was first entered on the list of lawyers was elected. The number of members of the council, including the president and the assistant president, had to be not less than five and not more than fifteen, according to the number of lawyers in the district. The general assembly decided on this number by a vote taken before the election

---

23 *Ibid.,* Art. 398.
24 *Ibid.,* Arts. 357, 358.
25 *Ibid.,* Art. 359.

of the council.[26] After the voting had taken place, the member of the *Palata* adjourned the general assembly, announcing the election of the council and the beginning of its functioning.[27] The list of the elected was handed to the President of the *Sudebnaya Palata* and published for everybody's information.[28]

The council had to be elected every year. A general assembly was called for this purpose by the president of the council. No member of the council, including the president and his assistant, could be chairman of the general assembly. The chairman had to be elected by the general assembly from among the other members of the bar present. Before the elections a report of the council on its activity in the past year was read to the general assembly.[29] When less than one half of all the lawyers registered in the district were present in the general assembly, the election did not take place, and a new assembly was convoked by the president of the council, who had to indicate in the invitation to this assembly that the council would remain in office for another year if a quorum of one half of all the members were not present in the second assembly.[30]

If more than ten lawyers resided in a city which did not have a *Sudebnaya Palata,* they could, with the consent of the council of the bar, elect a branch of the council of the bar attached to the circuit court. The council of the bar decided on the organization of the branch and the rights which it wished to delegate to the branch. The *Sudebnaya Palata* had to be notified about the creation of such a branch and the rights delegated to it by the council of the bar.[31]

2.   *Council of the Bar*

The rights and duties of the council were exactly regulated by the Laws of 1864 and had an administrative and disciplinary character. The council had to consider applications of persons desiring to be admitted to the bar or resigning their membership and notify the *Sudebnaya Palata* about its decision.

It had also to examine grievances lodged against lawyers and supervise the strict fulfillment by the lawyers of regulations, existing rules and obligations toward the clients. The council also had to appoint

---

26 *Ibid.,* Arts. 361-363.
27 *Ibid.,* Art. 362.
28 *Ibid.,* Art. 363.
29 *Ibid.,* Art. 364.
30 *Ibid.,* Art. 365.
31 *Ibid.,* Art. 366.

lawyers to serve their turn as counsels for persons entitled thereto because they were indigents, and to designate counsel for those who asked the council for such designation. In the absence of a written agreement concerning the remuneration of the lawyer, the council had to fix the amount of the remuneration in case of differences on this subject between the lawyer and the client. It distributed the fund collected for remuneration of lawyers appointed as counsels for persons entitled thereto because they were indigent, and inflicted penalties on lawyers on its own iniative or in consequence of grievances submitted to it.[32]

One of the most important rights of the council was that of disciplinary action. On its own authority, the council had the right to inflict the following penalties upon the members of the bar for violations of their duties: 1. Warning, 2. Rebuke, 3. Temporary suspension for a certain period of time not exceeding one year, 4. Disbarring, 5. Bringing to trial before a criminal court in especially important cases.[33]

If a lawyer was twice subjected to the penalty of temporary suspension and found guilty for a third time, he had to be disbarred.[34] The council had to notify the prosecutor of the court to which it was attached about every case of conviction or acquittal of a lawyer.[35] The infliction of penalities mentioned above could not take place without giving the accused time to present his explanations.[36] If the accused did not present explanations or did not appear on time for the hearing before the council without valid reason, the council had to render its decision according to records or circumstances known to it.[37] The council decided on the validity of the reasons for his absence according to its own discretion.[38] Conviction or acquittal by the council did not deprive the client of the right to sue the lawyer in court for damages.[39]

Every decision of the council required the votes of at least one-half of its members. In case of a tie, the president of the council cast the deciding vote. A majority of two-thirds of the votes was required for decisions inflicting penalties listed under paragraphs 3-5 of Art. 368.[40]

An appeal against the decision of the council inflicting a penalty

---

32 *Ibid.*, Art. 367.
33 *Ibid.*, Art. 368.
34 *Ibid.*, Art. 369.
35 *Ibid.*, Art. 370.
36 *Ibid.*, Art. 371.
37 *Ibid*, Art. 372.
38 *Ibid.*, Art. 373.
39 *Ibid.*, Art. 374.
40 *Ibid.*, Art. 375.

could be filed with the *Sudebnaya Palata* within two weeks, with the exception of warning and rebuke, against which there was no appeal.[41] Against other sentences of the *Palata* appeal to the Senate was permitted.

The prosecutor could also, within two weeks, lodge a protest against a decision of the council. With regard to complaints and protests, the decision of the *Sudebnaya Palata* was final.[42]

In cities where there was no council of the bar or branch thereof, the rights and duties of the council devolved upon the local circuit court.[43]

Thus the right of self-administration through a council of the bar was given to lawyers on condition that their number be not less than twenty; otherwise the functions of the council were fulfilled by the circuit court,—a body not elected by the lawyers themselves but appointed by the government.

In St. Petersburg, the petition to establish a council of the bar was filed on the same day when the Laws of 1864 were introduced, *i.e.*, on April 17, 1866. On May 2, 1866, the first Council of the Bar in Russia was elected by the General Assembly of the bar. In Moscow, the election to the Council took place Sept. 16, 1866. The third Council, that for Kharkov, was not elected until May 6, 1874. Then, in 1875, the formation of new councils of the bar was temporarily stopped, and in 1889 the opening of branches of councils prohibited. Those measures are to be explained by the growing discontent of the government with the activities of the lawyers and by a change in views concerning the Reform of 1864 in general. With this question we shall deal later.

The "temporary" stoppage lasted 30 years. In 1904, *i.e.*, when the revolutionary movement was accentuated and the reaction forced to retreat (also "temporarily"), the Imperial Ukase of July 21, 1904 permitted the creation of a council of the bar in Novocherkassk. Then, in accordance with Ukases of Nov. 10, 1904, councils of the bar were created in Kazan, Odessa and Saratov, and on Nov. 24, 1904, in Irkutsk and Omsk.

In 1905, still under the influence of the same revolutionary impact, the *Sudebnaya Palata* in Odessa decided that the Ukase of 1889, which prohibited organization of branches of councils of the bar, applied only to those councils which already existed and not to new

---

[41] *Ibid.*, Art. 376.
[42] *Ibid.*, Art. 377.
[43] *Ibid.*, Art. 378.

ones. Promptly the Odessa Council of the Bar established a branch in Kishenev. However, when in 1908 the reaction again took the upper hand, the Senate ruled that the Ukase of 1889 extends also to new councils, since "the defects of the organization of the bar which brought about the suspension of the opening of new branches were characteristic of all the districts, not only of those of Petersburg, Moscow and Kharkov." [44]

E. The Young Lawyer

1. *Admission*

It has already been emphasized that the Laws of 1864 mentioned the lawyer-in-training only in passing, in Art. 354 of the Statutes of Judicial Institutions in connection with the requirement of a five-year period of probation for admission to the bar. This article provided that the requirements were fulfilled when a person with high juridical education. . . "practiced law during five years under the guidance of a lawyer in the capacity of his assistant." We know also the reasons why the legislator of 1864 did not want to give to the lawyer-in-training the rights and privileges of a lawyer.[45] It is peculiar that also the subsequent legislation ignored the young lawyers almost completely, although they played an important role in the life of the country. Not a single law was published regulating the rights and duties of *the pomoshchniki prisyazhnykh poverennykh* during the entire period of their existence until the very end of the prerevolutionary legal profession, shortly after the October Revolution of 1917.

Due to the absence of legislation, the activity of young lawyers had to be regulated by the councils of the bar and, in places where there was no council, by the circuit court. This situation excluded a uniform regulation of their activity. Every council issued rules concerning lawyers-in-training attached to its district.

The St. Petersburg Council was the first to adopt some rules concerning admission to the practice as a lawyer-in-training in 1869, and then issued general regulations in 1872. These regulations contained rules concerning admission requirements, the rights and duties of lawyers-in-training, their disciplinary responsibility and other conditions to be observed during the time of probation. In the period pre-

---

[44] Quoted by P. S. Tager, "Organizatsiya sovetov," in *Istoriya russkoi advokatury,* II, 168-169.
[45] *See above,* pp. 122-123.

ceding the adoption of these regulations, every lawyer formulated his own rules for the lawyer-in-training whose services he accepted. He had only to notify the council about the admission. The council took it into consideration and entered the name of the lawyer-in-training on the list.

According to the regulations by the St. Petersburg Council of 1869, the admission of lawyers-in-training was taken over by the council. The candidate had to present a diploma or certificate of graduation from the faculty of law of a university or law school. The application of this rule was extended to those who were admitted before 1869. Not admitted as lawyers-in-training were persons excluded from admission to the bar by Art. 355 of the Statutes of Judicial Institutions,[46] with the exception of Paragraphs 1 and 4 of this Article, which excluded from admission persons under 25 years and those in government service; these rules could not be applied to young lawyers. The Council investigated every candidate.

In 1872 amendments introduced the requirement that the candidate should present a certificate of his future patron testifying to the consent of the latter for the admission of the candidate as a lawyer-in-training under his patronage. The name of the candidate was put on a blackboard in the lawyers' rooms in court in order to collect information about the moral qualities and the former activities of the candidate.

It is peculiar that until 1906 the Senate had no occasion to deal with these admission rules of the council. In a decision of December 14, 1906, the Senate ruled that the regulations of 1869 had to be amended so that persons coming under Paragraph 4 of Art. 355 of the Statutes of Judicial Institutions (*i.e.,* those in government service or serving in elected positions) should not be admitted as lawyers-in-training.[47]

In Moscow, the first regulations were adopted in 1878. Up to 1890 the practice of the Moscow Council of the Bar did not differ much from that of St. Petersburg in matters concerning lawyers-in-training. On March 3, 1890, the Moscow Council issued new regulations for the admission of lawyers-in-training with the purpose of making access to this profession extremely difficult.

The Moscow Council decided that, besides the requirements of the provisions of Art. 354 and 355 of the Statutes of Judicial Institutions

---

[46] See p. 124.
[47] See Kh. M. Charykhov, *"Pomoshchniki prisyazhnykh poverennykh,"* in *Istoriya russkoi advokatury,* III, p. 156.

the candidate had to meet the following requirements: he must have reached the age of 21, have served his time in the army or been released from military service, have permission from a judicial institution, be in possession of a license for soliciting in affairs of others[48] and, finally, not have practiced law independently before.

Such restrictions were due to the viewpoint that the mere fact of a young man's having a diploma is insufficient for his admission to the profession of lawyer-in-training; there should be also a lawyer who needs his services, a demand for his work—in other words, the law of demand and supply should regulate the situation.[49]

Five years later, the Senate abrogated these regulations by the Ukase of May 4, 1895. The Senate ruled that the requirement of the candidate's being 21 years of age contradicts the law providing that a lawyer must have reached the age of 25 in order to be admitted to the bar; since the period of probation was five years, the young lawyer must have the right to begin his training at the age of twenty. The Senate also found unlawful the restrictions concerning military service, permission from a judicial institution and previous practice. The Moscow Council had to change its regulations again and the requirements for lawyers-in-training were reduced to those existing before 1890.

In other districts, the regulations concerning the admission and activities of the lawyers-in-training were, in most cases, the same as in St. Petersburg and Moscow.

2. Probation

a. Corporative and Personal Patronage

Since the law gave no indication about the method of training young lawyers during the probation period, councils of the bar had to prescribe rules here also. There are various systems of training young lawyers: the system of corporative patronage, the system of personal patronage, a combination of the first and second, and still another system, which was applied in Germany and Austria.

The system of corporative patronage is applied in its purest form in France.[50] There the young lawyer—avocat stagiaire—takes the oath

---

48 A license given according to the Law of 1874 with which we shall deal later on pp. 155-159.

49 Otchet Soveta prisyazhnykh poverennykh pri Moskovskoi Sudebnoi Palate za 1899-90g. p. 21.

50 In Gt. Britain full rights of a barrister and member of a "Jun" are acquired after three years of probation and an examination in English and Roman law.

in the beginning of the probation period and is from this moment on in the possession of almost all the rights of a *maître,* and also has this title. The robe he wears in court differs only slightly—in the shape of the collar—from that of an *avocat.* If he has reached the age of twenty-two, he has the right to carry on suits in his own name, pleading in court on an equal footing with his senior colleagues.[51]

Since the Decree of May 5, 1851, the young French lawyers are divided into *colonnes* (units). In every *colonne,* two members of the council of the bar fulfill the duties of presidents. All the members of the *colonne* are obliged to attend its sessions, which take place at least twice a year. At the sessions, the presidents of the *colonnes* instruct the members about the usages, rules and rights of the guild. Beside the sessions of the *colonne,* the *stagiaire* is obliged to take part in conferences which take place once a week and are designed to develop his knowledge of practical and theoretical jurisprudence. At the conference, reports are made on subjects which are selected by the members of the conference and confirmed by the president, an *ancien* of the bar. After the reading of reports, discussions take place, and then the president sums up the opinions expressed without giving his own. The discussed questions are then solved by voting.

After three years of probation, the young French lawyer is entered on the list of the bar. For this he has to prove (1) that he has regularly attended the conferences and the sessions of the *colonne* during the three years of probation, (2) that he has an address in the city, and (3) that his behavior is beyond reproach. In matters of discipline, the *avocats stagiaires* are subject to the supervision and jurisdiction of councils of the *ordre* (bar), just as senior lawyers.[52]

The system of personal patronage is of quite another character. Under this system, the young lawyer is merely an aid of his patron, a clerk in his office, completely deprived of any professional independence. He passes his time of probation working under the personal direction of his patron, who has to instruct him in all the finesse of the profession.

The overwhelming opinion of the members of the St. Petersburg and Moscow Bars was in favor of personal patronage as against the desire of the lawyers-in-training, who wanted to work under a system of corporative patronage. Let us briefly describe the struggle of the young lawyers with the Councils of the Bar in St. Petersburg and

---

51 F. E. Mollot, *Règles sur la profession d'avocat,* I, 336.
52 *Ibid.,* p. 363.

Moscow, a struggle which they did not win *de jure* but which *de facto* led to the toleration of a combination of both systems.

The single provision of the law concerning lawyers-in-training —in Art. 354 of the Statutes of Judicial Institutions—and especially the official message to accompany this article, do not leave any doubt that the legislator of 1864 had personal patronage in view. That is why training started under this system. Already in 1871, the results of such training appeared inadequate to the young lawyers and they submitted to the Petersburg Council of the Bar a plan of training during the period of probation which was based on the principles of corporative patronage. This plan, which called for the creation of conferences of young lawyers similar to those of the French *avocats stagiaires* was accepted by the Council on November 9, 1871. On May 30, 1877, Regulations for Juridical Conferences of Lawyers-in-Training, worked out by a commission of young lawyers and confirmed at their General Assembly, were adopted by the General Assembly of the Bar in a somewhat altered form.[53] These conferences began to function alongside the personal patronage system.

However, the work of the conferences was unsatisfactory. In 1879 a commission of lawyers-in-training worked out new rules, according to which participation in the work of conferences was declared optional, and submitted them to the Council of the Bar. The Council rejected this suggestion. New regulations concerning the conference were adopted by the General Assembly of the Bar on November 21, 1880. The conferences were retained for pedagogical functions and participation in them remained obligatory. The attempt of the lawyers-in-training to free themselves completely from personal patronage by transferring the functions of patronage from individual patrons to leaders of the conferences had no success with the Council and the General Assembly of the Bar.

In 1883 the Council of the Bar adopted a completely negative position with regard to the system of corporative patronage and prepared a plan according to which the young lawyer had to work exclusively under the leadership of his patron during the whole time of probation. On the other hand, the lawyers-in-training, aiming at the establishment of corporative patronage in its pure form, suggested the creation of *colonnes* similar to those functioning in France.

The General Assembly of the Bar of December 11, 1883, rejected both proposals and elected a commission for working out a new plan.

---

[53] See Charykhov, *op. cit.*, p. 176, and A. A. Isayev, "Yuridicheskiya konferentsii v petrogradskoi advokature," in *Istoriya russkoi advokatury*, III, 299-300.

The commission elaborated a plan which was to be adopted by way of legislation and in which the systems of personal and corporative patronage were combined: personal patronage was retained as a foundation, and the lawyer-in-training received some freedom in exercising his profession—the right to carry on civil suits in court under his own name but only with the permission of the Council of the Bar in each individual case; although the corporative principle in its pure form was repudiated, the conferences were retained as an educational institution. The plan also called for the reduction of the period of probation from five to four years, and the extension of the disciplinary functions of the Council of the Bar over the lawyers-in-training; the Law of May 25, 1874[54] was not to apply to lawyers-in-training.

The plan of the commission was accepted by the General Assembly of the Bar in St. Petersburg with some insignificant amendments in 1885, and forwarded to the *Sudebnaya Palata* for further consideration. The *Palata* approved the plan, with the exception of the provision giving to the lawyer-in-training the right to carry on civil suits in his own name, and submitted it for final confirmation to the Ministry of Justice. There the paper was pigeonholed.

Since the attempt to resolve the problem in a legislative way had no success, the Council of the Bar decided to request its members to apply the rules which were adopted in 1885 for lawyers-in-training and sent a corresponding request, in the form of a circular, to all the lawyers of its district on May 1, 1889. A few months later, however, the Imperial Order introducing restrictions for admission to the bar of persons of non-Christian confessions created a change in the situation which made necessary the adoption of new regulations for the activity of lawyers-in-training.

On this occasion the Council revised the whole system, and in its decision of January 20, 1890, returned to the principle of exclusive personal patronage and rejected any form of corporative patronage. In an explanatory note, the Council gave the following reasons for its decision: under corporative patronage, fictitious relations between the patrons and the patronized developed in practice, and resulted in the fact that the young lawyers "remained without leadership in training for the profession of a lawyer and therefore acquired habits and views concerning their duties which are by no means in accord with the traditions established in the lawyers' guild from the very beginning of its existence. . ."; in order to avoid such fictitious relations it is neces-

---

[54] See pp. 155-159.

sary the Council held, that the lawyer-in-training "should be an assistant to his patron in the full sense of the word, *i.e.*, should work in his office on the preparation of cases, drafts of briefs and fulfillment of other assignments connected with the profession." [55] Independent law practice was to be completely prohibited for lawyers-in-training in civil cases; in such cases he was to be allowed to operate only with a power of attorney transferred to him by his patron and under his supervision.

In criminal cases he was not to plead before two years of his period of probation had expired. The number of young lawyers under the patronage of one lawyer was to be limited to three. The conferences were to be dropped.

It is natural that the young lawyers reacted violently to this decision of the Council. They prepared a note in which all the objections against strict personal patronage and the deprivation of professional independence were presented. The note was sent to all the lawyers of the district.

In the General Assembly of the Bar on February 4, 1890, the young lawyers achieved full victory: the decision of the Council was rejected by an overwhelming majority, and a commission, which for the first time included representatives of the lawyers-in-training, was created and received the assignment to work out new regulations. This commission prepared a plan which again was a compromise between the two systems—the personal and the corporative—and submitted it to the Council of the Bar. However, the Council did not deem it necessary to present the plan to the General Assembly, since the matter had to be resolved through legislation.

Thus ends the story of the various attempts on the part of the lawyers and the lawyers-in-training in St. Petersburg to make up for the lack of legislative provisions concerning the field of activity of the junior partners in the corporation of lawyers' guild.

The course of events in Moscow District was almost similar to that in St. Petersburg. The Regulation of 1878, although based on personal patronage, introduced conferences as an educational institution. When, in 1890, new regulations were adopted by the Council in St. Petersburg, the Moscow Council also declared itself in favor of the strict application of the system of personal patronage and the complete restriction of independence in matters of law practice. The regulations adopted by the Moscow Council on March 3, 1890, were even more drastic than those of January 20 in St. Petersburg: for instance, a

---

[55] Quoted by Charykhov, *op. cit.*, p. 182.

lawyer, as a rule, was allowed to have under his patronage one young lawyer only; for a greater number of trainees, he needed the permission of the Council. Furthermore, the regulations of the Petersburg Council were only a plan, which was not accepted by the General Assembly of the Bar, whereas the Council of the Bar in Moscow ordered the application of these regulations without the approval of the General Assembly. Those young lawyers who did not conform to these regulations were barred from the list of lawyers-in-training as of May 25, 1890.

Complaints against the decision of the Council were lodged with the *Sudebnaya Palata.*

The decisions of the *Palata* and later of the Senate concerning these complaints are of interest as a matter of principle. With regards to the right of the Council to make regulations concerning the internal order and control of the guild, the *Palata* found that the Council did not exceed the limits of its power and field of activity conferred to it by law, and with regard to the substance of the complaints, the *Palata* declared itself incompetent, since "the right of supervision over the lawyers and lawyers-in-training. . .belongs to councils of the bar only, and does not belong to the field of duties either of judicial institutions in general or of the *Sudebnaya Palata* in particular." [56]

Acting on a complaint against this decision, the Senate ordered the *Palata* to examine the complaints in substance. The *Palata* considered the complaints point by point and dismissed them, declaring that the Regulations of March 3, 1890, were within the limits of the law.[57]

Again a complaint was filed with the Senate against the decision of the *Palata.* On May 4, 1895, over five years after the regulations had first been enforced in Moscow, the Senate rescinded the decision of the *Palata* on the ground that the Regulations of March 3, 1890, were unlawful in two respects: the prohibition of law practice during the period of probation and the limitation on the number of lawyers-in-training under the patronage of one lawyer.

Thus the Regulations of March 3, 1890, had to be changed. This was accomplished by the Council in such a manner that the regulations remained, in general outline, as they were adopted on March 3, 1890, with the exception of the provisions rescinded by the Senate. According to an amendment to these provisions, the lawyer-in-training

---

[56] Quoted by Charykhov, *op. cit.,* p. 182.
[57] *Ibid.,* p. 149-50.

was bound to notify his patron concerning every case he took over, and to keep a register of those cases.

However, the fight for a radical change in the regulations did not stop at this point. On December 14, 1897, the General Assembly of the Moscow Bar decided that new regulations should be worked out. Adopted on October 7, 1898, these regulations restored optional conferences, but did not satisfy the lawyers-in-training. Finally, on June 2, 1900, new regulations were again adopted and remained in force during the last 17 years of the existence of the bar.

Such was the development of the problem in St. Petersburg and Moscow. In bars of other districts the state of affairs was almost the same.

Thus, after graduation from the university or other law school, the young lawyer had to enter his period of probation. During this period he had to acquire the necessary practical experience and be initiated in the rules and traditions of behavior which had to be his moral beacon in his future practice. In Russia the school gave no, or almost no, practical knowledge. The university supplied the students with a more or less voluminous stock of theoretical knowledge, but did not train him to make use of it.[58] This training had to be acquired by work under the supervision of a patron. Thus, the first task was the finding of a patron who not only had the desire and time to instruct a young lawyer, but also needed his help. This was not an easy task. Associations of lawyers were unknown in Russia. Law firms with a great number of members, huge offices, and numerous personnel are widespread in the United States and, on a smaller scale in Germany, but did not exist in Russia. There every lawyer practiced individually and only occasionally resorted to the collaboration of a colleague for consultation or joint handling of a concrete case. If a lawyer employed three or more young lawyers as his assistants, he was an eminent lawyer with a big clientele, very occupied and usually lacking time and desire to instruct the young lawyers more than was necessary for the completion of the work assigned to them. And still it was the dream of every young man entering the law career to work under the supervision of a prominent lawyer whose name often appeared in newspaper reports. Of course, only a small number of such dreams was

---

[58] Prof. Martin Wolff, of the Faculty of Law at the University in Berlin, was in the habit of telling his students that the scope of juridical study at a university does not go farther than to teach the future young jurist where he has to search for the solution of problems which will arise before him when he practices law.

realized. The great majority of the candidates had to be satisfied with the patronage of an unknown lawyer—if by chance he needed help. It was necessary to be registered for training with a lawyer, because if he was not on the list the candidate did not receive his title of lawyer-in-training, and the period of probation began on the date of registration. For those who could not find a patron or who were of the opinion that they could do better without working for a patron, the only way which remained open was to register fictitiously with a patron and, having obtained a certificate of private attorney,[59] to practice law independently.

Since the attempts of councils of the bar to limit the number of lawyers-in-training under one patron remained fruitless, it was easy to find a lawyer willing to enter the name of a candidate as his trainee without actually employing him. Thus the young lawyer was entered on the lists of lawyers-in-training and applied for a certificate which was granted to him without difficulty if he was not of a non-Christian confession (after the Law of 1889).[60]

With regard to criminal cases, the lawyer-in-training was free to plead in court, since this function could be assumed by any person considered qualified by the court. Several attempts by councils of the bar to limit the activities of lawyers-in-training also in this direction, by the requirement of two years of previous practice, had no success.

In the beginning, the courts even appointed lawyers-in-training as counsel in criminal cases, with the consent of the accused. But in 1871, a lawyer-in-training, Lyutse, refused to take over the defense in a case assigned to him by the Circuit Court, arguing that there were no provisions of law obligating lawyers-in-training to serve as appointed counsel. The Petersburg *Sudebnaya Palata* then ordered the courts of its district to discontinue such appointments. The other *Palatas* followed the same practice.[61]

As far as conferences were concerned, one of the major problems was the obligatory nature of attendance and participation.

The lawyers-in-training struggled against the obligatory nature of their work at conferences, but without success. When the revolutionary movement was at its peak in 1905, the lawyers-in-training in St. Petersburg decided in their General Assembly of December 1905 "to abrogate, at once, obligatory attendance and the submitting of reports."[62] However, this resolution was rejected by the Council of the Bar. Con-

---

[59] See below, p. 157.
[60] See below, pp. 275-276.
[61] See Isayev, *op. cit.*, p. 292; and Charykhov, *op. cit.*, p. 236.
[62] Quoted by Charykhov, *op. cit.*, p. 222.

cerning the question of compulsion, the distinguished lawyer P. N. Malyantovich wrote: "There is no organization without compulsion. An organization implies a certain form of compulsion, and duties with sanctions are the unavoidable foundation of every active organization. Without compulsion there is no norm of law. A rule without punitive sanction is a useless, trivial phrase." [63] But according to the rules adopted in the St. Petersburg District in 1880, which remained in force till 1917 (with insignificant amendments), the obligatory attendance of conferences and participation, in their work was reduced to the first two years of probation, in which period that lawyer-in-training had to attend 14 sessions (7 every year) and make three reports on topics assigned to him by the leader of the conference.

The conferences in St. Petersburg were divided into four and later five groups, with a leader at the head of each group. The leaders were elected by the General Assembly of the Bar from among the most eminent members of the guild. One of the permanent and most active leaders was the famous lawyer, A. Ya. Passover.

In 1912, attendance in St. Petersburg was 40-50 persons at every session and group, and 3,500 per year. The groups were divided according to law disciplines: 1st group—criminal law; 2nd—constitutional, administrative and civil law; 3d, 4th and 5th—civil and commercial law. On the suggestion of O. O. Gruzenberg and M. M. Winaver, systematic studies of criminal and civil procedures and laws, similar to those practiced in university seminars, were introduced in the first and third groups.

Though compulsory the conferences did not represent a heavy burden for young lawyers.

b. *Pros and Cons of Corporative and Personal Patronage*

Opinions on the relative merits of corporative and personal patronage differ widely.

"Well-organized professional training of young lawyers can be achieved only under corporative patronage," writes Charykhov,[64] who adheres to the opinion that efficient patronage is beyond the ability of individual patrons. "It is not exaggerated to assert that in the whole lawyers' guild only a small number can be found who are really able to transmit the necessary quantity of knowledge to the lawyers-in-training and to share their personal experience with them," Winaver

---

[63] Quoted by Isayev, *op. cit.*, p. 311.
[64] Charykhov, *op. cit.*, p. 218.

writes. He is of the opinion that the student—it may be the apprentice of the Middle Ages or the contemporary lawyer-in-training—assimilates not only the merits of his teacher, but also his manner, and that such a bond is the first sign of stagnation. According to Winaver, it is necessary for a young mind equipped with the apparatus of knowledge and looking for its application to be in a condition to use all methods for broadening his horizon, to have the opportunity to compare and choose, to let congenial persons join; only under these conditions is originality born or saved from destruction; the needs of a student do not always correspond to the abilities of the teacher; the first frequently outgrow the second. "It is frightful to think concludes Winaver, "that forced dependence on one teacher can kill what could be the source of our growth." [65]

I cannot agree with the authors quoted above. While recognizing the usefulness of corporative patronage, I regard personal patronage as absolutely necessary. The best way to prepare a lawyer-in-training for his future activity is to let him benefit from both systems.

What is the aim of personal patronage ? First of all, to acquaint the young lawyer with the technicalities of his profession. When he leaves school, he is completely ignorant of them. These technicalities he can learn best of all in the office of a lawyer—of his patron *de jure* or of another lawyer with whom he works and who becomes his patron *de facto*.

The attendance of conferences and reading of reports will not familiarize the young lawyer with the technique necessary for his activities. Traditions, customs and ethics, to which he has to subordinate his actions, can be assimilated only in practice, through cases which he has to handle in the office of his patron, or in the court as his patron's deputy. Of course, the work in conferences will enlarge and deepen the knowledge acquired in school. But the most eminent lawyer, elected as leader of a group, is unable to convey to the 40-50 attendants of the conference, the membership of which constantly changes, his skill and the particularities which made him eminent or even famous. Of course, the experience and knowledge of the leader will greatly contribute to the clarification of cases reported or questions discussed, but the leader of a conference lacks personal contact with his numerous listeners. And if sometimes such contact is established, it is with especially brilliant participants and remains the privilege of a very small number of persons who, thanks to their aptitude, would

---

[65] M. M. Winaver, *Ocherki ob advokature,* p. 87-88.

have made their way also without this very valuable help. For the great mass of lawyers-in-training the conferences were a burden and source of boredom.

A young lawyer who begins his career without the direction of an experienced colleague is completely helpless. To whom shall he revert with the innumerable questions which arise at every step? In France, the *avocat stagiaire* is legally not subordinated to a patron but he still has recourse, in the beginning of his career, to the advice of a senior colleague who actually fulfills the functions of a patron. And is this not also the case in the United States, where the young members of the bar, who just passed their bar examination, join the offices of older lawyers where they do the work of clerks until they acquire experience and maturity enabling them to assume a more independent position? In reality these young lawyers are for several years lawyers-in-training, but without being called so.

Even if Charykhov is right in saying that the great majority of patrons were far from ideal as mentors and advisers, there were very few who could bring real harm to the patronized young lawyers.

It is also difficult to share the opinion of M. M. Winaver that the assistants acquire the qualities and defects of their patrons. Unfortunately the best attribute of a lawyer—talent—cannot be transmitted even by the most gifted lawyer to his trainee. Eloquence, straight juridical thinking, ability to gain a proper understanding of people, relations and things, are innate qualities which can be acquired only to a certain extent by very capable students who would have found their way also without the help of a great patron. As for the faults of the patron, they are assimilated by such pupils who have a natural inclination for these defects. In the majority of cases this inclination will manifest itself regardless of the qualities of the patron. And as for the suppression of the originality of the lawyer-in-training by his patron, Winaver's apprehensions are unfounded. Brilliant personalities can seldom be suppressed. They always find means and occasions to reveal themselves. The personal patronage system does not oblige the lawyer-in-training to spend the whole time of his probation with the same patron. As we saw, registration with a patron does not always necessarily mean the obligation to work with him *de facto*. The lawyer-in-training has the freedom to make comparisons between his patron and other lawyers, to experiment with a variety of methods of training, and to enlarge his horizons. It is much more difficult to gather experience without the help of a patron, even a mediocre one. Without the assistance of his patron, a young lawyer who makes his first steps in the profession is simply lost in the dense forest of legal formalities, requirements and regulations.

Mistakes are inevitable under such conditions. Of course, *errando discimus*—"we learn from our mistakes"—but, unfortunately, it is the client who suffers. If a young lawyer can rely on the support and advice of a senior colleague, if he has a place where he can find guidance and information, he may assume the responsibility of carrying on civil and criminal cases in his own name. But imagine such a young man, fresh from school, sitting on the bench of the defense opposite the jury, intimidated to the highest degree by the surroundings, by the prosecutor who is a much more experienced jurist, by the feeling of responsibility toward his client, and above all, by his lack of practical knowledge. Quite different is the situation when his patron sits beside him: he has the opportunity to hear the patron's replies to the motions of the prosecution, to learn the art of cross-examination, to participate in the defense without carrying the burden of responsibility, and, eventually, to plead after the case has been prepared by a more mature jurist. That is the only way of acquiring the necessary experience of behavior in court, of familiarizing oneself with court atmosphere, of mastering the proper strategy in the battle which rages between the prosecutor and the counsel. There were in Russia, as well as elsewhere, good patrons and bad patrons, able teachers and inept ones, but even in the office of the most neglectful and ignorant patron the trainee could learn the practical essentials of his profession, and, after having acquired them, he could start to build up an independent practice.

Since the necessity of guiding the lawyer-in-training at least in the the first years of the probation period is beyond question, personal patronage is the best method of achieving this goal. Charykhov, who is an enemy of personal patronage, says himself: "There is no doubt that the lawyer-in-training needs leadership in everything." [66] And still he comes to the conclusion that "the present organization of the professional training of lawyers can be achieved only by means of corporative patronage." [67]

It seems to me that this opinion is rather the result of a very legitimate desire to see the lawyer-in-training as independent as possible than the consequence of an objective evaluation of corporative patronage. Can anyone seriously assert that the attending of 14 ses-

[66] Charykhov, *op. cit.*, p. 215.
[67] *Ibid.*, p. 218.

sions of the conferences in two years, and the reading of three papers, are sufficient to initiate a young man, completely ignorant of the practical aspects of the profession, into the *finesses du métier*, especially in view of the fact that Charykhov shares the opinion of the majority of the lawyers-in-training that participation in the conferences should be voluntary? I am not opposed to conferences. They did splendid work, especially when placed under the leadership of such a man as A. Ya. Passover, but they can be useful only when combined with personal patronage. "The lawyers-in-training, who prepare themselves to be lawyers, must become familiar with the traditions of the guild as soon as possible, be inspired by the idea of their solidarity with it and take its interests to heart," Arsen'yev writes.[68] How can they carry out these wise precepts without being admitted to practical work in a lawyer's office, under his patronage?

It must also be emphasized that a five-year probation period was too long for the training of a young lawyer. In France and Germany, a three-year period was considered sufficient. There is no necessity to deprive the trainee of the full rights of a lawyer for such a long time. Arsen'yev has substantiated this in detail.[69] A request of the St. Petersburg Council of the Bar that the law be changed accordingly, remained unheeded.

The Councils of St. Petersburg and Moscow were fully aware of the important role of personal patronage, and that is why all attempts to completely replace it with the corporative system remained without success.

The systems used in various districts were as follows: in Petersburg—personal and corporative patronage, both compulsory; in Moscow—personal and corporative patronage, the latter voluntary; Kazan District followed the Petersburg system; Odessa, Saratov, Novocherkassk, Irkutsk and Kharkov Districts adopted the Moscow pattern.[70] In districts where councils of the bar had not yet been introduced, as, for instance, in Kiev District, only personal patronage existed.

c. German System of Training

Aside from the systems of personal and corporative patronage for the training of young lawyers, another system functioned in Europe, *i.e.*, in Germany and Austria. For the sake of comparison it is not irrelevant to describe here the essential features of this system.

---

68 Arsen'yev, *op. cit.*, p. 37.
69 Arsen'yev, *op. cit.*, p. 40-41.
70 Charykhov, *op. cit.*, p. 211.

After three years of law study at a law faculty of a German university, the first state examination, given by a commission consisting of a member of the appellate court as president and several university professors and high judicial officials as members, conferred upon the candidate an appointment to an unremunerated position as an official of the Ministry of Justice, with the title of *Referendar*. This *Referendar* had to have three years of probation, which consisted of work divided into six stages—six months in each stage. The first one was at the *Amtsgericht* (a court the jurisdiction of which corresponded to that of justices of the peace). Every *Referendar* was attached to a judge who handled civil and criminal cases. The judge acted as the instructor of his *Referendar*. He let him prepare reports on cases, draft decisions and, sometimes, toward the end of the six-month period, the *Referendar* had the opportunity to act as the deputy of the judge, deciding unimportant cases. The second step was the *Landgericht*, which may be compared to the Russian circuit court. The *Referendar* was assigned to a civil division and attached to one of the three judges of the bench. The work of the *Referendar* was essentially the same as at the *Amtsgericht*: he participated in the preparation of cases for the court session, wrote the minutes of the sessions, took part in the deliberations of the bench (being the first to give his opinion) and wrote the motivated decisions which were then edited by his chief and the presiding judge.

The third half-year was spent at the offce of a lawyer chosen by the *Referendar*. With regard to the selections of this lawyer, the *Referendar* had the same troubles as the Russian *pomoshchnik*: he had to find a lawyer willing to undertake his instruction; but since the *Referendar* was not paid, it was not too difficult to find a patron. In the office of the lawyer the *Referendar* started by doing clerical work and preparing briefs and other papers. In the majority of cases he was allowed to attend conferences of his patron with his clients. Since there was a monopoly of lawyers at the *Landgericht* and *Oberlandesgericht*, no hearing could take place without the presence of a lawyer. According to the German system of civil procedure, all motions and claims must be formulated orally during court session. If a party is not represented in the session of the court by a lawyer or a *Referendar* with power of attorney transferred to him, the opposite party has the right to ask for a judgment by default *(Versäumnisurteil)* . (The custom existed among lawyers not to take a judgment by default against an absent colleague if the day before he had not been notified about the intention to obtain such a judgment.) Hence, it was not seldom that a lawyer with a large practice was obliged to attend sessions of several courts on the same morning. He solved this problem by sending his *Referendare,* with transferred powers of attorney, to the less important sessions.

During the six months with a lawyer, the *Referendar* became acquainted with the practical side of this profession.

The next stage was the criminal court. The work was divided into two parts: three months with the criminal department of the *Landgericht* and three months with the prosecution. In the criminal session of the court, the *Referendar* had to lay down the minutes of the sessions, to take part in the deliberations of the court (the bench of three judges and the *Schöffen*)—with a consultative voice, of course —and to prepare motivated drafts of the decisions.

The prosecution usually assigned the *Referendar,* in the beginning, to a prosecutor at an *Amtsgericht,* where the *Referendar* had to act also as his deputy, and then to a district attorney, where the *Referendar* became familiarized with the preparation of more important cases and with the usual office work of a district attorney.

The fifth stage was usually the Labor Court *(Arbeitsgericht),* which dealt with litigation resulting from labor contracts (the sequence of the fourth, fifth, and sixth stages could be changed according to the number of candidates and vacancies). It was composed of a professional judge and two representatives: one of the employers and one of the employees or workers, according to the case. In this court the *Referendar* got acquainted with labor relations and their treatment by the court.

The last stage was usually the appellate court (*Oberlandesgericht,* in Prussia *Kammergericht*). Here the *Referendar* had to work in several departments: the appellate departments for appeals against decisions of the *Landgericht* as the first instance and as the second instance and, finally, in the administration department, which handled cases concerning inclusion in cadastre books, and the like. In the appellate court the *Referendar,* working under the supervision of judges with great experience and broad knowledge, received in a manner of speaking, his final polish. The making of decisions, in which he had to participate, being the first to give his opinion, required extended research work and a thorough acquaintance with the questions at hand.

At every stage, a certificate was delivered to the *Referendar* in which his aptitude was graded and a detailed characteristic of his personality was given. If the grades were satisfactory, the *Referendar,* upon completing his time of probation, could present himself for the second juridical state examination, called *Grosse Juristische Staatsprüfung*. This examination in Berlin lasted for six months and consisted of two reports on topics of criminal and civil law and procedures, prepared at home, and several written and one oral examinations—the written ones in the appellate court and the oral one at the Ministry of Justice. The grading "excellent" in both state examinations gave the right to receive personal congratulations by the Minister of Justice and priority in obtaining an appointment according to personal desire with regard to place and court.

After having passed the second state examination, which conferred the title of *Assessor*, the young jurist had to decide whether he wished to remain in government service or to quit it and practice law as a *Rechtsanwalt*.[71] In the first case the *Assessor* was appointed judge or district attorney at a court, received a modest salary, and after some years of service (generally three years), was promoted to *Landgerichtsrat*—a position held for life, on good behavior.

The *Assessor* who selected the career of a lawyer had to apply for registration at an *Anwaltskammer* (council of the bar) and had to be attached to a court—*Landgericht* or *Oberlandesgericht (Kammergericht)*, according to his own choice. This was, *de jure*, the only court in which he had the right to plead. For that reason he associated himself with a colleague who was attached to another court. They mutually transferred their powers of attorney when it was necessary, and this proceeding was accepted by the courts. In this manner every lawyer had the *de facto* right to plead in every court.

In this manner, the future *Rechtsanwalt* received a solid practical training during his term of probation as an official, which on the one hand gave him a good knowledge of the technical aspects of judicial activity, but on the other hand injected bureaucracy into his psychology, deprived him of the flexibility and adaptability of mind necessary to a good lawyer, and reduced to six months his training period with a lawyer.

Criticizing the system of training of young lawyers in Germany, M. M. Winaver writes: "corporate patronage was not adopted by countries where lawyers are organized into hidden, or obvious, officialdom, not into a free guild." According to him, in such countries the basic principle of professional training is compulsory service in chan-

---

71 G. B. Sliozberg is mistaken when he writes that an Assessor had to assume juridical positions before joining the bar. See his *Dela minuvshikh dnei*, I, 191. The *Assessor* could at once choose the career of a *Rechtsanwalt*, or join the judiciary or the prosecution.

celleries, similar to service in workshops. In such countries the bar, even if it exists outwardly, is based, he claims, on foundations which deprive it of essential conditions of independent development.[72]

I cannot agree with M. M. Winaver that the lawyers' guild in Germany, prior to Hitler, was not a free one and was not capable of independent development. The bar in Germany was a self-governing institution with free elected councils and presidiums (*Vorstand der Anwaltskammer*) with disciplinary power over the members of the bar. Thus the bar was organized similarly to those of other European countries. Officialdom existed not in the bar, but in the system of training of the young jurists. This training was thorough and efficient. It produced good jurists—but not good lawyers.[73] The *Referendar* was well trained to be a district attorney or another kind of judicial official, but the profession of a lawyer requires acquaintance with all aspects of life, knowledge of people and relations between them in various fields of human activity, which are acquired by dealing directly with clients in a law office and not from the bureaucratic heights of a judicial bench.

On the other hand it cannot be denied that it is useful for the prospective lawyer to get acquainted through his own experience with the psychology of the judge, to work directly on the spot where decisions are being prepared. He becomes familiar with the ingredients and learns how to mix them. The German system brings the lawyer close to the judge; both have the same training—but, unfortunately for the lawyer, also the same psychology. That is the main defect of the system, which makes it inappropriate for the training of members of a free legal profession. The German lawyer always remains a semi-official. He is not imbued with the idealistic spirit so characteristic of the former Russian lawyer.

It seems to me that the prospective lawyer must spend the years of probation exclusively in preparation for the profession of lawyer, i.e., he must be trained in the office of a lawyer and by a lawyer.

3. Self-Government of Lawyers-in-Training

The law left the lawyers-in-training to their own resources in the matter of corporative organization as well. It is only natural, therefore, that they tried to work out a system of self-government and to impose

[72] Winaver, *Ocherki ob advokature*, p. 60.
[73] Vas'kovsky says that the *Rechtsanwalt* is "half an official and half an artisan." He is unjust toward German lawyers, whom he depicts as a guild "which uses all means to achieve material benefits." Vas'kovsky, Organizatsiya advokatury, I, 276.

their system upon councils of the bar. These attempts had more success in St. Petersburg than in Moscow.

In 1872, for the first time, a Commission was elected by the General Assembly of lawyers-in-training in St. Petersburg in connection with the regulations adopted by the St. Petersburg Council of the Bar in that year. The function of the Commission in the beginning was to collect information for the Council of the Bar about candidates for admission as lawyers-in-training. In 1873 an attempt was made to induce the Council of the Bar to admit two members of the Commission to deliberations in disciplinary proceedings against lawyers-in-training. The Council refused.

In 1898 the Council of the Bar decided to direct every application for admission to the profession of lawyers-in-training to the Commission for the collection of information about the candidate and for its opinion about him.

In addition to these activities, the Commission began to function as a disciplinary court for lawyers-in-training. Although formally the Council of the Bar never transferred this function to the Commission it did not protest against disciplinary proceedings by the Commission in cases when the deliquent agreed to be tried by the Commission.

On the occasion of the complaint of a lawyer-in-training to the *Sudebnaya Palata* in 1883 that he had been tried first by the Commission of lawyers-in-training and then by the Council of the Bar, the *Sudebnaya Palata* requested explanations from the Council. The Council declared that "persons with common interests and affairs may, for their convenience, entrust one or several persons among themselves with the administration of these affairs, and such an agreement contains nothing illegal." [74]

In 1900 the Commission asked again for permission to send a representative to sessions of the Council dealing with disciplinary cases resulting from appeals against decisions of the Commission. The Council rejected this request, excepting cases in which the accused himself requests the presence of a representative of the Commission. However, aside from the gathering of information and disciplinary proceedings, the Commission of lawyers-in-training in St. Petersburg assumed other functions as well, with the tacit consent of the Council of the Bar: solution of various problems of common interest to young lawyers, administration of funds of mutual aid, etc.

The self-government of the lawyers-in-training in Moscow devel-

---

[74] *Otchet Soveta prisyazhnykh poverennykh pri S. Peterburgskoi Sudebnoi Palate, 1882/1883,* p. 17-18.

oped in a less favorable atmosphere. Their Committee was much more restricted in its rights and functions than the Commission in St. Petersburg. Charykhov writes that the fate of the Moscow Committee "depended on the nature of the predominant policy in the guild:" when a reactionary trend won the upper hand in the guild and in society, the Committee was abolished; in the years of the triumph of liberalism, the Committee was revived as an organ of corporative administration of the lawyers-in-training.[75]

The Committee in Moscow was organized by the Regulations of February 4, 1878, mentioned above. Its activities were limited to the gathering of information for the Council of the Bar about candidates for admission to be a lawyer-in-training. Disciplinary powers were denied to the Committee. However, the Council conceded to the Committee the position of an organ "elected by lawyers-in-training among themselves to manage current affairs of common interest and facilitate the supervision of the activities of lawyers-in-training by the Council."[76]

The famous Rules of March 3, 1890, abolished the Committee. It was revived by the Rules of June 2, 1900, which conferred upon it extensive rights with regard to participation in the activities of conferences. The Committee had the right to draw up the work plan for the conferences, to formulate the program together with the leaders of the conferences to prepare the annual report on the conferences and to inform the Council of the Bar about the participation of individual lawyers-in-training in the work of the conferences. In 1908 its functions were enlarged with regard to the gathering of information about the candidates. In 1909 the Council acknowledged the right of the Committee to give its opinion on every candidate.

The activities of the Committee and its very existence came to a premature end in 1914, when the General Assembly of the Moscow *Sudebnaya Palata* issued an order to the effect that the Moscow Council of the Bar had no right to create an institution which was not foreseen by law.

The Committee of the lawyers-in-training in Odessa, organized in 1892, was similar, with regard to its activities, to the Commission in St. Petersburg (including disciplinary rights). In Kiev, where a council of the bar did not exist, the Council of the Consultation Office of lawyers-in-training fulfilled the same functions as the Commission in St. Petersburg. In Kharkov the Commission had no disciplinary func-

---

[75] Charykhov, *op. cit.*, p. 263.
[76] *Otchet Soveta prisyazhnykh poverennykh pri Moskovskoi Sudebnoi Palate, 1885/1886*, p. 5.

tions. However, the Committee in Kazan, established in 1906, in the revolutionary period, had disciplinary and other functions similar to those of the Commission in St. Petersburg. The Tomsk Commission shared the fate of the Moscow Committee: it was abolished by an order of the *Sudebnaya Palata* in 1911.[77]

The general assemblies of lawyers-in-training constituted the electoral bodies which chose the commissions and committees.

4. Young Lawyers Under Disciplinary Supervision of the Council of the Bar

According to Art. 367 of the Statutes of Judicial Institutions, councils of the bar had to examine complaints against lawyers and check on their strict compliance with law and established rules, as well as the fulfillment by lawyers of all obligations assumed in the interest of their clients. Disciplinary actions of council could be started as a result of a complaint lodged by a client against his lawyer or initiated by a council itself with regard to facts which came to its knowledge in any other way.

The disciplinary jurisdiction of councils extended to almost all the actions of a lawyer. In places where there was no council of the bar, disciplinary powers belonged to the circuit court. The appellate instance for the disciplinary decisions of the council and the circuit court was the general assembly of the *Sudebnaya Palata*. To the jurisdiction of the latter were subject all the lawyers who resided in the district of the *Sudebnaya Palata*. The disciplinary power of councils over the lawyers-in-training, not being stipulated by law, experienced some fluctuations in practice.

In 1870, the President of the Criminal Department of the St. Petersburg Circuit Court notified the Council of the Bar that a lawyer-in-training, Lyutse, had declined to assume the functions of counsel in a criminal case assigned to him by the President, asserting that, according to law, such functions could be assigned only to lawyers, not to lawyers-in-training. When the Council invited Lyutse to appear before it in order to explain his action, he refused to do so, declaring that he was not subject to the disciplinary jurisdiction of the Council and was not obliged to give explanations or to comply with any decisions and orders of the Council. The Council decided in October

---

[77] See Charykhov, *op. cit.*, p. 263-276, *passim*.

1870 to exclude Lyutse as a lawyer-in-training. Against this decision Lyutse filed a complaint with the *Sudebnaya Palata*.

Although the *Sudebnaya Palata* shared the opinion of the Council that its supervision over lawyers-in-training was very beneficial, it still found that the existing laws did not give the Council disciplinary power over lawyers-in-training and reversed the Council's decision of October 1870.

With regard to this decision of the *Palata*, the Council requested the patron of Lyutse to use his influence on his trainee not to decline the fulfillment of his duties and comply with the decision of the Council. However, the patron informed the Council that Lyutse obstinately refused to submit to the supervision of the Council and to give any explanation to the Council, even through the mediation of his patron. Then the Council requested the patron to drop Lyutse as his trainee. This request was fulfilled. When another lawyer expressed the desire to accept Lyutse as his trainee and Lyutse filed an application for admission, the Council rejected the application.

As a consequence of this affair, the Council in St. Petersburg adopted the following policy with respect to disciplinary supervision over lawyers-in-training: the candidate for admission to the profession of lawyer-in-training had to pledge in a written declaration to submit to all decisions and orders of the Council. When reasons for disciplinary proceedings came to the knowledge of the Council, it invited the lawyer-in-training to give oral or written explanations; if sufficient evidence for a disciplinary punishment was gathered, the punishment was inflicted through the mediation of his patron.

Meanwhile the *Sudebnaya Palata* refused to decide on complaints of lawyers-in-training against decisions of the Council, being of the opinion that the trainees did not stand in the same relation to the Council as the lawyers, since the relations of the trainees were not regulated by law, and that consequently the *Palata* was not competent to decide on such complaints.[78]

However, the Senate did not share the point of view of the *Palata*. On the ground of a complaint against the decision of the *Palata*, the Senate ruled that if a council extends its disciplinary powers to lawyers-in-training, the latter have the right to appeal to the *Palata* even if they are not mentioned in Art. 376 of the Statutes of Judicial Institutions,

---

[78] Decisions of the *Sudebnaya Palata* of May 26, 1876, and December 13, 1880. See P. V. Makalinsky, *Sanktpeterburgskaya prisyazhnaya advokatura*, p. 81-83; A. N. Trainin, "Distsiplinarnoe proizvodstvo v sovetakh prisyazhnykh poverennykh," in *Istoriya russkoi advokatury*, II, 290-295.

and that an opposite viewpoint would, on the one hand, give councils more power than they were entitled to and, on the other, would deprive the lawyers-in-training of a right which belongs to every accused namely, the right of appeal.[79]

Then the St. Petersburg *Palata* began to reverse decisions of the St. Petersburg Council of the Bar concerning the exclusion of lawyers-in-training.

But in 1902 the Senate ruled that since councils had the right of supervision, they also had the right of disciplinary punishment. And, finally, a decision of the Senate of 1905 declared that ". . .lawyers-in-training are under the jurisdiction and the closest supervision of council of the bar, and thus the actions of lawyers-in-training concerning the carrying on of lawsuits are unconditionally subject to appraisal by councils so that the councils can take measures, if necessary, to call the lawyers-in-training to account just as they do lawyers.

This last decision put an end to the fluctuations of the Senate in the question of the disciplinary competence of councils of the bar with regard to lawyers-in-training. It marks a final acknowledgement by the Senate of the lawyer-in-training as a junior partner in the lawyers' guild.

F.   MONOPOLY OF LAWYERS. OTHER MEMBERS OF THE LEGAL PROFESSION

1.   *Monopoly*

The Legislator of 1864 had also to solve the question of the monopoly of lawyers in matters of soliciting and pleading in court.

In criminal proceedings the accused had the right to select as his counsel a member of the bar or any other person "whom the law does not prohibit from carrying on other persons' lawsuits." [80] Thus, no monopoly for lawyers in criminal cases was established.

In case the accused did not choose a counsel and asked the court to appoint one, the president of the court had to appoint one of the lawyers of the district as counsel for the accused, or, if no lawyer was available, a "candidate for a judicial position" [81] who was known to the president as a reliable person.[82]

---

79 *Resheniya Obshchago Sobraniya kassatsionnykh s uchastiyem Pervago i Vtorogo departamentov Pravitel'stvuyushchago Senata*, 1880, No. 6 (in the Evreinov Case) .
80 *Ustav ugolovnago sudoproizvodstva*, Art. 565.
81 A trainee for the position of judge or prosecutor.
82 *Ibid.*, Art. 566.

The accused was free to make his choice of counsel among non-lawyers as well. In practice, cases when persons other than lawyers pleaded in criminal courts with jury were rare.

The exclusive right of members of the bar to represent their clients in civil proceedings exists in some countries. Thus, for instance, in Germany, the *Anwaltszwang* obliged a party in civil cases to have a lawyer in collegiate courts: *Landgericht, Oberlandesgericht (Kammergericht) and Reichsgericht.*[83]

As it appears from the provisions of the Law of 1864, the State Council desired to give lawyers an exclusive right to carry on civil lawsuits in court. However, the State Council feared that in the beginning there would be an insufficient number of lawyers to take care of all lawsuits. Article 387 of the Statutes of Judicial Institutions reads as follows: "In those cities where there is a sufficient number of resident lawyers, the litigants may give powers of attorney for carrying on lawsuits in the courts of those cities to lawyers only." Article 388 provides that the number of lawyers considered sufficient for district and province centers as well as for the capitals, was to be specified in a special roll which, on recommendation of the *Sudebnaya Palata,* the Minister of Justice was to submit to confirmation by the Tsar through the State Council. Thus until a sufficient number of lawyers was reached, as established by an act of the Tsar, the carrying on of lawsuits and pleading in civil cases actually remained open to everyone.[84] However, the Minister of Justice constantly declined to produce an imperial ukase setting the "adequate number" for every city, as he was required to do by Article 388.

A change was made by the Law of 1874.

2. *Private Attorneys*

On May 25, 1874, the Rules Concerning Persons Having the Right to Become Private Attorneys, confirmed by the Tsar, were published. These rules produced the first major break in the majestic edifice of the Laws of 1864. They created a new kind of attorneys, the so-called *chastnye poverennye* (private attorneys), as distinguished from the *prisyazhnye poverennye* (sworn attorneys, lawyers). These rules were introduced as an amendment to the Statutes of Judicial Institutions.[85] No educational requirements were set for becoming a private attorney. ✓

---

[83] The courts introduced by Hitler and after him are not discussed here.
[84] *Ustav grazhdanskago sudoproizvodstva,* Art. 245.
[85] *Uchrezhdeniye sudebnykh ustanovleny,* Art. 406¹-406¹⁹.

A person who desired to enter this profession had to file an application with the law court at which he intended to practice and to declare that none of the impediments listed in Art. 246 of the code of Civil Procedure existed in his case.[86] The court with which the application was filed had the right to make sure that the applicant had the necessary knowledge, in case he was not a graduate of law from a university or another institution of higher learning and no certificate of private attorney had been given him by another court of equal or higher instance.[87] The certificate of a private attorney could be granted by an assembly of justices of the peace, a circuit court and a *Sudebnaya Palata*, and conferred the right to practice only at the court which delivered the certificate. There were, however, two exceptions to this rule: (1) a certificate issued by an assembly of justices of the peace entitled one to plead before individual justices of the peace, and (2) a certificate issued by any one of the courts mentioned above conferred the right to carry on suits in the Senate if the suit had been examined in one of those courts in first instance.[88] The law permitted the possession of several certificates issued by various courts, so that a private counsel could represent his client virtually in all instances and courts in a manner similar to that of a lawyer.[89]

Article 406[13] provided that the court to which the private attorney was attached, *i.e.*, the court which issued the certificate, had the right, on its own initiative or as a consequence of a request by the prosecutor

---

[86] *Ibid.*, Art. 406[5]. Article 246, mentioned above, gives a general list of persons who do not have the right to act as private attorneys. These are: 1) illiterates; 2) those not of age; 3) monks, with the exception of cases when they solicit for their monasteries or through power of attorney granted by their monastic superiors; 4) priests of the secular clergy, with the exception of cases when they solicit for the Ecclesiastical Department or for their wives or children, as well as for foster children in their charge; 5) those declared insolvent, as long as the kind of insolvency is not defined; 6) pupils, students, people attending lectures and persons who attend educational and academic courses, as long as they had not graduated, with the exception of cases when they represent their parents, brothers or sisters; 7) those under tutelage; 8) members of judicial institutions and officials of the prosecution magistracy, with the exception of cases when they solicit for their children, parents or wives, provided the cases are not being heard in the courts where they serve or in places under the jurisdiction of these courts; 9) those excommunicted by decision of an ecclesiastical court; 10) those deprived of all civil rights or all special rights and privileges acquired personally or by virtue of their membership in a class, and also those freed from such punishment by an imperial manifesto; 11) those indicted for crimes punishable by the loss of all civil rights or all special rights and privileges acquired personally or by virtue of belonging to a class and not acquitted by court decision; 12) those dismissed from governmental service by virtue of a court decision, or excluded from communities and assemblies of the nobility by decision of those classes to which they belong; 13) those to whom the carrying on of cases is prohibited by court decision.
[87] *Ibid.*, Art. 406[6]
[88] *Ibid.*, Art. 406[2-4].
[89] *Ibid.*, Art. 406[2].

of the circuit court or *Sudebnaya Palata*, to investigate irregular acts by the private attorney and inflict the following disciplinary penalties upon him: (1) warning or reprimand; (2) rebuke; (3) temporary suspension from functions for a period not over one year; and (4) exclusion from the list of private attorneys. Thus, disciplinary power was conferred upon law courts and the punishments were similar to those inflicted by councils of the bar according to Article 368. However, an additional provision gave the Minister of Justice the power, independently of punishment inflicted by court, to bar, from soliciting, such persons on whom he received indubitable information to the effect that they are engaging in objectionable practices which do not accord with the rank of attorney.

Finally, the law provided that "Articles 406^1-406^{16} are fully applicable to lawyers-in-training." [90] This meant that a lawyer-in-training could apply for a certificate of private attorney and, if the certificate was granted, could practice law in the capacity of a private attorney, retaining his rank of lawyer-in-training. This was the provision of the Law of May 25, 1874, mentioned above, which, according to the 1895 decision of the Senate, had been violated by the regulations of the Moscow Council of the Bar which had prohibited the practice of law to lawyers-in-training.

Thus the Law of 1874 introduced into Russian administration of justice a new kind of attorney. The private attorney was not required to have the education of a lawyer or his experience, acquired during the time of probation. He was also free from supervision and control by a guild with a high standard of morals and traditions. Of course the private attorney too was subject to disciplinary sanctions by the court, but the court only prosecuted for infractions against professional duties on the part of private attorneys, not for moral transgressions. The latter could be determined and censured only according to moral standards developed and defended by a corporative institution such as the council of the bar. In Arsen'yev's opinion, the examination of applications for admission to the bar and of grievances against lawyers is a vital question for the council of the bar, to the correct solution of which all its efforts are directed; for the courts, supervision over the private attorneys is a secondary, accessory occupation among others much more important; the council as the representative of the guild is directly interested that no person should join the guild, or remain in it, if he is unworthy of belonging to it; the court has no such inter-

---

[90] *Ibid.*, Art. 406^{17}.

est because there is not and cannot be any solidarity between it and the private attorney; the council does not limit itself to the examination of grievances submitted to it, but initiates disciplinary proceedings on its own initiative.[91]

The Law of 1874 solved the problem of the monopoly of the lawyer. Article 406[1] of the Statutes of Judicial Institutions provided that the right to represent parties in court belongs to lawyers and private attorneys only. This important provision was somewhat qualified by Article 389 and Article 406[18]. [92] Thus, monopoly became a reality for the lawyers, but had to be shared with private attorneys.

The reason for introducing the institution of private attorneys into the Statutes of Judicial Institutions of 1864 was officially defined as due to the necessity for increasing the number of representatives in court, since the development of the profession of lawyers progressed too slowly. Indeed, the number of lawyers in the beginning was too small to handle all the civil and crinminal cases to be examined by the courts. But in 1874 the State Council itself admitted that in the two capitals and in cities where the *Palatas* had their residence the number of lawyers was sufficient.

Since the Laws of 1864 did not produce an actual monopoly for the lawyers, the old *stryapchiye* continued to represent the parties in court. The opinion of the State Council concerning their practices was no better in 1874 than in 1864. Here is what the State Council wrote in 1874:

> It appears from unanimous reports of many presidents of circuit courts and assemblies of justices of the peace that among these solicitors there are many who do not understand the basic principles of the Codes and the controversial and accusatorial proceedings, who submitted incompetent briefs,. . .failed to observe the deadlines prescribed for judicial actions and left the interests of their clients without any defense. These solicitors caused the courts much unnecessary work in examining unfounded petitions and reading useless papers, and also took up many cases of the most questionable character. For such attorneys the question whether a suit was well-founded was almost a secondary matter, the main interest being in the remuneration.

---

91 K. K. Arsen'yev, *Zametki o russkoi advokature,* p. 11.

92 Article 406[18] provided that everybody had the right to carry on three suits per year before a justice of the peace. If the justice of the peace, after the first case, found that the representative has not the qualifications necessary for a private attorney, he could request a decision of the assembly of justices of the peace prohibiting this person from further pleading in court. Article 389 conferred the right to issue a power of attorney to close relatives such as parents, spouse, children, as well as to persons involved in the same suit or managing the property under litigation.

The practices of such persons, who sometimes did not hesitate to forge documents, was an insuperable obstacle to the mediation of suits, because such attorneys assured their clients beforehand that they would win the suit without making any concessions. Finally, it often happened that the same man who brought in an action against somebody later appeared in court as the representative of the defendant. . .[93]

The old *stryapchiye* became in many instances private attorneys. One would think that having entertained as low an opinion of these solicitors as cited above, the State Council would definitely bar them from the courts and establish a monopoly for lawyers (this would have corresponded to the intentions of the Legislator of 1864). However, the State Council chose another way: it attempted to bring the solicitors under the control of the courts.

As a matter of fact, the main reason for establishing the institution of private attorneys was not the insufficient number of lawyers, but discontent with the practices especially political, of lawyers, which will be discussed later. It was therefore deemed necessary to create a competitor for the lawyer who would be free from the ideological character which the profession of lawyers assumed from the very beginning.

As far as the lawyers-in-training were concerned, the Law of 1874, instead of regulating their activities and their relations to their patrons put them on an equal footing with private attorneys in matters of law practice and subjected their activities to the supervision of the court. Thus the lawyers-in-training on the one hand received the right to practice law, which had been denied to them by the legislation of 1864, and on the other were made subject to a double disciplinary competence: that of the councils of the bar, as lawyers-in-training, and that of the courts, as holders of certificates issued by the courts.

The Senate tried to draw a line between the two competences, declaring that councils of the bar had the right of supervision and the Court had the right of disciplinary punishment. But the right of supervision without the right of sanctions is deprived of all significance. Still, in 1910, the Senate denied to councils of the bar disciplinary jurisdiction over lawyers-in-training who held certificates, but in a decision of January 28, 1912 reversed its viewpoint and came to the conclusion that the disciplinary power of the councils extends to such lawyers-in-training as well.

---

[93] Quoted by I. V. Hessen, *Advokatura*. . ., p. 230-231.

3. *Attorneys Attached to Commercial Courts*

It must be mentioned here that there was still another kind of solicitors, who were attached to commercial courts. They were a legacy of the old legislation, retained by the Reform of 1864.

The Law of May 14, 1832[94] had established a kind of attorneys who had the right to represent parties and carry on suits in the courts of commerce—the so-called *prisyazhnye stryapchiye*. The name *stryapchiye* the origin of which has been so well explained by Leroy-Beaulieu (see p. 110), was retained for them, apparently in memory of the old *stryapchiye*. In addition to that, they were called *prisyazhnye, i.e.,* "having taken an oath." According to Article 34 of the Law of May 14, 1832, only persons entered on a special list of the courts of commerce could represent parties and plead in those courts. In order to be entered on the list, a candidate had to present all the papers which in his opinion would support his candidacy.[95] Special education was not required. The court could reject the application without any explanation, even verbally.[96] *Prisyazhnye stryapchiye* could be dropped from the list also without any explanation, at the court's discretion, but the court had to give reason for its decision in the minutes.[97]

The Laws of 1864 did not make any change in the Law of 1832, so that the lawyers—the senior and the junior ones—had to be entered on the lists of the courts of commerce in order to have the right to practice as attorneys before them. This was only a formality, since members of the bar were entered without any objection. However, when restrictive measures were taken concerning admission of persons of non-Christian confessions to the profession of lawyers and lawyers-in-training in 1889, these restrictions were extended to admission as *prisyaznye stryapchiye* also.

Thus, beside the lawyers, the lawyers-in-training and the private attorneys, there was still another category of attorneys with a very limited field of action in the courts of commerce—attorneys whose functions were insignificant.

---

94 *Svod zakonov,* Vol. XI, Part 2: *Ustav sudoproizvodstva torgovago.*
95 *Ibid.,* Art. 35.
96 *Ibid.,* Art. 36.
97 *Ibid.,* Art. 37.

CHAPTER IV

DISCIPLINARY POWER OF THE COUNCIL OF THE BAR AND PROFESSIONAL ETHICS

A. Extent of Disciplinary Power of the Councils of the Bar

The disciplinary power of the council of the bar covered all the irregular actions committed by a lawyer or a lawyer-in-training. The council acted as a court of first instance. The *Sudebnaya Palata* functioned as an appellate court. The competence of the council extended not only to the sphere of the professional actions of the lawyer and his trainees, but also to actions committed not in the capacity of lawyer, with the exception of those in the field of private family life. Already in 1872 the Council in St. Petersburg decided that "the only sphere which does not and will not concern the Council is the sphere of private family life of the lawyer." [1] Decisions as to the limits of its competence rested with the council. Thus, in one case, the St. Petersburg Council decided that a personal clash between a lawyer and another person provoked by actions of the lawyer which had nothing to do with his professional activity could be examined by the Council only in cases when the behavior of the lawyer signified "such deviation from rules of behavior compulsory for every honest and respectable man as deprives him of the requisite consideration and confidence of others." [2]

But when in the General Assembly of the St. Petersburg Bar the question was raised as to how to interfere with card-gambling by lawyers, the extent of which had become a menace, the majority was of the opinion that the question was beyond its competence. [3]

How strict the councils were in matters of transgression of their duties by lawyers may be seen from the fact that the St. Petersburg

[1] Quoted by A. N. Trainin, *op. cit.*, p. 312.
[2] M. A. "Predely vedomstva distsiplinarnago suda v soslovii prisyazhnykh poverennykh" *Yuridichesky Vestnik*, 1891, No. 9, 115.
[3] Trainin, *op. cit.*, p. 316.

and Kharkov Councils ruled that there is no period of limitation for disciplinary proceedings, that disciplinary proceedings, when started, may not be discontinued because of a private settlement between the lawyer and the complainant, and that the disciplinary power of councils extends over actions committed by the lawyer before his admission to the bar.[4]

But it should not be forgotten that councils functioned only as tribunals of first instance in disciplinary proceedings, that over them stood the *Sudebnaya Palata* which sometimes rendered decisions which were completely opposed to those of the councils. Dissenting opinions were also adopted by circuit courts which acted in place of councils of the bar in districts where the latter were not introduced.

As an example of such dissenting decision of the *Sudebnaya Palata,* we may cite a case concerning the secrecy of the conferences between the accused and his counsel and advice given under the seal of this secrecy. According to Article 704 of the Code of Criminal Procedure, "lawyers and other persons who fulfill the duties of counsel to the accused are not permitted to testify with regard to confessions made to them by their clients during the proceedings in which they are involved." The accused B. testified in court that his lawyer P. had advised him, during a conference he had with him in jail, to withdraw the confession he had made in the preliminary investigation. The *Sudebnaya Palata* excluded P. from the list of lawyers of the Warsaw district. The *Palata* was of the opinion that the secrecy of the conferences of the accused with his counsel was a guarantee of the interests of the accused, not of the lawyer. The Council did not agree with the opinion of the *Palata* and made a report to the Minister of Justice and to the President of the Joint Bench of the Senate. In this report, the Council asserted that the secrecy prescribed by Article 403 of the Statutes of Judicial Institutions[5] must be extended also to the accused. The Council declared that if the obligation to keep secret the conferences of the accused with his counsel were not to be extended to the accused, the latter would have the possibility of charging his counsel with disreputable action, and the lawyer, bound by Article 704 of the Code of Criminal Procedure, would not have the possibility of defending himself against the charges of his client, since he is excluded from testimony. The report produced no effect whatsoever.[6]

With regard to the duty of the lawyer not to reveal the secrets of

---

4 Hessen, *Advokatura. . .* , p. 285.
5 For this provision of Art. 403 of the Statutes of Judicial Institutions of 1864 see above p. 125.
6 Trainin, *op. cit.,* p. 316-318.

his client, the Moscow Council of the Bar declared that "the secrets entrusted to the lawyer are sacred; never, to nobody and under no conditions should they be revealed by him, even if he is invited to do so by the court itself." [7] The Senate confirmed the lawyer's duty of secrecy in the following remarkable words: "The dignity of criminal procedure is determined mainly by the nature of the means which the law allows or does not allow to be used for reaching the principal goal, *i.e.*, the discovery of the real perpetrator of any crime or misdemeanor. It would be incompatible with the dignity of the administration of justice to make use, for this purpose, of sources which are clearly unreliable or dangerous for public morals. One such source undoubtedly is. . .testimony against the accused combined with the disclosure of secrets." [8]

The Circuit Court in Kiev did not share the opinion of the St. Petersburg Council that disciplinary proceedings cannot be discontinued by a settlement. By a decision of 1881, the Circuit Court quashed disciplinary proceedings against a lawyer because of a peaceful settlement of differences between him and his client. [9]

B. CASES INVOLVING PROFESSIONAL ETHICS

One of the cardinal questions of professional ethics, which repeatedly arose before the councils, was the following: may the lawyer assume the defense of any criminal, and is he allowed to carry on suits based on a formal right of his client acquired by an immoral action?

With regard to this problem, we shall discuss several cases which will acquaint us with the viewpoints on this subject of the council of the bar, the *Sudebnaya Palata,* the Senate, and some eminent writers.

1. *The Lokhvitsky Case*

N. Elkin, a lawyer-in-training, got acquainted with an elderly widow, Popova, and under a promise to marry her received from her 15,000 rubles in cash under a loan contract. Later Elkin persuaded her to return this contract, with a fictitious receipt showing that he had allegedly returned the 15,000 rubles. He also persuaded Popova

---

[7] *Otchet Soveta prisyazhnykh poverennykh pri Moskovskoi Sudebnoi Palate 1899/1900,* p. 141.

[8] *Resheniya ugolovnago kassatsionnago departamenta Pravitel'stvuyushchago Senata,* 1894, No. 2 (in the Popov Case).

[9] Hessen, *Advokatura . . .,* p. 285.

to transfer to him her house by means of a gratuitous deed. Then, Elkin not only did not marry Popova, but evicted her from her former house.

On account of these actions, the Circuit Court with jurors sentenced Elkin to jail. His counsel and patron A. V. Lokhvitsky, who defended him in court, submitted an appeal from this decision to the Cassation Department of the Senate. The Senate reversed the decision of the Circuit Court on grounds of a wrong application of the provision of the Criminal Code by the Circuit Court and remanded the case to the Circuit Court for a new examination. The latter again convicted Elkin, and his counsel Lokhvitsky appealed to the Senate for a second time. The Senate again reversed the judgment of the Circuit Court, this time for the reason that the imputed actions described in the questions submitted to the jury did not contain elements of punishable offenses specified by law. Thereupon he Circuit Court quashed the proceedings against Elkin.

However, Popova sued Elkin in civil court, demanding (1) restitution of the 15,000 rubles which she had lent to Elkin (2) restitution of the house, and (3) if she failed to get (2), another 15,000 rubles which, she said, he had later promised to pay her for the house. With regard to Claim (1), the suit was definitely won by Popova, but Claims (2) and (3) were rejected in the first and second instances.

A. V. Lokhvitsky was Elkin's counsel in all instances of the civil suit as well. Popova's counsel, Ordynsky, filed a complaint against Lokhvitsky with the Council of the Bar, in which he charged Lokhvitsky with maintaining notoriously unfair claims before the court.

The Council found that Lokhvitsky did not commit anything blamable by defending Elkin in the criminal court, but adopted the opposite viewpoint with respect to his activities in the civil suit, motivating it as follows: The civil suit had to solve the question as to whether Elkin should retain the fruits of his dishonorable actions; the *Palata* had confirmed the validity of the deed because of its formal legality and had left the house in Elkin's ownership; thus an unfair claim had been upheld because formally it was correct; this fact, however, does not justify a lawyer who defends such claims. The Council asserted that "the lawyer must be cautious, strict and scrupulous in the choice of cases he accepts, never defend unfair claims, and reject all doubtful cases. He is not a servant of his client, ready to do everything for money, but a defender and backer, who in civil cases defends and backs only those who act conscientiously." [10] The Council of the

---

[10] Quoted by Hessen, *Advokatura. . .*, p. 314-315.

Bar prohibited Lokhvitsky from practicing law for three months.

Lokhvitsky appealed to the *Palata* against the decision of the Council, and the Prosecutor, for his part, filed a protest with the *Palata* against the decision of the Council on the ground that the punishment was too mild.

Lokhvitsky's case gave rise to violent discussions and provoked a great diversity of opinion among the members of the General Assembly of the *Palata* who had to decide on the appeal and the protest. One member proposed that Lokhvitsky be merely reprimanded. Another member wanted to prohibit him from practicing law for one year. Three thought it necessary to confirm the decision of the Council. Seven members pleaded for the acquittal of Lokhvitsky, finding that he did not act in any respect against his professional duties. Eight members were of the opinion that Lokhvitsky should be disbarred. This last opinion, belonging to a relative majority, was finally adopted. In its reasons, the *Palata* declared: ". . .a lawyer who submits to a civil court a notoriously unfair claim in the interest of his client. . .must be considered as a person committing a dishonest action. . .In such a case there can be no indulgence, no sympathy. . .He has violated his most essential duty—to act honestly." [11]

Lokhvitsky complained to the Senate against the sentence of the *Palata* disbarring him. The Senate absolved Lokhvitsky from all responsibility.

This decision of the Senate is of great interest from the standpoint of principle. Analyzing the decision of the *Palata*, the Senate first of all pointed out that the *Palata* did not find that Lokhvitsky "wrote or spoke anything directed against good morals or tending to weaken the church, state, society or family," [12] and that it accused Lokhvitsky only of having accepted to defend Elkin's civil claims although he knew the immoral source of these claims, in which actions the *Palata* saw a serious violation of professional duties on the part of Lokhvitsky. But in order to establish the principle which must regulate the activities of the lawyer when he accepts a civil case, it is necessary, thought the Senate, to keep in mind that every litigation concerning a civil right is subjected to the competence of a court, the activities of which consist in applying the law which determines the right itself as well as the means for the identification of its validity. "The civil court," the Senate continued, "does not aspire to the finding of absolute justice;

---

[11] *Ibid.*, p. 316.
[12] *i.e.*, did not break the lawyer's oath. See *Uchrezhdeniye sudebnykh ustanovleny*, Art. 381, and above pp. 123-124.

it checks and defines the contested right by means set by law and in accordance with the evidence presented by the parties, and decides on it on grounds of laws which preserve and defend the contested right." And here the Senate made the statement that "the morality of civil law is less strict than individual morality," and that "if individual morality is not required from a party in a suit, the activities of a lawyer cannot be examined from the standpoint of principles of individual morality. . ." The lawyer, the Senate held, is a representative of a profession which is a kind of public service; it puts him in the position of mediator between the party and the court in matters of solving questions pertaining to rights. It also seemed clear to the Senate that the criterion of individual morality is too elusive and is understood by everyone according to his own concepts. It felt that the acknowledgment of the duty of a lawyer to refrain from the defense of rights which according to his opinion, have been acquired dishonestly, would leave a great number of rights based on law without defense. The *Palata* had established, the Senate emphasized, that Elkin's actions tended to misappropriate foreign property and nevertheless had rejected Popova's claim concerning the restitution of the house and had freed Elkin from any criminal responsibility; having thus freed him, it had proceeded to convict Lokhvitsky for having defended Elkin's rights. The Senate also pointed out that the possibility of prosecuting a lawyer for defending titles acquired immorally could convert the necessary supervision over the activities of lawyers into a means of retaliation: the losing party would have the possibility of persecuting the lawyer of the winning party. Thus, the present case was initiated by Ordynsky, Popova's lawyer, after the court had rejected a part of her claim, the Senate said. In the concluding portion of its decision, the Senate wrote: "Considering that. . .the principle of absolute morality cannot serve as a basis for judging the professional activities of a lawyer with regard to the acceptance of a civil suit; that the mere knowledge of the dishonest acquisition of rights which he undertakes to defend cannot serve as an absolute reason for the recognition of the activities of the lawyer in such a case as inconsistent with his rights and duties as defined by law; that, in spite of this, the conviction of Lokhvitsky as Elkin's counsel is based exclusively on Lokhvitsky's knowledge of the dishonest means of acquisition of the contested right by Elkin; and that consequently, the proceedings in this case, which does not contain elements of an act prohibited by law, must be quashed, the General Assembly of the Departments of Cassation of the Ruling Senate has decided as follows: since there were not found in the facts established by the *Sudebnaya Palata,* elements of acts calling for disciplinary punishment, the decision of the General Assembly of the Moscow *Sudebnaya Palata,* with all its consequences, is hereby reversed." [13]

Apparently, it was not easy for the Senate to supply reasons for this decision. According to Dzhanshiyev, it took from January 22, 1879, to January 11, 1880, *i.e.,* almost a year, to write it down. The draft of the decision was rewritten several times.[14] And indeed, it seldom happened that a decision of the Senate provoked such a tempest of conflicting opinions in the juridical and non-juridical literature.

In 1884 Lokhvitsky died, and his death provided the occasion for a revival of the whole controversy about his case. In an obituary, D. Nevyadomsky, a distinguished lawyer and President of the Bar in Moscow for a long time, wrote: "All the views of Lokhvitsky concerning the professional duties of a a lawyer correspond in their essence to the views of the legislator when he created the lawyers' guild—a new institution in our country."[15] The confirmation of this opinion Nevyadomsky sees in the official message by the State Council to accompany Article 394 of the Statutes of Judicial Institutions, which provides that a lawyer who is appointed as a counsel by a Council of the bar or by a court has not the right to refuse the appointment without weighty reasons. In the official message to accompany this provision, the State Council states: "Physicians have the exclusive right to treat sick persons; but at the same time they assume the duty of treating without fail everyone who resorts to them. A corresponding rule must be established also with regard to lawyers." [16] The law-makers of 1864 thought that they were creating a monopoly of lawyers similiar to that of physicians for medical treatment, and that is why they introduced the provision of Article 394. It is evident that in countries where the assistance of a lawyer is made compulsory by law (as in France and Germany), it must be made difficult for the lawyer to reject a case, since a party would be prevented from going to court if it does not find a lawyer willing to represent it. However, Nevyadomsky forgets that the provision of Article 394 refers only to appointed counsels and not to lawyers who accept a case under a free agreement with a party.

The Senate decision of 1879 in the Lokhvitsky Case was subjected

---

[13] *Resheniya ugolovnago kassatsionnago departamenta Pravitel'stvuyushchago Senata,* 1879, No. 1.

[14] Dzhanshiyev, *Vedeniye nepravykh del,* p. 20.

[15] D. Nevyadomsky, "A. V. Lokhvitsky," *Zhurnal grazhdanskago i ugolovnago prava,* 1884, No. 6, p. 50.

[16] *Sudebnye Ustavy. . .,* III: *Uchrezhdeniye sudebnykh ustanovleny,* p. 243.

to heavy fire by the press and especially by Dzhanshiyev, who published a special pamphlet, *Pleading of Immoral Causes,* dedicated to the Lokhvitsky Case and to the decision of the Senate, in which he entered into controversy with Nevyadomsky. The latter answered with a booklet,[17] and the general press took part in the controversy on one side or the other.

Dzhanshiyev considered the decision of the Senate as a striking example of a misinterpretation of professional obligations. The Senate he argued, was conferring upon a lawyer freedom from any moral duty and might bring about an end to aspirations for establishing standards of truth and honor in the guild. "There is only one morality; the civil laws do not have their own morality," [18] he wrote, and emphasized also that the Senate, in its previous decisions, had confirmed the disbarring of lawyers on grounds of dishonorable, although not criminal, actions committed by them.[19]

Dzhanshiyev's assertions are unfounded. He admitted himself, in another part of his pamphlet, that there are provisions of law which are not covered by "individual morality" (following the definition of the Senate), but by such juridical formulae as *dura lex, sed lex, praesumptio juris et de jure, summum jus,* etc., and that "the civil court which senses elements of fraud in a case is not always in the position to come to the aid of the deceived party." Does this not show that there is more than one morality and that the civil laws have a morality of their own? Furthermore, the previous ruling of the Senate quoted by Dzhanshiyev dealt with dishonest, although not criminal, actions committed by lawyers themselves, not by their clients.

2.   *The Kroneberg Case*

The Kroneberg Case, tried in 1876, is remarkable not only because one of the most famous Russian lawyers, V. D. Spasovich, the so-called "king of the Russian Bar", was accused of having assumed the defense of an unworthy man, and defended him in a despicable manner, but also because the charges against Spasovich were formulated, not by the council of the bar or by the courts, but by men of no less caliber than F. M. Dostoyevsky and M. E. Saltykov-Shchedrin.

Kroneberg, an educated and well-to-do man, had a liaison with

---

17 D. Nevyadomsky, *Vechnye voprosy advokatury.*
18 G. Dzhanshiyev, *Vedeniye...*, p. 23.
19 See, for instance, *Resheniya Obshchago Sobraniya kassatsionnykh s uchastiyem Pervago i Vtorogo departamentov Pravitel'stvuyushchago Senata,* 1870, No. 5.

a woman; when they parted, neither of them knew that she was pregnant. Several years later Kroneberg met his former mistress, who was already married. She told him that she had a daughter by him whom she left with a peasant family in Switzerland. Kroneberg at once declared himself ready to assume the education of the child, went to Switzerland, took her from the peasant family and entrusted her education to a pastor in Geneva, in whose house the girl remained for some time. However, the pastor's education showed no good results and Kroneberg decided to take the girl to Russia, into his home (he was unmarried), and to take charge of her education.

The girl was seven years old at that time, but had already acquired some bad habits, which the father undertook to eradicate. According to witnesses, she lied, committed petty thefts and was inclined to masturbation. As a pedagogical method Kroneberg chose slaps in the face and flogging. During one of such floggings, the girl screamed so violently that two women, the cook and the wife of the doorkeeper, alerted the police. Kroneberg was indicted on counts of torture, and V. D. Spasovich was appointed by the court as his counsel. The jury acquitted Kroneberg.

Dostoyevsky dedicated a whole chapter—twenty-eight pages—of his *Diary of a Writer* to the Kroneberg Case and especially to the speech of Spasovich. It is written in the style which is so peculiar to Dostoyevsky. The author repeatedly asserts that he is not competent to write on juridical matters, that he writes his *Diary* for himself and wants to speak about some thoughts which remained firmly in his mind— "hardly thoughts—rather some kind of sensations." [20] In reality it is a passionate accusation not only of Spasovich, but of lawyers in general. Dostoyevsky has the following to say on the subject:

In spite of the talent displayed in Spasovich's speech, this speech made an almost disgusting impression on him, because of the odd situation involved in the Kroneberg Case—an odd situation from which Spasovich, in his capacity of lawyer, could not free himself. Kroneberg had been accused of inflicting torture and faced extreme, excesive punishment. Therefore, Spasovich denied from the very beginning the fact of torture, and represented the severe beating of the child as merely an excessively severe paternal punishment. Spasovich said that he himself was not a proponent of corporal punishment and could very well imagine a system of education without the rod, but that he did not expect the complete eradication of corporal punishment any more

---

20 F. M. Dostoyevsky, *Dnevnik pisatelya za 1876 g.* In his *Polnoye sobraniye sochineny.* 6th ed. Vol. XI, p. 59.

than he expected the jury to cease functioning in court for lack of crimes.

Dostoyevsky is indignant at Spasovich's most unattractive picture of the child, whom the counsel represented as a lying, thieving, untidy girl with a bad secret vice. "The whole trick is somehow to destroy one's sympathy for her. Such is human nature: one will not pity a person one dislikes, for whom one has an aversion. It is compassion [for the girl] that Spasovich fears more than anything else, because if one begins to pity her, one might convict the father. Herein lies the falsity of the situation." [21] But Spasovich reaches "Herculian pillars" in his incriminating speech according to Dostoyevsky, in his reference to "the justified wrath of the father." When the father came to know, said Spasovich, that in addition to the habit of lying and other vices, the girl had been stealing, he felt great anger. Spasovich said that everyone would have felt similar anger; that to prosecute the father because he had severely but deservedly punished his child would be a disservice to the family and also disservice to the state, since the state is strong only when it relies on a strong family; that the father was fully justified in becoming indignant. "The father is tried," says Spasovich, "but what for? For the abuse of power. The question arises: where is the limit of this power?" [22] These last words bring Dostoyevsky to the climax of his indignation: "Do you seriously mean what you are saying, Mr. Spasovich?" Dostoyevsky exclaims.

> "Do you really not know what the limit of this power is?. . .
> If you don't know what this limit is, I shall tell you. The limit
> [of this power] lies in this—that it is not permissible to beat a
> little child of seven, who is not responsible in any way for any
> of her vices. . .—an angel-like creature who is incomparably purer
> and more sinless than you, Mr. Spasovich, and myself, than both
> of us, and than all those present in the courtroom, who tried and
> condemned this girl. The limit [of this power] lies in this—that
> it is not allowed to beat her for a quarter of an hour, disregarding
> her cries. . . Yes, clever counsel, there is a limit to everything, and
> if I did not know that you are saying all this deliberately, faking
> with all your skill in order to save your client, I would add,
> addressing myself to you personally, that there are limits to all
> poetic outbursts and to a lawyers' devotion [to his client], and
> that this limit does not allow one to go as far as to say things such
> as you have said, Mr. Councill" [23]

---

21 *Ibid.*, p. 69.
22 *Ibid.*, p. 77.
23 *Ibid.*, pp. 77-78.

Dostoyevsky's charges against Spasovich personally are accompanied by accusations directed against lawyers in general:

> I blush in advance at the naiveness of my questions and assumptions. It would be too naive and innocent on my part to expatiate, for instance, on the usefulness and pleasantness of the institution of the bar. Let us assume that a man commits a crime, but does not know the laws. He is ready to confess, but the lawyer appears and proves to him, not only that he is right, but that he is a saint. He finds the laws, or the rulings of the Department of Cassation of the Senate, which make the whole matter appear in another light, and he succeeds in pulling the unfortunate man out of the hole. A most pleasant thing! True, one might argue that this is somehow immoral. But suppose that an innocent man is before you, a completely innocent simpleton, and that the evidence is such, and the prosecutor summarized the facts in such a manner, that it seems the man must perish for somebody else's guilt. The man is ignorant, knows nothing about laws, and merely keeps mumbling: "I don't know, I know nothing"—which in the end annoys the jury and the judges. But the lawyer appears . . . manages to confuse the prosecutor, and—lo and behold—the innocent man is acquitted. That is useful.

Dostoyevsky adds ironically: "What would the innocent man do in Russia without a counsel?" [24] and continues elsewhere: "It is extremely moral and touching for the counsel to use his skill and talent for the defense of the unfortunate. But the thought flashes through your mind that he deliberately defends, and tries to acquit, a guilty person and that he cannot, moreover, act differently even if he would like to do so. . . ." [25] In the opinion of the famous writer, a lawyer is forced by his profession to be dishonest and unscrupulous. He says:

> It seems to me that it is as difficult for the lawyer to avoid falsehood, and to preserve honesty and conscience, as for anyone to enter paradise. . . . Did it not happen that we heard counsels in court almost swear, addressing themselves to the jury, that they had assumed the defense of their clients only because they became convinced of their innocence? When you listen to these oaths, the most nasty suspicion inevitably penetrates your mind: "What if he is lying and does this merely for money?" And, indeed, it often happened that the clients, defended with so much zeal, turned out to be absolutely and unquestionably guilty. . . . Whatever you may think, there is in this entire institution, in addition to all the unquestionably beautiful things, a kind of sad

---

24 *Ibid.*, p. 60.
25 *Ibid.*, pp. 60-61.
26 *Ibid.*, p. 61.

element. . ... And a nonsensical paradox flashes into one's mind, to the effect that a counsel is actually never able to act according to his conscience, that he cannot help playing with his conscience, even if he would like not to do so, that he is a man doomed to dishonesty, and that finally—and this is the most important and serious matter—this sad situation has actually been somehow legalized by someone and something, so that it is not considered as being in any sense a deviation [from the straight path] but, on the contrary, as a most normal state of affairs. . . ." [26]

Now let us hear the second accuser of Spasovich, Saltykov-Shchedrin, and then answer both. Saltykov-Shchedrin dedicates a whole chapter—seventeen pages—of his "Unfinished Talks" to the Kroneberg Case and to Kroneberg's counsel. Shchedrin also subjects Spasovich's speech to a detailed analysis. But his criticism is formulated in another manner, and he is shocked by other aspects of the case and of the speech than Dostoyevsky. He also begins with compliments to Spasovich and characterizes him as a brilliant lawyer:

> Mr. Spasovich has splendidly taken advantage of the vague character of the material gathered by the preliminary investigation. In general, independently of his gifts, he is the most reliable and sensible lawyer among the acting lawyers of the present time. He also stands on the sure ground of facts and is interested, first of all, not in the question as to whether the crime was really perpetrated, but in the question as to whether there are some excuses for it in the law and as to how the evidence presented can be refuted. He does not use fruitless excursions into the field of liberal babble. He does not forget that he is a lawyer, only a lawyer, not a philosopher or publicist, and requests the jurors to keep this in mind. In his eyes a crime has nothing monstrous, amazing about it. . . . He knows the provisions of the law with all their amendments and additions, can comment on them, and always keeps in store a reason for cassation. The witnesses have been studied by him most subtly, and therefore he does not lecture them and bother them with importunate questions, but only steers them gently; he knows that a witness, left to his own devices, will bring him pure honey more readily than a witness taken under the tutelage of a lawyer. He takes the jurors under his spell and simplifies their duties by explaining to them (usually in the course of his plea) that a crime is out of the question in the case at hand, because the indictment already failed to correspond to this or that requirement of the law. Moreover, Spasovich does not belong to the kind of lawyers who are agitated by a violent craving for rapid enrichment. This wins him the hearts of his clients even more. [27]

---

[27] M. Saltykov (N. Shchedrin), *Polnoye sobraniye sochineny*, XV, 369-370.

Having described the basic arguments of Spasovich's pleading in the Kroneberg Case, Shchedrin formulates his objections to the famous lawyer. The first is that Spasovich made a compromise with his own "artistic, juridical" ideas. Since Spasovich declared himself in the beginning of his pleading not to be a partisan of slaps in the face and the rod, it would be natural, thinks Shchedrin, to ask him the following question: "If you do not approve of slaps in the face and rods, why do you meddle in a case which entirely consists of slaps and rods?" [28] (Shchedrin forgets that Spasovich was appointed as counsel by the court.) And here the eminent writer enters into a long discussion of the "political and philosophical doctrine known by the name of compromise." Its essence consists in the assertion that "humanity must advance by retreating." Then Shchedrin draws an analogy between the political compromises of Louis Blanc and Gambetta, and those of Spasovich in the Kroneberg Case. Spasovich is charged with compromising because he says that he is not a proponent of the rod, that he does not believe a system of education by the rod can be established, but. . .at the same time asserts that he has little hope for a complete and absolute eradication of corporal punishment. "It is strange," exclaims Shchedrin, ". . .to make allusions to the possibility of 'slapless' pedagogical ideals and then to declare that these ideals have to be confined in a closet and locked up forever. . .It is clear that Mr. Spasovich has stepped out of his role and made a mistake." [29]

These are the chief things which Shchedrin says about Spasovich and his speech. But he takes this opportunity to express his views on the lawyer and his activities in general. In the beginning, he asserts, the bar in Russia had ideals similar to those of the liberal press, but later those ideals were lost and the lawyer became an ordinary professional man. In the beginning, literature, like "an elder sister in liberalism," took the bar under its wing. Criticism, reproaches, etc., were expressed very often. That was wrong. Even in France, the classical country of lawyers, the press does not pay much attention to lawyers as such. "The professional character of the bar must become much more evident in Russia, because our lawyers have definitely no relation to politics," Shchedrin says, overlooking the role of the bar in political trials and in politics in general. Not matters of life, but questions resulting from applying codes of law and decisions of the Cassation Department are important for them. A skillful handling of legal provisions is what come first, just as in other professions the

[28] *Ibid.*, p. 374.
[29] *Ibid.*, p. 378.

major emphasis is placed on the skillful handling of the needle, awl, spade, etc. "Why did nobody even think of accusing the cobbler of indignity who made shoes for Mother Mitrofaniya,[30] or the tailor who sewed clothes for Ovsyannikov,[31] but charges are heaped from everywhere on the lawyer who, seeing Ovsyannikov covered with the soot of the arson fire, undertook to wash him in the bath of resurrection?"

In the future, Shchedrin thinks, there can be no relation of comradeship between the liberal press and the bar, because they have no common ground, with the exception of words, which are the tools of both literature and the lawyer. But their aims and their character are completely different: "Literature is the servant of society, the lawyer— of his client. Honesty for literature consists in the development of ideals and prospects for the future. Honesty for the lawyer consists in complete harmony with reality and submission to ideals worked out in the past and left to be defended by codes. . ." [32]

In conclusion, Shchedrin gives his opinion that "since the bar has expressed the desire to renounce its sphere of intellectual and moral interests, which it has in common with literature, it is necessary to take advantage of this desire and not to force the bar to maintain liaison with literature; it is necessary to assign to the lawyers the place which they should occupy among men of various other professions." [33]

Shchedrin, like Dostoyevsky, is not a jurist. His charges against Spasovich and the bar are based exclusively on considerations of morals and decency. He even forgets that Spasovich did not "meddle" in the case voluntarily, but was assigned as counsel to Kroneberg by the court. Shchedrin is shocked by the "compromise" Spasovich made with his conscience by saying that, although he, Spasovich, is not a partisan of slaps and the rod, he does not believe that corporal punishment will disappear completely, because it is deeply rooted in society. Unfortunately, Spasovich was right. Over seventy years have passed

---

[30] Abbess Mitrofaniya, born Baroness Rosen, was accused of forging the signature of the millionaire M. G. Solodovnikov, and other persons, on documents. Her counsel was S. S. Shaikevich.

[31] Ovsyannikov, a wealthy merchant, was accused of arson of his mill, which was insured for 700,000 rubles. His counsel was P. A. Potekhin. The private prosecutor who represented the insurance company, was V. D. Spasovich. In reply to the defense, which asserted that the prosecution had produced evidence consisting of "traits" only, Spasovich said: "Yes, traits and traits, but from those traits contours are formed, and from contours—letters, and from letters—syllables and from syllables—a word, and this word is a r s o n." Both the Abbess Mitrofaniya and Ovsyannikov were found guilty by the jurors.

[32] Shchedrin, op. cit., p. 381.

[33] Ibid.,

since he pleaded for Kroneberg, and corporal punishment is still used not only in families, but also in schools, (in England, for instance), and, in two states of the United States, as a punishment for crimes. In spite of historical excursions into the field of the political compromise of Louis-Blanc and Gambetta, which he considers similar to the compromises of Spasovich, Shchedrin does not prove anything against Spasovich showing dishonorable defense methods, apart from his having assumed the defense of Kroneberg. In this respect Shchedrin disregards the recognized principle that every criminal has the right to be defended.

Dostoyevsky's philippic against Spasovich is purely emotional. In the beginning he says that talent is a useful thing, but that talented men become very responsive. "You must agree that in every talent there is always to be found this almost ignoble, superfluous 'responsiveness' which strives to lure the most sober man from the straight path," writes Dostoyevsky. ". . .It is a rare event that a man is able to control his talent. On the contrary, talent almost always enslaves its possessor." [34] Dostoyevsky cites Belinsky, who once described this excessive "responsiveness" as "prostitution of talent," and explains that Spasovich, being a talented man, was carried away by this "responsiveness" and said things which he should not have said. "I do not in the least deny that *even a lawyer*[35] may succeed in mastering his "responsiveness" when he possesses firm, honest principles and strength of mind. And yet, there are cases and circumstances when a man cannot resist. . .and is carried away." [36]

Dostoyevsky's remark about talented people is very true (but of course, not more so with respect to a lawyer than a writer). It is so true that Dostoyevsky, who is surely not less talented than Spasovich, has been carried away by his own "responsiveness" in his charges against Spasovich. What was the goal of Dostoyevsky's passionate unobjective, twenty-eight page diatribe? Dostoyevsky says that the case was so framed by the prosecution that if the jury brought in a verdict of "guilty," Kroneberg would suffer extreme and excessive punishment, and this would be a disaster: a distrupted family, and everybody miserable.[37] And indeed, according to the provisions of the Criminal Code covering cases of proved torture, Kroneberg would have been deprived of all personal and hereditary privileges and sent

---

34 Dostoyevsky, *op. cit.*, p. 62.
35 Italics mine. S. K.
36 Dostoyevsky, *op. cit.*, p. 63.
37 *Ibid.*, p. 65.

to Siberia for life.[38] What would have happened to the child? Would it really not be better to let Kroneberg go without punishment, since the law was too strict and left no possibility of a milder punishment for the abuse of paternal authority? Certainly Kroneberg, after his experience in court, would abstain from the pedagogical methods used by him before. The jurors understood the situation very well and acquitted Kroneberg, although he was a despicable person and merited punishment. Here again is a striking example of a juror's verdict correcting the inflexibility of the Criminal Code.[39]

Dostoyevsky uses, in his fulminous accusation, the method of Antonius speaking on the death of Caesar: "But Brutus is an honorable man. . ." He eulogizes Spasovich: "Already in the first words of the speech, you feel that you have to do with an extraordinary talent, with a power," and "I repent for having written all this, because it is known that Mr. Spasovich is a remarkably gifted lawyer. His speech in this case is, in my opinion, the climax of art," but being a climax of art, "it left in my mind an almost disgusting impression." [40]

In order to get Kroneberg acquitted, Spasovich had to prove that there had been no torture in the legal sense, that the severe punishment administered was only a misuse of the paternal power and that this paternal power was directed against a child with moral defects and vicious inclinations. Dostoyevsky is not concerned with the fact that there was no torture as defined by law. The girl had been unmercifully beaten, and that is why the perpetrator, the torturer of the "angel morally purer than Spasovich and Dostoyevsky himself," must be punished at any cost.

For Dostoyevsky the idea that Kroneberg was not punished is unbearable. Punishment, according to his philosophy, is necessary, because it gives to the criminal the occasion to suffer and, through this suffering, to expiate his crime. That is why everything done, directly or indirectly, to extenuate the guilt of Kroneberg, for instance, by emphasizing the defects of the child, is immoral and despicable. Thus, not only Spasovich personally, but the whole guild of lawyers who perpetrate such acts for money is despicable. Dostoyevsky is deeply shocked that the whole situation is sanctioned by "somebody and something," i.e., by law, by the judicial system. Since courts and judicial procedure exist, he understands that lawyers are not an evil (in the practical, or moral, sense), but even a necessary institution: "Yes,

---

[38] Ulozheniye o nakazaniyakh, Arts. 1478 and 1479.
[39] See above pp. 69-71.
[40] Dostoyevsky, op. cit., pp. 64-65.

the bar is a brilliant institution, but somehow a sad one," he repeats again. ". . .But am I really attacking the bar and the new courts? God forbid!" [41] He says it in the same sense as Antonius admitting that "Brutus is an honorable man." And the goal of his writing on the Kroneberg Case is formulated by Dostoyevsky in the following remarkable words: "The only thing I desire is that we all should become a little better. That is a most modest desire, but, alas, also a most idealistic one. I am an incorrigible idealist. I seek saintly objects. . ." [42] One of such "saintly object," the child, was bitterly offended by the accused and also, in Dostoyevsky's opinion, by the counsel, in the Kroneberg Case. This Dostoyevsky could not forgive.

With regard to some arguments used by Spasovich, namely, the charges formulated against the child, O. O. Gruzenberg, another star of the Russian Bar, apparently is inclined to take the side of Dostoyevsky.

> Dostoyevsky's painfully passionate conscience, which did not know the happy medium—either love or hatred—was deeply offended by Spasovich's pleading. . . . One feels that the speech of the counsel has completely bared the writer's nerves and he cannot master a torturing pain. Such a fit of compassion for the child does not persuade but subdues. . . . [After having read Spasovich's speech] I felt with all my heart that it is not the great teacher of the lawyers' guild who is right, but his passionate accuser. The famous professor and great master of the word based his speech on an obviously incredible foundation: he, an elderly, stocky man with a fiery glance through his spectacles, fulminated against a small human being as vigorously as if Kroneberg had been accused of having exceeded the limits of self-defense. Later when I became acquainted more closely with Spasovich, I understood the cause of his mistake: he remained unmarried all his life, had no children, did not know them, and, apparently, did not like them. . . . [43]

In other respects, however, Gruzenberg thinks that the jurors certainly did not acquit Kroneberg because of the arguments brought forward by Spasovich, "but they confirmed, by their just verdict, that Spasovich did not make any mistake in accepting the defense of Kroneberg, and that his moral striving to secure the acquittal of Kroneberg was not erroneous." [44]

Thus Gruzenberg admits that Spasovich was right in accepting

---

41 *Ibid.*, p. 84.
42 *Ibid.*,
43 O. O. Gruzenberg, *Ocherki i rechi*, p. 138.
44 *Ibid.*,

the defense of Kroneberg, that he was also right in striving for the acquittal of the accused, and reproaches him only for the fact that he "fulminated" against the child. What did these "fulminations" consist of? The fact that "an elderly, stocky man, with a fiery glance through his spectacles" accused a seven-year old girl of lying, stealing and having secret vices does not justify Dostoyevsky's "fit of compassion" for the girl, which Gruzenberg seems to share, and which induced Dostoyevsky to shower unjust accusations on Spasovich. Gruzenberg is too great a lawyer himself not to realize that the disclosure of negative features of the girl's character was necessary in order to mitigate Kroneberg's guilt, that Spasovich, as his counsel, was bound to bring out all the circumstances which could extenuate his guilt, and that Dostoyevsky's compassion belongs to the field of sentiment and philosophy. It is the father and grandfather in Gruzenberg,[45] not the talented lawyer, who took the side of Dostoyevsky against Spasovich.

Gruzenberg writes that "the jurors certainly did not acquit Kroneberg because of the arguments brought forward by Spasovich." Of course, it is hard to say which argument produced the decisive effect on the jurors. It seems to me that the jurors did not want to punish Kroneberg too severely for the sake of the child itself, who would have remained without support. Since the jurors had no means of sentencing Kroneberg to a more lenient punishment than that inflicted by law for torture, they preferred to free him completely. But the effectiveness of disclosing the child's real character from the viewpoint of Kroneberg's defense, cannot be denied. P. Sergeich, who calls Dostoyevsky's philippic "one of the most severe indictments of the misuse of speech," comes to the following conclusion after a detailed analysis of Spasovich's speech: "There is no doubt that, in acquitting Kroneberg, the jurors did not yield to reason but to the feeling of antipathy against the girl which had been fomented in them." [46]

In a meeting dedicated to the memory of Spasovich, another famous lawyer, S. A. Andreyevsky, said this about Dostoyevsky's criticism of Spasovich: "Our great mystic and searcher of hearts. . . was always below the level of his genius when he engaged in pamphleteering against persons whom he did not like (Spasovich, Turgenev)." [47]

I do not agree with Andreyevsky. Dostoyevsky was not "below

---

[45] Gruzenberg was married and had a daughter and a granddaughter whom he tenderly loved.
[46] P. Sergeich, *Iskusstvo rechi na sude,* p. 310.
[47] S. A. Andreyevsky. *Dramy zhizni,* p. 616.

the level of his genius" in his writing on Kroneberg and his counsel. Just the contrary is true. The whole Dostoyevsky appears in the pamphlet: the passionate pleader, the mystic, the moral prophet-preacher and, first and foremost, the great writer. And the same thing of which he accused Spasovich happened to him: carried away by his talent, he used all means to press home his charges. The pamphlet became a passionate accusatory speech (it also has the form of a speech), written with such power that it can be envied by any district attorney. Dostoyevsky himself did not see any practical solution to this "odd" situation. But what he could not understand, what he could not admit, what he could not become reconciled to, was that a child, "an angel," one of those who, according to Dostoyevsky, should not suffer, on whose suffering Ivan Karamazov refuses to construct the future happiness of the world, had been tortured, and the perpetrator had been acquitted and remained free, without punishment, and there were people who had assumed the right to discharge him of all guilt, and a talented man dared to speak in his defense. . .

A distinguished literary critic, Yu. Eichenwald, wrote concerning Dostoyevsky: "His peculiar hatred of lawyers. . .is to be explained not only by the fact that they have a 'hired soul,' but mainly because they are shallow, superficial defenders of the human soul, and remove a crime from it like a hat. . .If Dostoyevsky so often comes out, as an artist and a publicist, against the jurors with their acquitting verdicts, it is also because of the superficial levity of the acquittal." [48]

Neither Dostoyevsky nor Shchedrin were right in their criticism of Spasovich: he is not to blame for having taken over the defense of Kroneberg, and the means he used were effective and admissible.

3. Other Cases

We saw that Lokhvitsky was punished by the Council of the Bar and the *Sudebnaya Palata* on the grounds that he took a case he should not have defended. On the other hand, the Moscow Council censured the declaration of an appointed counsel to the effect that he had nothing to say in favor of his client. The lawyer, L. A. Kupernik, later a famous lawyer in Kiev, said in his pleading: "I consider the testimony of the defendant here in court as false, invented in jail, and, especially, contrary to the only expression of human feelings which he gave earlier. If the law permits the prosecutor to drop the

---

[48] Yu. Eichenwald, *Siluety russkikh pisatelei*, II, p. 117.

accusation according to his conscience, I consider that I have the right and the duty to renounce the defense. . .Since the criminal responsibility of the accused had been proved, and since a certain system of punishment exists, I can only say: let justice run its course." [49] The Moscow Council was of the opinion that Kupernik's behavior was improper and reprimanded him. Arsen'ev thought that such leniency on the part of the Moscow Council was incomprehensible and that the St. Petersburg Council would have taken a much more rigorous position.[50]

It is evident that Kupernik committed a great offense against the basic duties of a lawyer. There is always something to say in order to mitigate the guilt of the worst criminal. As Koni puts it: "There is no criminal or fallen person in whom everything human is irrevocably darkened and about whom it is quite useless to hear a word of indulgence." [51]

The viewpoint that the appointed lawyer has no right to decline the defense of an accused whose political opinion he does not share, or whose actions he condemns, was invariably upheld by councils of the bar. In 1906, the lawyer N. refused to defend soldiers of a regiment who had participated in the bloody suppression of political disorders in the town of X. He wrote to the President of the Court: "Since the defendants are soldiers of the . . . regiment, I consider it inadmissible for myself to come into any contact with them after the acts committed by this regiment in X. I ask to be dispensed from their defense." In his explanation, submitted to the Council of the Bar, the lawyer wrote that the defense has first of all a public character, and that he could not function as counsel of persons who had so deeply offended Russian society by their acts. In its decision, the St. Petersburg Council formulated the following principles: the public aspects of the acts of a lawyer consists, not in the fact that the counsel acts as a representative of society, but in the principle that, being a representative of a private person, the lawyer must render juridical assistance to everyone and cannot decline to fulfil this duty on grounds of any personal opinion about the defendant or the action committed by him; one cannot assert that a lawyer has the right to decline the defense of an accused in order to emphasize his disapproval

---

49 Quoted by Hessen, *Advokatura. . .*, p. 171.
50 Arsen'yev, *op. cit.*, footnote on p. 148.
51 Koni, *Na zhiznennom puti*, II, 517.
52 *Otchet Soveta prisyazhnykh poverennykh pri S. Peterburgskoi Sudebnoi Palate za 1905/1906g.*, p. 245-247, *passim.*

of the act of the defendant, since in the majority of criminal cases the counsels have to defend persons who committed acts violating public interests; the institution of obligatory defense created by law never supposed solidarity between the counsel and the accused; personal views and opinions cannot serve as grounds for the rejection of obligatory defense, because then the compulsory character of defense would lose all meaning; views, convictions and sympathies vary considerably: one lawyer may decline the defense because the act committed by the accused offends his sense of morality, another because it disagrees with his religious beliefs, a third one because of antipathy for this or that nationality, a fourth one because the previous activities of the defendant did not correspond to his political opinions, etc.[52] The Council decided to explain to N. the incorrectness of his behavior, and since the action of N. had no evil consequences for anyone, the Council did not deem it necessary to inflict punishment upon him.

The *Sudebnaya Palata* reversed the decision of the Council, acting on the objection of the prosecutor, and prohibited N. from practicing for one year (because of "political and professional reasons," Hessen thinks).[53]

The Ovsyannikov Case, mentioned above, led to two disciplinary proceedings. They were directed against V. N. Gerard and P. A. Potekhin—counsels of Ovsyannikov, members of the St. Petersburg Council of the Bar and eminent lawyers. Gerard was charged with having accepted, first the functions of a civil prosecutor for the insurance company, and then the defense of the accused; he received a severe reprimand. Potekhin was accused of having summoned Gerard as a witness for Ovsyannikov; he was reprimanded. Both resigned as members of the Council.[54]

Disciplinary proceedings were iniated against Spasovich, Vice-president of the St. Petersburg Council of the Bar at that time, because he submitted a petition to the Tsar asking him to reverse a decision of the Civil Department of Cassation of the Senate. The Council pointed out that "every complaint against a decision of the Senate, every demand for its reversal on the part of a private person, is improper, but on the part of a lawyer, who must protect the dignity of the court and the inviolability of its final decisions, it is not only

---

[53] Hessen *Advocatura. . .*, footnote on p. 471.
[54] *Ibid.*, pp. 172-173.

improper but also very blameworthy." Spasovich defended himself, arguing that he did not act in the capacity of a lawyer utilizing his power of attorney. However, the Council responded that its competence extended to the activities of a lawyer in the broadest sense.[55]

In September, 1914, shortly ater the beginning of the First World War, the attorney of the *Deutsche Bank* in Berlin, who was maintaining a claim for 11,000 rubles on behalf of the Bank against a private person, declared in the Petersburg *Sudebnaya Palata* that he considered it impossible for him to represent a German firm and asked that the hearings be postponed. The *Sudebnaya Palata*, after a deliberation, forced the lawyer of the *Deutsche Bank* to retain his power of attorney and to continue to fulfill his duties in connection with the suit.[56]

C.   SOME PRINCIPLES OF PROFESSIONAL ETHICS

Let us quote some decisions of the councils of the bar in which general views on the lawyer's behavior and his activities are reflected.

The Moscow Council held that not everything which is not forbidden by law and, hence, not punishable, is permitted to a lawyer.[57] The Council was of the opinion that lawyers have a broader mission than merely serving private interests, that their mission consists in organizing a guild of men who will act in the interest of society and justice, will abstain from the defense of obviously immoral claims and use only lawful and honest methods; that the profession of a lawyer should not be regarded only as a means of subsistence; that law, society and the guild of lawyers itself see in it a noble field for heroic deeds of high public service; that no lawyer worthy of esteem will be guided exclusively by mercantile considerations in his professional activities; that the mission of the lawyer consists not only in conducting lawsuits, but also in preventing them, and that his participation in a case is valuable, not only because of his knowledge, but also due to his tempering influence upon the development of the suit and the elimination of the passionate element which is brought by the parties into the fight for their economic interests.[59]

---

55 Hessen, *Adokatura*. . ., p. 173.
56 *Ibid.*, p. 472.
57 *Otchet Soveta prisyazhnykh poverennykh pri Moskovskoi Sudebnoi Palate za 1892/1893*, p. 76.
58 *Ibid.*, 1903/1904, p. 11.
59 *Ibid.*, 1902/1903, p. 385.

The Odessa Council of the Bar held that in their profession as well as in their private lives the lawyers must always remain the bearers of the idea of what is right and lawful, and show consideration for other people's rights.[60]

According to the Kharkov Council of the Bar, the activities of a lawyer are based on other people's confidence in him, and without this confidence his activities cannot be imagined; this confidence must be earned and upheld; confidence must be given to every member of the guild as such, and, thus, whoever undermines this confidence by his acts is guilty not only before his client, but also before himself and the whole guild; the public mission of the lawyer is to serve truth; according to the requirements of this public service, the lawyer must inspire confidence through every word he says.[61]

With regard to the means used by lawyers, the councils of the bar adopted the same requirements of high morality and honesty. The St. Petersburg Council worked out one main rule in this respect—namely, that in defending the rights of his client, the lawyer must not violate either the existing laws or rules of morality and honor, and must not resort to blameworthy methods to achieve his goal, even if his client requests this of him.[62]

The St. Petersburg Council declared in a decision that a lawyer may not lie deliberately when he pleads in a criminal or civil case. The Council held that the conscientiousness and veracity of a lawyer's declarations to the court are the essential conditions to the discharge of his duties; that only by complying with this requirement can the lawyer win the confidence and respect of the court and the public whose interests he is called upon to reconcile; that this requirement in no respect contradicts the rule according to which the lawyer is forbidden by law to divulge a secret entrusted to him by his client, even before the court; that whenever the lawyer may not reveal the whole truth to the court, he must be silent, but never may he assert the opposite of what he knows positively to be true; and that, obviously, the lawyer may also defend an accused who has pleaded guilty and even to demand his acquittal, provided the defense is not based on the denial of acts which the accused has confessed to the lawyer.[63]

A lawyer, said the Kazan Council of the Bar, must not forget that

[60] *Otchet Soveta prisyazhnykh poverennykh pri Odesskoi Sudebnoi Palate za 1908*, p. 190.

[61] *Otchet Soveta prisyazhnykh poverennykh pri Khar'kovskoi Sudebnoi Palate za 1906/1907*, p. 218.

[62] Arsen'yev, *op. cit.*, p. 179.

[63] *Otchet Soveta prisyazhnykh poverennykh pri S. Peterburgskoi Sudebnoi Palate za 1897/1898*, p. 139.

he is performing one of the most essential functions of the administration of justice, that he is paving the way for a correct decision by the court and in this sense is "the soul of justice," as important, in the administration of justice, as a judge.[64]

A lawyer—to quote, once again the St. Petersburg Council—should never resort to immoral means to defend the interests of his client; by his acts he must persuade the people who resort to his aid that they can expect from him no other methods of defense of their interests than moral and lawful ones.[65]

There is no moral rule, the same Council decided, which allows one to give deliberate help to an extortionist and blackmailer in getting money from someone; such help on the part of a lawyer is all the more inadmissible; a lawyer who is unable to inspire confidence any longer must not remain in the guild.[66]

It is impossible to give more examples here of the decisions of the councils of the bar on all questions subject to their jurisdiction. This would require an entire volume. A. N. Markov has collected and classified a great number of decisions of councils of the bar on questions of professional ethics.[67] Many decisions are quoted by P. V. Makalinsky,[68] Hessen[69] and Asen'yev.[70] These decisions of the councils deal with numerous questions pertaining to the behavior of the lawyer in his profession, and to a certain extent, his private life. If the fact is taken into consideration that the councils functioned for about fifty years and that during the first forty years they functioned in three districts only, it appears amazing that it was possible to enforce and develop rules and traditions of high morality among lawyers in such a comparatively short period of time.

Spasovich formulated his views on the lawyer and his virtues in a speech delivered at the General Assembly of the St. Petersburg Bar on September 8, 1876. "Our profession," he said, "consists in helping those who resort to our juridical knowledge, by means of a sharp word, by writing and speaking." He then compares the activities of writers, politicians and lawyers, and finds that since the moral value

---

64 *Otchet Soveta prisyazhnykh poverennykh pri Kazanskoi Sudebnoi Palate za 1908/1909*, p. 121.
65 *Otchet Soveta prisyazhykh poverennykh pri S. Peterburgskoi Sudebnoi Palate za 1881/1882*, p. 86.
66 *Ibid., 1909/1910*, p. 651.
67 Markov, *op. cit.*,
68 Makalinsky, *op. cit.*,
69 Hessen, *Advokatura. . .*
70 Arsen'yev, *Zametki o russkoi advokature.*

of a word is measured not only by its sincerity, but also by its veracity, literature holds first place; the writer is paid for his talent and his thoughts, not because he praises or scolds someone for money. Less honorable is the profession of a politician; he depends upon the party with which he identifies himself. But as a party man he acts for the common good, which can be realized, in his opinion, by the rule of his party only. The lawyer is in an even more dependent position. He either acts as a consultant, in which case he is obliged to tell the strict truth on the question he is consulted upon, or as a counsel in court, in which case he is never free from bias in presenting his case. According to Spasovich:

> The lawyer is, so to say, split in two parts. One part detects the truth by direct intuition, but [the other part] creates for him an artificial conviction, which he strives to inculcate in his listener's minds by power of his talent. I am expressing as best I can, what has been the inescapable evil, the fatal evil of our profession at all times and in all parts of the world, that which makes this profession unusually slippery and full of temptations. . . . If we take the viewpoint that words are services, that these services can be traded and the lawyer's profession is a trade in words like any other trade, we shall inevitably reach cynicism and Philistinism. . . . Our guild always fought against this Philistine opinion on the duties of the lawyer and assumed the opposite viewpoint, which was the cause of the great and profound esteem which it enjoyed, in spite of the animosity of the government and some kinks from literature. In our mind, the only chance of standing firm on a high level consisted, and consists at the present time, in seeing to it that the evil in the lawyer's profession, which I denounced, should be as small, as insignificant, as possible, that it should be reduced to the strict limits of necessity, that we should have a particularly strict moral code placed above the criminal code.[71]

On January 25, 1914, another famous lawyer, V. A. Maklakov,[72] delivered a lecture on "Tolstoi and the Court," which gave him the opportunity to characterize the mentality of the lawyer and his profession. This lecture, reproduced in the form of an article in the periodical *Russkaya Mysl'*, met, in that part of it which dealt with lawyers, with considerable disapproval among Maklakov's colleagues. Maklakov asserted that the profession of a lawyer has many negative features. Venality is not among them: it may be a defect inherent in

---

[71] Quoted by Hessen, *Advokatura. . .*, p. 222-224, *passim*.
[72] V. A. Maklakov was also a member of the Third and Fourth Dumas and Ambassador of the Russian Provisional Government in Paris. He is at the present time the only living representative of the group of great Russian trial lawyers.

individual representatives of the profession, but not in the profession itself. A negative feature of the profession is the fact that it puts the human mind in a position directly opposed to the purpose of the mind. The human thinking process leads from a fact to a conclusion. In the lawyers' profession, thinking takes the opposite direction: from a given conclusion to the fact. The conclusion is given *a priori* and the facts must be adapted to the conclusion: "The lawyer is trained in the skill of finding in facts just what he wants to find," writes Maklakov. "Positive facts are found where they are looked for; black spots—where they are expected to be. . .The opinion that the lawyer cheats other people is unjustified: more than anyone else, he cheats himself." Maklakov emphasizes that it never happens that a case is submitted to a lawyer and he is asked to defend the interests of one or the other side, according to his desire. He is always asked to represent a definite party, *i.e.*, to fiind out everything which speaks for that party. His normal work consists in just looking, with preconception, upon the interests he accepts to represent, and all his art consists in the defense of this preconceived position. "Lawyers are people without principles," asserted Maklakov. "I do not mean this in the evil sense of the word with which persons who change their convictions are branded. The lawyer simply has no convictions. He understands very well that every position, every thesis is relative. He understands that everything has two sides. In arguing, he develops a skill for discovering things which others do not see. But incontestable truth and concepts are almost non-existent for lawyers."

Maklakov is of the opinion that the lawyers themselves are not to blame for this, that this is a professional illness which is to a great extent responsible for the role the lawyers play in political life. The lawyer as such is biased with regard to the client who requires his help, and in political life he is biased with regard to the party to which he belongs.[73]

We see that Spasovich and Maklakov express very similar ideas. Both share the viewpoint that the lawyer is not objective, that he adopts and defends the position of his client even if "his other self," as Spasovich puts it, feels that objectively this position is wrong.

Spasovich and Maklakov correctly described the psychology of a lawyer. Of course, he is not objective. To be objective is not his task. Just the contrary is true. It is precisely by taking an openly one-sided position that the lawyer contributes most to truth-finding. Of course,

---

[73] V. A. Maklakov, "Tolstoi i sud," *Russkaya Mysl'*, March 1914, pp. 64-66, *passim*.

he must not lie. But to group the facts in the manner which is most favorable to his client is his sacred duty. "The counsel must be one-sided and subjective in his opinions. He is not obliged to be objective," writes Prof. Graf zu Dohna.[74] Another eminent German jurist, Wolfgang Heine, is of the opinion that the counsel must defend his client with even more energy than he would defend himself. He might give up his own interests if he dislikes to make use of certain means of defense, but he cannot sacrifice the interests of his client to his own sympathy or dislike, or even to his feeling of what is right.[75]

Indeed, the lawyer has to bring forward everything which speaks in favor of the defendant in a criminal case and everything which supports the viewpoint of his client in a civil suit. That is his *raison d'être*. To be objective is the duty of the court. The court—an umpire between the parties in a civil case and between the accused and the state in criminal proceedings—must be objective, and that is why it must be independent of the state and the parties. Thus, it is only natural that the lawyer should strive to come through with his viewpoint, using all his skill and talent, even if it seems that he is trying to convert "black into white and white into black." [76] Maklakov is quite right when he says that everything has two sides and that different opinions can exist about almost everything in the world. Indeed, that which is black in the opinion of one person is white according to another.

It seems to me that the dialectical method of Hegel is well applicable to a suit or a trial. The thesis is opposed by the antithesis, and the deciding synthesis is formed by the judge. A French proverb says *"Du choc des opinions jaillit la lumière"*—light springs from clash of opinions.

To bring about such a revelation is the task of the two lawyers, or of the prosecutor and the counsel. By generating a spark of truth for the judge through the contact of the positive and negative poles of accusation and defense, or of plaintiff and respondent, the lawyer accomplishes a public service and takes part in the administration of justice.

The eminent Belgian lawyer Edmond Picard gives a masterly description of the enlightening work of the lawyer in court and of the help which he renders to the judge: "In order to master the

---

[74] Graf A. zu Dohna, *Das Strafverfahren*, p. 57.
[75] W. Heine, "Wesen der Verteidigung," *Die Justiz*, 1925, No. 1, p. 43.
[76] As early as in the fifth century B. C., in the Athens of Socrates and Aristotle, a talker who could convert black into white and vice versa was called an advocate.

numerous and very complicated elements which lead. . .to a decision, it is necessary to submit the case to a detailed and deep analysis, to plough it up in all directions, to bring to the surface all it contains, all the pros and cons, to discuss it, to shake it and turn it inside out, in one word, to defend it. . .The process of purification, confrontation and isolation, after which only grains of pure gold remain on the field of battle, develops before the eyes of the judge; from these grains, the judge composes his decision. . .The only question the lawyer must put to himself is: is the case defendable?" [77]

Questions of moral obligations and professional duties are perennial questions for the lawyer.

One problem is whether the acceptance of dubious cases should bring about disciplinary punishment of the lawyer or be considered as nothing more than a lawful but immoral action, resulting in loss of respect for the lawyer.

Another question is: what are the methods which the lawyer should be allowed to use in the defense of dubious causes?

In the opinion of the present author, the decision of the Council of the Bar and that of the *Sudebnaya Palata* in the Lokhvitsky Case were unjust, and that of the Senate—correct.

The Council of the Bar wrote in its decision that it found nothing with which to reproach Lokhvitsky when he assumed the defense of Elkin in the criminal trial, but found a despicable element in the assertion of Elkin's civil claims against Popova. I think that this distinction is groundless. It is clear that the Council was of the opinion that a lawyer may defend a criminal independently of the degree of immorality of the act committed. Indeed, every criminal, be he the most immoral monster, has the right to have a defender, who must bring out in his defense everything which may extenuate the criminal act or the guilt of the accused. Why should it be different in a civil suit? Suppose that Elkin had killed Popova; Lokhvitsky would have had the right to defend him. Is the morality of a murderer higher than that of a man who tries to retain property which he acquired immorally? Why may a lawyer defend the perpetrator of an immoral act in a criminal court but not in a civil one?

As to the decision of the Senate, its opinion about the special morality of the Civil Code which does not correspond to individual morality is correct, and Dzhanshiyev is wrong when he asserts that

---

[77] E. Picard, *Scènes de la vie judiciaire. Paradoxe sur l'avocat*, pp. 20-22, *passim*.

there is just one morality, that civil laws do not have their own morality. In reality, morality and law are different concepts which do not always coincide. This has always been taught in the very first semester of law school. That some laws are completely immoral is so evident that it has become a truism. Morality is one of the most relative concepts formed by men.

The concept of *bonae mores* varies according to time, country and nation. Pascal was indignant that "we see scarcely any thing just or unjust that does not change quality in changing climate. Three degrees of higher latitude overturn all jurisprudence. A meridian decides the truth; fundamental laws change in a few years; right has its epochs." [78] And Pascal illustrates his thought by the following dialogue:

> Wherefore do you kill me? What! do you not dwell on the opposite side of the water? My friend, if you dwelt on this side, I should be an assassin, it would be unjust to kill you thus; but since you dwell on the other side, I am courageous, and it is just. [79]

Pascal asserts that "theft, incest, infanticide, parricide, all have had their place among virtuous actions." And he exclaims: "Can any thing be more ridiculous than that a man has a right to kill me because he dwells on the other side of the water, and because his prince has a quarrel with mine, although I have none with him?" [80]

Tolstoi was also deeply shocked by this duplicity of morality. He thought that if it is immoral to kill, it must *always* be immoral and impermissible to do so. He called soldiers murderers. This is true according to his concept of morality, but not according to that of the majority of people and not according to the law, which forbids killing in peace and allows it in war. Laws have been created just because morality is relative. They usually correspond to the concept of morality of the majority of the people for whom they have been created; they must be followed, and their transgression is punishable. However, Tolstoi denies to the state the right of punishment. [81]

---

[78] Blaise Pascal, *The Thoughts, Letters, and Opuscules*, p. 183.
[79] *Ibid.*, p. 211.
[80] *Ibid.*, p. 184.
[81] On Tolstoi's views on punishment, see the illuminating discussion of the problem in *Prestupleniye—kak nakazaniye, a nakazaniye—kak prestupleniye* by A. S. Goldenweiser, an eminent lawyer in Kiev. To the English translator of the book, E. A. Goldenweiser, Tolstoi wrote: "I cannot but say that your father's essay brings out with great force and clearness my thoughts dear to me, about the unreasonableness and immorality of that strange institution which is called trial." (A. S. Goldenweiser, *Crime a Punishment and Punishment a Crime*, p. 3.)

It is evident that the Civil Code has a morality of its own, not identical with "individual morality," as the Senate puts it. Take, for instance, the whole series of abstract transactions involving real property. Here the legislator is not interested in the circumstances under which the property was acquired, but only in the fact that it was acquired in accordance with the forms prescribed by law. Here morality is almost completely disregarded by law. The legislator had his reasons for doing so. He considered the protection of real property so important that he wanted the owner to be especially careful in transferring his rights: he should know that no dispute over rights (with some very insignficant exceptions) will help him to recover a piece of property if he has formally tranferred it to another, and the same applies in reverse, to the transferee of the property. That is why the *Sudebnaya Palata* rejected Popova's claim of restitution of the house transferred to Elkin according to established forms, although the *Palata* knew that Elkin had acquired his title to the house dishonestly.

Furthermore, the whole series of so-called *obligationes naturales* is not protected by law, but must still be carried out from the viewpoint of individual morality. According to the laws of many countries, a claim resulting from card playing is not protected by law, *i.e.*, cannot be brought to court, but individual morality requires a person to pay his card debts. The same is true for claims based on bets and some services, as, for instance, those of a marriage broker. A prostitute also cannot go to court over money promised to her.

The *Palata* said in the Lokhvitsky Case: "The lawyer who submits to the civil court a notoriously unfair claim must be considered as a person committing a dishonest act. . ." And what did the *Palata* itself do? On the one hand it rejected Popova's claim for restitution of the house and approved the retaining by Elkin of the fruits of his dishonorable act, and on the other disbarred Lokhvitsky for the defense of Elkin's claims! Now, are judges who confirm a right which is, as they know, acquired dishonestly, not more guilty than a lawyer who defends a claim to those rights? No, neither the judges nor the lawyer are guilty. The judges are bound by the provision of the law; *dura lex sed lex*. But the lawyer too cannot be punished if he makes use of the law in the interest of his client. If anyone may be reprimanded, it is the legislator who created a law which shields dishonest claims. The lawyer is not bound to be *plus catholique que le pape* or *plus royaliste que le roi*. He cannot be punished for maintaining formally lawful claims even if they are acquired dishonestly.

The Moscow Council of the Bar did not share this opinion, as may be seen from the Lokhvitsky Case. Also in a decision taken seven years after the Lokhvitsky Case, it declared: "A lawyer must serve only a just cause with [all] his knowledge and ability; he must not knowingly maintain unjust claims, defend an evidently unjust situation, although reasons for that could be found in the law; *he must prevent— as far as he can—collisions between formal law and justice and not provoke them.*" [82, 83] The Council disbarred the lawyer involved. It acted more strictly than in the Lokhvitsky Case because the lawyer had advised his client to demand a payment on grounds of a formal right, in spite of the fact that he knew that the payment had already been made once. This case is somehow different from the Lokhvitsky Case, but the principles governing the Council in its decision were the same: the lawyer was punished because he reverted to formal law in order to maintain an immoral claim.

In denying that disciplinary punishment for defending claims similar to those discussed above is called for, do we mean that every lawyer should undertake to defend such claims? Of course not. Morality, simple morality, "individual morality," should be considered by the lawyer when he accepts a case. Repeatedly, in their decisions, the Senate and the councils punished lawyers for actions committed in private life which were immoral, although not criminal; they required from lawyers a higher standard of behavior than from people of other professions. This is right, because the lawyer must enjoy confidence and respect and, therefore, his private life must be adapted to these requirements. It is beyond any doubt that many lawyers would have refused to defend Elkin's interests, and Lokhvitsky, being a distinguished lawyer, a professor of law before the Reform, should have turned down such a client. There were instances in which the accused was unable to find counsel even in a criminal case. In 1874, for instance, Kolosov and Yaroshevich were accused of counterfeiting railroad shares. Kolosov, who induced Yaroshevich to commit the crime and participated in all his criminal acts for a long time, later denounced Yaroshevich in his own interest. None of the lawyers of the Petersburg Bar was willing to assume the defense of Kolosov, and a counsel had to be assigned to him by the court.

Arsen'yev[84] sees a difference between cases accepted by the lawyer voluntarily and cases assigned to him by court. The first, Arsen'yev

---

82 Italics mine. S. K.
83 *Otchet Soveta prisyazhnykh poverennykh pri Moskovskoi Sudebnoi Palate za 1887/88 g.*, p. 148.
84 Arsen'yev, *op. cit.*, p. 177.

says, he should not accept "unless he is certain of the righteousness of his client." [85] Arsen'yev is right, because the lawyer may choose his clients and is not obliged to accept the defense of interests which are not in accordance with his sense of honor and morals. If, however, a lawyer accepts a dubious case but conducts it by using honest means and arguments, pointing out only the formal rights of his client, he should not, in my opinion, be prosecuted. A counsel assigned by court must take up every case. As Arsen'yev puts it, the duty of the counsel is "to find in the case, and to bring together in a proper light, all the circumstances which speak for the accused, *i.e.,* help to refute the accusation or mitigate its effect. Such circumstances can be found in every case, without distorting the facts and without attempting to pervert the truth. . . .Grave as the crime and great as the corruption of the criminal may be, the attempt to explain his moral decline and to find features which reduce his responsibility will seldom remain fruitless." [86]

Indeed, nobody thinks of punishing disciplinarily the counsels of the Nürnberg trial, who defended perhaps the greatest criminals known to history. But not every lawyer would have undertaken to assume the defense in this trial.

The same consideration should be applied to civil cases. A lawyer with a high moral standard will not defend dubious claims based on formal right: *non omne quod licet honestum est.* "To accept a case which better should be rejected may happen even to the most scrupulous lawyer for this or another reason which can not always be defined," writes Arsen'yev, "but a steady or often repeated selection of such cases gives the right to assume that it is based, not on casual circumstances, but on a system. The prestige of a lawyer who acquires such a reputation drops in the eyes of the judicial world and then in the eyes of the whole society. . .and the success of his activity is also endangered sooner or later, because the mere fact that he, the lawyer of *mauvaises causes,* as the Frenchmen say, has been selected as counsel, may discredit his client beforehand." [87]

Arsen'yev hits the nail on the head. The lawyer should not be held responsible for accepting dubious cases, or for defending a villain. He is responsible only for the means he employs in discharging his duty as a lawyer. However, by accepting cases dubious from the point of view of individual morality, he stains his good name and

85 *Ibid.,* p. 147.
86 *Ibid.,* p. 149.
87 Arsen'yev, *op. cit.,* p. 175-176.

should be punished, not by disciplinary measures, but by the loss of his reputation.

It must be said that the Moscow Council, so strict in questions of lawyers' ethics,[88] considered the control of the choice of clients by lawyers to be beyond its competence. Thus, the Council said in a decision: "In the selection of cases, the personal conviction of the lawyer must be decisive." [89] And further: "In general, the Council cannot control the convictions of a lawyer about a certain case: it is formed by a combination of imponderable and subtle data." [90]

Markov remarks on this problem that the question of how a lawyer came to accept power of attorney from this or that person, must be viewed as lying outside the competence of the Council.[91] M. M. Winaver is of the opinion that those who assert that a lawyer must defend only such interests as his conscience considers legitimate are wrong. "This is a false and pitiful maxim, which leads to arbitrariness and despair. The court is called upon to discover and assert truth; left to themselves, the most talented judges are unable to fulfil this task." [92]

The controversial question of whether the lawyer should accept any case offered to him, disregarding its moral foundation, has been very vividly presented by the eminent Belgian lawyer Edmond Picard. He discusses the problem of how it is possible that two lawyers, both equally honest, clever and upright, try to prove opposite assertions. "What is the value of our professional conscientiousness and knowledge if everyone of us every day disagrees with another, equally honest in questions of law, honor and liberty. . .Moreover, if my client had chosen me as his attorney, I would try to prove with the same impetus what I deny today, and *vice versa*. . .Thus, my conviction as to whether one and the same case is rightful or not has formed in accordance with the party which resorted to my services and not on the grounds of the case itself. Am I not a trader in words?"

However, Picard thinks that to accuse the lawyer of trading in words is paradoxical. The mistake lies in the initial assumption, *i.e.*, that every lawyer must accept undisputedly rightful cases only. "Human nature is limited and delicate, incapable of grasping the truth at once. We see the truth only from one side, and act as if this

---

[88] *See* p. 182.
[89] *Otchet Moskovskago soveta prisyazhnykh poverennykh pri Moskovskoi Sudebnoi Palate za 1896/1897,* p. 158.
[90] *Ibid., 1880/1881,* p. 115.
[91] A. N. Markov, *Pravila advokatskoi professii v Rossii,* p. 90.
[92] M. M. Winaver, *Ocherki ob advokature,* pp. 144, 159-160, *passim.*

truth were really on one side only. And just because each party clarifies its viewpoint, the judge understands the whole."

Of course, Picard is far from asserting that a lawyer should accept every case offered to him. He says himself that "there are cases the immorality of which is evident. They are not accepted by lawyers who respect themselves. These cases are the booty of those who as yet are not disbarred because of abundant indulgence." But he rightly stresses the fact that the lawyer, in the great majority of cases, is unable to decide on whose side the truth lies when he accepts a case. To judge is the job of the judge, not of the lawyer.[93]

Samuel Johnson spoke some very wise words on this subject. In his *Life of Johnson,* Boswell has recorded the following conversation: "We talked of the practice of the law. Sir William Forbes said he thought an honest lawyer should never undertake a cause which he was satisfied was not a just one. Sir, said Johnson, a lawyer has no business with the justice or injustice of the cause which he undertakes, unless his client asks his opinion, and then he is bound to give it honestly. The justice or injustice of the cause is to be decided by the judge. Consider, sir, what is the purpose of courts of justice. It is that every man may have his cause fairly tried by men appointed to try causes. A lawyer is not to tell what he knows to be a lie; he is not to produce what he knows to be a false deed; but he is not to usurp the province of the jury and of the judge, and determine what shall be the effect of evidence, what shall be the result of legal argument." [94]

Vas'kovsky made an attempt to determine almost mathematically when a counsel is bound to decline a case. First he divides all cases into three categories from the juridical point of view: (1) unconditionally sure cases, (2) hopeless cases, (3) dubious cases; and into three categories from the moral point of view: (1) just cases, (2) unjust cases, and (3) dubious cases. With this as a basis, Vas'kovsky classifies all cases into nine categories with regard to the acceptability. He summarizes his conclusions in the form of a "theory of moral scrupulousness" to which the counsel must conform.[95]

Vas'kovsky's reasoning is based on the conception that counsels are representatives, not of individuals, but of society. It will be shown below[96] that his assertion is erroneous.

---

[93] Picard, *op. cit.,* pp. 16-22.
[94] Quoted by James Ram, *A Treatise on Facts as Subjects of Inquiry by a Jury,* p. 278.
[95] Vas'kovsky, "O razborchivosti pri prinyatii del k zashchite," *Zhurnal yuridicheskago obshchestva,* 1894, No. 6.
[96] See pp. 197-198.

There are lawyers who have not the courage to refuse their services in cases which are well remunerated. This is the "slippery side" of the profession of which Spasovich speaks, and which inspired John Gay's humorous verses:

> I know you Lawyers can with ease
> Twist words and meanings as you please
> That language, by your skill made pliant,
> Will bend to favour ev'ry client;
> That 'tis the fee directs the sense
> To make out either side's pretense.
> When you peruse the clearest case,
> You see it with a double face:
> For scepticism's your profession;
> You hold there's doubt in all expression.
> Hence is the bar with fees supplied;
> Hence eloquence takes either side.[97]

and:

> Does justice, or the client's sense,
> Teach lawyers either side's defence?
> The fee gives eloquence its spirit;
> That only is the client's merit.[98]

However, a lawyer who desires to preserve his reputation and not to become an *avocat de mauvaises causes* must resist temptations.

With regard to Maklakov's assertion that lawyers are people without principles, Gruzenberg declared: "It is very sad that Maklakov's friends and colleagues, whom he encounters every day, failed to convince him that in the political, social and religious fields, the members of the guild are steadfast, even over-scrupulous, in their convictions and faith." [99] Hessen is of the opinion that such an assertion in literature as that of Maklakov threatens to upset definitively the notion of a lawyer's duties.[100]

It is evident that Maklakov chose his words badly when he asserted that lawyers lack principles. Did not Maklakov himself declare in a speech which he delivered as a member of the Third Duma in 1909 that thousands of Russian lawyers pleaded in countless political trials out of pure idealism, not for money or fame? [101] And did not Maklakov himself passionately take part in such trials? His assertion that lawyers

---

[97] Gay, *Fables*, p. 135.
[98] *Ibid.*, p. 189.
[99] Gruzenberg, *Ocherki. . .*, p. 90.
[100] Hessen, *Advokatura. . .*, p. 472.
[101] See p. 309.

have no principles must be understood in the sense that the lawyer defends his clients and their interests regardless of his own convictions and principles.

CHAPTER V

POLITICAL TRIALS

A. Government in the Fight
Against the Revolutionary Movement

1. *Interests of State and Society*

Are state and society two separate organizations?
Do the interests of state and society coincide?

According to Korkunov, it was Schlözer who in his *Staatskunde* first discussed the idea of an independent science of society.[1] Lorenz von Stein originated the theory of society as an organism not only separate from the state, but even in latent opposition to the state. Stein asserted that the state and society are engaged in a constant struggle. "The meaning of the life of a human community must be the constant struggle of the state against society and of society against the state." [2]

Marcell Frydmann thought that this fight finds its most evident expression in criminal proceedings. There the prosecutor, the representative of the state, is opposed by the lawyer, the representative of society. Society strives to emancipate itself as much as possible from the intervention of the state and the counsel attempts to prove that the act under indictment belongs to the sphere of free activity to which the punitive power of the state may not be extended. The counsel is the attorney-at-law of the society (*Gesellschaftsanwalt*).[3]

In Russian legal literature, prior to the Revolution, the defender of this idea was E. V. Vas'kovsky. He argued that it is the duty of society to take care of the accused as one of its members. "Consequently, society must, in its own interests, [and] in order to preserve its rights, take the accused under its protection, in the same way as the state protects the victim. Society sends a special representative [to court] to participate in the proceedings, just as the state is represented by the prosecutor. This accredited representative of society in the

---

[1] N. M. Korkunov, *op. cit.*, p. 230.
[2] Lorenz von Stein, *Geschichte der socialen Bewegung*, I, p. xxxi.
[3] Marcell Frydmann, *Systematisches Handbuch der Verteidigung*, p. 65.

criminal court is the lawyer." [4] Vas'kovsky further declared that "lawyers serve society in the same manner as the judiciary and the prosecutors serve the state. Thus. . .a staff of lawyers must be created for society. . .which depends on society for appointment, promotion, supervision and remuneration." [5]

Vas'kovsky's assertion was sharply criticized. "What kind of a theory is it," asks Professor Zagorovsky, "according to which the state appears as a bloodthirsty persecutor of the accused, *i.e.*, of a person who will, perhaps, be proved innocent, according to which the society must protect the accused from the attacks and 'abuses' of the state by sending a lawyer? . . . Is the state not as interested as society in seeing to it that justice is done to the accused? And is not society as interested as the state in the punishment of a criminal?" [6]

M. L. Goldstein asserted that Vas'kovsky is wrong in considering criminal proceedings as a struggle of society against the state, a struggle in which the state is the enemy of the accused and society his defender. The state, argued Goldstein, consists of power, territory and people.[7] To contrast the state with society is therefore to contrast the whole with one of its parts. The state acts, in criminal proceedings, in the interest of society, not in the interest of territory or power. If Vas'kovsky were right, Goldstein contended, society would be fighting society, i.e. itself.

Prof. N. N. Polyansky also repudiated Stein's theory and Vas'-kovsky's assertion that the lawyer is the representative of society against the state. In 1910, Polyansky wrote an article entitled "Defense and Accusation in Cases of Crimes Against the State." Criticizing Stein, he wrote that the idea of antagonism between state and society and the notion of criminal proceedings as a struggle between state and society, which was deduced from this idea, is in contradiction to modern conceptions, according to which the state is the most universal form (with respect to its aims) of the human community.[8]

Polyansky argued that the state is an organization which unifies the society it represents. Therefore, even though the concepts of state and society are not identical (society is conceivable apart from the

---

[4] Vas'kovsky, *Organizatsiya advokatury*, p. 7.
[5] *Ibid.*, p. 18.
[6] A. I. Zagorovsky, 'Otzyv ob uchenykh trudakh privat-dotsenta E. V. Vas'-kovskago," *Zapiski Imperatorskago Novorossiiskago Universiteta*, XCVII (1903) , 20.
[7] L. M. Goldstein, "Printsipy organizatsii advokatury," *Vestnik prava*, 1900, No. 1., p. 57.
[8] N. N. Polyansky, "Zashchita i obvineniye v delakh o gosudarstvennykh prestupleniyakh," *Pravo*, 1910, No. 36, p. 2121.

organization which unifies it), it is nonsensical to visualize these concepts as "completely opposed poles."

Polyansky admits, however, that the idea of antagonism between state and society makes sense if the state is identified with the predominant class, and society with the oppressed social groups. The state is then considered as synonymous with government, and society—with the governed.[9] Polyansky thinks that trials based on crimes against the state constitute a special case, by virtue of the following considerations: (a) whereas normal criminal proceedings are carried out in the interest of society, trials of political cases are often instigated in the one-sided interest of the government, when a split exists between government and society; (b) in political cases involving attempts against the political rights of the people, agents of the government [the judiciary in this case] are often guilty of acting in accordance with the "views" of the government, which, naturally, is inclined to treat its agents leniently.[10]

The controversy concerning Stein's theory of state and society and of a constant struggle between them is beyond the scope of our discussion. We shall see later, however, that the state has often been considered a living organism with its own aims and interests, which do not necessarily have to coincide, and often fail to coincide, with the aims and interests of society. This is especially true in the case of a totalitarian state.

Let us only emphasize here that Polyansky was completely right in his remark that in political trials the interests of the government, personifying the state, and those of society, are often opposed to each other.[11]

When the state has developed into an independent political organism, when it pursues its own aims, disregarding the will of the majority of the people—although asserting that it acts for the greatest benefit of the people—its interests do not correspond any longer to public interests and are opposed to them. But in the field of admini-

---

[9] See H. Ortloff, "Staat und Gesellschaft in der Strafrechtspflege," *Der Gerichtssaal*, XLVII (1892), No. 2-3, p. 282.

[10] N. N. Polyansky, "Zashchita i obvineniye v delakh o gosudarstvennykh prestupleniyakh," *Pravo*, 1910, No. 36, pp. 2121-2123.

[11] Prof. N. N. Polyansky, who after the Revolution remained in Russia and occupied a chair in one of the legal institutions of higher learning in the USSR wrote in 1927 a pamphlet entitled *Pravda i lozh' v ugolovnom protsesse* (Truth and Untruth in Criminal Trials), in which he repeated all his criticism of Stein and Vas'kovsky as formulated in 1910, omitting, however, his correct remarks concerning the antagonism between the state and society in political trials. Many of the bitter truths which one was permitted to state under the autocratic tsarist government must be hushed up under Soviet rule.

stration of justice one would think that state and society strive for the same goal—justice. The prosecutor, representing the state, also speaks for society, which is interested in the punishment of the criminal. However, even in the field of administration of justice there is no full harmony of interests. How often is an act declared punishable by the state when according to popular conceptions it is not reprehensible! The state inevitably tends to enlarge its repressive power with regard to the individuals who make up the society. This is particularly true when the majority of the people is opposed to the government. In the fight between the regime, which strives to retain power, and society, which seeks to escape from the grasp of the state in order to secure the necessary individual freedom for its members, the interests of both parties are opposed to each other. However, the lawyer is not the representative of society, but of the individual. That is why Vas'kovsky's conception of the lawyer as a servant of society, acting in its interest and under its control and supervision, is erroneous. Yet, serving the individual, the lawyer indirectly protects the interests of society and of the people, of which his client is a component part.

The conflict of interests becomes most evident in political trials. In Russia the nineteenth century, (beginning with the Decembrists on the Senate Square in St. Petersburg) and the first seventeen years of the twentieth century were marked by a more or less open struggle of the Russian people, first represented by its intelligentsia and then also acting directly, against the government (personifying the state) for liberation from the yoke of despotism and autocratic power. This fight had its ups and downs. The government had to make concessions when the outbursts of the revolutionary movement became particularly strong, but then took the upper hand again and tried by means of repression and political trials to check the movement and then to liquidate it together with its participants.

In those trials the Russian lawyer accomplished the noble task of defending the interests of the individual against oppression by the state.

2.   Policy of Administrative Repression

After the assassination of Alexander II by the terrorists of the *Narodnaya Volya* and the execution of the perpetrators of this crime, "the most monstrous in modern political history," as Graham rightly remarks,[12] the organization lost its ablest men and women and, what

---

[12] S. Graham, *Tsar of Freedom*, p. 314.

is still more important, its *raison d'être*. The *Narodnaya Volya* asserted that the forcible elimination of the Tsar will bring the fall of autocracy in Russia. Nothing of the kind occurred. In place of the "Tsar—liberator," a resolute reactionary mounted the throne. The *Narodnaya Volya* and its movement were definitely crushed.

The years of Alexander III's rule were marked by the most severe political reaction. Toward the end of his reign, when reaction was at its peak, the government sought to avoid political trials in its fight against the revolutionary movement. Under Alexander II, political criminals were tried by the *Sudebnaya Palata* with class representatives and, in the most important cases, by the Senate with the participation of the same representatives. The assassins of Alexander II—Rysakov, Zhelyabov, Mikhailov, Perovskaya, Kibal'chich and Gelfman were also tried in this manner. They had counsels (with the exception of Zhelyabov, who assumed his own defense) who pleaded for them and were allowed to bring forward everything they thought proper to mitigate the guilt of the accused.[13] However, every open political trial stirs public opinion and therefore is a powerful and efficient means of propaganda and agitation. The case is discussed in the press, pleadings of the counsel are reproduced and revolutionary ideas openly discussed. That is why the government of Alexander III preferred to fight the revolutionary movement in the dark, by means of administrative punishment, by banishments to Siberia and the Northern provinces of European Russia, by confinement in fortresses (the famous Peter and Paul Fortress and the Schlüsselburg Fortress) without public trial and much fuss. It is self-evident that the method of short shrift in the administration of justice opened the doors to every abuse.

After the death of Alexander III, his son, Nicholas II, the last Russian Emperor, pledged to follow in the steps of his father and to abstain from anything which could be deemed not in his father's spirit. Thus he continued the same policy of secret administrative repression,[14] with a few exceptions.[15] With regard to this policy, Lenin wrote in 1901: "It is physically impossible to make thousands and tens of thousands of people responsible for refusing to work, for

---

[13] *Protsess 1-go marta 1881 goda.*

[14] The last political trials in court under Alexander III took place in 1889 (the Yakutsk Case) and in 1891 (the Sofiya Ginzburg Case). See L. I. Goldman, *Politicheskiye protsessy v Rossii 1901-1917,* p. 6.

[15] In 1897, seven weavers were tried for striking. In 1898, ninety-five workers were tried for the same reason, and in 1900 fifty-eight and seventy-eight workers. Goldman, *op. cit.,* p. 17.

strikes, for gatherings. It is politically impossible to initiate court proceedings for every such case because, no matter how hand-picked the bench may be, no matter how castrated the publicity, nevertheless the shadow of a court will remain. . .and, of course, of a 'court' over the government, not over the workers. . . .Criminal laws. . .are being inexorably pushed into the background by direct political struggle and open street fighting. 'Justice' takes off its mask of impartiality and loftiness and takes to flight, leaving the field of action to the police, gendarmery and Cossacks. . ." [16]

However, this method was unable to check the revolutionary movement, which grew in strength and scope. The Russian Social Democratic Labor Party was founded in 1898 in Minsk, and the Socialist Revolutionary Party in 1902.

The government reverted again to political trials, without abandoning the administrative measures. After 1901, when three political cases were tried, the number of these trials and persons involved increased rapidly and reached its peak in 1907 and 1908. During the period of 1901-1907, hundreds of thousands of workers, peasants and representatives of the intelligentsia were indicted and tried for political offenses, according to data gathered by the All-Union Society of Former Political Convicts.[17] The Criminal Code was applied in political cases such as strikes, persecution of strikebreakers by workers, armed resistance during searches, clashes of armed demonstrations with police and gendarmes or armed forces, terroristic acts, expropriations, agrarian disorders, etc.

However, the Criminal Code and the ordinary courts created by Alexander II were deemed insufficient for the suppression of the revolutionary movement. Special laws were promulgated.

3. Law of August 14, 1881

On August 14, 1881, Alexander III confirmed a law, worked out by the Committee of Ministers, concerning "Measures for the Preservation of State Order and Public Tranquillity." [18] This law gave to the administration far-reaching powers in those provinces which were declared to be "in a state of reinforced or extraordinary protection."

---

16 Lenin, *Sochineniya*, 2d ed. IV, 116.
17 Goldman, *op. cit.*, p. 7. These data were collected in accordance with a decision of the Conference of the Society in 1928.
18 *Svod ustavov o preduprezhdenii i presechenii prestupleny, Izd. 1890 g.*, Art. 1, Note 1.

In the field of administration of justice, the local administrations of those provinces and their cities were empowered:

1. to transfer to the competence of courts-martial the trial of crimes, with the provision that the more important crimes should be tried according to war-time laws;[19]

2. to order the trial of criminal cases in closed session;[20]

3. to arrest persons on the ground of mere suspicion of having committed a crime against the state, of being involved in such a crime, or of belonging to an unlawful association;[21]

4. to search dwellings even without definite suspicions;[22]

5. to banish persons to various localities of the Empire under the open[23] supervision of the police for a term not exceeding five years.[24]

The "extraordinary protection" was an even more severe restriction of the civil rights of the individual than the "reinforced protection." In matters of administration of justice, the *Glavnonachal'-stvuyushchy* (Commander in Chief of a province) had the right to bring whole categories of criminal offenses under the competence of courts-martial and under military laws by a single order (in excess of rights granted under the reinforced protection).

The Law of August 14, 1881, was thought of as an "extraordinary but temporary measure," and it was limited to three years. In reality it functioned till the end of the monarchy, being extended every time it was to expire.   . . . . .

First it was extended over several provinces and city governorships. Subsequently, more and more provinces were added to the list, so that in 1901 almost all Russia was "in a state of reinforced protection." When, in 1905, the law was to expire, the first Russian revolution was in full swing. The law was not only extended, but considered inadequate and a new law, even more drastic, was enacted in 1906.[25] In 1905, those provinces which were under "reinforced protection" were put under "extraordinary protection."

As mentioned above, in the period of time between 1881 and 1901, the government preferred to eliminate its real or potential internal enemies by administrative measures provided for by the Law of August 14, 1881. But in 1902, when the revolutionary movement extended to the peasantry and agrarian disorders spread in the

---

19 *Ibid.*, Arts. 17 and 18.
20 *Ibid.*, Art. 17.
21 *Ibid.*, Art. 21.
22 *Ibid.*
23 In contradistinction to secret supervision.
24 *Ibid.*, Art. 24.
25 See pp. 205 ff.

Ukraine and the Volga Region, the government again reverted to political trials and made use of its right to bring some criminal offenses before courts-martial. To these courts were transferred the cases in which the administration desired to bring about a death sentence. According to the Criminal Code, capital punishment existed in Russia only in four cases: (1) criminal acts against the life and authority of the Emperor;[26] (2) criminal acts against the Empress or the Heir to the Throne;[27] (3) conspiracy and upheaval directed against the person of the Emperor and the State;[28] and (4) premeditated damaging of telegraph wires with the intention of committing the crimes covered by Art. 241, 244 or 249.[29]

However, Art. 279[30] of the Military Code provided the death penalty for many offenses of a general criminal character, such as robbery and arson.

A. A. Lopukhin,[31] Director of the Department of Police, wrote in a secret report to the Committee of Ministers on December 4, 1904, in which he criticized the Law of August 14, 1881: "The transfer of a case to a court-martial decided the question of the death penalty beforehand." [32] Lopukhin reported on the right to banish individuals to Siberia and other remote places of the Empire, saying that these banishments were impartially applied to "those who are really dangerous for the state and to those who only express independent opinions, and to the latter even more than to the former." He emphasized that during the last years administrative banishment was inflicted upon young people who participated in student disorders which did not have any political character, upon workers for strikes which were quite peaceful and pursued exclusively economic ends and, furthermore, upon peasants who, after long arguments about the land with landlords, occupied it arbitrarily. Persons who committed public offenses, the investigation of which would present too much trouble for the police, and even those persons who merely insulted officials, were also banished. "Using administrative banishment for

---

26 *Ulozheniye o nakazaniyakh*, Art. 241.
27 *Ibid.*, Art. 244.
28 *Ibid.*, Art. 249.
29 *Ibid.*, Art. 1145.
30 *Svod voyennykh postanovleny*. Kniga XXIV (1869) , *Ustav voenno-sudny*.
31 The same Lopukhin who revealed the identity of the famous *agent provocateur* Asef to the journalist V. Burtsev, in a train between Cologne and Berlin. Lopukhin was tried for revealing a state secret and banished to Siberia.
32 *Tsarism v bor'be s revolutsiei*, p. 25. The report was first published in Geneva in 1905 under the title: *Dokladnaya zapiska direktora departamenta politsii, rassmotrennaya v Komitete ministrov*, with an introduction by N. Lenin.

over twenty years," writes Lopukhin, "the administration got so accustomed to it that registration of banishments exists only for those persons who were put under open supervision of the police." [33]

4. Law of August 19-22, 1906

On August 19-22, 1906, between the sessions of the First and the Second Duma, the government of Stolypin brought out an Imperial Ukase based on Art. 87 of the Fundamental Laws of 1906 on the Establishment of Army and Navy Field Courts-Martial.These courts were to function in places put under "extraordinary protection" and under "martial law." The local administration in such places—the governor-general, the commander-in-chief and persons designated by them—were entitled to transfer cases involving private persons who committed crimes considered too evident to need an investigation to field courts-martial for trial according to martial law (Art. 1). The court consisted of a president and four army or navy officers (Art. 2.) Young officers, being considered politically unreliable, were not admitted as members of the court. The names of the members of the court remained secret. Notification of the appointment to membership of a field court-martial was handed to the officer in a sealed envelope on the morning on the day of the session. The court records were made available to the members of the court just before the beginning of the session, so that they did not know in advance whom they were going to try and for what offense.

The session of the court took place behind closed doors. Publicity was excluded.[34]

An instruction on the procedure to be followed in field courts-martial was published on September 11, 1906. According to it, the accused had no right to have a counsel. Also, no prosecutor was admitted. The accused was simply notified by the presentation of an indictment that he is subject to trial by a field court-martial. There was no appeal against the sentence, and no cassation. The sentence came into force immediately and had to be carried out not later than twenty-four hours after its pronouncement.

The evident aim of the government in creating field courts-martial was the turning out of a great number of death sentences and increased repression to intimidate the people. In the collection of documents published in Moscow in 1936, under the title *Tsarism in*

---

[33] *Ibid.*, p. 30-31.
[34] *Ibid.*, Art. 5.

the Fight Against the Revolution, one paper attracts particular attention. It was a secret circular letter dated August 27, 1906, from the
Minister of War, A. F. Rediger, to the Commander-in-Chief of the
Guard and of the St. Petersburg Military District, Grand Duke
Nikolai Nikolayevich, which reads as follows: "In the course of my
personal report on August 26, His Majesty the Emperor deigned to
give me the order to inform all the Military District Commanders that
His Majesty requires the unconditional application of the new law
concerning the field courts-martial. . .to all crimes mentioned in the
regulations of these courts. The military district commanders and
governors general who will tolerate deviations from the Imperial
Order will be responsible to His Majesty personally. The military
district commanders must take care that no telegrams with pleas of
pardon be sent to His Majesty the Emperor in these cases." [35]

This Imperial Order does not need any comment. Indeed, the
field courts-martial applied almost no other punishment than death.
In the first six months of their functioning, 960 death sentences were
pronounced.[36]

S. Usherovich calculated that between August 19-22, 1906, and
April 20, 1907, when the law expired, more than 1,000 persons were
executed on grounds of sentences passed by the field courts-martial.[37]

As mentioned above, the Law of August 19-22, 1906, was passed
by the government under Art. 87 of the Fundamental Laws of 1906.
This article enabled the government to enact laws when the Duma
was not in session. However, Art. 87 also provided that "the adopted
measure ceases to be in force if the competent Minister does not bring
before the Duma a bill corresponding to the adopted measure during
the first two months after the Duma resumes its activity, or if the bill
is rejected by the Duma or the State Council." [38] The Second Duma
was called to order on February 20, 1907. Thus the field courts-martial
had to cease their activity on April 20 if a bill was not passed in the
meantime. However, the Duma desired to eliminate the field courts-
martial before this date, as soon as possible. Therefore, a bill concerning the abolition of the field courts-martial was prepared by the Duma
itself and introduced on March 9. The President of the Council of
Ministers, P. A. Stolypin, said in the Duma on March 13:

---

[35] Tsarizm v bor'be s revolutsiei, p. 82.
[36] S. Orlovsky. "Voenno-polevye sudy," in Bol'shaya Sovetskaya Entsiklopediya,
XII, 290-292.
[37] S. Usherovich. Smertnye kazni v tsarkoi Rossii, Footnote 1 on p. 104.
[38] Svod osnovnykh gosudarstvennykh zakonov. Izdaniye 1906 goda (Svod
zakonov, Vol. I).

... We have heard here accusations against the government; we have heard that it has bloody hands. We have heard that it is a shame and disgrace for Russia that such measures as field courts-martial have been resorted to. ... But when in danger, the state must revert to the most rigorous, the most exceptional measures in order to avert disintegration. This was, this is, and this will be so always and everywhere. This is the principle of human nature which also lies in the nature of the state itself. When a house burns, gentlemen, you break into a strange apartment, you break the doors, you break the windows. When a person is sick, he is treated by poisons. When a murderer attacks you, you kill him. This system is recognized by all the states. ... Gentlemen, there are fateful moments in the life of a state, when state necessity is above the law and when one must choose between the integrity of theories and the integrity of the fatherland ... I am asking myself ... has the government the right with regard to its faithful servants, who are subjected to deadly danger every moment, to make an open concession to the revolution? After having considered this question, after having weighed it thoroughly, the government came to the conclusion that the country expects from it a demonstration not of weakness but of faith. We wish to believe, we must believe, gentlemen, that we will hear words of appeasement from you, that you will stop the bloody madness,[39] that you will pronounce the word which will force us all to start, not the destruction of Russia's historical building, but its rebuilding, remodeling and adornment.[40]

Stolypin's speech was answered by V. A. Maklakov:

In our country we practice a method of repression which remains a puzzle. ... You wish to fight the revolution by strong repression. Speaking from my point of view, I would say that this is an unreliable method: it has already been applied without any success. But I shall assume your viewpoint ... and ask: what does repression mean? What are the rights of a state which wishes to apply repression? It may pass a new law, i.e., publish a general rule, increase punishment for everyone who commits a certain offense. Yes, you may decree that not only an attempt on the life of officials, but also abuse of them, is punishable with death. It would be a lawful action. ... But the government did not choose this legal way when the sad law concerning the reinforced protection was adopted in 1881. The general criminal laws have not been abolished. We even sometimes take the opportunity to boast

---

39 Stolypin had in mind the assassinations of officials by revolutionaries.

40 Gosudarstvennaya Duma. Vtoroi sozyv 1907 g. *Stenografichesky otchet*, I, 513, *passim*.

41 We quote a large part of Maklakov's speech because he was one of the most eminent Russian lawyers in the last period of the existence of the bar in Russia. Although not delivered in court, this speech gives a brilliant analysis of the administration of justice in the years after the Revolution of 1905.

of them before Europe,[42] we even point to England, where a man
can be hanged for theft. We act differently: the right to transgress law has been granted to the administration. This was
achieved by the law on reinforced and extraordinary protection
and, to a monstrous degree, by the law concerning the field
courts-martial.

Here Maklakov explains how, according to these laws, the Minister of
the Interior or his local representative may choose the kind of court
which will decide upon the fate of a defendant. Then he continues:

Thus, we practice a method of repression which is a puzzle
for us, for Europe, and especially for the jurists. For the same
crime committed under similar conditions—the murder of a minister—the perpetrator in one case is tried by the court-martial and
hanged, and in another case—by the *Sudebnaya Palata* and is not
hanged. In the same year, a man was hanged for the assassination
of a policeman, and the murderer of a minister was not hanged.
And this occurred, not under law but at the discretion of the
minister [of the interior] or even a governor-general. . . . Where
there is no law equally applicable to everybody, where there are
three laws, there is no legality at all. Court-martial justice is the
negation of law and its obligatory power against every man, the
negation of the main pillar of statehood, a blow against the state
itself. . . . However, the defenders of these courts put a naive or
malicious question, saying: 'You condemn field courts-martial, but
is the underground revolutionary tribunal better?'. . . Don't you
realize that by trying to justify field courts-martial by referring to
the underground revolutionary tribunal you give the most anni-
hilating characterization of your own courts? . . . In comparing
yourselves with revolutionaries, remember that, however terrible
the deeds accomplished by the terror from beneath may be, they
are less terrible than your terror of the field courts-martial. I am
an enemy of death, I understand the horror of people who are
shot in the street, who are torn to pieces by bombs. I understand
how terrible all this is, but it is nothing in comparison with what
is done by field courts-martial. Indeed, there is nothing more
repulsive than the legal solemnity of an execution. . . . [In the
case of terroristic murder,] there is the possibility to fight, there
is a hope to escape, even if it proves vain. But what happens during our countless executions? A man is caught, disarmed, tied,
brought [to court] and told that in several hours he will be
killed. His relatives are admitted; they take leave of him, of their
dear, their beloved one who is young and healthy and who must
die because of the will of men. He is led to the gallows like an
animal to the slaughterhouse; he is dragged to the place where
a prepared coffin awaits him and, in the presence of a physician,

---

[42] Maklakov has in mind the boast that the Criminal Code in Russia did not
apply capital punishment in cases of general, non-political crimes.

prosecutor and clergyman who are blasphemously convoked to attend this procedure, he is calmly and solemnly killed. This horror of a legal murder exceeds all the excesses of the revolutionary terror. With regard to ignoring human values, the record has been broken by the government, not by the revolution . . . Military laws are strict. Article 279 of the Military Code provides the death penalty for robbery, arson and murder. But this law, even though strict, is still a law, a lawful phenomenon, and when judges judge according to this law, they are still judges. They may apply Article 906 of the Military Code, which permits mitigation of punishment in accordance with the degree of guilt. The law on "protection" has changed everything: . . . instead of Article 279 of the Military Code, Article 18 of the Law of 1881 is applied when the governor-general desires it. According to Article 18, not only murder but also attempted murder, not only the taking of life but even the causing of injury, as well as careless manslaughter, are punishable by death. But that is not all. The court has been limited in its legal rights: Article 906, which provides the right to mitigate punishment, has not been abrogated, it exists; but in 1887 a secret circular was brought to the knowledge of the judges by the Minister of War, a secret order of the Tsar that the judges may not apply Article 906. Thus was produced this deeply anti-state phenomenon, according to which a law was not abrogated but the judges were forbidden to use it. Then began the passing of those sentences against which protested the conscience of the judges, which the judges did not desire, in which they, the judges, were not judges but toys in the hands of the governor-general. . . . Look, gentlemen, what you are doing. There are two pillars of the state: the law as a general rule, obligatory for all, and the court as the defender of the law. When these pillars—law and court—are intact, the state itself stays firm. And you [the men in the government] must defend these pillars, you, the defenders of statehood. But you have undermined the law, you have trampled the court into mud, you have sapped the foundations of the state—and all this was done in order to defend statehood. You say: in hitting back at the revolution, we could not spare private interests. . . . But we are not speaking of private interests. Indeed, they are spared neither by the government nor by the Maximalists. . . . But there is something else which you were bound to defend: it is statehood, court and law. In hitting the revolution, you did not hit private interests, but that which defends all of us—court and legality. I think that this is an erroneous way of hitting the revolution. . . .

At the end of his speech, Maklakov said that he understands that the government should defend itself, that he also understands that severity is sometimes needed, but that there is something else which cannot be forgotten: the state must live according to law, law courts must be law courts, arbitrariness cannot be sanctified. He emphasized that field courts-martial are disgraceful, and that even if they are not to be used any more in the future, the bare possibility of their existence is completely incompatible with Stolypin's words about statehood. His concluding words were prophetic: "If you deal with the revolution in such a manner, you will finish off the state at the same time. *Not a lawful state will emerge from the ruins of the revolution, but people gone wild and the chaos of state decomposition. . .*"[43,44]

Finally, Stolypin declared that he did not wish to defend field courts-martial as a judicial institution and promised that they would no longer be used—not even before the expiration date of the Law of August 19-22, 1906, *i.e.*, April 10, 1907.

Since, however, the field courts-martial, when created were included as an institution into the Military Code of 1869 (Book XXIV), they continued to function in places proclaimed under martial law. In these places they existed until 1917.

The First Duma passed unanimously and without debate a bill excluding the death penalty completely from the Russian books of law. It was, perhaps, the shortest bill ever presented to a legislative body. It reads: "Art. 1. The death penalty is abolished. Art. 2. In all cases when the death penalty is provided for by laws in force, execution is commuted to the next punishment in order of importance." That is all. But the government opposed the bill. It passed to the second chamber, the State Council, in which it was discussed from the end of June to July 9. On July 9 the First Duma was dissolved, and the bill thus remained a *pia desiderata*.

A new bill concerning the abolition of the death penalty which was worded exactly like the bill adopted by the First Duma, was brought before the Second Duma on March 19 and 22, 1907. The Duma had no time to pass the bill before June 19, 1907, when it was dissolved.

A third bill reached the Third Duma on June 19, 1908. It was referred to the Judiciary Committee, where it remained for two years, and only in May 1910 was the bill brought before the plenary session of the Duma, which rejected it on November 12, 1910.

In the meantime the work of the executioners did not stop. Particularly abundant in executions were the twenty-three years of Nicholas II's reign. S. Usherovich, who wrote a book of 500 pages on capital punishment in Russia, gives a list of 3014 names of persons executed

---

[43] Gosudarstvennaya Duma. Vtoroi sozyv 1907 g. *Stenografichesky otchet*, I, 385-391, *passim*.
[44] Italics mine. S. K.

in the period 1905-1917 and adds to this number several thousand men whose names he could not identify. According to the same Usherovich,[45] the number of persons executed during the reign of Alexander I was 24, of Nicholas I, 41, and from 1881 to 1894 (Alexander III's reign), 33.

It is difficult to say to what extent the statistical data of Usherovich are reliable. Professor M. N. Gernet remarks in his introduction to Usherovich's book, which he praises very highly, that the figures given by various authors writing on these subjects are not identical.[46]

The number of death sentences pronounced by the ordinary courts-martial in the period 1875-1908 was calculated by O. O. Gruzenberg according to official annual reports of the Main Court-Martial Administration. In these 34 years, 2,678 persons were executed by these courts, including 268 military and 2,410 civilians; from this total, 2,239 were executed between 1905 and 1908, and the figure for 1908 alone was 1,340, i.e., more than during the previous 33 years taken together. After 1908, the number of executions falls abruptly: in 1909—617.[47] "If we take into consideration the fact that the slightest revolutionary outbreaks were suppressed by punitive expeditions and field courts-martial," writes Gruzenberg, "the aforementioned number of executions pursuant to sentences of courts-martial which functioned regularly must be considered monstrous." [48]

The penalties of the Military Criminal Code were much more severe than those of the general Criminal Code. It is sufficient to mention that the death penalty was imposed by the Military Criminal Code in 19 cases as the exclusive punishment and in nine cases as one of the possible punishments, whereas the general Criminal Code mentioned only four cases of death penalty—for offences which actually occurred very seldom.

The Laws of August 14, 1881 and August 19-22, 1906, represent a profound breach in the majestic structure created by the Laws of November 20, 1864. The basic principle of separation of the judicial power from the administrative, promulgated by Alexander II, was sharply violated by these laws. The Administration, in the persons of the minister of the interior, the governor-general and their representatives, was empowered to refer criminal cases to special courts at its

---

45 Usherovich, op. cit., p. 104.
46 Ibid., footnote on p. 10. For statistical data, see also G. V. Filat'yev, "Dorevolyutsionnye sudy v tsifrakh," Katorga i ssylka, 1930, No. 7; and Ya. L. Berman, "Deyatel'nost' voenno-okruzhnykh i polkovykh sudov," Pravo, 1913, Nos. 36 and 37.
47 Ibid., p. 2063.
48 O. O. Gruzenberg, "K voprosu o smertnoi kazni v Rossii," Pravo, 1910, No. 23, p. 1437.

discretion, thereby predetermining the sentence. It received the right to choose the punishment for a political act or a criminal act suspected of having a political character by directing the case to a special court. Furthermore, the governor-general had the right to deny to the defendant the right of appeal to the Main Court-Martial against a sentence of the circuit court-martial and thus to send directly to the gallows an accused whose death sentence would, perhaps, have been reversed by the cassation instance.

B.   THE LAWYER IN POLITICAL TRIALS

1.   *Position of the Defense in Political Cases*

What was the position of the defense in political cases? We have seen that the lawyers were not admitted to field courts-martial. But in ordinary courts-martial and, of course, in the *Sudebnaya Palata* with class representatives which tried political cases, the lawyers could freely exercise their profession. "Every Russian who has been brought to court," writes Leroy-Beaulieu, "has seen a man rise by his side who has dared to oppose, in his name, the representative of authority over the charge brought against him. In this vast Empire, which has no political assemblies, the honor of having been the first to speak up freely belongs to the lawyers. In a country where military courage is quite common, the lawyers were the first to be called upon to give an example of something hitherto unknown: civic courage." [49] Those heartfelt words give a vivid picture of the situation at the time when Leroy-Beaulieu made his four trips to Russia in 1879-81. They remained true subsequently with respect to the battle the lawyer fought for the accused in criminal and political trials. In his pleading in the Gillerson Case [50] before the *Sudebnaya Palata* in Vilna in 1908, O. O. Gruzenberg said: "For six years[51] the Russian bar has had to take part in political trials. Hard and painful years. In every corner of this huge country, our colleagues accomplish their task, humble perhaps, but great—the defense of the individual against the impact of the state, against the mistakes and injustices of the prosecution. Half of this task had to be accomplished in courts-martial, foreign to us, frequently

---

[49] Leroy-Beaulieu, *op. cit.*, II, 364.
[50] *See* below pp. 286-291.
[51] He had in mind the period after 1902, when the government again reverted to political trials. See p. 202.

behind closed doors, without support of intimates and dear ones; surrounded by cold walls, one is alone with one's client, alone among indifferent and alien people." [52]

And sixteen years later, as a political refugee in France, Gruzenberg wrote in his reminiscences of these political trials the following pathetic lines:

> Arise, my unforgettable ones, you whom I shielded with my own chest, for whom heavy blows are showered upon me . . . I remember my scurrying all over the country with my colleagues. I remember the somber courtrooms, the morose judges coldly calculating human sinfulness. Opposite them, behind my back, young life, merciless toward its own self, is palpitating feverishly, with the joy of self-immolation. Another moment, and the hangman's noose will choke it. . . . No, no, I will not give them up. I will bring the hangman no offering. How often as I neared the end of my pleading did a mad thought shoot through my brain like lightning: what, you are finishing? You are letting the judges off to the conference room? They will go away and take with them the fate of the one who is, at present, the only person in the whole world for you. . . . Do not finish. You cannot do it. Do not let them go. Do not further shorten the already short young life. . . .[53]

Depicting the joy of saving the life of a political defendant threatened with a death sentence, Gruzenberg writes:

> Listen, you wise, steady, cold people, for whom there are no riddles, for whom life is clear as a market price schedule, you who know the fixed price of things, people and even ideas: did you ever experience such happiness? To give life, not in the fire of passion, not in carnal lust, but in the pangs of struggle, in the trembling of responsibility, . . . to cut the noose on the neck of a completely strange man—is there a deeper and higher joy in the world? . . . My defendants are passing before my eyes one by one—rootless and sleepless bustlers for human happiness. Were they good or bad? How can I judge? Didn't I give myself to them piecemeal?[54]

It must be emphasized that the Russian lawyers were free to say nearly anything they deemed favorable to their client almost during the entire fifty years that the free Russian bar existed, in those thousands of trials of peasants for rural upheavals, workers for strikes and

---

[52] O. O. Gruzenberg, *Ocherki i rechi*, p. 74.
[53] O. O. Gruzenberg, "Poruchik Pirogov," *Sovremennye zapiski*, XXI, 230-232, *passim*.
[54] *Ibid.*

other political criminals which were held in Russia from the end of
Alexander II's reign to the last days of Nicholas II. In defending the
accused in political trials, the lawyer was bound to accuse the regime
against which his client had risen. Speeches like those delivered by
the Russian lawyers would be impossible in any other autocracy, and
what the lawyers said during the trials would never have been tolerated in tsarist Russia anywhere but in court. In the courts the freedom of speech conferred by the Reform of 1864 remained in force,
notwithstanding the fact that the stenograms of the pleadings were
allowed to appear in the press uncurtailed by censorship, thus making
the free words of the lawyers known throughout the country.

By way of exception, several cases of interference with the lawyer's
freedom of speech occurred in the years when the reaction undertook
the task of suppressing political upheavals by the increased use of
gallows and firing squads. Although in this period the defense in
political cases became perilous for counsels, political prisoners did
not cease to find lawyers ready to defend them and to accomplish their
mission, thereby showing much civic courage.

In the following, some examples of the pleadings in political
trials are given. Of course, only a few can be quoted in these pages
from among thousands of cases.

2.   The Vera Zasulich Case

On January 24, 1878, Vera Ivanovna Zasulich, daughter of a
captain, twenty-eight years old, appeared in the reception room of
General Fyodor Trepov, Governor of the City of St. Petersburg, allegedly in order to present a petition to the General. When Trepov
approached Zasulich, she fired a shot, which wounded him. He recovered after a short convalescence.

Arrested, Zasulich declared that she had fired at Trepov because
he had given an order to flog a political prisoner, Bogolyubov, for
rude behavior.

According to the records and the testimony of witnesses, General
Trepov on July 13, 1877 entered the prison yard where several prisoners were taking their morning walk. A political prisoner, Arkhip
Bogolyubov, took off his hat when the General passed him the first
time. But when the General went through the yard again, Bogolyubov
failed to doff his headgear. "Hat off!" shouted Trepov, and knocked
off Bogolyubov's hat. Trepov ordered that twenty-five strokes of the
rod be administred to Bogolyubov.

Although Bogolyubov had already been sentenced to forced labor and deprived of all rights for having taken part in a politcal demonstration, Trepov's order was unlawful, since the sentence was not yet in force.

Three hours later the flogging took place in the corridor of the jail under the frantic protests of all the political inmates.

Vera Zasulich was indicted for attempted murder. Count Palen, Minister of Justice, who shortly before this case had been sharply criticized because of the "trial of the 193," [55] was anxious to avoid another political trial and decided to present the case of Vera Zasulich as a pure act of vengeance devoid of any political character. Therefore, he assigned the case to the St. Petersburg Circuit Court, with the participation of the jury.

Anatoly Fyodorovich Koni was President of the Court, and presided at the session at which Zasulich was tried. In his memoirs on Case Zasulich, written in 1904 and published in Russia in the form of a book of 563 pages in 1933, after his death (1927), Koni relates to what pressure he was subjected on the part of Count Palen, who wanted to obtain conviction at all costs. Palen asked Koni whether he could guarantee him a verdict of guilty, and when Koni answered that he could not do it, Palen said that he would report this attitude of the President of the Court to the Tsar. When Koni emphasized that as a judge he must be objective and impartial, Palen retorted ironically: "Yes, justice, impartiality. . ." and continued: "but in this damned case the government has the right to expect special services from the court." "Count," replied Koni, "let me recall to you the words of d'Aguesseau to Louis XIV: 'Sire, la cour rend des arrêts et pas des services.' " (Sire, the court renders decisions, not services)[56]

Palen wanted his best prosecutors to take care of the case. He assigned it to V. I. Zhukovsky, who declined the assignment under the pretext that his brother lived abroad as a political emigrant and could be endangered if he prosecuted Zasulich. Then Palen offered the prosecution to S. A. Andreyevsky, who stipulated, as a condition, that he be permitted to blame Trepov in accusing Zasulich. This condition was not accepted by Palen. Both Zhukovsky and Andreyevsky had to leave government service because of their refusal to accuse Zasulich. They joined the bar and became eminent lawyers; Andreyevsky es-

---

[55] The "trial of the 193" was conducted by a special bench of the Senate for more than three months, from October 18, 1877 to January 23, 1878. The indicted were accused of revolutionary propaganda. See A. Yakimov, "Bol'shoi protsess ili protsess 193-kh," *Katorga i ssylka*, 1927, No. 8.
[56] A. F. Koni, *Vospominaniya o dele Very Zasulich*, p. 69-72, *passim*.

pecially distinguished himself as one of the foremost criminal counsels of Russia.

During the trial, the defendant and her counsel told the jury the story of her life. This biography is characteristic, of the revolutionary youth of that time and also bears eloquent witness to the measures by which the government sought to check the revolution in Russia.

In 1867 Vera Zasulich graduated from school at the age of 17 and passed the examination for the certificate of private teacher. In the fall of 1868 she arrived in St. Petersburg with her mother. She found a job as clerk to a justice of the peace and attended courses at a teachers' school. There she made the acquaintance of S. G. Nechayev, the famous revolutionary, who was at that time a student at the University of St. Petersburg.[57]

Nechayev introduced her to his political friends, and when he left Russia he asked for permission to send letters for other persons to her address. In April 1869, the police searched her apartment, but did not find anything compromising. Nevertheless, when she left St. Petersburg for Moscow, she was arrested at the Moscow station on April 30 and sent back to St. Petersburg under the custody of two gendarmes, directly to the Third Division of His Majesty's Own Chancellery.[58] She was incarcerated without any explanation of the cause of her arrest and remained in prison till May, 1870. From prison she was transferred to the Fortress of Peter and Paul and was implicated in the case of Nechayev.[59]

In the preliminary investigation Zasulich was found completely innocent and was released from the fortress in March, 1871. Several weeks later, however, she was again arrested and banished by administrative order to the Province of Tver'. From the deportation jail in St. Petersburg she was sent under the custody of gendarmes to Krestsy (Province of Tver') and released there with two rubles in her pocket and one dress which she had on. In the summer of 1872 she was again arrested on suspicion of having spread proscribed literature among students of the Theological Seminary and banished to Soliga-

---

[57] Zasulich relates her romance with Nechayev in her memoirs. Nechayev fell in love with her, but she did not reciprocate his feelings. V. I. Zasulich, "Vospominaniya," *Byloye*, 1919, No. 14.

[58] Political police.

[59] Nechayev returned to Russia in the fall of 1869 and organized revolutionary societies in Moscow and elsewhere. On his order and with his active participation a student, Ivanov, whom Nechayev accused of treachery, was murdered. Nechayev escaped to Switzerland, but some of his accomplices were tried in July-August, 1871. Nechayev himself remained abroad till August, 1872, when he was extradited to Russia as a common criminal, tried and sentenced in 1873 to 20 years of forced labor. He died in the Fortress of Peter and Paul in 1882.

lach, Kostroma Province. In December, 1873, she was transferred to Kharkov, where she remained under the supervision of the police and without the right to leave the city until September, 1875. In Kharkov she obtained a midwife's certificate, but could not find a job because of the stigma of police supervision. Finally, at the end of 1875, she was released from police control and could leave Kharkov for Penza and St. Petersburg.

Zasulich was tried on March 31, 1878. The counsel for the defense, P. A. Aleksandrov, asked the court to summon as witnesses several persons who were present at the incident which took place in the prison yard on July 13, 1877, and those who were in prison when Bogolyubov was whipped. The court rejected this demand. However, Article 576 of the Code of Criminal Procedure provided that a defendant had the right to summon witnesses at his own expense if he filed the demand not later than a week after the refusal of the court. Zasulich's counsel made use of this provision, and the court summoned and heard these witnesses.[60]

The impression made by these witnesses is well described by Elisabeth Naryshkin-Kurakin (Naryshkina-Kurakina), Lady-in-Waiting of one of the Grand Duchesses at that time who was present at the trial: "The appearance of a number of young political prisoners created quite a stir. They had been brought into the courtroom from the Peter and Paul Fortress merely as witnesses of the incident in prison. Their pale faces, their voices trembling with tears and indignation, the details of their depositions—all these statements made me lower my eyes in shame. Then the strong, bombasting voice of the attorney for the defense, Alexandrov, rang out. First, he elucidated the depositions, and then he mercilessly disclosed the whole despotism of government power." [61]

The counsel based his plea in defense of Vera Zasulich on the tremendous impression produced on her by the unlawful order of Trepov to whip Bogolyubov, which she got to know from newspaper accounts. In order to expand on this impression Aleksandrov turned to a description of the defendant's former life.

> The years of youth are justly regarded as the best years of human life. The recollections and impressions of these years last for the rest of your life. The child is preparing himself for

---

[60] This episode is important because the Senate reversed the verdict of *not guilty* on ground of violation of Art. 576 by the court, giving a very peculiar interpretation to this provision. See Decision of the Senate of May 20, 1879, quoted by Koni, in his *Vospominaniya . . .* Supplement IX, p. 415.

[61] Elisabeth Naryshkin-Kurakin, *Under Three Tsars,* p. 55.

adult life. Life is seen from afar from its alluring side, pure, without dark shadows and spots. . . . This is the time of first love, of light-hearted days, merry hopes, unforgettable joy, the time of friendship, the time of all those dear, fleeting, elusive things which both mature matron and old granny alike enjoy recalling.

It is easy to imagine how Zasulich passed the best years of her life, what fun she had, what happiness she enjoyed during this precious time, what rosy dreams stirred her behind the prison wall and in the casemate of the Peter and Paul Fortress. She suffered complete isolation from everything and everyone behind the prison and fortress gates. For she did not see her mother, her relatives, her friends. No work . . . From time to time a book, which passed the prison censorship, reached her. She could take some steps in the cell, but could see nothing through the window. The squeak of opened and closed doors, the clank of rifles of guards being relieved and the monotonous music of the fortress clock were the only sounds which reached her. No human being, except the warder who brought her meals and the guard who looked from time to time through the door slot. Instead of friendship, love, close association with the world—only the consciousness that behind the wall, to the right and to the left, were fellow-sufferers, victims of an equally miserable fate.

Indeed, during these years of nascent sympathies, Zasulich forever created and strengthened in her soul one sympathy—a selfless love for everyone who, like herself, was forced to drag out the miserable existence of a political suspect. The political offender, whoever he might be, became a dear friend to her, the companion of her youth, the comrade in upbringing. The prison was her *alma mater*, which strengthened this friendship, this association.[62]

Then, after describing Zasulich's unhappy life in banishment under the supervision of the police, the counsel reverted to the punishment of Bogolyubov:

Fifteen years after the abolition of corporal punishment a political prisoner was subjected to the ignominious punishment of whipping, This circumstance could not have remained hidden from the public. It was discussed in St. Petersburg, notices appeared in newspapers. These notices gave the first impulse to Zasulich's thoughts. The short newspaper accounts of the punishment inflicted on Bogolyubov could not but have an overwhelming impression on Zasulich. A man to whom, by birth, upbringing and education, the rod was alien; a man who felt and understood all its infamous and disgraceful significance; a man who according to his frame of mind, convictions and feelings could not witness and endure the fulfillment of the infamous punish-

---

62 Koni, *Vospominaniya* . . . , pp. 160-166, *passim*.

ment upon another without shuddering—this man had to bear
on his own flesh the overpowering execution of this shameful
punishment. "What terrible torture," thought Zasulich, 'what
scornful profanation of everything which constitutes the most
essential values of an intellectual, and not only of an intellectual,
but of everyone to whom the sense of honor and human dignity
are not foreign. . . ."

Then Aleksandrov analysed the character of crimes against the
state:

> Attention should be paid to the typical moral features of
> crimes against the state. The nature of such crimes changes very
> often. What was considered a crime yesterday, becomes a glorious
> deed of civil valor today or tomorrow. A crime against the state
> is often the expression of a doctrine aiming at premature reforms,
> at propagation of something not yet grown to full maturity and
> for which the time is not yet ripe. . . .

> Zasulich reacted to the punishment inflicted on Bogolyubov
> with a feeling of deep, irreconcilable insult. Who was Bogolyubov
> to her? He was neither her relative, nor a friend, nor even an
> acquaintance; she had never known or seen him. But is it neces-
> sary to be a sister, a wife or a mistress in order to be indignant
> at the picture of a morally crushed man, in order to revolt against
> a disgraceful mockery of a defenseless human being?

> Bogolyubov was for Zasulich a political prisoner, and this
> word meant everything. A political prisoner was for her not an
> abstract notion, taken from books, known from hearsay, from
> court sessions, a notion which in an honest heart generates the
> feeling of pity, compassion and heartfelt sympathy. A political
> prisoner meant to Zasulich her own self, her bitter past, her own
> story, the story of irretrievably ruined years, the best and dearest
> in the life of every man who is not afflicted by a fate similar to
> that of Zasulich. A political prisoner was for Zasulich the bitter
> recollection of her own sufferings, of her terrible nervous excite-
> ment, constant apprehension, wearisome incertitude, everlasting
> thought: "What crime did I commit? What will happen to me?
> When will an end be put to all this?" A political prisoner was her
> own heart, and every rough contact with it produced a painful
> repercussion in her agitated nature.

Aleksandrov gave a dramatic description of the whipping as
Zasulich had mentally reconstructed it, according to information she
gathered upon arriving in St. Petersburg. When he said the words:
"Everything stood still in the anxious expectation of a moan, and this
moan was heard; it was not a moan of physical pain—it was the poign-
ant moan of a suffocated, humiliated, insulted, crushed man. . . ," passionate applause and bravos shook the hall, which was overcrowded
by a select audience.

Aleksandrov went on to picture Zasulich's feelings when she learns all the shocking details of the affair.

The fateful question confronted her: "Who will stand up for the insulted honor of a defenseless political convict? . . . Who will stand up for the fate of other wretches? . . . Where is the guarantee that such an abomination will not be repeated? . . . Bogolyubov has many companions of distress . . . must they live in fear of the latent possibility of being exposed to Bogolyubov's fate? . . ." Zasulich expected intercession on the part of the press, she expected that the question which tortured her would be raised there. But, mindful of the restrictions, the press remained silent. Zasulich also expected help from public opinion. However, public opinion did not crawl out of the seclusion of private studyrooms, intimate circles and conversations among friends. She expected, finally, a word of justice . . . but justice remained silent. Hopes remained hopes. But her gloomy thoughts and the anxiety of her heart did not cease. Again and again the picture of Bogolyubov and all the circumstances of the affair rose before her. It was not the clank of his chains which troubled her soul, but his shameful scars caused her cruel pain. . . And suddenly, an unexpected thought brightened her mind: 'Oh, I myself! . . . All is silent around Bogolyubov! A shout is needed. I have enough strength to utter such a shout! I shall utter it and force everybody to hear it!" Instant determination responded to this thought. . . . "If I commit a crime," Zasulich thought, "the silenced question about Bogolyubov's punishment will arise; my crime will provoke a public trial, and Russia, in the person of her people's representatives, the jury, will be compelled to pronounce a verdict not on me alone . . . and in the sight of Europe, this Europe which likes to call us a barbarian state, in which the attribute of the government is the knout. . . .." It was irrelevant to her goal whether the shot directed against a certain person would cause any harm. Zasulich did not want to inflict physical pain on General Trepov. To take his life was not her real aim. She wanted to appear in the dock in order to raise there the question of Bogoloyubov. . . . When she entered the house of the Governor of the City with the decision to solve the question which tortured her, she knew and understood that she was sacrificing everything . . . her liberty, the rest of her broken life, the little that was given her by a merciless destiny. And it is not to bargain over this or that extenuation of her guilt is she here today, gentlemen of the jury. She was and she remains the selfless slave of her idea, in the name of which she raised the bloody hand. She came in order to submit to you all the burden of her grieved soul, to release before you the mornful story of her life, to relate honestly and truly all that she had endured, thought and felt, what had moved her to commit a crime and what she expected from her action.

Gentlemen of the jury! It is not for the first time that a woman appears before the court of the people's conscience in this dock of crime and oppressive moral suffering. Women who have retaliated [for wrong done them] by killing their seducers have appeared here. Women who have steeped their hands in the blood of their lovers or their more fortunate rivals, have been here. These women left this place acquitted. These sentences were just, an echo of divine justice, which takes into consideration not only the external side of an action, but also its inner meaning— the real guilt of the accused. These women did bloody, summary justice, they fought for and avenged themselves. But for the first time there appears here a woman who had no personal interest in her crime, a woman who bound up her crime with the fight for an idea, for the sake of a man who was for her no more than a companion of distress. If these reasons for crime prove lighter on the scale of public justice, if she must be punished for the sake of general welfare, the triumph of justice and public safety— then let your chastizing justice take place! Indeed, she may leave this court condemned, but not disgraced, and one may only wish that circumstances which provoke such actions and generate such culprits should not be repeated.[63]

The jurors did not deliberate very long. When they re-entered the court hall, their foreman read the questions and started to read the answer of the jury. But when he pronounced "Not guilt. . . . ," he was unable to continue: "One who was not present," writes Koni, "could not imagine either the burst of sound, which covered the voice of the foreman or the movement which seized the hall like an electric current. Shouts of unrestrained joy, hysterical sobbing, terrific applause, stamping of feet, shouts of 'Bravo! Good boys! Vera, Verochka, Verochka'[64]—all this merged into a continuous noise, scream and howl. Many crossed themselves. In the upper rows, a section occupied by a lower-class public, people embraced one another; but even on the places behind the bench[65] zealous applause was heard. . .Somebody was especially active in the demonstration of his approval, just beside my ear. I turned my head—the Deputy of the Master General of the Ordnance, Count Barantsov, an old, stout man, red in the face, violently clapped his hands. When our eyes met, he stopped, disconcerted, but as soon as I looked away, he started his exercise again." [66]

As Elizabeth Naryshkin-Kurakin puts it: "The judges, jury, digni-

---

63 Koni, *Vospominaniya* . . . , p. 166-193, *passim.*
64 Diminutive of Vera.
65 Reserved for high dignitaries.
66 Koni, *Vospominaniya* . . . , p. 215-216.

taries and officials grown grey in the service, the whole public—everyone was carried away by the mood of the moment. One could not analyse it, but it swept over everyone, without exception, even the soberest of them, in that dramatic moment." [67]

Aleksandrov was carried on the shoulders of the crowd from the court to his house.[68]

In the field of the administration of justice the trial of Vera Zasulich had an important consequence: a further limitation of the competence of the jury.[69] The only political trial which the government took the chance of entrusting to the jury[70] ended with a defeat of the government. Indeed, the acquittal of Zasulich was a condemnation of the régime. The trial revealed the deep dissatisfaction of the people with the government and its methods. The great majority of the intelligentsia and even a part of the bureaucracy approved the verdict. It was felt that the verdict of the jury was a solemn public expression of indignation against administrative violence.

G. K. Gradovsky, a talented journalist, gave in the Golos his impression of the trial, which undoubtedly corresponded to the feelings of an overwhelming majority of the people. Gradovsky described the court hall filled with a "select public," glittering with "stars" [decorations] "pressed against one another as in the milky way," and near them the pale defendant. And Gradovsky had a hallucination: it seemed to him that not Zasulich, but he, and with him society as a whole, were on trial, and that the defense was delivering an accusatory speech which deprived them of any hope of acquittal. And when the word of acquittal resounded, muffled by the outburst of enthusiam, again it seemed to him that not Zasulich but he himself was being acquitted, that now everything would be all right after many failures and much distress. . .[71]

In the camp of the reactionaries, on the other hand, the verdict

67 Naryshkin-Kurakin, op. cit., p. 55.
68 Already the next day after her acquittal, Zasulich was sought by the police and would have been arrested if found. But she had fled abroad. In 1883 she took part in the activities of the group Osvobozhdeniye Truda (Liberation of Labor) and collaborated in the publications of this group. She was also a member of the editorial board of the Iskra (Spark) and Zarya (Dawn). After the splitting of the Russian Social Democratic Party into Mensheviks and Bolsheviks, she joined the Mensheviks. In 1917 she was a member of Plekhanov's group Yedinstvo (Unity) and an enemy of the October Revolution. She wrote on Voltaire and Rousseau and the history of the First International. She died in 1919.
69 See p. 80.
70 As said above political crimes (crimes against the state) were excluded from the competence of the jury already by the legislator of 1864.
71 G. K. Gradovsky. Itogi, p. 430-436, passim.

produced the effect of an exploding bomb. Prince V. P. Meschchersky wrote in his memoirs:

"The solemn acquittal of Vera Zasulich happened as in a nightmare. . . . Nobody could understand how such a frightful mockery of the highest servant of the Tsar and such an impudent triumph of faction could take place in the courtroom of an autocratic empire. The sad and fateful acquittal of Vera Zasulich showed, alas, too eloquently the disposition and mood of the contemporary society. I can say without exaggeration that there were very few of us in St. Petersburg at that time who were extremely shocked by this fearful act of violence against justice. We were an insignificant minority, and it must be said that up to the highest hierarchy, including the Senate and the State Council, the verdict of acquittal, which honored Vera Zasulich, was accepted by some with loud transports, by others with quiet approval and by almost everyone with sympathy. I remember how persons who later, under Alexander III, spoke about this acquittal with loud indignation, had quite forgotten that in 1878 they had joined those dignitaries who had dared to shout 'bravo' when they heard about the acquittal of Vera Zasulich, and lifted their glasses to the victory of justice, at home and in their clubs." [72]

The unexpected outcome of the trial was attributed by the government to the attitude of Koni, the presiding judge of the court, who permitted the discussion of the whipping. A. E. Perets, State Secretary at that time, noted in his diary: "Not less tactless was Koni, the President of the Court, who allowed the discussion of Trepov's behavior toward prisoners, which was shown in a very ugly light." [73]

And Elizabeth Naryshkin-Kurakin writes: "Society has been deeply impressed by the Zasulich Case. Many regarded and celebrated her as a second Charlotte Corday, and did not see the danger that lurked in the pardoning of a political murderer. Conservative circles, on the other hand, were indignant beyond measure, and their rage turned on Koni. Although such experienced judges as Chicherin, Dimitriev and Shamshon thoroughly approved of his tactics, the public opinion of the reactionary groups branded him mercilessly, and all those doors which had stood open to him hospitably before, were now suddenly closed." [74] And much later in the 20's of the present century, as a political exile in Germany, she entered into her memoirs: "I own to this day a letter from Anatole Fyodorovich Koni, in which he thanks me for my unchanged attitude toward him. . . .To this day,

---

[72] V. P. Meshchersky. *Moi vospominaniya*, II, 402-403.
[73] A. E. Perets, *Dnevnik*, p. 49.
[74] Naryshkin-Kurakin, *op. cit.*, p. 56.

there are narrow and superficial minds who claim that Koni acutally let loose the revolution and that all the later catastrophies would not have happened if Vera Zasulich had not been pardoned." [75]

Count Palen, the Minister of Justice, asked Koni to resign from judicial service, but Koni refused and could not be dismissed because of the tenure of judges introduced by the Reform of 1864. However, he had to abandon his activity as judge in criminal cases and accept the presidency of the civil division of the *Sudebnaya Palata*.

Describing Koni's attitude in the Zasulich Case, O. O. Gruzenberg writes: "His summing up for the jury was and remains a masterpiece of this most difficult kind of juridical work, surpassed by no one. . .Koni has broken his judicial career because as President of the Court he carefully treated the interest of the defendant and tried to recreate before the court the conditions of life which brought her into conflict with the law." And about the case itself Gruzenberg observed: "The only political case in Russia tried by the jury ended with an acquittal scandalous for the government. Koni granted the defense the possibility of extending limits of judicial investigation and putting into the limelight the question of the lack of rights of political prisoners, of lack of rights which alone can explain the cruel mockery of the political prisoner Bogolyubov ordered by General Trepov." [76]

Koni was never forgiven for the case of Vera Zasulich. When in 1885, he was named as a candidate for the position of Chief Prosecutor at the Criminal Department of Cassation of the Senate. K. P. Pobedonostsev wrote to Alexander III: "One hears from all sides that the present President of the Civil Division of the *Sudebnaya Palata*, Anatoly Koni, will be appointed Chief Prosecutor of the Criminal Department of Cassation of the Senate. This appointment would produce a very unpleasant impression because of the case of Vera Zasulich, in which, you remember, Koni was President at the trial and displayed utter weakness. . ." [77] However, Koni's exceptional talents made his services so valuable that they could not be dispensed with. In an audience on the occasion of this appointment, the Tsar told him: "I have appointed you to such an important and responsible position because of the assurance of the Minister of Justice about your outstanding qualifications for this position. I hope that your further services will be successful and will make me forget the painful impres-

75 *Ibid.*
76 Gruzenberg, *Vchera,* pp. 198-199, *passim.*
77 K. P. *Pobedonostsev i ego korrespondenty.* II, 497.

sion produced on me by your activity in a certain case known to you." [78]

Reactionary circles thought that the acquittal of Vera Zasulich would stimulate terroristic actions. Perets wrote in 1881: "The late Tsar understood very well all the mistakes which were committed by the Minister of Justice in this miserable case, which was a signal for further attempts on the part of socialists. When shortly after this case, he dismissed the Minister of Justice, Count Palen, the Tsar said to Grand Duke Konstantin Nikolaevich that Palen was discharged because of the negligent handling of the Zasulich Case." [79]

3. Trial of the Murderers of Alexander II.

On March 1, 1881, Alexander II was assassinated. Six persons were indicted; Nicholai Rysakov, Timofei Mikhailov, Gesya Gelfman, Nicholai Kibal'chich, Sof'ya Perovskaya and Andrei Zhelyabov. The defendants, except Zhelyabov, who defended himself personally, had five counsels: Unkovsky, Khartulari, Gerke 1st, Gerard and Kedrin, all appointed by the court. The court,—a special bench of the Senate with class representatives—began its session on March 26, 1881.

The defense in this trial was a very difficult task, since the horrible crime was committed against the person of the Great Reformer. Unkovsky, Rysakov's counsel said: "Is it necessary to speak about the difficulties which the defense has to overcome in this case. One is still under the impression of the event of March 1st. . . I understand very well that many think a defense completely impossible in this case. Indeed, such thought may enter one's mind in the present case. However, the duties of counsel appointed by the court are sacred. We are bound to fulfill this duty because the great creator of the Judicial Reform, on the basis of which this trial is taking place, said in the law promulgated by him that no one may be accused of crimes otherwise than on the basis of these statutes, according to which the defense is on an equal footing with the prosecution in the administration of justice. It is self-understood that I am not defending the crime which has been committed. I am defending only the person who committed it. . . The counsel who gets to know the accused privately may find in him the characteristic features which explain the committed crime, as mean as it may be, more easily [than the prosecutor]. . . I do not speak about the horror of the committed crime, but I think that we can by no means convert this case into an act of vengeance. . .I think

---

[78] Koni, *Vospominaniya*. . ., Footnote 236 on p. 554.
[79] Perets, *op. cit.*, pp. 49-50.

that the accused must enjoy all the guarantees which have been established by the late Emperor. That is why I consider it my duty to present everything which may be favorable to the accused Rysakov." [80]

Gerard, the counsel of the accused Kibal'chich, began his speech by pointing out that even those people who are in the habit of analyzing events seriously and searching for their causes cannot react as usual in this case of a monstrous crime against the Emperor. They see only the horrible fact of the murder of the Emperor and are unable to look into the past or future of it . . . "But you, the judges, you must be free of every passion; the court cannot act under the impact of passion; it cannot judge the fact only; it must also consider the causes. In judging the accused, the court must necessarily enter deeply into the conditions which brought him from the path of legality to the [path of] crime. And the graver the crime, the longer the way from legality to the committed crime, the more strictly must you fulfill this duty." [81] Then Gerard gives a picture of what his client experienced as a political suspect at the age of 17, how he was persecuted by the police which brought out an indictment against him and put him in jail, where he remained for almost three years before his first political trial took place. In this trial no evidence could be brought against Kibal'chich and he was condemned to only one month in jail, which was equivalent to an acquittal in a political trial. Thus, Kibal'chich remained in jail for three years on account of an action which even in the opinion of the special bench of the Senate did not deserve more than one month of confinement. "Then," Gerard continued, "in August 1878, General Mezentsev was killed in St. Petersburg. One of the first administrative measures was the eviction from St. Petersburg of all persons who ever had been indicted for political offenses, whether or not they had been found guilty by the court . . . Kibal'chich was also subjected to this measure. I will not speak about the injustice of this measure, since I think that it has already been condemned . . . " Here Gerard was stopped by the President of the Court. " . . . but I will only point out the practical uselessness of the measure . . . ; stopped again, he continued: "I would like only to say that such measures almost never affect those who are really energetic and ready for an active fight against the government. The way to the underground is open to them, and it is precisely the underground conditions which have brought Kibal'chich into the dock, where you see him now. Having followed the previous political trials and taken part

---

[80] *Protsess 1-go marta 1881 goda,* p. 192.
[81] *Ibid.,* p. 207-208.

in some of them as a counsel, I tried to understand how such a phenomenon [a terroristic party] could have originated in Russia, and I
came to the conclusion that measures which were taken against political offenders by the administration have greatly contributed to it
. . . . Look at the previous political trial of the 193 accused, and you
will see that more than 1000 persons were involved in this case, as
suspects of political crimes . . . " Here Gerard was energetically called
to order by the President. Then he continued: " . . . I ask you to
consider the trial of the 193 accused. That trial will give you much
material for the comprehension of the causes which brought about a
terroristic party in Russia . . . " [82]
All the six accused were condemned to death.

4. *The Sazonov Case*

On July 15, 1904, the Minister of the Interior, V. K. Pleve, was
assassinated in St. Petersburg. He was killed by a bomb thrown into
his carriage by Yegor Sazonov, who executed a death sentence pronounced by the "Combat Detachment of the Social Revolutionary
Party." Sazonov was tried by the St. Petersburg *Sudebnaya Palata* on
November 10, 1904, behind closed doors. He was indicted under the
provisions of Art. 100 and Art. 102 (Parts 1 and II) of the new Criminal Code, as well as Art. 13 (Part II) and Art. 1453 of the old Criminal Code. As stated above, a part of the new Criminal Code, confirmed by the Emperor on March 22, 1903, was introduced in June
1904. It contained provisions, such as the aforementioned, concerning
crimes against the state which were punishable by death. Article 1453
of the old Criminal Code provided forced labor for from 15 to 20
years, or for life, as the penalty for murder.

N. P. Karabchevsky, Sazonov's counsel, tried first of all to spare
his client the death penalty by proving, with the help of a juridical
analysis, that the application of the articles of the New Criminal
Code was unlawful in this case. In this he succeeded, and Sazonov was
condemned to forced labor for life.[83]

In his pleading, Karabchevsky said: " . . . It was pure accident
that Minister Pleve was killed precisely by a Social Revolutionary. He
could have been killed by any fanatic in the stifling political atmosphere in which the whole of Russian society lived at that time . . . "
Interrupted by the President, Karabchevsky then continued: "The

---

[82] *Ibid.*, pp. 210-212, *passim.*
[83] Sazonov committed suicide on Nov. 28, 1910, in the Zorentuisky Forced
Labor Jail in Siberia (Goldman, *op. cit.*, p. 78) .

prosecutor exclaimed with ironical indignation: 'they [the Social Revolutionaries] preach things unheard of.' Indeed, we Russian citizens seldom hear appeals on behalf of what is considered the final ideal by the Socialist Party: the reconstruction of society on principles of broad freedom, collective labor, complete equality and sincere brotherhood, in one word—on principles of 'general happiness.' For us it is really something unheard of, since any Social-Democratic propaganda, even if it is peaceful, is prohibited in our country. If the methods to which the Party sometimes is forced to resort sicken our moral feelings, the aims none the less remain pure. Who would not desire heaven on sinful earth, who would not adhere to such an ideal if it could be realized at once, in one brotherly embrace. What stormy happiness would overcome our hearts . . . Are we not so excited by the words equality, freedom and brotherhood because we feel in them an imperious appeal on behalf of this common happiness, which is still far ahead of us but which is always striven for, and a belief, . . . '

President: "I ask you to desist. Return to the case."

Karabchevsky: ". . . You cannot deny his [Sazonov's] selfless bravery. He knew that the effect of the bomb is absolutely destructive within a range of 15-20 paces, and he stood just eight paces from the place of the explosion. If, stunned and covered with wounds, he still survived, this was not his will and desire. I will be his true spokesman if I say: against his will and desire. In taking the life of another man, a life which he considered dangerous and disastrous for his fatherland . . . "

President: "I ask you not to use such expressions."

Karabchevsky: " . . . full of strength, he gave away for it his young life, in payment for his gallant determination. What else, which other, more precious, equivalent could be offered as testimony of all the sincerity and disinterestedness of the motives which prompted him? . . . Although it is generally hard to excuse a murder, there are many facts similar to the one under consideration which found an historical explanation a long time ago. No one shudders any more at the names of William Tell or Charlotte Corday, and everyone understands very well why their names are surrounded by the sorrowful halo of martyrdom . . . " [84]

Reverting to Sazonov's biography Karabchesky repeated the assertion made years ago by Alexandrov concerning Vera Zasulich, and by Gerard with regard to Kibal'chich, to the effect that police measures drive the youth into the camp of the terrorists. "It is a sad phe-

---

[84] N. P. Karabchevsky. Delo Sazonova, pp. 16, 19, 20, 21, passim.

nomenon," he said, "that we have to look for biographical information about our young people exclusively in the files of the Department of Police. This is a sign of our time which must be taken into consideration when we evaluate the motives which inspire these young people to take over the burden of this or that terroristic action. Such is the story, beginning with Vera Zasulich. Always the same story. Worn out, morally and physically, by the 'illegal' life, with nerves shattered by perpetual 'inquiries,' searches and persecutions for their convictions and views, they finally go over to the camp of the 'active' revolutionaries and immolate their young lives as a purifying sacrifice to atone for the lawlessness of the administration, the inertia of society and . . ."

President: "We did not investigate that. I forbid you [to do so]!"

The last part of the pleading is dedicated to a characterization of Pleve. "After the assassination of Minister Sipyagin,[85] the vacant post was occupied by Pleve. Balmashev was hanged. Deathly silence and apparent quiet reigned over society. The press, the only mouthpiece of the state of the public mind, maintained a forced silence or fawned and cringed before the powerful minister . . . "

President: "I shall forbid you to speak if you will again allow yourself to use such expressions."

Karabchevsky: "The press unfortunately was silent."

President: "Didn't I stop you? (Pause). Continue."

Karabchevsky: "In the free foreign press, of course, no words were spared in the description of the gloomy figure of the late statesman, the former leader of Russian internal policy . . . All the horror which overtook Russia in the last years was attributed to him. It was he who insisted on the hanging of Balmashev. He jailed and banished thousands of innocent people. He flogged and shot peasants and workers. He scoffed at the intelligentsia, he instigated mass massacres of Jews in Kishenev and Gomel, he choked Finland, he oppressed the Poles, he exercised his influence to bring about the war with Japan in which so much blood has already been shed and will continue to be shed in the future . . . Sazonov's imagination pictured Pleve as a fatal, sinister, nightmarish figure, pressing its imperious knee against the chest of the fatherland and mercilessly choking it. It seemed to Sazonov that this monster can be annihilated only by another monster —death. And grasping with trembling hands the bomb which was destined for Pleve, Sazonov believed, piously believed, that it was filled

---

[85] Sipyagin was assassinated on April 2, 1902 by the student Stepan Valer'yanovich Balmashev, who was tried on April 26, 1902 by the St. Petersburg Circuit Court-Martial. His counsel was V. O. Lyustikh.

not so much with dynamite and fulminate of mercury as with the tears, sorrow and calamity of the people. And when its splinters burst and scattered in all directions, it seemed to him that he heard how the chains which bind the Russian people are jangling and breaking to pieces . . . "

President: "I forbid you! You do not submit. I shall be obliged to remove you!"

Karabchevsky: "So thought Sazonov . . . I finish . . . That is why, when he regained consciousness, he shouted: 'Long live liberty!' " [86]

5. *The Lieutenant Pirogov Case*

The following case shows how much depended upon the talent, ability and erudition of the counsel and what important services a skillful and brilliant lawyer could render to his client, and, thus, to society.

In this case one letter—*i*—which in Russian means *and* or *also*, saved the life of Lieutenant Pirogov.

On a gloomy Petersburg December morning in 1908, a colleague called on O. O. Gruzenberg and told him that he had just received a telegram from Vladivostok containing a power of attorney to represent a certain Lieutenant Pirogov before the Main Court-Martial. Pirogov had been sentenced to death by the Circuit Court-Martial in Vladivostok, and his appeal of cassation from the sentence was pending at the Main Court-Martial. The case had to be pleaded on the same morning, and Gruzenberg's colleague had not a single paper on the case in his hands. He did not dare to assume the responsibility of defense under such circumstances, and asked Gruzenberg to plead in his place; he thought that the defense would be in better hands than his, if Gruzenberg agreed to plead.[87] Gruzenberg left at once for the court.

Gruzenberg relates in his memoirs about his thoughts on the way to the court, before the battle for the life of his client: how the fighting spirit of the defense attorney took possession of him—this spirit full of pain and ineffable happiness; and he asked himself: how did it happen that he, no longer a young lawyer, with the reputation of a lawyer especially skilled in cassation procedure, joined the camp of political defense attorneys? What brought him there? Political pas-

---

[86] *Ibid.*, p. 25-27.
[87] O. O. Gruzenberg was particularly known for his ability in cassation proceedings.

sions? No, he was always far fom politics. Ambition? Even less: ambitious people go through politics to fame, but never *vice-versa.*

When on his way he passed the edifice of the Circuit Court-Martial, again a question arose in his mind: why, when he thought about this building in which he knew every corner, every turn of the corridors, only one room appeared to him: a tiny room, without windows, completely dark, into which the defendants were brought during court recesses. The defense attorneys were allowed, with special permission of the president of the court, to show relatives of the accused into this room for a few minutes. The relatives and the accused could not see one another, but all the more tender was the music of the voices, all the more delicate the hand which stroked the hair, the face, the clothes. "I frequently thought," writes Gruzenberg, "that vengeance will be wreaked for this room when the days of the great wrath come . . . "

When Gruzenberg arrived at the Main Court-Martial he heard that the records were not yet there and that the reporting judge would bring them directly to the session. Thus faded the last hope of becoming acquainted with the records before the session. The only thing which remained to be done was to listen attentively to the report in the session and then to plead without any preparation.

The judge entrusted with the report started out, reading rapidly: "The case of the Nikol'sko-Ussuriisk Military Organization. By decision of the Priamursk Circuit Court-Martial, the former Lieutenant of the Turkestan Strelkovy Regiment, Vyacheslav Pirogov, and also the civilians Kastorsky, Teben'kova and Ivanov, are found guilty of having organized a secret society in Nikol'sko-Ussuriisk which aimed at the overthrow of the existing regime, the introduction of the republican form of government and the assassination of the reigning Emperor if necessary . . . The Court has sentenced: Pirogov to the death penalty by hanging, the others to various terms of forced labor . . . All the defendants have appealed for cassation . . . . Pirogov complains that . . . "

This was the decisive moment. Gruzenberg heard for the first time the grounds of cassation and had to decide on the spot, in a few seconds, which grounds ought to be maintained in the pleading. He concentrated all his power of attention on the words which were to follow.

The judge reported all the reasons in support of cassation, one after the other: "The first . . ." ("Nonsense," thinks Gruzenberg.) "The second . . . " ("Nonsense too.") "The third . . . " ("Same.") "The fourth: Pirogov complains that no civil counsel had been appointed for his defense as he had asked" ("This objection is childish," thinks Gruzenberg. "Since Pirogov is accused of a military offence under Articles 112 and 110 of the Military Criminal Code, he is not entitled to a civilian defense attorney.") "With regard to Pirogov's complaint concerning his right to select a counsel," the reporting judge continued, "the conclusions of the indictment are decisive: Ivanov, Kastorsky and Teben'kova have been indicted according to Part 3 of Article 102 of the new Criminal Code and Pirogov also [in Russian: *i*] according to Art. 110, 112 of Book XXII of the Military Code."

The report was finished. The President called on the defense.

"I had the floor . . . but I could not begin," writes Gruzenberg. "What was it? Perhaps I didn't hear correctly. Was I dreaming? Did not the reporting judge pronounce the conjunction '*i*' before citing the military provision? Certainly, I was dreaming. It was impossible that so many people saw the records before me and nobody noticed the main thing . . . " With some inflection of astonishment in his voice, the President called on the defense for the second time.

I have to make up my mind, thought Gruzenberg, and said: "Mister President, a man's life is at stake. Forgive my somewhat unusual demand: could not the conclusions of the indictment be read once more?"

The reporting judge read the conclusions for the second time, and Gruzenberg heard that he had not been mistaken.

"A wave of happiness mounts, seethes, begins to boil . . . " writes Gruzenberg. "The small hall with low vaults is full of blinding sunlight in spite of the late hours of a December day. Everything in me sings: Pirogov is saved, saved . . . "

Indeed, the magic letter *i* produced the wonder. Since Pirogov had been indicted under the Military *and* the general Criminal Codes, he had the right to have a counsel according to his choice.

"No speech is necessary," said Gruzenberg, "The most effective pleading for the defendant consists of one conjunction, more accurately of one letter . . . Pirogov was threatened with death and at the same time deprived of his legal right to select his counsel."

The court retired for deliberation. During the recess, a member of the chancellery of the court said to Gruzenberg: "Do you know against whom you fought in this case? Against a marginal note by the Tsar!" Thereupon he revealed to Gruzenberg the contents of the records which the latter had not seen.

Pirogov, an excellent officer, fought bravely in the Russo-Japanese War. Deeply impressed by the defeat of the Russian Army and the senseless loss of thousands of Russian officers and soldiers in the dishonorably initiated and carelessly conducted war, Pirogov threw himself into the revolutionary movement with all the energy of a passionate and active nature. Soon he was arrested, tried and sentenced to death before a firing squad. His appeal for cassation of the sentence was barred by the Commander of the Armed Forces of the Priamursky Military District. However, he commuted the death penalty to forced labor for life in consideration of Pirogov's services in battle and personal qualities.

In accordance with the law, the Commander reported the commutation to the Minister of War. The Minister of War submitted the report to the Tsar, who wrote in the margin: *"Naprasno"* (Too bad)."

When this expression of disapproval from the top became known to the Military Prosecutor of the Priamursk Court-Martial, a new indictment was formulated against Pirogov in the same court. He was again tried and sentenced to death. This time the Commander did not dare to exercise his right of commutation, but agreed to the appeal for cassation.

These were the circumstances which preceded the trial in the Main Court-Martial described above, and which were unknown to the counsel during the trial.

After a two-hour deliberation, the Main Court-Martial reversed the sentence because of the denial of Pirogov's request to be allowed to select a defense attorney, to which he was entitled, and remanded the case to the Priamursk Court-Martial for a new trial. Pirogov's life was saved—but seemingly for a short time only.

On July 19, 1909, Gruzenberg had to defend a second appeal in cassation after the Priamursk Court-Martial had sentenced Pirogov to death for a third time.

This time Gruzenberg had studied the records. What he had not known at the time of his first pleading now became clear to him. The second indictment was unlawful, since it was based on the same crime as the first one. It violated the rule *ne bis in idem.*

Gruzenberg's pleading[88] was on strictly juridical grounds. The court deliberated for several hours and not only reversed the sentence but quashed the indictment. Pirogov's life was definitely saved.[89]

---

88 See *Pravo*, 1909, no. 28.
89 Pirogov was liberated by the Revolution of February 1917.

6. The Case of Workers Accused of Robbery of Arms

Another example which clearly shows what a talented counsel was able to achieve in Tsarist Russia is the case related by V. Bernstam, a noted trial lawyer. The main actor is again Gruzenberg. This is what Bernstam writes:

"Once we [Bernstam and Gruzenberg] pleaded in the main Court-Martial in St. Petersburg. The courtroom was empty. Even the workers, the defendants in the case, were not there. They remained in a province jail, and waited. . . . Present were the main Court-Martial Justices—grim-faced generals and old men who had seen life; the Assistant Chief Military Prosecutor, also an old man, a general; the secretary, a Councillor of State and the two of us . . . nobody else. Only walls—cold stone walls. . . . Four persons had been sentenced to death by a province court-martial. It was up to the Main Court-Martial to reject the appeal in cassation, and by some strokes of pen on paper to tighten definitively the loop around the neck of the defendants, at a distance, as by an electric knob." The case was as follows:

At a small railroad station, in the tempestuous days of December 1905, notice was spread that a freight car with arms had arrived. The crowd ran to the car and snatched away the arms. Four persons were noticed in the crowd—"maybe because they were taller than the others," remarks Bernstam,—and indicted according to Art. 279 of the Military Criminal Code for robbery. They were sentenced to death.

"When the reporting judge," Bernstam continues, "presented the case, it became clear that the question of life or death for those four persons accidentally picked up which alarmed me the most, did not in the least impress the court, and that the sentence would be upheld. . . . The prosecutor was also indifferent. 'It is evident,' he said, 'that the provisions of Article 279 must be applied,' and sat down.

"Then Gruzenberg began to speak. He began to argue passionately against the indictment on the robbery count. 'Where is robbery?' he exclaimed. The insurgent people did not take the arms for the purpose of gain or profit, not to appropriate them! They took them in order to deprive the police of them and to defend themselves. . . . The trial court did not even raise the question as to why the workers took the arms. This question, which is precisely the main one, did not interest the court. There is no robbery without appropriation or attempt at appropriation! There is no death penalty for insurrection, and therefore the lovers of the scaffold need [the accusation of] robbery. Let the prosecutor, this eye of the law, give us an answer: where is the law in all this? The indictment is juridical nonsense! If it is necessary to hang people, you cannot hang them ignorantly. Why, then, use courts and not simply torture chambers? Open them!' And he dashed around like an infuriated lion, strong and powerful in his great indignation. It seemed that he forgot where he was, that he was the strict judge and they [the justices] the accused. The wave of protest grasped him, and his speech grew in power and sharpness." [90]

The sentence was reversed.

7. The case of the Dolbenkovo Peasants

This case is typical of the kind of trials which occurred in the period 1902-1914. The counsel of the accused, V. A. Maklakov, delivered in this trial an inspired speech remarkable not only for the force of expression, but also for the accusations which he directed, through the judges, against the ruling class and for his almost prophetic words concerning the chaos into which Russia will be plunged as a result of its policy.

The peasants of Dolbenkovo Village were very poor, having about three *desyatinas* of land for every adult person. The land was not very fertile. Their village was surrounded by the huge estate of the Grand Duke Sergei Aleksandrovich, uncle of the Tsar. The peasants were completely dependent economically on the estate of the Grand Duke, from whom they had to lease land, buy grain and other agricultural products, and work under conditions very onerous to them. This resulted in tense relations between the peasants and the administration of the estate, which became even worse due to a system of fines used by Filat'yev, the supervisor of the estate, against the peasants for every violation of the interests of the estate, even very light ones.

A crowd of about 70 peasants came to the doors of the estate office on the evening of February 27, 1905 and requested the abolition of fines, dismissal of several employees, permission to drive cattle through the estate and lowering of the price of wheat, which the peasants had to buy from the Grand Duke. Filat'yev, scared, agreed to all these demands and also promised to give the peasants two buckets of vodka. [91]

On the next morning, peasants moved in a huge crowd toward the estate. On their way they met Filat'yev. In the beginning, the

---

[90] V. Bernstam, *V ogne zashchity,* pp. 279 ff, *passim.*
[91] One bucket—21 pints.

crowd was in a peaceful mood. Filat'yev chatted with the peasants. The promised vodka was brought and consumed. Filat'yev drank to the peasants' health, to steady peace and good-neighbor relations. But then the drunken peasants looted the store of the leaseholder Orlov, who rented a plot of land on the Grand Duke's estate which the peasants had wanted to buy at any price but did not get. Then they sacked the office of the estate, the apartment of the supervisor and the liquor distillery. Filat'yev was slightly beaten.

Sixty-three persons were indicted on counts of riot and some of them also for arson. The trial took place in the city of Dmitrovsk, Province of Orel, before the visiting assizes of the Moscow *Sudebnaya Palata,* with class representatives. The counsel of the accused, V. A. Maklakov, depicted the desperate situation of the Dolbenkovo peasants, which brought them into the dock, in the following words:

> This is not an ordinary criminal affair, but a page of history. No matter how much we close our eyes and plug up our ears, we know that the peace was not broken in this estate alone. We know that three judicial chambers met in Orel Province alone to try the cases of breach of peace, and that there is a wide flood of similar and much more terrible events outside of this province.
> ... That is why we may regard these peasants otherwise than as accused individuals who are answerable to their judges for their individual guilt. They are only a small part of a large whole; they are an unsubmissive part of society, which is now giving its reply to the state power which you represent. And as long as you, i.e., this state power, find that they are responsible for everything, that *they* deserve to be made the object of revenge for what is happening, allow me to address you, not as judges, but as that [state] power, and to reply to you briefly as such.
> ... There are two sides to this crime: the deeds themselves are criminal—damage, robbery, violence . . . but the *motive* is also a criminal one from the standpoint of law: it is enmity growing out of economic relations.
> That is what you accuse them of.
> But who is guilty of all that?
> Their deeds were criminal—there can be no two opinions on the matter. It would have been better, of course, if the 'peaceful demonstration' of which Filat'yev told us had ended differently. It would have been better, more typical, more usual if the peasants, having stated their wishes, had peacefully gone home; if, while they were awaiting, at their homes, the fulfillment of the promises made to them, military forces had burst in upon them, had dragged them from their homes, had picked out the instigators, used extreme measures on them and terrorized the rest. Had the 'insurrection' been suppressed in this manner, the misdeed would have been punished and good would have prevailed.

It would, perhaps, have been better. But Filat'yev himself saw to it that this should not happen.

'They have sown the wind and they shall reap the whirlwind.' He did not appease the feelings of the peasants, but excited them. After the pogrom had started with Orlov's house, there was no restraint, no limit any longer. 'A Russian riot started—senseless and merciless.'[92] It is useless to look for a plan, for leaders, for instigators. An infuriated, half-drunken mob destroyed everything it could, beat everyone who crossed its path. Its actions were senseless, wild and rude. But could it have been otherwise? What could have been expected from this mob? Indeed these people are always rude—rude in their kindness, rude in their jokes, rude in their arguments; could they have been different in their spite and anger? Can they be blamed for it?

Let history blame them when it describes our sad time. Let a foreigner blame them, censuring our temper and customs. Let them blame them, if they desire; but if you, representatives of the state power, start to blame them, I shall ask: you, who are blaming them, what did you do to cure them of rudeness? The state has cared for many things: that they (the peasants) should be submissive, devoted to the regime, humble before their superiors, meek before their chiefs. But did it seek to soften their customs, to drive the savagery out of them and to inspire them with disgust for rudeness? When and how was a cure applied for these purposes? Maybe when the peasants were threatened with rods during the investigation in the 'volost.'[93] Maybe when the Cossacks' whips were cracking in the streets without any discrimination, without sparing either children, as it happened in Kursk, or clergymen, as in the Caucasus. Our customs are cruel, but they are cruel both at the top and at the bottom. We reap in cruelty what we have diligently sown ourselves. Punish them, therefore, if you can, because they have finally revolted, because they have lost patience. Be aware that every mob, when worked up into a fit of temper, inevitably would have done the same. It is bitter mockery on the part of the state power to blame them for rudeness. They are such as you have yourselves made them, and you have as little right to blame the peasants for rudeness as to blame, for illiteracy, the people whom you deprive of the possibility of getting an education. . . .

Learn from this example what is awaiting us, but in the name of elementary justice, do not make them responsible for it. Quoting provisions of the law, Maklakov proves that Filat'yev and the administration of the estate had no right to impose fines. The *zemsky nachal'nik,* who had to protect the peasants, testified in court that he did not know about the fines, otherwise he would have stopped the unlawful practice.

---

[92] A quotation from Pushkin's *Kapitanskaya dochka* (The Captain's Daughter).
[93] Peasant district administration.

Maklakov said:

No, law is not honored in Russia! Before the eyes of everyone, openly, law is violated, lawlessness flourishes, and this embarrasses nobody, no one thinks about it. And now that you, the
representatives of the state power, came here to punish these persons, I have the right to ask you: you came when they violated
the law, but where were you when the law was being violated
with regard to them? You accuse them of having violated the
law, but why were you silent when it was violated by Filat'yev?
Did you not yourselves tolerate the conditions for the consequences of which you are going to punish them?

We know that the law protected their rights. They suffered
only because the law was violated. But they were not aware of
this and thought that the law itself allows the oppression under
which they suffocated. . . . They thought that the law is against
them, that the administration is against them and for Filat'yev.
Then, before these helpless people, in their ignorant minds, the
fateful question arose in all its horror: 'What can be done if
truth is helpless? What can be done if truth is undoubtedly on
our side but law is against us, when the administration protects
injustice? What can be done then? Should we submit?' But to
submit to injustice means to disavow justice. A people who would
promote this to a system, would perish. A state which would
demand this of a people, would perish. And if they did not want
to submit, it meant that they had to fight against that which
embodied the injustice, to fight the administration which was a
manifestation of it. They did it. Their fight was unreasonable,
their means were absurd. I condemn with all my heart what they
did. But in condemning their actions, I would like to ask you
calmly, with the sad conviction that such a question cannot be
resolved by words: what methods of struggle would you have
suggested to them instead of those they used?

As judges you will condemn [the peasants] according to the
Criminal Code. But as representatives of the state power, try to
be just. You did not defend them when they were unlawfully
ruined in their village; you closed to them the ways and means
for a legal defense of their interests; you systematically cultivated
rudeness in them. The results are known to you. You must
acknowledge that if they are guilty, we are all guilty before
them. . . .[94]

The *Palata* acquitted 18 of the 63 accused and submitted a petition to the Tsar asking that the condemned should not be deprived
of rights and not subjected to police supervision and other measures
hindering their free movement. The Tsar granted the request.

---

[94] V. A. Maklakov. *Rechi*, pp. 36-41, *passim*.

8. The Trial of the Signers of the Viborg Manifesto

After the dissolution of the First Duma on July 8, 1906, a group of members of the Duma went to Viborg, Finland and as a protest against the dissolution, signed an appeal "To the People from the People's Representatives." In this appeal they called on the people not to pay taxes and not to obey military conscription until the Duma convoked again.

The signers of the appeal were arrested and tried by the St. Petersburg *Sudebnaya Palata* with class representatives from the 1st to the 18th of December, 1907.

The 169 accused had more than 100 counsels. Only three of them pleaded in court: Teslenko, Pergament and Maklakov. The defense denounced the competence of the St. Petersburg *Palata,* since the appeal was signed in Finland and thus the Finnish courts were competent.

The accused were indicted according to Article 129 of the new Criminal Code, which provided for the loss of political rights, so that the defendants, if convicted, would not be eligible to the next Dumas.

The counsels argued that Article 129 could not be applied to the signers of the appeal, since it punishes only those who *disseminate* criminal appeals.

Punishment of signers of criminal appeals was provided by Article 132 of the same Code, but this fact was disregarded in the indictment, because this punishment was not combined with the loss of franchise.

Since no evidence of spreading of the appeal by the signers had been produced in the preliminary investigation, the count of the indictment setting forth a violation of Article 129 was unlawful. To make it possible to use Article 129, the act of accusation asserted that the signing of a criminal appeal involves complicity in the dissemination of the appeal as well.

The group of 169 members of the Duma, with the President of the Duma, Muromtsev, at their head, was the elite of the Russian intelligentsia of that time. Their aim was to start a political protest against the dissolution of the Duma, which they deemed unlawful. They reserved for themselves the right to speak in court (sixteen of them pleaded) to the Russian people. The counsels were confined to the juridical aspects of the case.

Maklakov's speech, although strictly juridical, produced a tremendous impression on his listeners. The excerpt from his speech which we reproduce below will not, perhaps, have the same effect upon the American reader. Perhaps his speech is of the kind "which must be heard" in order to be appreciated for its real value, as Aldanov writes in his Introduction to *Speeches* by Maklakov, published on the occasion of Maklakov's eightieth birthday in 1949.[95]

Maklakov said: "If we look upon the Viborg Manifesto from the historical or political point of view, this Manifesto becomes an inexhaustible theme for discussion and thought. But if we look upon it from the point of view of . . . the practical jurist, who is concerned exclusively with the correct application of the law, this entire case becomes extremely simple."[96]

Maklakov pointed out that the government's handling over of this case to an ordinary court, which serves the law and not the changing types of government, was something unexpected, and that many regarded it as something fortunate.

> . . . the handling over of the case to an ordinary court seemed to be a confirmation of those official announcements in which the government declared that it had irrevocably embarked on the path of law and legality. Recourse to a court from which the government may expect sentences and not services (as once the French courts were proudly saying), to a court for which there is no distinction between those who are invested with power and those who are subjected to it—recourse to such a court appeared to be a triumph of justice, no matter how narrow and formal the problem presented to the court for solution.
>
> But the brighter the [original] hopes, the sadder is the end toward which we are now coming. Indeed, the accusation into which this recourse to the court has degenerated does not call forth the former feeling in us. There is not even a mention of legality in that accusation.[97]

Having shown very convincingly that it is incorrect and illegal to bring the action of the accused within the scope of Article 129 of the Criminal Code, as the prosecutor demanded, Maklakov asked the question:

> Why was such a manifest violation of criminal law necessary? I will not analyze why it was necessary. Here the sphere of guesses begins. But we know only too well what happened as a result. The result is that these people have already been deprived, for a year and a half, of that which is dearest to them—political rights; that they will be forever deprived of these rights, no mat-

---

[95] M. A. Aldanov, "K 80-letiiu Maklakova," in V. A. Maklakov, *Rechi*, p. 14.
[96] Maklakov, *Rechi*, p. 53.
[97] *Ibid.*, p. 54.

ter what the punishment inflicted upon them under that article is. Thus the criminal court becomes a weapon of political struggle, and its goal is to drive the opponents from the political arena....

And such a formulation of the indictment is not a triumph of justice. I shall call it a public calamity. And I am speaking at the moment, not as a person who holds the same political views as they, who treats them with the same respect now that they sit in the dock as when they sat on our [legislative] benches; not as a jurist for whom it is painful to see law lacerated before his own eyes. I am speaking as a man who has the weakness to think that the court is the highest organ of state power, just as law is the soul of statehood. The woe of the country resides, not in bad (or, as we usually say, imperfect) laws, but in the fact that lawlessness is allowed to go unpunished in our country. No matter how good the laws which are published, no matter how good the legislative apparatus which has now been set up, the laws will be of no benefit to Russia if there is no one to defend them. But the defense of law from any violation from above or below is the task of the court. One may be angry at the court for this, one may drag the court into the struggle between political parties, one may threaten the irremovability [of its judges], but as long as the court, even if (its judges) are very removable, is independent and is guarding the law—as long as this is true—the state lives on.

And when I see that the prosecutor—the guardian of the law—is publicly asking for its violation; when he is asking for the application of an article which cannot be applied—not for the sake of the triumph of justice, but for political purposes— then there arises that political temptation which leaves one desperate and impoten. And I am thinking at this moment, not of the fate of these men—no matter how close and dear they are to me. Your decision cannot do much for them, but I await from this decision an answer to the tormenting question with which many Russian people view this trial—does our law have its defenders?[98]

With regard to this pleading, Maklakov was accused of not having touched upon the main political question at stake: how could a court sit in judgment over the Duma and decide upon differences between the Duma and the government? This reproach was addressed to Maklakov by A. A. Goldenweiser in his review of Maklakov's *Speeches*. "In his speech," Goldenweiser writes, "Maklakov thought it unnecessary to touch upon questions of principle," and "there was something to say 'for history' at this historic trial." [99] Also Aldanov

---

98 *Ibid.*, pp. 56-59, *passim.*
99 A. A. Goldenweiser, "Perechityvaya rechi V. A. Maklakova," *Novoye Russkoye Slovo* (New York, Apr. 23, 1950), p. 8.

remarks that "such a speaker as Maklakov . . . could have made his speech historic. . . . But he did not want to speak in court as he spoke in the Duma. This is, however, only my supposition. Maybe, as a virtuoso, he allowed himself the luxury of shaking Russia by an analysis of Articles 129 and 132 without any '*Quousque tandem*' and 'Higher, higher build your walls. . . .' " [100, 101]

Maklakov was certainly capable of making a historic speech Perhaps he abstained from "historic words" for the simple reason that the defendants themselves limited their lawyers to arguments against the description given to their action by the indictment.[102] No reproach may be addressed to him on the ground that he disregarded an opportunity to pronounce "historic words." Indeed, he succeeded in "shaking Russia" with the analysis of Article 129 and 132. We have the narrative of the impression produced by Maklakov's speech from the pen of a co-defender in this trial, the distinguished lawyer M. L. Mandelstam, who wrote: "Maklakov's speech produced an especially strong impression. He gave only a juridical analysis of the case, but the peculiarity of his oratorical talent consisted just in the fact that he, as no one, could be inflamed by juridical pathos. Psychological experiences, scenes of everyday life did not touch Maklakov, did not affect his temperament, and, speaking of them, he rose only slightly above the level of a good orator. But as soon as a right had been violated, Maklakov became transfigured. His speech reached a great force and pathos, captured and subjugated his listeners. I had the occasion to plead together with the best Russian orators, but should I be asked which speech made the greatest impression on me, I would answer without hesitation: Maklakov's speech at the Viborg trial. When he finished, the entire hall was still, and then, after a moment, a thunder of applause broke the silence." [103]

This juridical pathos of Maklakov is well characterized by M. M. Karpovich in his review of Maklakov's *Speeches*. "What does Maklakov's enthusiasm consist of?" asks Karpovich. And he answers: "It is the enthusiasm of legality to the defense of which are dedicated most of his pleadings and political speeches. If F. I. Rodichev[104] was a champion of freedom, V. A. Maklakov may be called the knight of legality—but not of that self-sufficient legality for the sake of which

---

[100] Famous words by Spasovich in his pleading in the Abbess Mitrofaniya Case, mentioned on p. 174, Footnote 30.
[101] Aldanov, *op. cit.*, pp. 14-15.
[102] Maklakov, *Rechi*, p. 52.
[103] M. L. Mandelstam, *1905 god v politicheskikh protsessakh*, p. 357.
[104] F. I. Rodichev, a member of the Duma and famous orator.

one could become reconciled with the world's ruin, according to a well-known expression. For Maklakov, the living human being always occupied the first place, and the main enemy was always the omnipotent state." [105]

The sentence of the *Palata* was three months in jail and the loss of franchises.

9. *The Beilis Case*

The indictment and trial of Mendel Beilis is one of the darkest spots on the high reputation of the administration of justice in Russia in the period 1864-1917, and at the same time a glorious page in the annals of the Russian jury and the Russian bar. "For those who love justice it was one of the great trials of history . . ." said R. Gordon Wasson.[106]

It was the policy of reactionary circles and of the government to use the Jews as a lightning rod for the people's anger. One of the methods was the fostering of the old and absurd legend that Jews made use of Christian blood for ritual purposes. This legend originated in the first centuries of the Christian era, lived through the Middle Ages and was the cause of innumerable persecutions, tortures and executions of Jews. Abandoned in Western Europe as result of enlightenment and culture, the legend was revived in Russia every time when the occasion presented itself. After one such trial during the reign of Alexander I, the Emperor issued a special Ukase on March 6, 1817, in which he ordered that no trials should take place on the sole basis of the belief in ritual murders committed by Jews. However, this ukase remained without effect, and trials of such a kind took place again and again during the subsequent reigns. It must be emphasized that these trials in Russia never resulted in a definitive verdict of guilty against the accused. Still they served to excite hostile feelings among the masses against Jews.

But the Beilis Case was outrageous not only because the Jewish religion and the Jewish people were accused of a horrible crime, but also because of the pressure exercised by the Minister of Justice on judges, the investigating magistracy and jurors to produce a verdict of guilty against a clearly innocent man and screen the actual perpetrators of the murder. Beilis had to wait in jail for almost 2½ years for his trial, until the administration considered the case sufficiently prepared for the purpose it had to serve.

---

[105] M. M. Karpovich in *Novy Zhurnal*, XXIV (1950), p. 289.
[106] R. Gordon Wasson, *Toward a Russian Policy*, p. 14.

The case will not be described here *in extenso*, but just three short excerpts will be given from the speeches of some of the defense counsels, the most distinguished members of the Russian bar at that time.

In order to evaluate their speeches, it will be necessary, however, to become acquainted with the results of the preliminary official and private investigations and 33 days of court sessions, including the testimony of witnesses and learned experts. The trial is recorded in three volumes of a verbatim report. Here is a short narration of the circumstances of the case, the contents of some testimony and the data on pressure and abuses by the administration as reported by the lawyers A. Margolin and O. Gruzenberg. (The latter was the principal counsel of Beilis and had the opportunity of examining the secret records of the Police Department after the February Revolution of 1917.)

The corpse of Andrei Yushchinsky, a boy of 13, was discovered in a cavern on the outskirts of Kiev on March 20, 1911. He was the illegitimate son of Aleksandra Prikhod'ko, the wife of a worker. He left his home for school on the morning of March 12, did not reach the school and never returned home. According to the medical examination, the corpse had 17 wounds in the form of openings and pricks of oval and rectangular shape. Yuschchinsky had lost two-thirds of his blood. Since no traces of blood were found in the cavern, it was concluded that the corpse was brought in after the boy had been murdered elsewhere. In the pocket of his blouse there was a blood-soaked strip from a pillow slip.

In the beginning, the public did not pay any particular attention to the news of the murder in newspapers. The ministries of Justice and of the Interior, however, became deeply interested in the case at once. K. Lyadov, a high official, was sent with special instructions to Kiev by Minister of Justice Shcheglovitov. The preliminary investigation was entrusted to V. I. Fenenko, Judicial Investigator for important cases. Fenenko was first of the opinion that the murderer of Andrei Yushchinsky must be sought among members of his own family: his father had bequeathed him money and the desire to appropriate the inheritance seemed to be the cause of the crime. Yushchinsky's mother, stepfather and an uncle were arrested, but later released.

On August 3, 1911, Mendel Beilis was also arrested. He was a janitor of a brick factory belonging to a Jew and adjacent to the plot of land on which the corpse of the murdered boy had been found. Beilis was 39 years old and the father of five children.

The arrest of Beilis took place under the following circumstances. First, the Prosecutor of the *Sudebnaya Palata*, Chaplinsky, gave Fenenko a verbal order to arrest Beilis, which Fenenko refused to execute since in his opinion there was no evidence against Beilis. Then Chaplinsky issued an official written order that Beilis should be charged with the crime. Fenenko had to resign or to submit to the order. He knew that if he resigned another more submissive magistrate would be appointed, and he decided to obey. Margolin relates that Fenenko said to him: "The proofs against Beilis are ridiculous and absurd . . . I am convinced that he will be released within a few days." [107]

Since the days passed and Beilis was not released, a special commission was formed by the Jewish Community of Kiev to assist Beilis in his defense. Margolin became a member of this commission.

The preliminary investigation uncovered the fact that Andrei Yushchinsky did not go to school after having left his house. He went to see his friend Zhenya Cheberyak. This friend of the murdered boy and his sister Valya Cheberyak, two very important witnesses, died suddenly of dysentery in the beginning of August. Vera Cheberyak, their mother, was a very suspicious character. According to police records she was in constant contact with the criminal world. Her half-brother, Singayevsky, was a recidivistic burglar. Her apartment was a meeting place of criminals. She herself resold stolen goods. Fenenko said that "her home is a hiding place for stolen property and a den for the most dangerous criminals." [108]

Aside from official investigations, private inquiries were conducted, one by the journalist Brazul'-Brushkovsky, another by the former Chief of the Secret Police in Kiev, Krasovsky. Fenenko, who himself was greatly hampered in his investigation by the pressure on the part of Chaplinsky and others, gave Margolin to understand that every attempt to uncover the actual murderers of Yushchinsky by the efforts of Brazul'-Brushkovsky and other independent persons would be highly desirable and timely.[109]

Brazul'-Brushkovsky, who worked in close contact with Margolin was of the opinion that Vera Cheberyak knew the circumstances of the case, and tried to get the truth out of her. He learned that she had been badly beaten by a certain Mifle, her former lover, on whom she had some years ago thrown sulphuric acid in a fit of jealousy. Now she accused Mifle of being one of the murderers of Yushchinsky. She

---

[107] A. Margolin, *The Jews of Eastern Europe,* p. 164.
[108] *Ibid.,* p. 167.
[109] *Ibid.,* p. 168.

said to Brazul'-Brushkovsky that she was ready to tell the truth about the crime, but that first she must go to Kharkov in order to see some criminals there from whom she would obtain important information, and asked him to finance her trip. Margolin, who had to go to Kharkov on business, advised Brazul'-Brushkovsky to bring Cheberyak there. He wanted to have an interview with her in order to get a personal impression of her knowledge of the crime. His name had to remain secret to Cheberyak. During the interview in Kharkov, in the presence of Brazul'-Brushkovsky and Vygranov, a private detective, Cheberyak declared to Margolin that Mifle, his brother and three other persons were the actual murderers of Yushchinsky. They wanted to eliminate the boy because he knew about their crimes and could have reported to the police. Cheberyak also described the cave in which the crime had been committed. However, Margolin had the impression that she herself, was involved in the killing and was seeking a way out from the suspicion of Magistrate Fenenko, who at that time abandoned his first supposition that the murderers were among the members of the boy's family, and also suspected Cheberyak.

The preliminary investigation against Beilis was closed on January 5, 1912 and the case turned over to the District Prosecutor. At that time, on the advice of Margolin, Brazul'-Brushkovsky published a statement in the newspapers of the capital and Kiev about the declaration of Vera Cheberyak on January 18, in which she had accused Mifle of the murder. The next day Mifle denounced Vera Cheberyak for fraud and resale of stolen goods. On the ground of this accusation she was tried by jury in February 1913, found guilty and condemned to imprisonment and loss of certain rights. It is interesting that in the first indictment against Beilis, Vera Cheberyak was called an "unstained character." [110]

Krasovsky, former Chief of the Secret Police in Kiev, who conducted the second private investigation, was also persuaded that the crime was committed by burglars from the gang which met in the apartment of Vera Cheberyak, and in that very apartment. Yushchinsky often visited the Cheberyak home in order to see his friend Zhenya and had threatened to disclose to the police the presence of stolen goods in the apartment.

Krasovsky found out that three burglars of the gang of Vera Cheberyak—Rudzinsky, Latyshev, and Singayevsky, Vera's half-brother, were in her apartment on March 11 and 12, 1911 (the day of the mur-

---

110 *Ibid.*, p. 178.

der). At the time of Krasovsky's investigation, only Singayevsky was free. Rudnitsky and Latyshev had meanwhile been arrested for burglaries. In order to obtain the confession of Singayevsky, Krasovsky resorted to the help of an anarchist, Karayev, who had served a term for a political case in the jail of Kiev and had become popular among the criminal inmates and was also on good terms with Singayevsky. Karayev and his friend, the student Makhalin, succeeded in gaining the complete confidence of Singayevsky. During a conversation with Singayevsky, Karayev told him that he, Rudzinsky and Latyshev were suspected of being the murderers of Yushchinsky, that it was assumed that the crime had been committed in the apartment of Vera Cheberyak, and that he would soon be arrested. This information alarmed Singayevsky greatly, and he said that a certain D'yakonova must be killed because it was she who entered the apartment of Vera Chebehyak in the morning of March 12 and saw him and his two accomplices there. Then, in the presence of Makhalin, Karayev pointed to Singayevsky and said: "This is the real murderer of Yushchinsky. His accomplices were Rudnitsky, Latyshev and Vera Cheberyak." And he asked Singayevsky: "Is it true?" Singayevsky confirmed Karayev's words saying "Yes, that is our work," and said that on March 12 in the morning "they did this work." [111]

All this was said by Karayev in his testimony before the preliminary investigator. Makhalin fully corroborated Karayev's testimony and added that Singayevsky related that soon after the killing, the D'yakonov sisters entered the apartment but the murderers had the time to run to another room and cover the corpse with the boy's overcoat and that he, Singayevsky, assumed that the visitors had not seen either them or the corpse. [112]

Singayevsky was wrong in his supposition. Yekaterina D'yakonova, a woman who often visited Vera Cheberyak, testified in the preliminary investigation that when she entered Cheberyak's apartment about noon on March 12, she saw Singayevsky, Rudnitsky, Latyshev and Lisunov (another member of the gang) rapidly entering another room as soon as they noticed her. D'yakonova also testified that Vera Cheberyak had told her that the killers took care that the blood should not splash on the floor and walls and therefore soaked up the blood with rags. Finally, the witness related that Cheberyak's ten-year old daughter, Lyudmila, had said to her: "Mother did not kill Yushchinsky. She

---

[111] *Delo Beilisa. Stenografichesky otchet,* I, 24.
[112] *Ibid.*

was on the staircase at that time," and added that Yushchinsky was killed with the thick sewing needles belonging to her mother and Mifle, but that later the needles were thrown away in order that no suspicion should arise that Yushchinsky had been killed in her mother's house.[113]

In their testimony at court both sisters, Yekaterina and Ksen'ya D'yakonov, asserted with the greatest assurance that the strip of pillow slip found in the pocket of Andrei's blouse belonged to Vera Cheberyak. Ksen'ya D'yakonova had sewn pillow slips for her, and Yekaterina D'yakonova saw them because she slept several times at Cheberyak's.

It must be noted that during the search in Cheberyak's home one of her four pillows was found by the police in the apartment without a slip. It is peculiar that Mashkevich, the preliminary investigator who replaced Fenenko, who had been removed because of his lack of complaisance to the views of the Ministry of Justice in this case, did not show the pillow slip to the witnesses D'yakonov during the preliminary investigation, although he was obliged to do so according to law.

Another witness, Malitskaya, whose apartment was situated under that of Cheberyak, testified that several days before the corpse of Yushchinsky had been found, she had heard, one morning the noise of a child running in the apartment above her from one room into another, and also the steps of two grown-up persons. Then she heard the screams of a child and the sounds of bustling. She understood "that something very unusual and queer was going on in the apartment above . . . that a child had been grabbed and something was being done with him." [114] Later, when she heard about the murder of Yushchinsky, she became convinced that the crime "had taken place in Cheberyak's apartment." [115]

On March 13, the day after the murder, Singayevsky, Rudzinsky and Latyshev suddenly left for Moscow. Several days later they were arrested in Moscow and sent back to Kiev to be judged for thefts and burglaries which they committed there some time ago. While in jail in Kiev, they heard about the testimony of Karayev against them, whereupon they accused themselves of a burglary committed on the night of March 12 to 13 and said that they went to Moscow in order to sell the stolen goods.[116] Gruzenberg writes in his memoirs that one

---

[113] *Ibid.*, p. 25.
[114] *Ibid.*, p. 26.
[115] *Ibid.*
[116] This proved to be a lie and false self-accusation for the purpose of creating

of the most pathetic moments of the trial occurred when he asked Singayevsky why he and his companions had all three left for Moscow precisely on the day after the murder and how they could afford to spend money for three tickets when the sale of the goods they alleged to have stolen could bring in an insignificant sum only. Singayevsky lost his head and answered that they had wanted to visit Moscow.[117]

Another witness, Shvachko, who had been accidentally arrested and had spent a night in the police station, testified that he woke up at night and overheard a conversation between two criminals, who lay on the same plank-bed with him. One of them, who was Rudzinsky, was asked by the other fellow: "And how is it with the bastard?" Rudzinsky answered: "We finished him off." [118]

In December 1911, Latyshev testified before the preliminary investigator that he knew neither Cheberyak nor Singayevsky and confirmed his testimony in an affidavit. However, when another criminal was brought into the office of the investigator Latyshev tried to snatch his affidavit, but was prevented from doing so. Then he ran to the window and jumped from the fourth floor to his death.

On January 20, 1912, the indictment against Beilis was confirmed by the *Palata*. He had to be tried on May 17. However, on May 6, 1912, the reports of Brazul'-Brushkovsky and Krasovsky on their private inquiries was handed to Colonel Ivanov, who led the police investigation. The trial was postponed. On May 30 and 31 the private reports were published in the press of Kiev and St. Petersburg with the photos of Cheberyak, Singayevsky, Rudzinsky and Latyshev. Public opinion was shocked by the fact that Beilis remained in jail. Even the editor of the very conservative anti-Semitic newspaper *Kievlyanin*, Professor Pikhno, wrote a series of articles condemning the actions of the administration. The fact that even this staunchly pro-government paper was protesting Shcheglovitov's action made a great impression everywhere in Russia. A few days later the case was returned to the preliminary investigator for a new investigation.

The police and a new investigating magistrate, Mashkevich, specially sent by Shcheglovitov from St. Petersburg to substitute for Fenenko, who received two months' leave, began to check on the material gathered in the private investigations. Beilis remained in jail.

In the spring 1913, a new indictment against Beilis was submitted by the prosecutor for confirmation to the *Sudebnaya Palata*, the Cham-

---

an alibi. They were never indicted for this theft.

[117] Gruzenberg, *Vchera . . .* p. 121. Gruzenberg writes by mistake "Rudzinsky" instead of "Singayevsky." Cf. *Delo Beilisa*, II, 71.

[118] *Delo Beilisa*, II, 83. Yushchinsky was an illegitimate child.

ber of Accusations of which fulfilled a function similar to the grand jury in this country.

In the session of the Chamber on this case, the reporting judge, Ryzhov, moved that the case should be dismissed because of lack of evidence against Beilis. The presiding judge, Kamentsev, was of the same opinion. But the other three judges, who constituted a majority, were for confirmation, declaring that it would hurt the prestige of justice to free without trial a man who had been in jail for nearly two years. Kamentsev and Ryzhov filed a dissenting opinion in which they emphasized that there was no evidence against Beilis, not even of an indirect nature. They announced that they would not disgrace their last years by trying an innocent man. Of these two judges Margolin says: "May they rest in peace—these courageous, fearless champions of law and justice, who refused to be intimidated by the threatened revenge of Shcheglovitov and all the Black Hundreders of Russia!" [119]

The indictment charged Beilis with having "killed Yushchinsky with premeditation after previous agreement with persons who remained undisclosed by the preliminary investigation, moved by motives of religious fanaticism, for ritual purposes." [120]

Let us now consider the evidence gathered against Beilis according to the indictment.

The house in which the Cheberyaks lived was adjacent to the very extensive grounds of the brick factory in which Beilis was employed. The factory was neighboring on the other side, to an unoccupied plot of land on which the corpse of Yushchinsky was found.

The wife of a lamplighter, Ul'yana Shakhovskaya, testified that on the morning of March 12, 1911, she had seen Andrei Yushchinsky together with Zhenya Cheberyak at a street corner, eating candies, and that her acquaintance, Anna Zakharova, had told her that on that morning while Andrei, Zhenya and a third boy were playing on the grounds of the factory, before her eyes a man with a black beard[121] grasped Andrei and dragged him to the kiln. (Anna Zakharova flatly denied having seen such a scene or having talked about it to Shakhovskaya.)

Kazimir Shakhovsky, the lamplighter, testified that he too had seen Andrei and Zhenya together on that morning. When three days later he asked Zhenya Cheberyak whether they had played well on that

---

[119] Margolin, *Ibid.*, p. 210.
[120] *Delo Beilisa*, I, 37.
[121] Beilis had a black beard.

day, Zhenya answered: "No, because when we were playing on the ground of the factory, we were frightened by a man with a black beard." Before the preliminary investigator however, Zhenya testified that he had seen Andrei for the last time about ten days before the body of the latter was discovered: it was when Andrei dropped in at about two o'clock in the afternoon and invited him to take a walk. He declined and Andrei went by himself.

A detective, Polishchuk, testified that Ul'yana Shakhovskaya had told him in a state of drunkenness that her husband had seen how Beilis dragged Yushchinsky to the kiln. But Shakhovskaya declared that she does not remember what she had said when she was drunk but that her husband had never told her of having seen how Beilis dragged Andrei. Also Kazimir Shakhovsky said that he had not seen such an episode.

A convict, Kazachenko, who was in prison in the same cell with Beilis, declared that Beilis gave him a letter to his wife when he, Kazachenko, was released from the prison. In this letter Beilis wrote: "Dear wife, the man who will give you this note should be received by you as a friend . . . he can help you very much in my case. Tell him who else is testifying against me falsely. Why does nobody act as counsel for me? . . . If this man asks you for money, give him [money] for expenses which will be necessary . . . Those who falsely testify against me are my enemies." Kazachenko also declared that Beilis had proposed to him that he should poison two witnesses and bribe a third one, for an amount of money upon which it was not agreed, and promised him that his wife would give him 500 rubles for expenses from the money collected by Jews. The Jews would also provide the poison —strychnine. The witnesses who had to be poisoned were Kazimir Shakhovsky and Mikhail Nakonechny.

An idea as to the veracity of this testimony may be gotten from the fact that Nakonechny had testified favorably to Beilis. Nakonechny also declared that Shakhovsky had said to him on the way to the pre-liminary investigator that he, Shakhovsky, would frame an accusation aggainst Beilis because the latter had denounced him to the police for having stolen wood in the factory.

Vasily Cheberyak, the husband of Vera Cheberyak, testified that his deceased son Zhenya had told him that several days before the corpse of Yushchinsky had been discovered he had played with him on the factory ground but Beilis had chased them from the premises and that at about the same time he had seen two Jews in peculiar attire arriving to visit Beilis. He had also seen them praying. As soon as the corpse was discovered, said Zhenya, these Jews left the apartment of Beilis.

Finally, the nine-year-old Lyudmila, the third child of the Cheberyaks, corroborated the assertion about the presence of two strange Jews in Beilis' apartment. She said also that the last time she had seen Andrei was when he came to their house and suggested that they go to the factory in order to ride on the brake (machine for grinding clay). Andrei, Zhenya, Valya, another girl and herself went to the factory, while they were riding on the brake ,they saw Beilis and the two Jews running toward them. The children began to run away, but Zhenya and Andrei were grasped by Beilis. Zhenya managed to free himself and to escape, whereas Andrei, as she saw, was dragged by Beilis toward the kiln. She said that Valya told her that she also had seen how Andrei was dragged toward the kiln by Beilis.[122]

Lyudmila gave her testimony for the first time on July 10, 1912, *i.e.* 16 months after the murder of Yushchinsky.

This was all the evidence gathered against Beilis during the two years of the preliminary investigation. But this was enough to hold in jail, for 2½ years, a man of irreproachable reputation and a father of five children on the charge of murder and to accuse the Jews and their religion of the use of Christian blood.

The Ministry of Justice searched all over Russia to find experts who would prove that a ritual of using Christian blood, based on the Bible, the Talmud and other religious books, is being observed among Jews. Finally, a Catholic priest, Pranaitis, Master of Divinity, former lecturer on Hebrew in St. Petersburg, transferred for bad behavior to Turkestan, was entrusted with this task. He was confronted in the trial by such world-famous scholars as Professor Kokovtsev, member of the Academy of Sciences, Professor Troitsky, and Maze, Chief Rabbi of Moscow, who were summoned by the defense.

Also, medical experts produced by the prosecution were opposed by experts of the defense.

F. A. Boldyrev, President of the Circuit Court in Kiev, was the presiding judge. O. Yu. Vipper, Assistant Prosecutor of the St. Petersbrug *Sudebnaya Palata,* was sent to Kiev to act as trial prosecutor. The extreme-rightist organization *Dvuglavy Orel* (two-headed Eagle) managed to obtain a power of attorney from the mother of Yushchinsky for the representatives of the organization: A. S. Shmakov, attorney-at-law in Moscow, who specialized in anti-Semitic affairs and G. G.

---

122 *Delo Beilisa,* I, 33-36, *passim.*

Zamyslovsky, rightist member of the third *Duma,* the latter not being a member of the bar, was appointed private attorney by the circuit court in order to take part in the trial. Shmakov and Zamyslovsky functioned as private prosecutors. The defense was in the hands of O. O. Gruzenberg, V. A. Maklakov, N. P. Karabchevsky, D. N. Grigorovich-Barsky and A. S. Zarudny.

From twelve jurors, seven were peasants and five were small officials. The trial lasted from September 25 to October 28, 1913.

Three excerpts from the pleadings of Maklakov, Gruzenberg and Karabchevsky follow.

The strength of Maklakov's speech lies in his summing up of the evidence against Vera Cheberyak and her gang:

". . . Gentlemen jurors! If there is anything certain in this case, . . . if there is something which has been suggested by the entire development of this case, it is one thing: Vera Cheberyak is involved in the murder. I do not know who killed, I do not assert that she killed, but that she somehow participated in it, this must be now acknowledged beyond any argument. I shall rely neither on the testimony of Malitskaya nor of that of the D'yakonov sisters. . . . I shall follow a trail which does not present any doubt. . . . Andrei Yushchinsky came to see Zhenya Cheberyak (on the morning of March 12), but for a long time she did not say anything about it. . . .[123] She knows everything, she knows that on this morning he went a long distance to come from Slobodka, where he lived, to Luk'yanovka, where she lived, in order to see her or Zhenya. She alone has the key to the problem. And she is silent. However, if she were just silent, one could say that she did not do enough thinking. But she does not remain silent, she lies. . . . The witness Kirichenko[124]testified that when he was making a search at Cheberyak's and began to speak with Zhenya, Zhenya suddenly became silent, and when he, Kirichenko, turned his head, he saw the mother who, pointing at her tongue, made signs to Zhenya not to chatter. He said also that, when Zhenya and his mother were interrogated, the mother flew at her son, urging him not to chatter. But why should he not chatter? What had he to disguise? And unexpectedly this came to light. The first witness, the lamplighter Shakhovsky, testified first against Cheberyak, asserting he had seen Andrei and Zhenya together on the morning of March 12. . . . The key was found. Thus the solution of the problem is around Zhenya, somewhere close to him. Certainly, it might be that it was not the Cheberyaks who killed, but they know who did it. . . .But Zhenya denies, Vera

---

[123] Let us recall that Zhenya Cheberyak, when interrogated for the first time by the preliminary investigator, declared that he did not see Andrei on this morning.

[124] The police officer who made a search in Cheberyaks' apartment.

Cheberyak denies, all of them are silent. Why? Let the prosecutor say why they are silent. . . . But I ask: why were they silent at that time, what were they afraid of? She belongs to a gang of thieves. Were it a case of theft, she could remain silent, but . . . when there is a murder here, a bestial murder, how could she think that she would be suspected if she had nothing to do with it? . . . Nevertheless she was suspected . . . and arrested by the end of July. But why did she not recollect then everything she knew about the case? If at that time she really had known not only that Andrei was with Zhenya on that morning but that they went to the factory for riding on the brake and that Beilis had grabbed Andrei, why didn't she, the innocent one, shout in self-defense: "Why do you molest me? Here is what I know: he was seized by Beilis at Zaitsev's factory." But no, she remained silent; not only did she remain silent, but she forbade Zhenya to speak. . . . Gentlemen of the jury, I come to the most terrible episode of this case. It is Zhenya's death. . . . The sick Zhenya was brought to the hospital when Vera Cheberyak was under arrest. Then she was released and informed that Zhenya is not at home, that he is very sick, on the critical list, and . . . she takes Zhenya from the hospital and brings him home. She says there was no more hope, and she wanted him to die at home. Gentlemen, where is the mother who does not hope till the last moment that her child will be saved? Where is the mother who would drag her dying child through the whole town on the quiet assumption that he will die anyhow. What mother would dare to bring him even one breath nearer to the grave? What mother would do it? (Stir in the audience.) Why did she do so? I do not think that she does not love her children. But here, along with the natural feeling of a mother there was another feeling; fear and terror for herself and for those close to her. She knew that Zhenya could spill a secret in the hospital, that there he is far away from her. Indeed, the detectives were around him and did not leave him. She wanted to shake her finger at him when he was dying as she had done when he was in good health. And thus she takes him home from the hospital. Here starts a fearful, disgusting and mournful episode. Zhenya dies, dies painfully. He is dreaming of Andrei, and he shouts: "Do not scream, Andryusha." Andryusha is before his eyes, with his unsolved problem. Zhenya is in distress, he calls for a priest, he wants to tell him something, but when the priest arrives, he is again silent. Why? Something happens in the meantime. During these moments he is redeeming other people's sins, but detectives are around him. . . . And here is what the miserable Cheberyak is obliged to do: she has to think at this moment, not about the salvation of her son's life, about his rest. She cannot shout to the detectives: "Get out of here! There is death here, God's work is being done here." She cannot do that! Then she wants to make use of her son. She asks Zhenya: 'Zhenya, say that I have nothing to do with it.' At the last moment she wants to employ Zhenya for her salvation: 'Say that I have nothing to do with it! But what does Zhenya answer? He says: 'Mother, leave me alone, I am in distress.' The dying boy did not fulfill her request, the dying son did not say: 'She has nothing to do with it, this other one is guilty.' He did not say what was so easy to say: 'I have seen how Beilis dragged Andryusha.' No, he says: 'Leave me alone, mother, I am in distress.' And when he wants to speak out, this miserable mother, according to the testinmony of witnesses, kisses him, prevents him from speaking, and when he is passing away, she seals his lips with a kiss, a kiss of Judas. (Stir in the audience).

. . . Much later,[125] Vera Cheberyak remembered that her late son Zhenya confessed to her a very simple thing: that Mendel Beilis had dragged Andryusha to the kiln before Zhenya's eyes . . . there you have a piece of evidence against Beilis, and that is all the evidence. . . .

However, there is still the testimony of the child Lyuda.[126] This unfortunate child, who came forth and word by word recited the lesson she had been taught, answered the following to the question of whether or not she had seen Andryusha long before [the murder] 'God forbid, I did not see him for a long time.' This 'God forbid' from a little girl! It is not she who asks God to preserve her from acquaintance with Andryusha." [127]

Then Maklakov speaks about the shielding of Vera Cheberyak and her gang by the administration and about the shortcomings of the preliminary investigation, which did not want to discover any other perpetrator than Beilis and wanted Beilis as the perpetrator at any price. . . . He asks why the preliminary investigator has used everything which could fasten the guilt on Beilis and has stopped every time the tracks turned in another direction. Maklakov continues:

. . . Hair was found on the body of Yushchinsky. This is a piece of evidence. If you find whose hair this is, you will know where to look for the culprit. This is not proof, but evidence. Thus a thorough investigation of the hair was made. It has been compared with Beilis' hair taken from all parts of his body. But with the hair of Singayevsky, Rudzinsky and Latyshev it was never compared. Such analysis was never made, as if one were afraid of something. . . . Why, if there is no preconceived notion, is the hair of one suspect compared and that of others not? Then the clay on Andrei's clothes. . . . Samples of the clay from all

---

125 Zhenya Cheberyak died on Aug. 8, 1911 (*Delo Beilisa*, I, 36) and Vera Cheberyak's testimony that Beilis dragged Andrei was made before the preliminary investigator on July 10, 1912.
126 Nine-year-old daughter of Vera Cherberyak.
127 *Delo Beilisa*. III, 136-140, *passim*.

sections of Zaitsev's factory were taken and compared with the
clay on the clothes. Clay from one of the places resembled, just
resembled, that on the body. . . . But why was the same not done
with the clay from Cheberyak's cellar in which the corpse could
possibly have been kept? The preliminary investigator. . . . took
all conceivable measures to fasten the guilt on Beilis, but why
did he not do the same for checking the testimony of Cheberyak?
And the carpet? Suspicious spots were found on Cheberyak's
carpet. It was assumed that it was blood. An analysis was made,
but how? Only naps of the carpet were analyzed. But what could
remain on these naps after months, after years, what could remain on them? Why was not the whole carpet analyzed? It was
not necessary to spare a carpet! A great deal has not been spared
in this case, a man's life has not been spared, and you spared a
carpet. (Stir in the audience). It is very strange that Singayevsky
and Rudzinsky were brought from Siberia to the trial, but
not Karayev,[128] who is also in Siberia. We did not see him
[here]. . . .[129]

Gentlemen of the jury . . . if the assertion of the prosecutor
were true, if Andryusha had been dragged to the kiln before the
eyes of all these children and his corpse had been found in the
cave, then all Luk'yanovka[130] would have risen. These simple
people, the simple Russian people would have risen, and there
would have been no need for the trial of Beilis. Then Zaitsev's
factory would not exist any more, nor Beilis himself, and no trial
would have taken place. It was said that these people, fathers and
mothers, know that their children are dragged to the kiln and
are silent because they are scared. It is strange to look at the
soul of a Russian man. The prosecutor said that everyone here
is bribed, even these witnesses, these coachmen from the province
of Chernigov, who said that they transported bricks on the morning of March 12 [and did not notice anything unusual in the
factory]. But the prosecutor does not realize one thing: it is that
a Russian may sin against his conscience, but not under every
circumstance. I do not believe that it can be said about all these
Russian coachmen that they are lying—lying in a case in which
a child of theirs has been tortured. No, gentlemen; had they
thought that it really happened, they could never have been
bribed. I cannot believe that all the district knew that the Jews
tortured and murdered Andrei and were afraid, and did not
tell. . . .[131]

The counsel analyzes the charges against Beilis. We omit this part

---

[128] Karayev is the man to whom Singayevsky confessed that he is one of the
murderers.
[129] *Delo Beilisa*, III, 141.
[130] The district of Kiev where the event took place.
[131] *Delo Beilisa*, III, 141-146.

of his pleading completely since we will quote Gruzenberg on this subject. Maklakov continued:

> I tried to compare the evidence against Cheberyak [and her gang] with that collected against Beilis. We have examined many pieces of evidence produced against her, which are unquestionable, indubitable—even the prosecutor does not reject them. Evidence has been found also against Beilis. But you cannot believe it unless you assume that in Luk'yanovsky District every one is a bribee who knew that the child had been dragged into the kiln by Jews and did not tell. This cannot be assumed. And at the same time we see that Cheberyak is shielded, we see the expression of every sympathy toward her, of full confidence [in her]; but from him (Maklakov points at Beilis) everyone has turned away. . . . You have heard here that the case is an outstanding one, that not the unfortunate Beilis is the point in this case . . . but world Jewry. . . . Yes, here is an optical illusion, and we all overlook it. . . . Behind the back of Beilis something strange occurred—the collision of some external forces. And this became the misfortune of justice. And if we desire a just verdict, if we all equally serve the administration of justice, we all, beginning with the defense and the prosecutor and ending with the bench, we all must tell you: do not repeat this mistake, gentlemen of the jury, achieve a heroic deed, put yourselves above these passions, be able to understand that all our faults, all the faults of the Jewish leaders, the mistakes of the Jewish people, all the faults which someone may have committed do not concern Beilis when he is on trial. . . . If, however, you yield [to these passions] . . . Russia's administration of justice will suffer. Beilis is a mortal. Should he be unjustly condemned, it will be forgotten. Many people have been unjustly condemned. Human life is short. Men die, Beilis too will die, his family will die, everything will be forgotten, everything will be forgiven, but this verdict,—this verdict will not be forgotten, this verdict will remain as a sentence passed by the jury on a man whom it has been tried to picture as your enemy. You are told that the Jews are your enemies, that they laugh at you, that they do not consider you as human beings. You are required to do the same toward them. Do not give way, gentlemen of the jury. Should you sentence Beilis in spite of the absence of evidence, should you sentence him for our sins, for their sins, for anything else, should he become an atonement for sin and should there be some people who will cheer at the sentence you pass, they will be sorry afterwards, and your verdict will remain a mournful page in the history of our justice. Remember that when you decide Beilis' fate, gentlemen of the jury![132]

---

[132] *Ibid.*, p. 151-155, *passim.*

O. O. Gruzenberg was the chief counsel of Beilis. He was the only Jew among Beilis' lawyers, and he felt that, beside Beilis, he had to defend the Jewish people.

A ritual murder. . . . The use of human blood. . . . A terrible assumption. Dreadful words, already buried long ago. But they are strong and of great vitality, and, as we heard, they rise from the cemetery to [haunt] the present. They contaminate everything living. And people who live peacefully, know one another, unexpectedly become enemies. Even now, as I stand before you, when I have to speak on the dreadful accusation. . . . I do not know whether I still enjoy your confidence, whether I may claim your attention. What does it matter that I was brought up among you, Christians and Russians? I shared your sorrows, your pains, your griefs. But, you see, the fateful hour has come, the words of the bloody slander have resounded and we have been torn apart and face one another as enemies. And at this moment it might seem to some that I wish to muffle by my pleading the mortal gurgle of this unfortunate martyr, the poor Andryusha. No, I do not want to muffle it, I do think of it. It is up to you to believe me or not, but should I for a single moment be aware or even just suppose that the Jewish religion tolerates or encourages the use of human blood, I would not remain in this religion any more. I say it loudly—knowing that these words will be heard by Jews of the whole world—that I would not think it possible for one moment to remain a Jew. I am deeply convinced, I know it perfectly well . . . that we have no such crimes and could not have them.

Gentlemen, you see that this accusation, which arose from a cemetery, has dragged us back to the cemetery. There we dug into millenial tombs and from these tombs, long ago fallen to pieces and covered with mould, we have extracted all the past. Think, gentlemen, here we have spoken of things which happened over three thousand years ago, when Jews went to war against certain Amalikitians and treated them cruelly, and now Beilis is in the dock and we discuss the question of what happened three thousand years ago, of whether the Jews handled them cruelly or not, of whether people fought cruelly or not at that time. Yes, gentlemen, 3,000 years ago people walked naked in the woods, people ate one another as barbarians, but Jews already recognized the single God, and if they sacrificed in temples, the offerings were always animals, never human beings. We dug into old reminiscences, spoke of the destruction of the temple, of the kind of sacrifices which had been offered. We rummaged in the past, we were all the time on a cemetery created 3,000 years ago, which, one might think, we had left forever.

We have seen that Beilis has played the part of a scapegoat. He has to answer for everything that happened at any time during these 3,000 years among the millions of Jews. And there were millions and millions of Jews during 3,000 years. Perhaps a crazy, insolent or offended man said a sharp word about foreigners or Christians—for all that Beilis is now responsible . . . You have heard that the prosecutor . . . did not call for the punishment of the perpetrator in strict accordance with evidence, but called for the redemption of [the death of Yushchinsky] and consolation of the unfortunate mother. Yes, the unfortunate mother needs consolation, but not by sacrifices, not by the condemnation of an innocent [man] . . . Look at this poor Aleksandra Prikhod'ko, [133] at this simple woman—we must learn from her how carefully we must handle human life. Do you remember how she came into the court and said holy words—which could, of course, not be understood by detectives and reporters who collect insignificant information—she said: "I have no tears, I cannot cry anymore." And this tortured woman, who has no tears, who cannot cry, was asked by the preliminary investigator and by us: "Whom do you suspect?' Not a word about Beilis, not a word about Jews. A holy woman! Thus, in these moments of wrath and despair, she was not intoxicated by the general hatred, she told the truth as she understands it. She suffers for her son, but she does not wish the ruin of another, innocent man.

What do you know about this Beilis? What did you hear concerning him? Gentlemen, different things are said about Jews, different things are thought about them, but is there anyone here who will not say that Beilis is one of those Jews from the class who should be dear to every Christian, and every Jew? Indeed he is an honest toiler . . . You heard that he got up at four o'clock in the morning, and at six o'clock work began and lasted till six in the evening. Not a minute of rest . . . Witnesses—Christians, workers, coachmen—many people were here, and what did they say about him? You know yourself: when a man is in distress, there is always somebody who remembers that this man offended him. But you did not hear a single word of reproach. Workers passed before you: look how warmly, humanely and sympathetically they spoke of him. They all consider him as an unfortunate, crestfallen, half-crushed man, who, with God's help, will recover, and you did not hear a single word of reproach.

Remember the children who came here. It was a touching episode when little Yevgeniya Voloshchenko, being asked about Beilis, looked at the dock and to the question, 'Did he chase you, offend you?' laughed and said: 'No, he never offended.' Nobody, neither grown-up people nor children, neither those summoned by us or by the prosecutor, uttered a word of complaint or reproach against Beilis, and still he is in the dock before you, and still he is 2½ years in jail, tortured, lacerated, crushed, and his condemnation is demanded here in the name of criticism of the Bible, in the name of criticism of Zahar, —a ghostly kind of book, which 9/10 of Jews have never seen and of which they have never

---

133 Andrei Yushchinsky's mother.

heard, on the ground of the testimony by drunken women for whom the investigation had to search in a den . . . The whole underworld was here and an attempt was made to find evidence against Beilis. . . . Is it possible that on the basis of evidence heard from a drunken woman; from Shakhovsky, who changed his testimony 17 times during the preliminary investigation and as many times here before you in this hall . . . on the basis of this testimony, often senseless, completely unfounded, related to nothing, confusing, scattered, it was suggested here that a man be sentenced to penal servitude . . . I ask: what is this for, what is the man guilty of? You have heard what the prosecutor said: since there is a chapel at the hospital, human blood was perhaps necessary in order to build this chapel on it. This is what the prosecutor said, this is recorded, we all have heard it. I address, therefore, the prosecutor and say: if you think that the chapel must have been constructed on Christian blood, if you think that for this chapel the unfortunate boy was sacrificed, why are you silent, why don't you act according to your conviction? Look, then, for the man who constructed this chapel. You have seen this man ,he stood before you. It is Zaitsev, the son of the old Zaitsev, the millionaire. He has built it, and if the prosecutor thinks that the chapel was erected on human blood, I ask you: why does not the builder of the chapel sit in this dock, why do those who contributed money for this chapel not sit there? . . . Should you [really] belive it, you would certainly put into the dock those who erected this chapel, who demanded this blood. But you did not do it, of course, because you understand very well yourselves that this is not true . . . And still you spoke here about it in order to create a suspicion: perhaps the blood of the unfortunate Yushchinsky was necessary for this purpose. Yes, gentlemen, for the poor mother Andryusha's blood, his shirt splashed with blood is not a combat banner. For her it is the last blood of her child. Not the cave which has all our attention is dear to her, but the two yards of the tomb where her boy lies, the tomb which, perhaps, no one of us visited. She goes there alone, beats [her breast], cries and seeks solace on that earth, but does not accuse anybody because she knows that there, before the throne of the Almighty, it would not help her son if another innocent man suffers, that beside her boy the children of this unfortunate Beilis will languish and suffer . . . She knows it, and I want those who are accusing to know it also. Discussing this case, they should see in this tomb a really sacred thing, a really martyred child, and this shirt should provoke real sorrow and one should not swing it as a banner and call people to mutual irritation and hatred.[134]

Then Gruzenberg refuted all points of the evidence against Beilis

---

[134] *Ibid.*, p. 155-158, *passim.*

one after the other. To the testimony of Vera Cheberyak and her nine-year-old daughter he opposed the testimony of several children who—the Cheberyaks themselves asserted—went with their children and Andryusha to the factory in order to ride on the brake on the fateful morning. These children flatly denied that Beilis had chased them from the factory and denied also the presence of two other Jews there. When Beilis was shown to them, they said that he never chased them. But Cheberyak asserted that these children were on the brake when Beilis and two other strange Jews arrived and dragged the unfortunate Andryusha. Said Gruzenberg:

> The boy Zarutsky says it is not true, Yevgeniya says it is not true, Sofiya says it is not true, children of the Nakonechnys also deny it. But who is it that does the affirming? See what a trick Vera Cheberyak played with her daughter, Lyudmila. She arranged things so that this child, who was six to seven years old at that time, allegedly saw how Jews dragged Andryusha. But how did the girl testify before the preliminary investigator, and how did she testify in court that Beilis and some other people came, shouted at them, that they all began to run away and Andryusha was afraid and Beilis' son Pinka was standing and laughing. But she did not conclude with the words which her mother said: that the Jews dragged the boy toward the kiln. Why? Because this is a lie, and a lie is dangerous, although the responsibility of a ten-year-old child is not the same as that of a grown-up. The mother told her: you will say that you played on the brake and then were chased, but do not say that the Jews dragged Andryusha, but tell that Valya—who is now dead,—told it to you that way. The mother herself said here that this and that had been related to her by the late Zhenya,[135] and the girl says—by the late Valya. Go now and ask the unfortunate Valya."

Father Cheberyak also quoted his late son, Zhenya. Gruzenberg showed the discrepancy in the father's testimony.

> Before the preliminary investigator he said, on December 20, 1911, that [according to Zhenya] the children played on the brake, that Beilis saw them, chased them and they ran away, and Pinka [Beilis' son], seeing it, stood and laughed. And not another word . . . Nothing about the fact that Andryusha was seized— not a word; that he was dragged—not a word; that there were other strange Jews with whiskers—not a word. And do you remember what he said in court? He said Zhenya had told him that Beilis and two rabbis—then he corrected himself—not two

---

[135] Zhenya himself did not mention a word about it to the magistrate—S. K.

rabbis but two Jewish teachers of religion had rushed at the children . . . all of them escaped; only the unfortunate Andryusha was seized and dragged . . . Perhaps you will say that at the preliminary investigation he did not remember all the details, but he came home, talked to Zhenya and Zhenya told him everything. But remember that he testified on December 20, 1911, and Zhenya died on August 8, 1911 . . . so that Zhenya was lying in the grave for four months already and could not have told him anything more. Why, then, between December 1911 and the day when he testified here under oath, did these two strange Jewish teachers of religion appear, and also Mendel Beilis who together with them [allegedly] caught the child? Then Cheberyak said that Zhenya told him this on March 12 about 11 o'clock. I inquired at the post office where Cheberyak is employed; they say that Cheberyak had worked that day from 9 A.M. to 3 P.M. and then from 9 P.M. to 9 A.M.[136]

We cannot follow Gruzenberg in all the details of his brilliant pleading. Let it be said that he refuted the points of the testimony against Beilis one after the other and emphasized the evidence which pointed to the home of the Cheberyaks as the place of the crime and to the gang of Vera Cheberyak as the perpetrators.

About the accusation directed against the Jewish religion, he said: "You heard how the Bible was spoken of here . . . exposing its cruelty accusing it of hatred toward men, of shedding human blood. . . . And there were minutes when I thought: My God, what is happening? Is it possible that the God of the Bible, who is equally holy to all religions, Christian and Jewish—is it possible that the God of the Bible became a Kiev Jew who is rounded up, chased and about whom it is said that in his books . . ." [137]

At this point Gruzenberg was interrupted by the presiding judge and asked not to make offending comparisons. Gruzenberg continued: "They are raiding the Bible, the holy books, tearing out individual parts and words which are equally dear to you Christians and to Jews, which are read in all temples and churches—Orthodox, Protestant, Catholic. . . . And when I suffered, hearing this, I still proudly said to myself: how good that among the Orthodox priests among Orthodox scholars, there was not one—at least not here in the court—who came and supported these terrible tormenting fables, this bloody slander, in his capacity of priest, Orthodox Christian or Russian scholar . . . Gentleman of the jury! The Jewish religion is an old anvil against

---

136 *Ibid.*, p. 168.
137 *Ibid.*, p. 189.

which many hammers were crushed—heavy hammers of enemies—and the Jewish religion came out of these ordeals pure, honest and steadfast. Do you really think, gentlemen of the jury . . ."

At this point Gruzenberg was again interrupted by the presiding judge, who explained that not the Jewish religion, but Beilis is accused of wild fanaticism and false interpretation. . . .

Gruzenberg continued: "The President has explained that the Jewish religion and the Jewish holy books were not accused of anything, that nobody suspects the Jewish religion, but only the wild fanatics. Then a completely worthless task occupied us during three days. For three days we did not inquire about fanatics, but discussed the Bible, Zahar and the Talmud. These are Jewish religious books, not books of fanatics. . . . You have seen how Pranaitis[138] stood here and made merciless reproaches against these books. . . ." [139]

At the end of his pleading, Gruzenberg said:

> I examined all the evidence. There is not a single piece of evidence against Beilis, but 20 years of forced labor await him, this honest man who for two and a half years has been suffering this torture . . . I am so convinced of the innocence of Beilis; I am so convinced that all this is obvious that I do not admit the possibility of differences of opinion; I do not admit that someone could be found in this hall who would say that Beilis is guilty, who would say that there remains a single piece of evidence, a single shred of proof against him. I profoundly believe it, but I ask myself: if I am wrong, . . . if he whom I consider innocent will perish, what then? . . . In order to say to a guilty scoundrel that he is a scoundrel, no courage is necessary. But to say of an innocent man that he is guilty when the contrary is obvious requires not courage, but violation of the courts' oath. God forbid such courage to the Russian judge. . . . I am firmly convinced that Beilis will not perish. He cannot, he must not perish! But if I am wrong? What if you, gentlemen of the jury, will subscribe to the horrible accusation in spite of the evidence? What can be done? Hardly 200 years have passed since our ancestors were burned on bonfires as a consequence of such accusations. Humbly, saying prayers, they submitted to an unjust execution. Why are you better than they, Beilis? You too must submit. And in days of unbearable sufferings, when despair and distress take hold of you, stand firm, Beilis, repeat the words of the prayer for the dying: "Hear, oh, Israel, I am thy God, the only God for every man." Horrible would be your end but still

---

138 The Catholic priest, expert on Jewish theology, who was summoned by the prosecution.
139 *Ibid.*, p. 189-190, *passim*.

more horrible is the mere possibility of such accusations here, under the protection of reason, conscience and law." [140]

Unfortunately, lack of space does not permit us to quote the brilliant speeches of N. P. Karabchevsky and other counsels of Beilis. Let us cite just the final sentence from Karabchevsky's speech, who, after having refuted in his turn all the evidence produced against Beilis and pointed to the real perpetrators of the crime, said: "If till now there was a pure and holy institution, which did not yield to any outside influences, it was our court, the court with jury, which we venerated, of which we were proud, and which we protected as something sacred. Gentlemen of the jury, I beseech you, keep it as such also by your verdict. May God help you." [141]

The jury had to answer two questions. The first one was whether Yushchinsky had been killed in such a manner as to inflict upon him great suffering and to drain his body of blood. The second question was: if the event described in the first question did occur, is Mendel Beilis . . . guilty of having killed Andrei Yushchinsky on March 12, 1911, acting with premeditation and stimulated by religious fanaticism in agreement with other persons who remained undiscovered?[142]

The jury answered the first question in the affirmative and the second one in the negative. Beilis was acquitted.

The confirmation by the jury of the fact that the character of the wounds inflicted upon Yushchinsky permits the supposition that the murder had been committed for ritual purposes had no importance whatsoever. First of all, jurors are not experts who can authoritatively decide upon the controversy on this question, examined by the experts of the prosecution and the defense. Then, even if it was admitted that the wounds were of such a character as to inflict upon Yushchinsky great suffering and to drain his body of blood, they could have been inflicted upon Yushchinsky with the purpose of simulating ritual murder. Finally, if Yushchinsky was murdered for ritual purposes, that could have been done by other fanatics, not Jews, since Beilis was acquitted.

Shcheglovitov and the "Black Hundreders" lost the Beilis case. Revenge was taken against those who contributed to the failure of the governments aims, and reward given to its obedient servants.

We mentioned above the article of Prof. Pikhno, the editor of the rightist paper *Kievlyanin*. Pikhno died in the summer of 1912,

---

[140] *Ibid.,* p. 193.
[141] N. P. Karabchevsky, *Rechi 1882-1914.* 3d ed., p. 580.
[142] *Delo Beilisa . . .* III, 300.

and Shul'gin, his son-in-law, a distinguished journalist and member of the Duma, assumed the direction of the newspaper. He was tried for an article describing the activity of Chaplinsky, Prosecutor of the *Sudebnaya Palata* in the Beilis Case. Shul'gin was sentenced to three months in jail. As to Chaplinsky, he was promoted to the position of Senator in the Department of Cassation of the Senate. Boldyrev, Presiding Judge in the Beilis Case, was appointed President of a *Sudebnaya Palata*. Several other newspaper editors of St. Petersburg and Kiev were tried for "spreading deliberate misinformation about the Beilis Case." Vera Cheberyak sued a contributor to *Kievlyanin*, Trifonov, for slander. The Investigating Magistrate, Fenenko, who testified as a witness in this trial, emphatically declared to Vera Cheberyak in the court session: "Today, as before, I am firmly convinced of your guilt in the murder of Yushchinsky." [143] Trifonov was acquitted. Krasovsky, whose private investigation produced the testimony of Karayev and Makhalin, was accused, by order of Chaplinsky, of having "without reason" arrested a peasant and of having destroyed the official correspondence in a case involving the collection of an unpaid tax of 16 kopecks when he was police captain in 1911. Krasovsky was acquitted, since his wife found the "correspondence" forgotten in a trunk when the Krasovsky's moved from one apartment to another. Brazul'-Brushkovsky was accused of having remained seated during the performance of the national anthem in a park in Kiev. He was sentenced to one year of confinement in a fortress on count of lese-majesty.[144]

The trial lawyers of Beilis were also accused: Maklakov for an article on the Beilis case entitled: "Salutary Warning. The Significance of the Beilis Case." [145] In this article Maklakov wrote: ". . . Persons who are convinced anti-Semites, but who still were not blind, could not help noticing that anti-Semitism which reaches such dimensions, which brings one to the profanation of the Statutes of Judicial Institutions; which sacrifices on the altar of the ritual not only the innocent Beilis but also Russian justice itself—that such anti-Semitism commits suicide, *discredits*—this word may sound strange—*anti-Semitism* itself. This sad and evil trial carried anti-Semitism to an absurdity . . . alienated from the accusation those for whom Jewry is an evil, for whom the struggle against Jewry was and is a matter of polit-

---

[143] Margolin, *op. cit.*, p. 233.
[144] *Ibid.*, p. 203 and 207.
[145] V. A. Maklakov. "Spasitel'noye predosterezheniye. Smysl dela Beilisa," *Russkaya Mysl'* (November, 1913), p. 135-143.

ical creed, but who still do not believe that *everything* is allowed for the achievement of their goal, that the distortion of Russian justice in this case may remain unpunished, who understood that the conviction of Beilis meant suicide. . . . The simple sense of equity and conscience revolted against this campaign against Beilis in which nothing was respected: either law, or truth, or dignity of the human being. Persons who were not blind became ashamed of the campaign in which they were involved, of the means used against Beilis. They became ashamed of *such* anti-Semitism, of such a fight—and this was the first sound reaction generated by this trial." [146]

Gruzenberg had to face disciplinary proceeding because he had declared during the testimony of the witness, Gendarmery Colonel Ivanov, that "there are no witnesses of the prosecution and the defense; there are honest and dishonest witnesses."[147] Gruzenberg was reprimanded by the council of the bar for this sentence.

Disciplinary proceedings were also taken against the lawyer, Arnold Margolin. Let us recall that Margolin directed a private investigation on behalf of a Jewish committee. He agreed to have an interview with Vera Cheberyak in Kharkov. Later Cheberyak declared that Margolin, together with other Jews, had offered her 40,000 rubles if she would assume the guilt of the murder of Yushchinsky. Margolin was tried displinarily by the General Assembly of the Circuit Court (there was no council of the bar in Kiev). He was found guilty and disbarred, although the court admitted that the attempt to bribe Cheberyak was not completely proved. The court found that the interview with her was incompatible "with the basic requirements of his professional activity: to serve the idea of justice by means and measures set by law." [148] In a dissenting opinion several judges wrote that Margolin did not commit any crime and that he had done everything which a lawyer and a man was "in duty bound" to do.[149] Margolin's appeal against the sentence of the Circuit Court was dismissed by the *Sudebnaya Palata*. After the February Revolution the Senate reversed the sentence of the *Palata*, considering it as a "perversion of justice," and Margolin was reinstated in all the rights of a member of the bar.[150]

O. O. Gruzenberg, who was appointed by the Provisional Govern-

---

146 *Ibid.*, p. 139.
147 *Delo Beilisa* . . . II, 116.
148 *Delo prisyazhnago poverennago A. D. Margolina*, pp. 24, 27.
149 Margolin, *op. cit.*, p. 231.
150 The Ukranian Central *Rada* appointed A. Margolin to the Ukranian Supreme Court, called also Senate, in 1918.

ment Senator of the Criminal Department of Cassation of the Senate, of which A. F. Koni was named President, got the opportunity to inspect the secret files of the Department of Police concerning the Beilis Case. On grounds of information gathered there, Gruzenberg relates in his book *Vchera* how the Ministry of Justice ran around looking for an expert willing to assert that Jews use Christian blood; how no one, except Pranaitis, could be found for this job; how all the prosecutors of Russia were ordered to collect written materials about alleged ritual murders. Every person who had sent sympathizing telegrams to the counsels of Beilis was immediately put under police supervision. Gruzenberg read the correspondence between the Governor of the Kiev Province and the Department of the Police. Being convinced of Beilis' innocence, the governor recommended postponement of the trial, since the acquittal of Beilis would have an unfavorable effect on the elections to the Duma. Gruzenberg found in the files letters which had been written to him and never delivered, as well as copies of letters he wrote during the trial. When Singayevsky and Rudzinsky were brought from Siberia to Kiev, they were held back at the last station before Kiev, and Chaplinsky, Vipper, Zamyslovsky and Boldyrev met in order to decide whether they should be brought to the trial as witnesses. He found in the files proof that Boldyrev had introduced a policeman into the room of the jury in the disguise of a judicial attendant. Finally, he saw reports by two officials specially sent by the Department of Police in order to report on the trial. One of them, D'yachenko, wired every day to the Police Department. In every telegram he emphasized that there is no evidence against Beilis, and in one of these telegrams he expressed the hope that "although there is no evidence, the ignorant jurors will still condemn [him], inspired by hate against Jews." But in his last report D'yachenko wrote: "The partisan behavior of the presiding judge became especially evident in his summing up, which had an obviously accusatory character, although evidence against Beilis, according to my opinion as former investigating magistrate and prosecutor, was very weak or, to put it better, non-existent. When the jury retired to discuss the verdict, Boldyrev asked me how I found his summing up, and I told him frankly that I expected more impartiality from him." When Beilis was acquitted the other official, Lyubimov, wired in despair: "A judicial Tsushima[151] has occurred." [152]

---

[151] The Russian naval disaster in the Russo-Japanese War in 1905.

[152] Gruzenberg, *Vchera* . . . p. 126-129, *passim*.

I cannot end the narrative of Gruzenberg's role in the Beilis Case without

When the Bolsheviks occupied Kiev in 1919, Vera Cheberyak was shot without trial.

O. Yu. Vipper, the trial prosecutor in the Beilis Case, who was promoted to Associate Prosecutor of the Criminal Department of Cassation of the Senate by Shcheglovitov, was tried in the Moscow Revolutionary Tribunal on September 18-19, 1919. After the October Revolution, Vipper occupied the insignificant position of auditor in the Province Food Committee in Kaluga. The Bolsheviks discovered him there.

Vipper was accused, first, of having accepted on the personal proposition of Minister Shcheglovitov the role of trial prosecutor in the staging of the accusation of ritual murder against Beilis, clearly realizing the aims of the trial and the means by which it was staged; secondly, of the fact that he, in his capacity as trial prosecutor, fully maintained the accusation against Beilis and thus contributed to the achievement of the main goal pursued by the government in staging this trial, to wit: to create by the sentence animosity against Jews in the masses of the population and to divert their attention from the real perpetrators of the calamities and the miserable conditions of life to which the Tsarist government subjected the toiling masses of the population. In his accusatory pleading, N. V. Krylenko said: "I do not accuse him [Vipper] of having been the prosecutor in the Beilis Case, but of having put all his talent, all his abilities in the service of Tsarism, of having desired the achievement of political aims necessary to Tsarism by means of bloodshed."[153]

The Tribunal condemned Vipper to confinement in a concentration camp "until the Communist regime is definitely strengthened in the Republic."[154]

---

quoting a witty remark he made many years later. A political refugee after the Bolshevist Revolution, Gruzenberg was dying in Nice, France, in 1940. He had to be operated on and a blood transfusion was necessary. A Christian colleague of Gruzenberg volunteered for the transfusion. After this had been done, Gruzenberg said: "Now, how could one assert that Jews do not use Christian blood?" He died the same night. Told by I. L. Tsitron, lawyer-in-training under Gruzenberg. In Gruzenberg, *Ocherki i rechi*, p. 56. On the role of the government in the Beilis Case see also A. S. Tager, *Tsarskaya Rossiya i delo Beilisa*.

153 N. V. Krylenko, *Za piat' let. 1918-1922 g.g. Obvinitel'nye rechi*, p. 366.
154 *Ibid.*, p. 368.

CHAPTER VI

GOVERNMENT AND COURT VERSUS THE LAWYERS

A. Relations Between Administration and Bar

1. *Administrative Tampering with the Bar*

The attitude of the tsarist government toward the lawyers, the jury, and the entire Reform of 1864, was closely related to the general political climate of any given period. Thus, in 1874, during the period of reaction in the reign of Alexander II, when the rightist press under the leadership of Katkov waged war against the jury, the law concerning private attorneys was issued—the first indirect blow against the lawyers. A direct blow was dealt in December 1874, when the Emperor decreed to postpone the further establishment of councils of the bar in juridical districts other than in those three in which they already functioned. The third council, that of Kharkov, began its functions on May 6, 1874; the next was established 30 years later, in 1904.

After the acquittal of Vera Zasulich, the competence of the jury was limited by the Law of August 1878, as mentioned above.[1] Moreover, the Ministry of Justice submitted to the State Council a bill tending to confer on the Ministry supervision over the activities of lawyers. The Minister of Justice was to have the right to prohibit individual lawyers from practicing if, in his opinion, their behavior was not compatible with their duties. In this Bill of April 21, 1878, it was said: "It cannot be denied that devotion to the chosen profession and its problems, which consists, in criminal cases, in full cooperation to find the truth, is not the most characteristic feature of the activities of the majority of lawyers . . .; on the contrary, this function of private persons acting as representatives in court somehow completely disappeared from the consciousness of the majority of lawyers and was replaced by aims of pecuniary gain, the striving for which does not stop before any moral considerations in matters of selection of clients or means of defense. . . . Such motives and action directed toward the achievement of acquittal of undoubtedly guilty persons, or even con-

---

[1] See pp. 79-80.

269

fessed perpetrators, by obscuring the case by all means, could not remain without a certain effect upon confidence in the administration of justice itself, and inevitably gave rise to the conception of the counsel as a hired protector of every kind of falsehood and crime." [2]

We see that one of the arguments brought forth by the Ministry of Justice was that lawyers sometimes asked for acquittal of a criminal who confessed his deed. How this fact was later used by the Senate for the indictment of counsels was described above. The State Council however, did not approve the bill and returned it to the Ministry "for harmonization with other measures planned concerning the Bar." [3] Although the political reason for this measure was not mentioned in the bill, one must agree with Hessen and Platonov that the desire to eliminate a free profession was being concealed by arguments of a moral nature.[4]

After the elimination of the *Narodnaya Volya*, which was responsible for the assassination of Alexander II, the reaction during the reign of Alexander III stepped up the fight against the revolutionary movement and also against every institution which had a liberal character.

The Law of 1881 on "The Reinforced and Extraordinary Protection," which referred to the competence of courts-martial a great number of criminal offenses in many provinces of Russia, was a serious blow to the Reform of 1864.

Political offenses were eliminated from the competence of courts for a long time, since these offenses were punished by means of administrative banishment to Siberia and other remote parts of the Empire.

In 1890, a commission was created under the presidency of the Director of the First Department of the Ministry of Justice, M. V. Krasovsky. This Commission worked out the draft of a law concerning the institution of lawyers and the bar. This draft was submitted to the State Council by the Minister of Justice, N. A. Manasein. However, Manasein resigned and his successor, N. V. Murav'yov, withdrew the draft.

Murav'yov formed a new Commission for the Revision of Laws Concerning Administration of Justice, in which senators, high judges, professors of law and representatives of the bar took part. This Commission worked out complete drafts of new laws in all branches of the

---

2 Quoted by Hessen, *Advokatura. . .*, p. 238-240, *passim*.
3 Vas'kovsky, "Advokatura," in *S. U.*, II, 273.
4 Hessen, *Advokatura. . .*, pp. 230 and 243.

administration of justice. These drafts were finally submitted to the State Council in 1904, when the political climate was once more in the process of changing. The drafts remained in the Council without consideration until the Fundamental Laws of the nation were changed in 1906 and legislative power transferred to the Duma together with a reorganized State Council.

Thus, five years' work by this Commission (503 sessions in sections and 35 general assemblies), which published 12 volumes of its work remained fruitless. Still it is not without interest to get acquainted with some opinions of the Commission concerning the lawyers and their organization.

The Commission started with the assertion that it holds firmly to the principles of the Reform of 1864. It called for the creation of councils of the bar in all the judicial circuits (with the exception of two) in which the councils had not yet been introduced. However, the councils should be established only "on suggestion of the Minister of Justice," [5] which means that the establishment of new councils was left to the discretion of the Minister of Justice. It was suggested in the Commission to remove from the disciplinary competence of the council of the bar offenses committed by lawyers in open court and to give jurisdiction to the bench in the case of such offenses. The Commission rejected this suggestion. The Commission decided to extend to the councils of the bar the provision of Article 265 of the Statutes of Judicial Institution which enabled the Senate to issue warnings and observations to courts when they were guilty of collective offenses. The Commission found it advisable to admit professors of law to the legal profession (we know, that the State Council was opposed to such admission in 1864).

The suggestion to establish two categories of lawyers (avocats and avoués, or solicitors and barristers) was debated in all detail. It was emphasized that since the avoué is the master of the suit (dominus litis), the avocat has more liberty and free time for scientific research, for the study of forensic oratory and participation in public life. However, the dependence of the avocat on the avoué,[6] who alone is in touch with the client and prepares all the briefs and other documents, was the reason which caused the majority of the Commission to reject this suggestion.[7]

---

[5] Vysochaishe uchrezhdennaya kommissiya dlya peresmotra zakonopolozheny po sudebnoi chasti. Ob"yasnitl'naya zapiska, III, 177.

[6] See on this question Odilon Barrot, De l'organisation judiciaire en France, who also deplores this dependence.

[7] For the categories of lawyers, see V. D. Spasovich "Ob organizatsii advo-

The Commission also took up, among others, the question of the training of lawyers. It adopted a resolution recommending the strict observation of the personal patronage principle. Moreover, the Commission excluded every kind of self-government by lawyers-in-training, i.e. their general assembly, commissions and committees. On the other hand, the Commission shortened the probation period from five years to three, deemed it necessary to exempt the lawyers-in-training from the obligation of a court certificate for the right of soliciting in their own name, and subordinated them to the disciplinary power of the council of the bar.

Further, the Commission made a very energetic decision in the question of the monopoly of the profession of lawyers in matters of soliciting and representation in court. The Commission disapproved of the policy of the government in introducing a new kind of attorney —the private attorney—who had the same rights as the lawyer but was not obliged to meet the requirements of education, morality and juridical experience demanded of the lawyer.

The Commission also decided that the number of lawyers foreseen by the Laws of 1864[8] (Art. 388 of the Statutes of Judicial Institutions) should be established immediately.

The problem of lawyers' remuneration was also examined by the Commission. It decided that the agreement between the lawyer and client determining the remuneration in relation to the result obtained is immoral in criminal cases. According to the Commission, the task of the counsel in criminal cases is "not to whitewash the defendant or to shift the responsibility from the culprit to an innocent person, but to cooperate with the court in the task of finding the truth . . . It is evident that to permit an agreement which determines the amount of the remuneration in relation to the outcome of the trial means to allow an unworthy bargain with regard to justice and the fate of the accused." [9] As to civil suits, in which the court examines the case within the limits of evidence produced by the parties, such an agreement between the lawyer and the client contains nothing objectionable, according to the opinion of the Commission.

This decision provoked a tempest of indignation among the lawyers, not so much because of the decision itself but because of the

---

katury," *Zhurnal ministerstva yustitsii, 1896, No. 3.* The strongest supporter of this system in Russia was E. V. Vas'kovsky. See Vas'kovsky, "Znacheniye advokatury i zadachi eya organizatsii," *Zhurnal ministerstva yustitsii,* 1895, No. 9, and his *Organizatsiya advokatury. . .,* II, 208-213.

8 See above, p. 155.

9 Vysochaishe uchrezhdennaya kommissiya. . .*Ob"yasnitel'naya zapiska,* III, 120.

arguments on which it was based. The differentiation between the role of the lawyer in civil and criminal cases was described as completely erroneous.[10] "If the role of the trial counsel in criminal cases is to cooperate in finding the truth and not to whitewash the defendant, does it follow that in civil cases the task of the lawyer consists precisely in whitewashing?" asks Winaver.[11]

The differentiation is, as a matter of fact, unjustified. The functions of a lawyer are determined by law in both criminal and civil proceedings, and within the limits set by law the lawyer is an organ of the administration of justice. In criminal cases he is obliged to bring forward everything which can influence the court in favor of the accused, but must certainly remain within the limits of truth and decency. In civil cases too he must observe the rules of morality and probity. Thus, if the agreement about the *quota litis* is deemed immoral, it is immoral in civil and criminal cases alike, and must be prohibited, as it was done in Germany, for instance, for both civil and criminal proceedings; otherwise it must be allowed for both civil and criminal cases, as in the United States.

The Commission was also concerned with another very controversial question: it adopted the draft of a law concerning the admission of Jews to the bar. The problem of anti-Semitism will, however, be discussed under a separate heading.

2. Anti-Semitism in the Administration of Justice

A very active anti-Semitic policy was adopted in Russia by Alexander III and even intensified by Nicholas II. It was a change from the policy of Alexander II; in the last years of the latter's reign, in the so-called period of the "dictatorship of the heart" of Loris-Melikov, the complete abolition of even the few restrictions to which Jews were subject at that time was considered.[12]

The first pogrom took place in Yelisavetgrad in 1881. In 1882, pogroms were repeated in several localities. "The experience of the later years has made it evident that if a governor of a province did not wish a pogrom, the police prevented it, and if the police opposed a pogrom, the crowd never initiated it," Sliozberg writes.[13]

Anti-Semitism became one of the main features of Alexander III's

---

10 See Hessen, *Advokatura.* . ., pp. 358 ff., in which he quotes exhaustively the very well founded objections of the St. Petersburg Bar against this decision.
11 Winaver, *Ocherki.* . ., p. 30.
12 See G. Sliozberg, *Dela minuvshikh dnei,* I, 97.
13 Sliozberg, *op. cit.,* I, 103.

internal policy, which his son later inherited and developed. The leading ideas of Alexander III's reign—nationality, autocracy and orthodoxy—proclaimed in his Manifesto, remained dominant during the
time he occupied the Russian throne. "Nationality" involved predominance of the Great Russians and opporession of the minorities, the
Jews first of all. "Orthodoxy" meant supremacy of the Greek-Ortho-
dox religion over other religions, and especially of Christian religions
over the non-Christian ones. This last principle determined the nature
of anti-Semitism in Russia: it was based officially on religious grounds.
The restrictions to which the Jewish people were subjected in tsarist
Russia and which were greatly increased in the reigns of the last two
Tsars were eliminated if a Jew abandoned his religion and became
a Christian. Every Jew who came to the conclusion that "Paris vaut
une messe," that equality of rights is worth a baptism, had only to
submit to such a baptism and come out of the Church—Orthodox, Catholic or Lutheran—as a citizen enjoying all the rights of a
subject of the Russian Tsar. The Gobineau-Chamberlain-Hitler race
theory was not yet applied, and the possibility existed for a Jew in
Russia to have an official career, to marry a Christian or enjoy other
rights withheld from his former co-religionists—if he became a
renegade.

It was not long before Alexander III's anti-Semitic policy was
applied to the administration of justice. Jews were excluded from
service as judges, prosecutors, investigating magistrates and officials of
the Ministry of Justice.

On November 8, 1889, the following Order of the Tsar was
promulgated: "The admission to the bar and to the profession of
private attorney of persons of non-Christian religion[14] by councils of
the bar and courts is subject to authorization by the Minister of
Justice, given on suggestion of presidents of the institutions mentioned above, until the publication of a special law on this subject." [15]
The Order was issued on the report of Minister of Justice Manasein,
in which he expressed the opinion that the bar was overflowing with
Jews who were forcing Christians out of this profession and introducing into the lawyers' activities a course of action which endangered
the moral purity of the lawyer's profession. It was also said in the
report, but not made public, that the Minister of Justice will not make

---

14 Only Jews were affected by this measure, since there were only four Moham-
medan lawyers in all Russia according to the Official Register of 1896.
15 *Sobraniye uzakoneny i rasporyazheny pravitel'stva*, 1889, No. 127, p. 1031;
the provision was introduced into the *Uchrezhdeniye sudebnykh ustanovleny* as
Note to Art. 380.

use of his discretional power of issuing permits until a law fixes the permissible percentages of Jewish lawyers in every judicial circuit, and until this percentage is reached in reality.[16]

The Imperial Order of November 8, 1889, was another breach of the Reform of 1864.

The ministers of justice who succeeded Manasein, especially Shcheglovitov, faithfully adhered to the Order of 1889 and its secret instruction: no permission for admission was granted to non-Christians until 1905, when the political atmosphere produced a change also in this field, and such lawyers as M. M. Winaver, O. O. Gruzenberg and G. B. Sliozberg, who were already famous in all Russia, but remained lawyers-in-training, were admitted as full members of the bar.[17] However, the political springtime of 1904-1905 was soon over, and the ministers of justice resumed the former practice. The bar again became hermetically closed to Jews (i.e., those who did not change their religion) until the February Revolution of 1917.

The Imperial Order of November 8, 1889 did not mention lawyers-in-training. The St. Petersburg Council of the Bar tried to fill this gap and on January 20, 1890, adopted the following provision: "Persons of non-Christian religion who do not obtain a certificate from court for conducting suits within three years after admission as lawyers-in-training will be dropped from the lists of lawyers-in-training." [18] The Council was of the opinion that the Order of November 8, 1889, would de facto prevent the Jewish lawyers-in-training from obtaining the certificates from the courts. The Council considered it necessary that a lawyer-in-training should, during the last two years of the probation period, conduct suits in his own name, remaining under the direction of the patron, in order to acquire the indispensable experience. Thus the Council thought it inadmissible to keep, among lawyers-in-training, persons who within three years did not obtain the necessary certificate.

The General Assembly of the Bar rejected this provision on February 4, 1890.

As we know, the Council of the Bar in Moscow introduced a similar provision concerning the admission to the profession of law-

---

[16] Murav'yov's Commission of 1894 on the Review of Legislation Concerning the Administration of Justice prepared a project of a law on the admission of non-Christians to the Bar. See below p. 276.

[17] O. O. Gruzenberg remained a lawyer-in-traing for 16 years, and M. M. Winaver for 15 years.

[18] Otchet Soveta prisyazhnykh povezennykh pri S.-Petersburgskoi Sudebnoi Palate za 1899-90 g., p. 23.

yers-in-training on March 4, 1890, and this provision was voided by the Senate only five years later, on May 4, 1895. In the meantime, since Jews did not receive certificates from court because of the Imperial Order of November 8, 1889, and the showing of such a certificate was required for admission, Jews were not admitted to be lawyers-in-training in Moscow in the period of 1890-1895.

Admission as lawyers-in-training was stopped for Jews in all Russia when the Joint Departments of Cassation of the Senate ruled in answer to a question of Minister of Justice Shcheglovitov, on March 12, 1912[19], that in cases of admission of persons of non-Christian confessions to the profession of lawyers-in-training, the provision of Art. 380 of the Statutes of Judicial Institutions had to be applied, *i.e.*, that the admission of such persons is conditional upon a previous permit of the Minister of Justice.

This decision definitely closed the doors of the legal profession to Jews. Those who were already lawyers-in-training were frozen in this position. The doors were reopened by the Revolution of February 1917.

With regard to the views of official circles, and some groups of lawyers, concerning anti-Semitism in the legal profession, it is interesting to quote the draft of a law adopted by the above-mentioned Murav'yov Commission. This was to be the "permanent law" announced in the Imperial Order of 1889.

The Commission emphasized the increase in the number of Jews among lawyers and lawyers-in-training by the end of the eighties. According to the statistics of the Ministry of Justice, the number of Jews among lawyers of all circuits increased from 201 to 249 in 1885-1890, *i.e.*, up to the time of the Law of November 8, 1889. The number of all other lawyers increased from 1,549 to 1,771 during the same period of time. Among lawyers-in-training, Jews showed an increase from 135 to 456, and members of other creeds from 710 to 1,069; the percentage of Jews grew from 19% to 42.6%. As of January 1, 1896, 389 out of 2,149 lawyers were Jews. The Commission was of the opinion that "it is evident that an effective danger is constituted, not by the presence among the lawyers of individual Jews, who have renounced to a great extent views which are peculiar to their nation and adverse to Christian morality, but by the presence among the lawyers of such a number of Jews as could give them a predominant importance and could exercise a pernicious influence on the general

---

19 *Resheniya Obshchago Sobraniya kassatsionnykh s uchastiyem Pervago i Vtorogo departamentov Pravitel'stvuyushchago Senata,* 1912, No. 4.

moral level and the nature of the guild's activity. Thus, in order to prevent this danger, it is sufficient to set a limit to participation of Jews in the bar which should not be exceeded in any circuit." [20]

The reason why Jews allegedly exercise a bad influence on the morality of their Christian colleagues consists according to the Commission, in the following: "Independently of the support and moral leadership which are given to an individual by a correctly organized society, . . . the most important and decisive cause which determines his behavior is the stimulation of his personal will, his consciousness, i.e., his internal life, which finds expression in religion. However, moral principles of various non-Christian creeds . . . rarely correspond to the demands which the life of a Christian state makes on the activity of administrative and public institutions. While individual persons belonging to non-Christian religions may often very satisfactorily fulfill their duty in positions at some of the aforementioned institutions, still it is necessary to keep in mind the danger represented for state and society by the submission of the activity of an entire institution to opinions which are foreign to Christian morality." [21]

Thus the Commission accused Jewish lawyers of behavior incompatible with Christian morality, to which Jews, presumably, cannot subscribe, since they belong to a non-Christian religion. What this behavior allegedly consisted in may be seen from the aforementioned arguments of Manasein's report, which led to the Imperial Order of November 8, 1889. Evidence of such behavior was produced neither by Manasein nor by the Commission. Even when some lawyers of non-Christian religion did behave badly, there is no reason to suppose that they did so because of their religion. Who could deny that some Christian lawyers did not behave according to the postulates of the Christian religions? It is evident that the behavior of this or that lawyer is seldom conditioned by his religious creed, but by other motivations independent of his religion. With regard to the bad influence allegedly exercised by Jews, the St. Petersburg Council of the Bar wrote in its "Remarks" on the opinion of the Commission that, according to statistics quoted by the Commission, 16 out of 346 lawyers in the Moscow Circuit were Jews (less than 5%), whereas in the St. Petersburg Circuit 57 out of 419 lawyers were Jews (less than 13.4%). "However," writes the Council, "nobody who is acquainted with the life of the bar will assert that the lawyers of St. Petersburg

---

[20] Vysochaishe uchrezhdennaya kommissiya. . .Ob"yasnitel'naya zapiska. . ., III, 36-37.
[21] Ibid., p. 33-34.

Circuit are in any respect inferior to lawyers of Moscow Circuit." [22]

Noteworthy was the attitude adopted on this question by lawyers who were members of the Commission. Only V. O. Lyustikh was against any restriction with regard to Jews. The other lawyers in the Commission (P. A. Korsakov, A. A. Kryukov, P. V. Makalinsky, and V. D. Spasovich) voted for a limitation of 10% or 15%, and Plevako wrote a dissenting opinion. Senators A. F. Koni and V. A. Zhelikhovsky were against any legislative restriction of Jews' admission to the bar, but, if a restrictive measure should be adopted, the figure should, they thought, be not less than 20%. The Commission adopted 10% as the percentage of Jews who could be admitted to the bar in every circuit. The Commission also decided that Jews could not be elected president and vice-president of councils of the bar.

F. N. Plevako, one of the most talented trial counsels in Russia, who was nicknamed "golden tongue," wrote a dissenting opinion on the decision of the Commission about the admission of Jews which is interesting because its argumentation is characteristic for that time. Plevako wrote:

> Every people who created their own name and fatherland as a result of their historic struggle . . . leave the imprint of their spiritual personality in their greatest sacred institutions— religion, state and law. These peculiarities constitute the nature and character of a nation and are expressed in its pattern and way of life, in its moral and public mode of life. These principles . . . have been created in Russia by the Russian people. These people, who have put their own world outlook into the foundations of their state system, have the right to demand that the safeguarding of these foundations should be entrusted, not to those who only know, but to those who also believe, who are completely imbued with the national character . . . But the difference in the world outlook, in the juridical and moral laws, reach the point of irreconcilability between people educated in the school of two thousand years of Christianity and people who denied Christianity for the same period of time . . . This is particularly true of Jews. How, then, can they be entrusted with the representation of interests which must be evaluated from the viewpoint of Russian law? How can they be the bearers of the fatherlands' legal consciousness with exhaustive completeness? Law is like religion: it can be the object of knowledge. But can he who knows our teachings in all their minutest details, but who remains outside of them because he does not accept their truth, be a teacher of religion? No, he cannot, because he *knows*, but does not *believe* . . . The same is true of Law. It is not enough to know it.

---

[22] Quoted by Hessen, *Advokatura. . .*, p. 348.

One must live it, embody it with the help of ideas which are conveyed by the native language, native customs, native surroundings . . . We admit to the bar neophytes recently converted to the Christian religion . . . This is a mistake . . . It is not a secret that the conversion of Jews to Christianity for the purpose of being admitted to a guild is an outward conversion . . . The Jew of yesterday, who in the morning is still a son of the Synagogue and in the evening a child of the Christian church . . . is a bad Christian. The change of religion without faith, apostasy —the first step with which a young Jew begins his career as a lawyer—is a bad guarantee for the stability of his character, the earnestness of his thoughts, the incorruptibility of his soul, the purity of his heart—in a word, for all those qualities which are so necessary to the future legal advisor and the fighter for justice and honor . . . I suggest the replacement of the words 'non-Christian' by the words 'persons of non-Christian origin.' I assert that it is better to increase the percentage of non-baptized Jews to 15%, even to 20%, than to limit the number to 10% and at the same time admit Jewish neophytes without any limitation. I also move the following amendment: Those born of baptized parents or of mixed marriages of Christians with non-Christians and, thus, baptized at birth, are considered to be of Christian origin." [23]

Thus, F. N. Plevako anticipated the racial theory as it was applied in Hitler's Germany. Discrimination based on differences of religion did not satisfy him, because morally unstable persons could avoid it by conversion. On the other hand, he was convinced that Jews, belonging to another religion, lack the moral virtues practiced by the Russian people and pertaining to them. He did not use the word "race" and did not refer to characteristics of specific races. He wrote at a time when specific characteristics were attached to a religion and not to a race. But in essence his viewpoint is that of Hitler's theory. The Nazis were also of the opinion that Jews cannot be lawyers or judges because, as non-Germans, they cannot understand German law, and law applied by them would be Jewish and not German law, and that they lack the moral qualities necessary for the legal profession because they are Jews and not Germans by race. However, Plevako was more tractable with regard to children of mixed marriages, called in Germany *Mischlinge*. Plevako was ready to grant them full equality of rights, whereas the Germans treated them much more roughly.

The reaction of the press to discrimination against Jews in the

---

[23] Vysochaishe uchrezhdennaya kommissiya. . ., *Ob"yasnitel'naya zapiska,* Vol. III, pp. 1-7, *passim*.

lawyer's profession depended, naturally, on the political orientation of a given paper. Hessen quotes to that effect the "Journal of Civil and Criminal Law," which as a professional periodical tried to observe neutrality in such questions. The Journal was of the opinion that the increase in the number of Jews among lawyers is an abnormal phenomenon. The paper wrote: "Not being anti-Semitic, we still cannot deny some characteristics [of Jews] which make it desirable that they should not prevail in any guild. Worthy men among Jews are few individuals in the mass. Of course, it is not the Jews who have created the bad reputation of lawyers . . . and large sums are snatched by several Russian names. Moreover, Jewish lawyers are more talented, have more knowledge and are more attentive to their duties than Russians; they defend their clients by all means. It is not the fault of Russians that history did not develop their [the Russians'], resourcefulness, and that competition with Jews is dangerous and even impossible for them." [24] The periodical *Russkaya Mysl'* was of the opinion that "The real reason for all discrimination is competition. But the lawyers carefully hide this reason behind the morally dubious characteristics of Jews." [25] Hessen comes to the conclusion that "indeed the entire press explains . . . the measures against the Jews by motives of competition." [26]

The great bulk of the juridical literature, as well as of the juridical associations, disapproved of the decision of the Commission concerning Jews.[27] Vas'kovsky wrote on the decision of the Commission: " . . . Such a restriction [i.e., percentage of Jews admitted] is beneath criticism, since it is in contradition with the principles of relative liberty of the bar, according to which all persons who meet certain juridical, mental and moral requirements must be admitted to the profession of lawyers. Neither religion nor nationality can play a role in this question, just as they do not play any role in the professions of physician, architect, literary man and others." [28]

---

24 *Zhurnal grazhdanskago i ugolovnago prava*, 1889, no. 6, p. 146.
25 *Russkaya Mysl'*, 1890, No. 4, p. 210.
26 Hessen, *Advokatura.* . ., p. 298.
27 See Vas'kovsky, *Organizatsiya advokatury.* . ., II, 111-113; Volmke, "Zamechaniya na proyekt ob izmenenii v ustroistve advokatury," *Zhurnal ministerstva yustitsii*, 1898, No. 5.
28 Vas'kovsky, *Organizatsiya advokatury.* . ., II, pp. 111-112.

B. Persecutions of Lawyers Illustrated

1. *Sanctions Against Lawyers*

The relations between court and lawyer were subject to fluctuations according to the course of government policy. The Minister of Justice, as an exponent of this policy in matters of administration of justice, managed to find obedient judges who, as in the Beilis Case, were ready to adapt themselves to his demands.

Almost all the interference with the rights of the defense occurred in political cases. There the counsel, although personally not necessarily sharing the radical opinion of his client, had to defend a perpetrator of criminal acts against the government and its representatives. Conflicts between the lawyers and the presiding judge occurred often. However, the presiding judge, the master of the session, had no discretionary power to sentence the counsel to prison on the spot for contempt of court, as is the case in this country. According to Art. 611 of the Code of Criminal Procedure and Art. 157 of the Statutes of the Judicial Institutions, the presiding judge had the right to issue warnings, reprimands, and, as the severest punishment, order the removal of the lawyer from the session. This, of course, did not preclude the right of the bench to ask the council of the bar (or the circuit court in districts where the bar had not yet been introduced) to initiate disciplinary proceedings against the lawyer.

2. *Trial of the First Soviet of Workers' Deputies*

In many political cases, the defense resorted to the strongest measure at its disposal: it walked out under protest. As an example we may cite the trial of the First Soviet of Workers' Deputies, which during 52 days of the year 1905 exercised real governmental power in Russia. The Soviet was tried by the St. Petersburg *Sudebnaya Palata* with class representatives for 30 days beginning on September 19, 1907. One of the tasks of the defense was to prove that the Executive Committee of the Soviet was not a self-styled organization, but had been elected by more than 300 representatives of St. Petersburg plants and factories. The defense succeeded in having these 300 representatives testify in court. Every one of these witnesses began his testimony with the reading of a declaration by the workers he represented. The declarations read approximately as follows: "We, the workers of such and such plant, declare to the St. Petersburg *Sudebnaya Palata* that we plead guilty to all the crimes of which our comrades, indicted in the case of the Soviet of Workers' Deputies, are accused. Acting as they did, they only fulfilled our will. That is why we also demand to be tried in the same manner as they." [29] There were more than 120,000 signatures on these declarations.

During the trial, Gruzenberg, who was the counsel of Leon Trotsky,[30] the Chairman of the Soviet after Khrustalev-Nosar', received two letters from the former Director of the Department of Police, A. A. Lopukhin. To the first letter had been added the copy of a letter by Lopukhin to the President of the Council of Ministers, P. A. Stolypin, about the pogrom agitation of the Department of Police, which printed in an official place, on printing machines confiscated from revolutionaries, proclamations calling for pogroms against Jews throughout the country.[31] In the second letter, Lopukhin offered

---

[29] Gruzenberg, *Ocherki i rechi,* p. 93.

[30] In his article "To the Memory of O. O. Gruzenberg," A. Ya. Stolkind reports a curious dialogue which took place in the summer of 1917 between Gruzenberg, who was at that time Senator of the Department of Cassation of the Senate and his former client. In a political meeting in the Aleksandrinsky Theatre, in which both took part, Trotsky delivered a speech in favor of an immediate peace with Germany. In the intermission Trotsky asked Gruzenberg how he had liked his speech. The latter answered : "During your stay abroad . . . you have not lost your erudition and your brilliant oratorical talent. But in my capacity of Senator I have a forced labor sentence ready for you." Trotsky responded: "You want to correct the mistake you made in having defended me." Stolkind "Pamyati O. O. Gruzenberga" in Gruzenberg, *Ocherki i rechi,* p. 21.

[31] Evidence about the organization of pogroms by the Department of Police of the Ministry of Internal Affairs was provided by some officials of the Department itself. Councillor of State Makarov presented a report to the Minister of Internal Affairs, P. N. Durnovo, on February 15, 1906 (printed *in extenso* by the St. Petersburg *Rech'* on May 5, 1906, No. 63), in which he declared that in a remote room of the Department of Police, under the guidance of the Official of Special Assignments, Komissarov, "proclamations were written, composed, printed and disseminated by the Department; these proclamations were designed to excite some classes of the population against other classes." (See Yu. Lavrinovich, *Kto ustroil pogromy v Rossii?* Berlin, n. d., p. 217). These proclamations were printed on machines confiscated from revolutionaries and disseminated in thousands of copies. Komissarov, the author of the proclamations, declared to Makarov: "Any kind of pogrom can be arranged. If you wish—against ten persons, and if you wish—against 10,000." (*Ibid.,* p. 288). Durnovo, however, did not act on Makarov's report. Then A. A. Lopukhin, at that time Director of the Department of Police, reported about Makarov's revelation to the President of the Council of Ministers, Count S. Yu. Witte, Witte personally questioned Komissarov who declared that he had acted on the order of Rachkovsky, Director of the Political Division of the Department of Police. Witte ordered the destruction of the secret printing office, and Rachkovsky was dismissed. The government was interpellated on this subject in the Duma. Several Deputies—Prince Urusov (former governor of Bessarabia and Deputy Minister of Internal Affairs). M. M. Winaver and F. I. Rodichev—presented in their speeches in the session of the Duma of June 8, 1906, overwhelming evidence on the participation of the Department of Police in St. Petersburg, and of local police forces, in the organization of pogroms. Explanations presented for the government by P. A. Stolypin, who had succeeded Durnovo as Minister of Internal Affairs, were considered inadequate by the Duma, which passed a resolution on June 9, 1906, in which it was said, among other things: "In the pogroms and mass beatings of peaceful citizens which have taken place, and are taking place, in Russia, indubitable signs

to testify in court that St. Petersburg was saved from a "Black Hundreders' " pogrom toward the end of October 1905 thanks only to the measures taken by the Soviet of Workers' Deputies.

Gruzenberg asked the *Palata* to summon Lopukhin and the officials named by him as witnesses. The *Palata* refused. Then the defense walked out. A short excerpt from Gruzenberg's speech explaining the step taken by the defense follows:

. . . Already in the first days of the trial we were turned down by the court in matters which pertain to the main issue of the case . . . We asked for the testimony of Count Witte, Durnovo, the War and the Navy Ministers, City Governor Dedyulin, of all those who witnessed the activity of the Soviet and who sanctioned its activity. This was rejected. We submitted, in the hope that by remaining in court we shall still be in a position to reveal the truth, for the sake of which we came here. The Soviet was not an impostor and was not 'created by outside forces.' It was born as leaves grow on trees in the spring, taking the place of the old, obsolete foliage faded in the fall. We wanted to show . . . and make clear that it was thought possible to select this handful of people from the mass of 200,000 St. Petersburg proletarians and make them responsible for the deeds of the mass. We asked for permission to produce evidence by the testimony of witnesses. This demand was denied . . . One of the fundamental questions of the case is the participation of the authorities in the organization of progroms and the action of the 'Black Hundreders,' since the Soviet of Workers' Deputies organized the working masses for defense against these pogroms everywhere in Russia, and first of all in the capital. In confirmation of the participation by the government in the organization of pogroms, we produced an irrefutable argument—the letter of one of the highest representatives of the government to another representative—and asked that it be put on record. This was refused. We

---

of a common organization and obvious participation of officials who remained unpunished can be observed. (Gosudarstvennaya Duma. Pervyi sozyv 1906 g. *Stenografichesky otchet,* St. Petersburg, 1906, pp. 1129 ff., and Viktor Chernov, "Tainye sovetniki i yavnye pogromshchiki," *Mysl',* 23/VI-1906).

The following episode is very characteristic. When the Minsk Governor, Kurlov, and the Odessa City Governor, Neidgardt, were tried by the Senate on account of inaction during pogroms which took place in Minsk and Odessa, the former Minister of Internal Affairs, Durnovo, testifying before the Senate in favor of the accused, said: "Such persons as Kurlov and Neidgardt should never be tried and made responsible in court, since in their actions they took into consideration the views and aims of the government and were interpreters of its desires." (Lavrinovich, *op. cit.,* p. 290).

It seemed to A. A. Lopukhin that the explanations given by Stolypin to the *Duma* were incomplete because Stolypin had not been correctly informed by his subordinates about all the circumstances of the affair, and he wrote Stolypin a letter which contained all the material available at that time. This is the letter a copy of which Lopukhin sent to Gruzenberg.

asked for permission to summon the author of the letter to court. This was also rejected. And now we have the right to say that we were put in a position which does not allow us to continue our work, since under present conditions we are threatened with the same thing which happened some days ago, when the secretary of the court read to us in a low voice the words of the workers' Marseillaise: 'Arise, arise, ye working people . . .' The reading of these words did not in the least recall the powerfully resounding hymn which rang out in the streets of St. Petersburg a year ago and assembled millions of people. The court desires that we also should tell the court in a low voice, in a quiet hall, in secret, how the revolution happened in St. Petersburg and how the Soviet of Workers' Deputies, the first workers' parliament in the world, was created and worked. We will not stand for that. The voice of the defense must sound loud and powerful—or not at all. That is why we are walking out with the firm conviction that neither the country nor history will blame us for it.[32]

The walkout had no unpleasant consequences for the defense. However, in some other cases the prosecution treated the walkout as a political demonstration.

3. *Agrarian Disorders in Valki*

In the case of the agrarian disorders in Valki, Kharkov Province, the defense under the leadership of N. V. Teslenko tried to prove that the defendants had been severely beaten by the police. But the Presiding Judge overruled every question to witnesses tending to establish evidence of the beating, although according to a ruling of the Senate the defense had the right to put such questions. Teslenko declared in the name of the defense that the defendants, before having been indicted, had been whipped by gendarmes, and that soldiers had been billeted in their homes, which caused heavy material losses to the defendants; that since they could not be punished twice for the same offense and the court had prevented the establishment of these facts, which must have a decisive influence on the sentence, the counsels were deprived of the possibility to defend the accused and had to walk out.[33] The *Sudebnaya Palata* submitted the case to the Council of the Bar in Kharkov, which did not find in the behavior of the counsels any reason for disciplinary proceedings. However, Tes-lenko was ordered to St. Petersburg by the Minister of Internal Affairs, V. K. Pleve, for a personal interview. Teslenko was received

---

[32] Gruzenberg, *Ocherki i rechi*, pp. 98, 100-101.
[33] Goldman, *op.cit.*, p. 25.

by the Director of the Department of Police, A. A. Lopukhin, the same Lopukhin who three years later wrote the letters mentioned above. Lopukhin declared to Teslenko, in the name of Minister Pleve, that the latter regarded the walkout by the defense as a political demonstration; that in case of repetition of such acts, very strict measures would be taken against the defense; and that Teslenko should also transmit the point of view of the Minister to other lawyers involved.[34]

4. The Savitsky, Plaksin and Kal'manovich Cases

Warnings by the government were no empty threats. The lawyers Savitsky and Plaksin, who had to defend workers in Ufa, were arrested and banished to Archangel Province by the police on the eve of the trial.[35]

On December 23, 1905, S. E. Kal'manovich, a distinguished lawyer, arrived in Tambov, where he had to participate in the defense of the murderers of General Bogdanovich. During the session of the court-martial, the officer on duty approached Kal'manovich and told him that somebody wanted to speak to him in the corridor. It was a gendarmery officer who declared to Kal'manovich that he was under arrest. Kal'manovich answered that he could not submit to the arrest before having fulfilled his duty as counsel. He returned to the session-room and informed the court about the incident. The court retired for deliberation and decided to free Kal'manovich from his duties as counsel of the accused. Kal'manovich was arrested; the two defendants were sentenced to death; the Governor-General denied the right of a complaint in cassation, and the perpetrators were executed the same night in the yard of the jail.[36]

With regard to the arrest of Kal'manovich during the performance of his duties, the Vice President of the St. Petersburg Bar, V. O. Lyustikh wrote to the Minister of Justice as follows: "Such an extraordinary measure which is, I believe, for the first time recorded in the annals of the administration of justice, cannot help but produce the most painful and depressing impression on all friends of order and peaceful development of our fatherland. . . ." [37] After remaining in jail exactly one month without any accusation having been brought against him, Kal'-manovich was released on January 25, 1906, and it was declared to him that his arrest was the consequence of a misunderstanding. The Gover-

---

[34] Hessen, Advokatura. . . , pp. 409, 411.
[35] M. V. Bernstam, in Pravo, 1905, pp. 355-356.
[36] Goldman, op. cit., p. 166.
[37] Quoted by Hessen, Advokatura. . ., p. 449.

nor of Tambov Province explained the misunderstanding by the fact that the police had information "about another Kal'manovich." [38]

In the same town of Tambov, Governor Muratov fined the lawyer Shatov for a speech delivered in court. True, this order was cancelled.

In Irkutsk, the Council of the Bar was arrested *in corpore* in 1906 and its functions were transferred to the Circuit Court. [39]

5. The Gillerson Case

The cases of arrest mentioned above were but a few scattered cases of administrative measures by over-zealous officials. Two years later, however, the administration instigated criminal proceedings against the lawyer A. I. Gillerson. He was indicted and tried for a speech delivered in court. This unprecedented attack against freedom of speech in court stirred the entire lawyers' guild in Russia.

In June 1906 several persons were tried by the Circuit Court in Grodno for having participated in the pogrom which took place on June 1-3 1906, in Belostok. Gillerson represented, in the trial, the victims of the pogrom, as private prosecutor. After having emphasized the fact that pogroms were instigated by the "Black Hundreders," Gillerson declared that his clients withdraw material claims against the accused since they are not really responsible for the progroms. Thereupon he walked out. The sentence was pronounced the next day in his absence. On October 2, 1908, Gillerson was summoned to the gendarmery in St. Petersburg, where he was interrogated as a defendant and then released on a bond of 5,000 rubles. He was accused of having committed, by his speech, the crime specified in Paragraphs 1, 2, and 6 of Article 129 of the New Criminal Code. [40]

Gillerson made a written report of the incident to the Council of the Bar in St. Petersburg. In the meantime, rumors about the impending indictment of Gillerson spread among his colleagues. A petition signed by a great number of lawyers demanded the convocation of a

---

[38] *Otchet Soveta prisyazhnykh poverennykh okruga S. Peterburgskoi Sudebnoi Palaty za* 1905-1906 g., p. 42.

[39] Hessen, *Advokatura. . .,* pp. 449-450.

[40] Article 129 reads: "He who is found guilty of public oral delivery or reading of a speech or a literary work, or of publicly displaying a literary work or picture, which incites:
1. to the perpetration of a seditious or treacherous act,
2. to the overthrow of the political structure of the State,
3. to animosity among individual sections or classes of the population, or among the estates, or among the employers and workers, is punishable. . . [banishment and various jail terms]."

General Assembly of the Bar. The General Assembly took place on October 19, 1908. The Council made a report and made known the explanations of Gillerson. After prolonged debates in which all of the speakers were of the opinion that Gillerson did not transgress his rights of free speech, and that the indictment represents an act of political vengeance and an atempt against the rights of defense in court, the Assembly decided to elect a commission of 12 lawyers for assembling material and formulating conclusions concerning the indictment of Gillerson. The Commission held several sessions. The research work and gathering of material from Rusian and foreign sources was taken over by O. O. Gruzenberg.

The second General Assembly of the Bar concerning the Gillerson Case took place on December 21, 1908. Gruzenberg made a detailed report. After very animated discussions, the Assembly decided:

1) to approve Gruzenberg's report.
2) to assert that a lawyer cannot be held responsible for a speech delivered in court session in fulfillment of his professional duties.
3) to declare that the unlawful indictment of A. I. Gillerson is an attempt to submit the court to external control and represents an act of political struggle.
4) to recommend that all the presidents, vice presidents or other representatives of all the bars take part in the trial of Gillerson [as his counsels].
5) to ask the Petersburg Council to make an agreement with other councils in order to carry out this decision.
6) to ask the St. Petersburg Council to send copies of Gruzenberg's report and of the material gathered to all other Councils.
7) to prolong the functioning of the Commission elected on October 19 . . . up to the end of the prosecution to which Gillerson was being subjected.[41]

Gillerson was tried at a special session of the *Vilenskaya Sudebnaya Palata* in Grodno on October 26-27, 1909.

The accusation was based on the following words of Gillerson:

1. That there was no animosity between Jewish and Christian workers, because the slogan of the former and of the latter is the same: "Proletarians of all countries, unite!" but not "Devour one another," which is the slogan of the bourgeoisie and the bureaucracy.
2. That the "Black Hundreders' " propaganda in the army was being carried on already at the time of the pogrom in Brest;

---

[41] *Protsess A. I. Gillersona* (St. Peterburg, 1910) , p. 18-19.

that he, Gillerson, succeeded in getting hold of an appeal to the army in which it was said that "Japanese, Jews and Poles are the source of all evil," that the officials' club *Otdykh* (Rest) in Belostok spread pogrom proclamations and agitated against Jews.

3. That the defendants are only victims of provocation, and that the real culprits of the pogroms remained free. Having dropped material claims against the accused, he asked for their acquittal, since they would be pardoned anyway, he said, on the grounds of a report by the Minister of Justice.[42]

4. Speaking of the love for freedom of the Russian people, he cited as an example the Republic of Novgorod the Great and expressed the desire that the times of Novgorod the Great should return and its precepts—which were legality, freedom and order—should be realized.[43]

That was all. But on the ground of those expressions, the indictment carried the conclusion that Gillerson had "publicly delivered a speech in which he had knowingly excited the animosity of the working class of the population against the officials and called for the overthrow of the existing form of government and public structure in Russia."[44]

Gillerson was defended by nine lawyers, headed by Gruzenberg, who represented all the Councils of the Bars in Russia.

In the following we give an excerpt from Gruzenberg's speech, which reflects the viewpoint of the guild on the lawyers' rights and activities. He said:

It is not for the personal defense of our honorable colleague Gillerson that representatives of the Russian Bar arrived here from all parts of the country. Not a few of our colleagues, carried away by the revolutionary tempest, languish in banishment, jail and forced labor. They were defended by individual colleagues and their cases never acquired sufficient importance to concern all the lawyers . . . But today not an individual lawyer but the whole guild is on the dock. The blow is directed against Gillerson, but, having wounded him, it will kill freedom of speech in court. We will not surrender this freedom without struggle, without an obstinate fight . . . The word is the only weapon of the defense . . . But it rings true, conclusive and strong when it is born in the atmosphere of fearlessness and duty. The word is not a goal. It is not a self-sufficient art. It is only a tool for finding the truth.

---

[42] He alluded to the fact that the Tsar systematically pardoned the perpetrators of pogroms condemned by courts. See *Molodaya Advokatura* (St. Petersburg, 1908) and Lavrinovich, *Kto ustroil pogromy v Rossii,* 199-202.

[43] *Protsess A. I. Gillersona. . .,* pp. 4, 24-25.

[44] *Ibid.,* p. 25.

We would look in vain for an analogy between a court hall and a public meeting . . . If a comparison is necessary, this hall is like a dissection room where no one is ashamed of nudity, because it no longer tempts. No one is afraid that passion will be excited there, because it dies down before the mystery of death. And in the court hall everyone and everything serves only one aim . . . the solving of the controversy between the accusation and the defense . . . Like the scalpel of an anatomist, the examination by the counsel, and his speech, cut asunder all the veils which envelop truth and justice. In the striving for acquittal, or alleviation of the guilt of the defendant, the counsel has the right to lay open the motives which agitated the soul of his client and placed him in opposition to the law. And for this purpose the counsel must penetrate into the mysterious world of his client's ideas and dreams, and, if necessary, to depict their magic power. The counsel has not only the right but the duty to do so. Justifying these ideas, if the crime has been caused by them, the counsel fulfills the duty entrusted to him by law, and must not pay any attention to the effect his speech may produce on the public. The circle of persons to whom the defense directs its words reaches no farther than the bench. The court hall is not open to the public as a place of performance. Publicity is only a means of control . . . It is preferable to close the court doors than to seal the lips of the defense.[45]

Then Gruzenberg emphasized that the presiding judge is the only power which has the right to interfere and stop the counsel or censor his speech. But the presiding judge did not reprove Gillerson's words which provided the ground for the accusation. Only the court before which the pleading is delivered can judge its admissibility. The case is developed step by step in the hearing. The court absorbs the impression produced by the investigation in court, and, following not only the words of the orator but the tone of the whole speech, the court alone can distinguish an unlucky expression from an intended misuse of speech.

Gruzenberg gave the example of the Anglo-Saxon countries, where lawyers enjoy full freedom of speech in court and cannot be subjected to criimnal prosecution for their pleadings.[46] He quotes French, Belgian, German and Italian legislation according to which only the court before which the speech is delivered can decide upon the punishability of its author.

In appraising the speech delivered by Gillerson on behalf of the victims of the Belostok progrom, Gruzenberg said:

---

[45] *Protsess Gillersona. ..,* p. 60-63, *passim.,*
[46] Gruzengerg has in mind cases other than contempt of court.

Today, gentlemen judges, you do not know the most essential thing, without which a just decision is not possible: you do not know either the truth of the facts disclosed in court, or the feelings lived through by the participants in the trial. Scraps of ideas, fragments of sentences from Gillerson's speech, incorrectly understood or distorted—that is all that has reached us. This speech was born in the gloomy session hall where the picture of the animal hatred of some, the enlightened cruelty of others and the senseless indifference of many, very many, was unrolled day by day, trait after trait, during two weeks . . . To you, gentlemen judges, children of a great sovereign nation which occupies one of the first places on the world arena, the feelings of a vanquished people, oppressed by the tragedy of history, is not known. Now is not the time to speak about it. I will say only that the Belostok slaughter, as all the other organized mass destructions of Jews, did not remain without effect on the Jewish intelligentsia. Blood, innocent blood was splashed on its sensitive soul, and kindled pain and despair there . . . Do not demand exactly calculated words and accurately weighed sentences in such cases. It is impossible to record the beating of an agitated heart with the help of a prosecutor's chronometer. There are moments when not to forget oneself means to forget one's human dignity." [47]

Then Gruzenberg analyzed the relevant pasages of Gillerson's speech and came to the following conclusion:

Is it not clear that there is nothing to support a well-founded accusation [of Gillerson], but only prosecution [for the sake of prosecuting]; no crime, but the threat of punishment? I know that our judicial family, strong through its unity in the past, has been split by political creeds. But always there has been a slogan which reassembled us under our banners: it is legality and our service to it. . . . . The bar realizes very well that the reaction which sweeps away every free institution will also not spare the bar. It feels that hostile waves press on it from all sides, as on a diving bell on the sea bottom: a single crack, and everything is lost . . . It is possible that these waves will today also engulf the bar, one of the few forces serving the public with utter devotion. But as long as this has not happened, as long as the place from which I speak is still holy, we declare to the public that it is in danger. Defense in political cases must be free, or it should not exist at all! However rigorous your sentence may be, the Russian bar will not be intimidated by it.[48]

Gillerson was sentenced on two counts based on Article 129 of the *Ugolovnoye Ulozheniye* to one year's confinement in a fortress.

Complaints in cassation were submitted to the Senate. The Crim-

---

[47] *Ibid.*, pp. 66-76, passim.
[48] *Ibid.*, p. 78.

inal Department of Cassation of the Senate decided on the complaint in its session of January 14, 1910. The session was attended by the Council of the St. Petersburg Bar *in corpore* and by the Commission on the Gillerson Case. Only Gruzenberg spoke for the defense. His speech was limited to the juridical analysis of the case and the grounds for cassation. The Senate rejected the complaint. In the reasons in support of the decision it was said that "pleadings in court may not be cloaked in the guise of legality in order to commit, with impunity acts otherwise forbidden by law under penalty." [49]

6. *Maklakov versus Shcheglovitov*

The animosity of the administration toward the bar found its expression in a speech by the Minister of Justice, Shcheglovitov, delivered in the Duma on November 22, 1909.

The occasion for the speech was the following: On January 18, 1908, the Administration of Prisons issued a circular order to all jail wardens not to admit counsels suspected of illegal transmission of letters to prison inmates to have *tête-à-tête* meetings with their clients. According to Article 569 of the Code of Criminal Procedure, the president of the court had to issue a permit to the lawyer to see his arrested client *en tête-à-tête*.[50] Thus, a jail warden had no legal right to refuse to a lawyer in possession of a permit issued by the court president admission to a private meeting with the inmate, even if he had grounds for suspicion that the lawyer was guilty of clandestine carrying of letters or other things to his client and *vice versa*. If a lawyer did not behave during his visit to the prison as he was supposed to do, the jail warden could notify the court president, who could cancel the permit and start disciplinary proceedings or notify the prosecutor if the lawyer had committed a criminal offense. However, discretionary power not to admit a lawyer in possession of a permit could not be conferred to the jail wardens by an administrative order. The circular order was a curtailment of the rights of the defense by the administration. The Duma therefore voted to put the following questions to the Minister of Justice: "1. Did the Minister of Justice know about the Circular Order of January 18, 1908? 2. If so, why did he not

---

[49] *Ibid.*, p. 104.

[50] In the official message to accompany this article, the State Council declared that: "to forbid a tête-à-tête between the arrested defendant and his counsel would mean to return to the inquistorial procedure. It may occur that the accused. . .must tell his counsel such details concerning his action as he cannot and even should not make known publicly (*Sudebnye Ustavy. . ., III: Ustav ugolovnago sudoproizvoidstva,* p. 217).

292   COURTS, LAWYERS AND TRIALS UNDER THE LAST THREE TSARS

take measures to rescind the Circular Order in due time? What measures did he adopt to prevent the fulfilment of this clearly illegal order?" [51]

Shcheglovitov declared to the Duma, in answer to the questions, that: 1) the order was issued with his knowledge and approval, and that 2) he would not rescind or change the order even if the Duma adopted a motion disapproving of his action.

In his explanations to the Duma, the Minister said: "The master of a house has the right not only to turn out of the house, but also not to let in, such visitors who will disturb the order in the house." This approach to the question the Minister himself described as Philistine, "but sufficient to justify the measure. The jail warden, being the master of the house, has the right not to let in a person suspected of illegal actions." Then the Minister declared that the order was caused by the behavior of some lawyers who carried leftist newspapers and letters to their clients in jail and agreed to take letters from defendants without the permission of the jail warden. In his speech, Shcheglovitov said: "Politics has become such an alluring occupation that it pushes questions of morality completely into the background. This phenomenon of our public life is also reflected, to a certain extent, in the activities of the lawyers. Complaints . . . that the defense sometimes distorts its purpose, converting itself from the defender of the accused into the defender of crimes, concern political cases especially. Defense in this respect has undoubtedly come down from the high position which was assigned to it by the fathers of the Judicial Institutions." [52] Thus, according to the Minister, "the lawyer is no longer an organic link in the administration of justice, but only a visitor tolerated [or not tolerated] by the master of the house," as Hessen remarks. [53]

V. A. Maklakov brilliantly replied to the Minister. His speech can be found on pages 2830-2841 of the verbatim report of the Duma session. A part of his speech concerning the role of the defense in political cases is quoted below. [54]

Indeed, the Minister of Justice, Shcheglovitov, had gone a long way in distorting the Judical Institutions of 1864, to which he continued to pay lip service in his writings. It was a long stretch on the road of reaction which separated the speech by the Chief Prosecutor

---

[51] Gosudarstvennaya Duma. Trety sozyv 1909 g. *Stenografichesky otchet*, p. 2508.
[52] *Ibid.*, p. 2520.
[53] Hessen, *Advokatura. . .*, p. 457.
[54] See p. 309.

of the Senate Shcheglovitov in the Semyonov Case[55] from the speech by Minister of Justice Shcheglovitov in the Duma in 1909! But the peak was reached by him in 1913 in the Beilis Case and the trial of the twenty-five lawyers as an aftermath of this case.

After extended debates, the Duma adopted, by a majority of 176 against 80, the following resolution: ". . . Considering that . . . the explanations presented by the Minister of Justice in the session of November 25 of the current year constituted not only an attempt to justify the illegality committed by the Circular Order of January 18, 1908, but also the proclamation of a whole system of equal infractions in the future, the State Duma declares the Order of January 18, 1908 illegal and the explanation of the Minister of Justice inadequate. . ." [56]

7. Trial of the Twenty-Five Lawyers

The major clash between the bar and the administration occurred in connection with the Beilis Case.

On October 23, 1913, while the trial of Beilis was going on in Kiev, a General Assembly of the St. Petersburg Bar was summoned for the purpose of electing a Council for a new term. During the Assembly a group of lawyers, headed by N. D. Sokolov and A. F. Kerensky, moved the passing of a resolution, and the sending of a telegram to Beilis' counsels in Kiev, containing a categorical protest against the circumstances of the trial. The majority of the Council opposed the passing of a resolution, since the question was not on the order of the day. A minority of the Council was, however, of the opinion that a resolution concerning the Beilis trial was not only admissible but even a sacred duty of the guild.

The resolution was carried by the General Assembly, and a telegram containing the resolution was sent to Kiev. It read: "The General Assembly of the lawyers of the Circuit of the St. Petersburg *Sudebnaya Palata* considers it to be its civic and professional duty to express its protest against the distortion of the foundations of justice evident in the staging of the Beilis trial; against the slander of Jewish people in court, a slander which is rejected by the entire cultured world; and against the charging of the court with the task, unusual for it, of propagating the ideas of racial and national animosity. This outrage against the foundation of human society debases and dis-

---

[55] See p. 68.
[56] See above Footnote 51, p. 2896.

graces Russia before the whole world, and we raise our voice in defense of Russia's dignity and honor." [57]

This resolution produced the effect of an exploding bomb. Action against the Bar and the lawyers who voted for the resolution was taken in two directions: the prosecution started an investigation for the purpose of indicting those who voted for the resolution according to Art. 279 of the old Criminal Code,[58] and the *Sudebnaya Palata* discussed the question of disciplinary proceedings against the Council of the Bar and the individual lawyers involved in the resolution.

The *Sudebnaya Palata* declined to start disciplinary proceedings against the Council, but ordered it to take disciplinary action against the lawyers who voted for the resolution, and opened disciplinary proceedings against the Chairman of the General Assembly of October 23, 1913.

The Council of the Bar examined the case of the lawyers involved in the resolution and the sending of the telegram, and acquitted them, finding that the resolution and the telegram protested only against a fact which was asserted in them, without any indication as to who should be considered responsible for the fact.

The General Assembly of the St. Petersburg Bar of October 23, 1913, had been attended by two hundred to two hundred and fifty lawyers. From this number the prosecution picked eighty-six, but indicted only twenty-five. They were tried on June 3-6, 1914, by the St. Petersburg Circuit Court without a jury. The defense was in the hands of eight counsels. A verbatim report of the sessions, with the testimony of witnesses and speeches of all the accused and their counsels, appeared in the press and in the periodical *Pravo*.[59]

The Court sentenced N. D. Sokolov and A. F. Kerensky to eight months, and the other accused to six months, in prison.

The sentence produced a tremendous effect on all classes of the population. On the evening when it was pronounced, the Council of the Bar *in corpore* honored the condemned lawyers with a dinner. D. V. Stasov, President of the Council, was chairman.

The next day a dinner in which more than two hundred lawyers

---

[57] *Pravo*, 1914, No. 24, p. 1838.

[58] Art. 279 of the *Ulozheniye o nakazaniyakh ugolovnykh i ispravitel'nykh* reads "Whoever will be proved guilty of having deliberately composed, displayed publicly or disseminated abusive letters or other writings, papers or pictures offensive to highly placed persons in the state, will be sentenced to jail for a period of one year and four months to two years, and deprived of some rights and privileges, according to Art. 50 of this Code."

[59] See *Pravo*, 1914, No. 23, pp. 1837-1849; No. 24, pp. 1911-1912; No. 26, pp. 2023-2052; No. 27, pp. 2098-2127; No. 28, pp. 2161-5185; No. 29, pp. 2229-2258; No. 30, p. 2300.

and members of the Duma participated gave an opportunity for speeches in which the 25 lawyers were praised as heroes and political martyrs. In an address signed by 141 of the most eminent members of the Bar, full solidarity with the condemned lawyers was expressed. It was said there that "the condemned 25 lawyer-citizens defended elementary rights without which the existence of a cultured society is impossible." [60] The chairman of the second banquet, Yefremov, a member of the Duma, who started the series of speeches, said: "We, the representatives of various shades of political opinion, could not keep silent about this trial. You, having been condemned, can proudly raise your heads." [61]

When A. F. Kerensky entered the session hall of the Duma on June 9, he was greeted by a tremendous ovation. For several minutes the hall was shaken by terrific applause.

Hundreds of telegrams were received from all corners of Russia from bars,[62] groups and private persons. The newspaper *Odesskiye Novosti* wired: "You left the court, not defeated, but victorious. The real sentence was passed by Russian society, and will be passed by history, one of the glorious pages of which will be represented by your trial, henceforth the historical Trial of Twenty-Five St. Petersburg Lawyers." [63]

The workers in St. Petersburg decided to protest in defense of those who had often defended them so faithfully. A great number of plants in St. Petersburg went into protest strikes. Thousands of workers demonstrated in streets and were dispersed by the police. A mass meeting at the factory "Erikson" adopted the following resolution: "We greet the condemned lawyers who defended truth with honor from anti-semitism." [64]

The trial of the 25 lawyers gave Russian public opinion an occasion to express what it thought about the Beilis trial and its staging. The indictment, the trial and the sentence rendered by the Circuit Court were a manifestation of the attitude taken by the administration, and thus by the regime, toward lawyers and their activities.

The war pushed the internal frictions between the administration and the lawyers into the background. It brought to lawyers many cases of defense in spy trials. War intoxication caused a great number of

---

[60] *Pravo*, 1914, No. 24, p. 1912.
[61] *Ibid.*
[62] The telegraph office in Kiev refused to transmit the telegram of the lawyers. It had to be sent by mail.
[63] *Ibid.*, p. 1914.
[64] *Ibid.*, p. 1915.

trials of persons who had nothing to do with spying or treason. Many of these trials occurred in regions under the jurisdiction of military authorities, for the most part in field courts-martial, to which counsels were not admitted. Russia experienced great military reverses in the beginning of the war. Responsibility for them was sometimes shifted from those who should have shouldered it onto imaginary "spies." In some cases, lawyers succeeded in saving the accused.[65] However, such trials are usual phenomena of war and also occurred in other countries at war. Products of wartime cannot serve as a description of typical Russian features of the administration of justice and the activity of Russian lawyers.

It must be emphasized that between 1864 and 1917, Russia had courts second to none in the world as far as civil and criminal cases without political character were concerned. It is the illegal interference of the administration into political cases, the arbitrary limitations on the jurisdiction of general courts, the use of courts-martial and the pressure brought upon the judiciary which produced the sentences and decisions that were not worthy of Russian courts as created by Alexander II. The Russian judiciary in general bears no responsibility for them.

The February Revolution of 1917 produced an important change in the administration of justice. As mentioned above, the Provisional Government appointed a commission for the restoration of judicial institutions as they were created by the Reform of 1864. The field courts-martial were reorganized: they now consisted of judges elected by soldiers and three judges elected by officers, with a presiding officer.

All religious and racial restrictions were abolished by a Decree of the Provisional Government of March 21, 1917; thus, the way to the bar and to the judiciary was reopened to Jews. Very prominent lawyers received high judiciary and administrative positions, beginning with A. F. Kerensky as Minister of Justice and then President of the Council of Ministers.

The task of carrying out a more fundamental reform in the field of the administration of justice, as in the other branches of government, was left to the Constitutional Assembly.

But the fate of the Russian people took another direction. The October Revolution put an abrupt end to a democratic and peaceful evolution and also brought about the end of the free guild of Russian lawyers.

---

65 See Gruzenberg, *Vchera* . . . , pp. 51-96.

CHAPTER VII

THE RUSSIAN LAWYER AS A CHAMPION
OF THE INDIVIDUAL

A. The Problem of Individualism and Individual Rights in Political Thought

The political history of mankind revolves around the problem of finding the just measure of independence, or freedom, which the individual may possess within the state. The individual and the collective confront each other, shaping the political history of mankind by their respective rights.[1]

Political philosophy tries to explain the relations between the individual and the state, and to define their reciprocal rights and duties. Every epoch, every stage of development of these relations had its philosophers and apologists.

At the time of Plato and Aristotle, the founders of political science, the state had already absorbed the major share of the individual's rights. The individual was oppressed by the state. Liberty was understood, in Greece, as the right of participation in the life of the state, whereas individual liberty as a sphere of activity with which the state could not interfere was unknown to Greek philosophy.[2]

It was Christianity which for the first time proclaimed the equality of men. They are all equal because they have an immortal soul, and because of the Fall. However, the church did not free the individual from the oppression of the state. On the contrary, it got hold also of his internal life. The individual became the subject not only of the state but also of the spiritual world empire founded by the church in addition to its secular state in Rome.

These secular and spiritual domains of the popes grew and were strengthened.

---

1 Hans Kelsen writes: " . . . the individual engaged in an apparently insoluble conflict with society is nothing else than an ideology fighting for certain interests, against their limitation by a collective system." (Hans Kelsen, "The Pure Theory of Law," *Law Quarterly Review*, L (1934) , 497).

2 Jellinek tried to show that the Greek State actually recognized some individual rights of its citizens, but that this was not realized by Greek philosophers.

297

The Middle Ages were oriented by history toward a struggle between kings and popes and between Catholics and Protestants. Finally the popes could not resist the double attack from the outside and the inside: the rising monarchies and the Reformation destroyed their secular state and disrupted their spiritual empire. In this struggle of states and religions, however, the individual did not participate as a champion of his personal rights. He fought for a state or a religious conviction, for the political or religious collective of which he was a member, but his personal rights within these collectives were not at stake. The majority of the people were serfs, deprived of elementary personal and political rights, subjects of a small or powerful lord. The nobility fought against the king for class privileges and not for individual rights. In the end, the nobility lost the fight and, after Louis XI in France, and by the time of Henry VIII in England and Emperor Charles V, in Germany and Spain, omnipotent states, small and large, with the *imperium* in the hands of an autocratic ruler, were firmly established.

The genius of Aristotle produced the cyclical theory of history. He asserted that all governments become corrupt sooner or later, generating the source of revolution. Thus, according to him, regular changes in government must occur. It is true that the political pendulum of history swings sharply from one side to the other, remains for a certain time somewhere in the middle, then resumes its movement. These sharp oscillations were also produced in the everlasting struggle of the individual against the state.

At the end of the eighteenth century, political thought asserted that man is good by nature, that the state was not created in order to curb his evil instincts, that the state is a product of a free compact between free men, born equal, and that within the state the individual possesses inalienable rights given to him by nature and confirmed by the compact he entered into in order to create the state.

The last quarter of the same century saw a very important movement of the political pendulum. It went from the extreme right to the extreme left in France in 1789-1793. The French Revolution was the first revolution made in the name of the individual liberating himself from the oppression of the state. "Liberté, égalité, fraternité" was its motto, the "Déclaration des droits de l'homme et du citoyen"— its charter. The revolution in the United States, which took place even before the French Revolution, was inspired by the same principles; it was, however, primarily an act of liberation of one state from the yoke imposed by another state, rather than an emancipation of the individual from enslavement by the state.

The individualistic principles proclaimed by the political philosophy of the seventeenth and eighteenth centuries were incorporated in the declarations of the American and French Revolutions and had the greatest influence on the shaping of the state in the United States and in France.

"We hold these truths to be self-evident, that all men are created equal, that they are endowed by their creator with certain inalienable rights; that among these are life, liberty and the pursuit of happiness. That to secure these rights governments are instituted among men, deriving their just powers from the consent of the governed," says the Declaration of Independence.

In the introduction to the *Déclaration des droits de l'homme et du citoyen* of August 26, 1789, it is asserted that the only reason for public disasters and corruption of the government is the neglect of natural inalienable and holy rights of men. In the following seventeen articles of the *Déclaration*, the foundations of a new political order are established and the rights of man are enumerated: personal immunity, judicial guarantees, freedom of thought, religion, speech and press, equality of taxation, etc.[3]

Cosmopolitan ideals, which originated in the Middle Ages, when Christianity created the idea of a world empire and when national states were weak, developed in political philosophy during the eighteenth century. Thus, Voltaire thought that individuals should not be restrained by patriotism or nationalism, and that loyalty to a nation and its culture must be produced by respect for its cultural contributions and its social order rather than by the accident of birth. Patriotism and nationalism, he felt, often produce immoral actions; they create a striving toward success without regard to morality. His ideal was cosmopolitanism and the greatest possible freedom of thought and religion. Power was for him a trust and not the instrument of the ruler's desires. David Hume wrote: "I should venture to acknowledge that not only as a man but as a British subject, I pray for the flourishing communes of Germany, Spain, Italy and even France itself."[4] Goethe said he did not know what patriotism was. He was "Der grosse Europäer" and not a German patriot. "The eve of the French Revolution found every wise man in Europe—Lessing, Kant, Goethe, Rous-

---

[3] See F. Hélie, *Les constitutions de la France,* p. 30-32.
[4] Quoted by Walter Lippmann, *An Inquiry Into the Principles of the Good Society,* p. 194.

seau, Lavater, Condorcet, Priestiey, Gibbon, Franklin—more a citizen of the world than of any particular country," W. Clarke wrote.[5] In his project of a lasting peace Kant asked for the complete abolition of restrictions on movement and settlement. He asserted that no one has more or less of a right to live on a certain spot of the globe than anyone else.

In the first half of the nineteenth century, individualism and the individual remained victorious in their fight against the state. Great Britain inaugurated in 1830 a period of reforms which gave her the final democratic form she has at the present time. "English Law", as Engels put it, "is the only one which kept and transplanted to America and the colonies the better part of that personal freedom, local self-government and protection from any, except judicial, outside interference—in one word, of those old German liberties—which completely disappeared on the Continent under the power of absolute monarchies, and have not yet been recovered to their full extent anywhere up to the present time." [6]

Freedom of trade as established in Great Britain and already advocated by Adam Smith in 1776 was accepted in France and even in Bismarck's Germany. Carlyle proclaimed hero worship and the hero as the maker of history. John Stuart Mill[7] and Herbert Spencer brought the exaltation of every kind of liberty to a climax. Spencer desired to limit state interference with individual freedom to punishment of crimes against the person and property. No other restraint upon the individual should exist, according to him. Dostoyevsky, Max Stirner and Nietzsche attempted to release the individual from almost every spiritual bond and to create the superman to whom everything is allowed.

The trend toward the emancipation of the individual was also reflected in the legal philosophy of the seventeenth, eighteenth and nineteenth centuries. It was the classical school of law-of-nature which conducted the fight for the rights of the individual. According to the principles of this school (Grotius, Montesquieu, Rousseau and Kant are its most important representatives), the rights to freedom, independence and pursuit of happiness are innate, inalienable rights given to the individual by nature, and these rights cannot be restricted by

---

5 Quoted by J. A. Hobson, *Imperialism,* pp. 7-8.
6 F. Engels, *Anti-Dühring,* p. 329.
7 Mill asserted that "the sole end for which mankind are warranted, individually or collectively, in interfering with the liberty of action of any of their number, is self-protection. That the only purpose for which power can be rightfully exercised over any member of a civilized community, against his will, is to prevent harm to others." (John Stuart Mill, *On Liberty,* p. 23).

the state beyond the strict necessity of preserving the liberty and happiness of other people. As Bentham put it: "It is the greatest happiness of the greatest number that is the measure of right and wrong." [8] He called this principle a fundamental axiom. The happiness of the community is, according to him, the totality of happiness of all its individual members.

The legal philosophy of the school of natural law revolves around the individual. It is he, his rights and happiness, not the interests of the state, that are the subject of care and protection. Limitations on the rights of the individual for the benefit of the community or the state must be reduced to a minimum and must be defined by law. The rule of law was proclaimed as the basic principle. The postulates of this school, which became predominent in the eighteenth and the first half of the nineteenth centuries, inspired the authors of law codes in France, Austria and Germany.

Some police states were changed into *Rechtsstaaten*—which means according to the German definition, that the state is ruled by law and not by arbitrariness. The rights of the individual are protected in such a state by laws which are, again according to the German definition, *"zweiseitig verbindende"* (mutually binding) norms. By this, Jhering understood norms which are binding not only on the people but on the state as well. The *Staatsgewalt* (state power) is brought into subordination to its own laws, and the real *Rechstszustand*—rule of law— is thus created. [9]

In such a state the court is independent of the administration and of the people and plays the role of an umpire between the state and the individual. Under such a political order the judicial power, as one of the three independent powers, acquired special importance, since the court applied the laws and commented upon them, and was the main support of legality. Of course, the courts did not assume in Europe the unique position they hold in the United States. Still, some European courts also became strongholds of legality in their respective states. Courts took over the task of safeguarding the personal rights of the individual. A court decision became necessary for almost every coercion of the person in those countries where the principles of freedom and legality were predominant and where administrative power with regard to the citizen was reduced to the inescapable minimum in cases of emergency and evident necessity—and even then the adminis-

---

[8] Jeremy Bentham, A Fragment on Government, p. 93.
[9] Jhering, *op. cit.*, p. 344.

tration was to remain responsible for illegal interference with personal rights.

B. Individual Rights and the Russian Judicial Reform of 1864

There cannot be any doubt that the wave of individualism which reached its peak in Europe about the middle of the nineteenth century influenced the reforms of Alexander II. Indeed, all his great reforms were constructed on the principle of the rights of the person. He liberated the serfs, which meant personal freedom to millions of Russians. He created the *zemstvo*, a kind of local self-government. He broke the shackles which bound the individual in court, by means of the Laws of November 20, 1864. Russia became a *Rechtsstaat* in the field of the administration of justice.

This emancipation of the individual by the Judicial Reform is brilliantly defined by Prof. Foinitsky: "Something new in the understanding of legality itself must have been brought about by the Laws of November 20, 1864, if these laws had the power to change our life to such an extent that the historian finds a greater and deeper difference between 1900 and 1860 than between 1860 and the time of Catherine II and even Peter the Great. Such was the influence achieved by the new spirit which entered Russian life in the sixties. This new spirit, which was characteristic of the codes and which, like the Emancipation Law of 1861, was created by a wave of liberating thought, consisted in the *idea of the individual*. This idea not only gave a definite form to the principle of legality itself, which was greatly different from the conception of legality as it was understood by previous codes, but also insured its wide and steady spreading in our fatherland." [10]

Indeed, we have seen that the conditions which preceded these laws, especially the inquisitorial procedure, were a complete negation of the individual and even of the person of the judge, who did not decide according to his conscience, but on grounds of formal rules of evidence against which he was completely powerless and could not transgress even if he was persuaded that these rules were leading him to injustice and iniquity. Persons were elected to courts, not because of their individual merits, but as representatives of classes to which they belonged. The person of the defendant was completely absent from the trial. The judges did not see him. He did not have a counsel

---

[10] Foinitsky, "Ideya lichnosti v sudebnykh ustavakh i kodifikatsionnoye ikh znacheniye," *Pravo*, 1899, p. 2283.

to defend him. He could not appeal the sentence, since the review procedure was prescribed by law and applied automatically.

We have also seen that the Laws of 1864 introduced general guarantees for the benefit of the individual: publicity in court, controversial procedure, jury, counsels, irremovable judges to a great extent independent of the administration. "The Codes of 1864 are our first constitutional charter," writes Polyansky.[11] In addition to their general spirit, these codes contain specific provisions in defense of the individual and acknowledgement of his personal rights.

Not enough attention is usually paid by the reviewers of the Laws of 1864 to the provisions of Arts. 9, 10 and 11 of the Code of Criminal Procedure. This is perhaps due to the fact that these provisions were not applied in the sense desired by the legislator of 1864 and were thus neglected and forgotten for a long time. As a matter of fact, if correctly applied, they could have assumed the importance of a Habeas Corpus Act.

These articles read: "A demand for the arrest of a person must be fulfilled only in case the demand was issued according to the provision of this Code" (Art. 9); "Every judge and every prosecutor who finds that a person is being detained within the territory of the judge's or prosecutor's precinct or district without a decision of a competent agency or person must immediately set free the person unlawfully deprived of liberty" (Art. 10); "A judge or a prosecutor who is informed that a person is being detained in an improper place of detention within the limits of his district or precinct must take measures for detention in a correct place" (Art. 11).

The duty of a judge to free a person who is unlawfully arrested and detained in his district corresponds to the right of Habeas Corpus. That precisely such a right was contemplated by the legislators of 1864 is indicated in the official message to accompany these articles. It is said there: "In some foreign countries, very strict laws have been adopted in order to defend the personal freedom of every member of society. Everyone knows the English Habeas Corpus, according to which the liberation of a person unlawfully arrested is carried out by the 'Queen's Bench' . . . The French Code also protects private persons from unlawful arrests . . .Articles 9, 10 and 11 clearly and positively specify the cases in which the arrest of a person is unlawful . . . Thus, every deliberate arrest of a person by an incompetent official represents a criminal act, the prevention of which must be the duty

---

11 N. N. Polyansky, "Mirovoi Sud," in *S. R.*, II, 206.

of every judge or prosecutor who has the necessary means for that purpose." [12]

Thus, these provisions were a powerful means of curbing arbitrary arrests. However, they were never resorted to before the first Revolution. In 1904-1905, several justices of the peace tried to apply these provisions; they visited jails and other places of detention and ordered the freeing of persons detained without valid legal grounds. However, these measures were speedily blocked by the administration, which simply did not obey judicial orders[13] and finally obtained a ruling of the Senate on September 21, 1906 (no. 21) to the effect that the justices of the peace have no right to make checks at jails.[14]

It is interesting to note that Catherine II attempted, under the influence of the liberal ideas of her time (she was also acquainted with legal literature, such as the works of Beccaria and Blackstone), to introduce a kind of *Habeas Corpus* in Russia. The *Uchrezhdeniye o guberniyakh* of 1775 created the *Sovestnye Sudy* (a kind of equity court) to which every man could appeal if under arrest for longer than three days without having been interrogated. The court was obliged to question the arrested person and free him on bail if he was not accused of lese majesty, treason, murder, robbery or theft. However, the *Ustav blagochiniya* of 1782 introduced thirty-seven exceptions to this provision. The provision itself remained on the books till 1864.[15]

The Laws of 1864 freed the judge from the rules of formal evidence. His conscience became sovereign in any decision on the guilt or innocence of the accused and on the appraisal of the facts which led to his decision. But also in the solution of legal questions the judge became free to comment on the provision of the law according to his convictions, whereas the old laws prescribed for him the "literal" application of the law. We have seen above that Arts. 12 and 13 of the Code of Criminal Procedure and Arts. 9 and 10 of the Code of Civil Procedure not only gave the judge the right, but made it a matter of duty for him, to decide according to the general spirit of the laws

---

[12] *Sudebnye Ustavy* . . . , II: *Ustav ugolovnago sudoproizvodstva*, pp. 30-31.

[13] Examples are given by Polyansky, "Mirovoi sud," in *S.R.*, II, 208 and footnotes 1, 2 and 3.

[14] M. P. Glebov, President of the Assembly of Justices of the Peace in St. Petersburg, declared: "Conditions of public life were such that this law lost its importance, and the judges ceased to visit the places of detention, and, thus, the check by the judicial power on the legality of arrests made by the administration ceased to exist." *Pravo*, 1906, p. 1945.

[15] See, for details, P. I. Lyublinsky, *Svoboda lichnosti v ugolovnom protsesse*, pp. 235-237.

when the provisions in the books were incomplete or unclear, as well as in the cases of absence of laws or contradictions in them. Finally, the judge was freed from the duty of gathering evidence and was made a free umpire between the parties in civil proceedings and between the accusation and the defense in criminal trials. The parties in both proceedings had to produce the evidence they deemed necessary.

Jury, publicity, controversial proceedings, and a free bar were the guarantees of the rights of the individual. The jurors were individuals and not representatives of different classes.

Personal freedom was guaranteed by Article 8 of the Code of Criminal Procedure, which read: "Nobody may be arrested other than in cases prescribed by law," a provision which was almost literally reproduced in Article 73 of the Fundamental Laws of 1906.

Summarizing the rights of the individual according to the Laws of 1864, Lyublinsky comes to the conclusion that "in the Laws of 1864 the individual was invested with definite rights in his relations to the state for the first time in our history, and a court was created in order to protect these rights."[16]

A state is governed by three powers: the legislative, the executive and the judiciary. A constitutional state is a state where all three powers are administered "by the people and for the people." A totalitarian state is a state where all three powers are concentrated in the hands of the monarch, the Führer or an oligarchic group. "In every state," writes Leroy-Beaulieu, "be it absolute or constitutional, monarchical or republican, the citizens or subjects can have no better guarantee than a good administration of justice. If there is no justice, there may be said to be no true freedom; if there is justice, one may venture to assert that despotism, or at least tyranny, is impossible." [17]

The Laws of November 20, 1864, did not transform Russia into a constitutional state, but they brought about the abolition of despotism in one of the three fundamental powers of government, namely, in the judiciary. The Monarch himself relinquished all judicial powers except that of pardon, he separated judicial power from the other two powers, and made it to a great extent, independent of the administration, especially by means of the irremovability of the judges. *Between 1864 and 1906, Russia offered the example of a state unique in political history, where the judicial power was based on democratic principles, whereas the legislative and executive powers remained completely autocratic.*

---

16 P. I. Lyublinsky, "Sud i prava lichnosti," in *S. R.*, II, 13.
17 Leroy-Beaulieu, *op. cit.*, II, 277.

Thus, in the judicial field, the Russian people reached a goal in 1864 for the achievement of which, in the legislative field, they had struggled and died for many years, and for which they were going to struggle and die in the future. This goal—the participation of the people in all branches of the government and the securing of the rights of the individual—was not fully achieved until the Revolution of February, 1917.

The individual, still under the despotism of the state in all other aspects of life in Russia, became free from it, in 1864, in matters pertaining to the administration of justice. In court, he had his well-established rights as against the government, and he was judged, not by justices resembling those of the old courts—where, according to the expression of Leroy-Beaulieu, "the symbolic scales of justice served to weigh the offers of the interested parties rather than rights and titles." [18]— but by independent men from the people, in accordance with their conscience and their sound sense of justice. And at the side of the individual stood the lawyer, whose task was to defend him and his rights from the encroachments of the totalitarian state.

Naturally, Vyshinsky gives a different characterization of the bar. According to him, "the bar was a bourgeois institution, which shared the fate of the bourgeoisie. . . When the bourgeoisie fought against feudalism and played a progressive role, the same role was performed by its bar." [19] "But," Vyshinsky continued elsewhere, "when confronted by the proletariat and the proletarian revolution, the bar invariably and everywhere turned out to be counter-revolutionary, beginning with the thirties and forties of the nineteenth century; . . . it was counter-revolutionary to the same extent as its master, the bourgeoisie." [20]

It seems to me that enough evidence has been cited in this book to show that Vyshinsky's assertion is not correct, at least with regard to the Russian bar of 1864-1917.

However, the importance and magnitude of the Reform became at the same time the source of its defects. The Reform, this *"insula in flumine nata"* according to Koni's witty remark, did not entirely fit into a state where the other two branches of government remained despotic. As Nabokov, writing in 1915 on the Laws of 1864, put it, "features of another regime which we had not yet lived to see were

---

[18] *Ibid.*, p. 285.
[19] A. Ya. Vyshinsky, *Revolyutsionnaya zakonnost' i zadachi sovetskoi zashchity,* p. 31.
[20] A. Ya. Vyshinsky, "Advokatura" in *Entsiklopediya gosudarstva i prava,* I, 57.

distinctly apparent in them." [21] And as Winaver wrote, "the judicial Reform was the first attempt to establish in life the principle of rule of law. It was directed toward the taming of the boundless arbitrariness of the administration and the defense of the individual's rights."[22]

Indeed, the subjects of the Tsar, deprived of rights in the other branches of government, were suddenly endowed with rights in the judicial branch. There is no doubt that the ideas embodied in the Reform could have served as a basis for the administration of justice in a really democratic state; in Russia, they were destined from the beginning to come into conflict with other branches of the administration and their representatives.

That is why the reaction which devastated Russia in subsequent years, up to the first Revolution of 1917, could not remain without effect upon the Reform of 1864 and its functioning. We have seen above to what distortions and violations it was subjected. Still, the main features of the Reform survived. The first concern of the Provisional Government after the Revolution of February 1917 in the field of the administration of justice was to restore the Reform of 1864 in its original scope. A special commission, in which the most eminent Russian jurists participated under the presidency of A. F. Koni, were to revive the basic principles of the Reform and to adjust them to the new order. The commission abolished the class representatives in criminal courts and transferred their competence to the jury, definitively abolished the zemskiye nachal'niki and the borough justices of the peace, and completely revived the system of elected justices of the peace.

The October Revolution of 1917 destroyed the Reform of 1864 and its institutions.

C. The Russian Lawyer as a Defender of the Rights of the Individual

The lawyer stood at the side of the individual in the latter's fight for the protection of his acquired rights and in his struggle for political rights and liberty. Let us recall the words of Leroy-Beaulieu: "Every Russian who has been brought to court has seen a man rise by his side who has dared to oppose, in his name, the representative of authority over the charge brought against him. In this vast Empire, which has no political assemblies, the honor of having been the first

---

21 Nabokov, op. cit., p. 344.
22 M. M. Winaver, Nedavneye, p. 19.

to speak up freely belongs to the lawyers. In a country where military courage is quite common, the lawyers were the first to be called upon to give an example of something hitherto unknown: civic courage." [23] But the lawyers were not only the *first* ones to raise their voices in free speech; they were, for a long time, the *only* ones permitted to do so in Russia.

The struggle of the Russian people for liberty and against despotism was carried on in the second half of the nineteenth century and in the first seventeen years of the twentieth. Count M. M. Speransky, undoubtedly one of the most brilliant statesmen tsarist Russia has ever produced, wrote in the Introduction to the Code of Laws of 1809 that the "Russian constitution will owe its existence, not to the excitement of passions and the exigency of circumstances, but to the blessed inspiration of the Supreme Power. . . ." [24] He was wrong. The "blessed" Supreme Power granted reforms to the Russian people only reluctantly and, with few exceptions, always under the pressure of the revolutionary impact. As a matter of fact, the regime sought to curtail, distort and paralyze every reform it was forced to grant. In its fight against the revolutionary movement, the tsarist government used all repressive means at its disposal. Administrative banishments, courts-martial, field courts-martial, special laws, [25] punitive expeditions, scaffolds and firing squads were employed. The rope of the executioner (called "Murav'yov's collar" and "Stolypin's necktie" by the people) was designed to choke the revolutionary movement. Indeed, the government succeeded in suppressing the revolutionary outbursts which culminated in the upheavals of 1904-1905. The wave of strikes and rural disorders which threatened to sweep away the regime was held down. The period of "liquidation of the revolution," which began under Stolypin, was the period of revenge taken by the government against the subversive elements.

This period, and the activity of the lawyers in it, were brilliantly characterized by Maklakov in his speech in the Third Duma on December 2, 1909, which he delivered in response to the charges formulated against the lawyers by the Minister of Justice, Shcheglovitov. Maklakov said:

> I am willing to accept the challange of the Minister of Justice and remind him of what the lawyers did in these difficult,

---

23 Leroy-Beaulieu, *op. cit.*, II, 364.
24 Speransky, *op. cit.*, p. 15.
25 *I.e.*, laws which suspended some civil rights as well as the ordinary administration of justice.

ill-fated years, those years when, indeed, began the liquidation of what was called the liberating movement, in those years when the *Sudebnye Palaty* were filled with trials, when the *Palaty* were short of time in spite of the fact that similar trials were taking place—invariably and ceaselessly—before courts-martial . . . It was the time when the notion of morality was shaken . . . because the Minister of Justice began to threaten recalcitrant judges. It was the time when the Second Duma was being told about irremovability [of judges], while in reality presidents of the *Palaty* were being removed and displaced. It was the time when disciplinary proceedings were being conducted against Judges who had made undesirable utterances in court. It was the time when . . . one could only ask oneself whether the judges were not becoming simple tools of politics. Thus, at that time, at that really terrible time, there were so many trials, there was such a number of defendants, that one could think that no time, no persons, no desire could be found for their defense. And the Russian lawyers may be proud of the fact that in those bad times the accused did not remain without counsels, and some day the tremendous work which was performed by the Russian lawyer of that time will be appraised in its true value. Also that will be appraised which cannot be expressed in figures, *i.e.*, the mental anguish suffered by everyone who saw what had become of the administration of justice, who saw how politics were victorious over justice, who saw how sometimes nothing remained of justice and law in some famous and very significant trials . . . And I shall say now that what was done [by the lawyers] was not done because of self-interest—no self-interest was involved. It was not done because of vanity, since those trials attracted nobody's attention at that time. . . . In reality, it was done out of a feeling of deep pity for those who suffer sometimes out of temporary enthusiasm, out of a feeling of deep compassion for those who were persecuted in spite of law and right, who were pursued in a political fight; and sometimes because of a strong desire to defend right, court and law from politicians.[26]

Defense in political trials became perilous for the counsel. Nevertheless, political prisoners did not cease to find counsels ready to defend them, and to accomplish this mission with great civic courage. The lawyers were inspired by idealism. They considered their profession to be a kind of ministry. They saw their mission in the defense of the individual assaulted by the state, in the preservation of his rights with regard to the state. O. Ya. Pergament wrote in 1905: "Was there during this last decade, a single so-called public case caused by

---

[26] Gosudarstvennaya Duma. Trety sozyv 1909 g. *Stenografichesky otchet*, pp. 2830-2840, *passim*.

a strike, or by religious sectarianism, or by mass movements due to class, economic or religious motives, or by political crimes, in which representatives of the Russian guild of lawyers did not take part—disinterestedly, valiantly and bravely? In spite of the hard work, time and responsibility involved, not sparing their strength and expenses, [lawyers] raised their voice in all these cases, . . . awakening the public by its appeal, from its somnolence and Philistinism. Public consciousness was awakened to a great extent by the voice of the lawyer which rolled over the entire country. Created in the public interest, the guild of lawyers really served the public's welfare." [27]

This role fell to the lawyer historically as a consequence of the position assigned to him in the administration of justice by the legislator of 1864—a position which, although shaken by subsequent legislation and administration, was retained, in spite of all, until October 1917.

"The fight for the rights of the individual, his defense against the unmitigated rule of the state—this is the field of action of a free lawyer," Winaver writes. "The Laws of 1864 gave to the individual a means with which he could defend his rights against oppression through arbitrariness of the government. However, he was not yet given any [political] rights that could be defended, and was obliged to procure these rights by a struggle with a regime which had survived [the Revolution of 1905] and was fighting back blindly with the despair of self-defense." [28] Or, as Borodin puts it: "Lawyers are specialized jurists who defend, in court, the rights of individuals, in the name and in the interests of the public good." [29]

Such a viewpoint on the role of the lawyer was shared by the majority of the members of the guild and expressed in decisions of the councils of the bar.. Thus, the Moscow Council wrote in its Report of 1903-1904: "It is quite natural that the guild of lawyers should give rise . . . to a team for the most experienced and capable fighters for the public ideals, since no one else comes into such close contact with all aspects of life and can personally ascertain its real needs and necessities. . . . The predominant role of the guild of lawyers in every fight in which public interest is involved becomes not only comprehensible but also inescapable."[30]

It must be emphasized that the guild of lawyers as such, never

---

27 O. Ya. Pergament, *Obshchestvennyya zadachi advokatury*, p. 29-30.
28 M. M. Winaver, *Nedavneye*, p. 56.
29 N. D. Borodin, *Istorichesky ocherk russkoi advokatury* p. 70.
30 *Otchet Soveta prisyazhnykh poverennykh pri Moskovskoi Sudebnoi Palate za 1903/1904 g.*, p. 466.

pursued political interests. In the majority of cases, the individual ✓
lawyers pleaded in political trials, not because the accused were persons whose political convictions they shared, but because it was their
function to defend the individual against the state regardless of the
crime he had committed. The lawyer had to produce everything which
could be used in defense of his client. The political opinions of Karabchevsky for instance, had nothing in common with those of Sazonov.
But Karabchevsky, in order to defend Sazonov, had to explain the
crime from Sazonov's point of view. That is why Karabchevsky's
speech sounds as revolutionary as the political convictions of Sazonov.
Karabchevsky's picture of Pleve as he appeared to Sazonov is so vivid
that, when reading the speech, it becomes clear that Sazonov *had* to
throw the bomb which tore Pleve to pieces, that he *could* not act differently, that in his eyes this was a just retaliation for all the evils which
this Minister had inflicted upon the Russian people.

Maklakov, a moderate liberal, was opposed, as a matter of principle, to any revolution, even that of February 1917. This did not prevent him from defending rioting peasants and revolutionaries. Such
examples could be provided in great number. To be able to perceive
the psychology of his client, to transplant himself into his mentality,
independently of his own convictions, is one of the most valuable assets
of the lawyer.

In the fight of the individual against the state, the lawyer was
naturally on the side of the individual, not only because this function
had been assigned to him by the Laws of 1864, but also because he was
definitely convinced that the individual person is the greatest value
society possesses and that to be his knight and defender is the noblest
function a man can fulfill in society.

In his speech in the General Assembly of the Petrograd Bar on
the occasion of the jubilee marking its fiftieth anniversary (1866-1916),
Gruzenberg said: "Does our guild understand that where the state
puts pressure with its entire unlimited might, with all its inexhaustible resources, on a grain of sand— on the individual—there, first of
all, is the lawyer's place? It is there that must be employed the greatest
virtues of a counsel: fearlessness, readiness to take the blows directed
against the defendant and the ability not to fear loneliness in the
court hall. We must be overjoyed and proud that the Russian lawyers,
who are just beginning to live, have from the very first day taken a
place beside the oldest European guilds. . . .

And in spite of the reaction, in spite of the administrative penalties which were inflicted upon them, our colleagues pleaded with the same passion and courage fifty years ago as in the famous years after 1900."

Towards the end of his speech, Gruzenberg came back to the same idea: "Hundreds of cases involving peasants, workers, pogroms, thousands of purely political cases were pleaded by steadfast and courageous counsels. With the greatest efforts, often forgetting their own interests, our colleagues in all corners of Russia fulfilled their modest but great office—*the office of the defense of the individual against the onslaught of the state.*" [31]

The political trials were only one of the lawyer's fields of activity. The regular criminal and civil proceedings were other fields for his daily fight for the individual. In criminal proceedings, the lawyer was able to denounce the economic and social injustices which often bring a man into the dock. Here again he defended the individual against the punitive power of the state. In civil proceedings he defended the material rights of his client. "Thus the Russian lawyer . . . fought for principles whose defense constituted his vital task. In alliance with other public forces, but going his own way, he prepared the path for the future rule of law in the state," Winaver writes.[32]

Foinitsky has brilliantly characterized the profession of the lawyer: "Coming to the help of the oppressed and often of the innocent man in the most critical period of his life, the defense is one of the most noble fields of juridical activity. It is capable of stimulating all the best spiritual forces of man. That is the explanation why persons of high intellectual and moral caliber dedicate themselves to this profession, and of the undeniable sympathy of the public toward the pure essence of this activity." [33]

Noble aims always find people ready to dedicate their lives to them. When the Reform of 1864 opened up administration of justice as a real public service, the Russian intelligentsia rushed into this field of activity. Judges, prosecutors, lawyers—all were inflamed by the new spirit created by the great reform of Alexander II. As Koni says on this subject: "It was an activity . . . like a calling, like a *first love.* Such a love exists, not only in the personal life of a man, but also in his public life. In both cases, it is the *first* thing to enter his heart and the *last* thing to leave his memory." [34]

It is a striking phenomenon that this love was revived over and

---

31 Gruzenberg, *Ocherki* . . . , p. 82-89, *passim.* See also E. Kulischer, "Gruzenberg kak advokat," in Gruzenberg, *Ocherki* . . . , p. 17-18.
32 Winaver, *Advokatura i pravovoye gosudarstvo,* p. 32.
33 Foinitsky, *Zashchita v ugolovnom protsesse* . . . , p. 62.
34 Koni, *Za posledniye gody,* p. 483.

over again in the hearts of subsequent generations. An imposing number of very prominent orators, jurists, and scholars adorned the ranks of the Russian bar in the short period of its existence. Enthusiasm for their profession, idealism, devotion to the freedom of the individual and its defense, which took possession of the lawyers at the beginning of their activity, lasted for the fifty years during which the guild existed in Russia.

It is self-evident that, speaking of "lawyers" and "guilds," I do not intend to assert that 100% of them were altruistic and self-sacrificing idealists. When it is said of Napoleon's soldiers that they were brave, this does not mean that there were no cowards among them. But the exceptions only confirm the rule. The great majority of lawyers were filled with love and enthusiasm for their profession.

Even more striking is the fact that this love did not die in the hearts of the few survivors among those who took part in the administration of justice in Russia before the Revolution of October 1917 or were educated in a spirit of love and veneration for the principles embodied in the Reform of 1864. Every year, before the October Revolution, on the birthday of the Reform, members of the judiciary and the bar assembled in Russia to speak about the Reform and the great deeds accomplished by it. Ever since the Revolution of October 1917, on every November 20, groups of Russian émigrés in Paris, New York and other cities gather to pay tribute to the memory of the now buried Reform. They are former Russian judges, prosecutors or lawyers. They have lost their positions, their property, their fatherland, but they keep in their hearts the love of which Koni spoke so well. Speaking at an assembly of the Association of Former Russian Lawyers in Paris in 1929, M. L. Goldstein, a former eminent trial lawyer in Russia, said: "We are an association of former Russian lawyers, not only because we have a mutual aid fund, but because we have a fund of *moral* mutual aid [italics mine—s.к.]. The past of the Russian guild of lawyers has left priceless values: in the dark days of our present life, we may find moral help and comfort in these values."[35]

In his speech in the General Assembly of the Petrograd Bar on the occasion of the jubilee marking its fiftieth anniversary, Gruzenberg said: "Comrades! twenty-five years ago on this same day of April 17, V. D. Spasovich said: 'Let us shake hands in reminiscence of the valiant past years, and let us cry as our successors will not cry—those who will live to see the next twenty-fifth jubilee in 1916.' He was

---

[35] M. L. Goldstein, *Rechi i stat'i*, p. 12.

right. We do not cry, but not because the conditions of our life have improved, or because our wounds do not ache. We do not cry. . . . Be blessed our sorrows, the offenses we endured, the persecution we were subjected to: they have toughened our spirit, made our will unconquerable. We want to live and we will live. . . . But for the bar, to live means to fight tirelessly—without fear of defeat and without self-delusion in victory—for justice and liberty without which there is no justice." [36]

The fight for liberty and justice, as well as for the rights of the individual, was lost in October 1917.

Decree No. 1 on Courts of the Council of People's Commissars, dated November 24, 1917,[37] abrogated all the existing judicial institutions and the guild of lawyers. It is one of the supreme ironies of history that the free Russian lawyer and the democratic administration of justice were born by the will of an autocratic Tsar and destroyed by a decree of a revolutionary government, as the life of Alexander II himself, who was the creator of the greatest democratic reforms in Russian history, was destroyed by revolutionaries.

The abrogation of the institution of lawyers and of the bar had its precedent in history: the French *Constituante* declared in its Decrees of August 16 and September 2, 1790, that those who "call themselves *avocats* may no longer form a class, or association, or wear special clothes during the performance of their duties." As mentioned above, this measure was intended, on the one hand, as a liberation of the lawyer from the restrictions imposed on him by the guild of lawyers, on the other hand, as a destruction of the lawyer's professional monopoly. In the bill concerning the reorganization of the administration of justice, it was said that "everyone will have the right to carry on his suits personally if he finds it convenient, and, in order to enjoy the necessary liberty, the lawyers will cease to form an association. . ." [38]

When the bill was discussed in the *Constituante,* a single man raised his voice against the abrogation of the lawyers' guild. It was Robespierre. He pronounced words which can be applied to the pre-revolutionary lawyers in Russia as well. He said: "This profession alone . . . escaped the absolute power of the monarch. I admit that this profession also was not free of the abuses which will always

---

[36] Gruzenberg, *Ocherki . . .* , p. 91.
[37] *Sobraniye uzakoneny RSFSR*, 1917, No. 4, Art. 50.
[38] Joachim, Gaudry, *Histoire du barreau de Paris depuis son origine jusqu'à 1830*, II, 336.

afflict people who do not live under a régime of freedom; but I am obliged to recognize . . . that this association contained the last vestige of liberty, which had been banished from other parts of society. This association alone retained the courage to speak the truth, dared to maintain the rights of the weak victim against his mighty oppressor. You will no longer see, in the sanctuary of justice, these men who were receptive and capable of becoming inflamed by their interest for other people. . . . These men, fearless and eloquent, the defenders of innocence and the terror of crime . . . will retreat, and you will see in their place coarse lawyers, indifferent to their duties and prompted to their noble activity by base calculation. You are perverting and abusing an activity valuable to humanity, necessary for the spiritual development of society. You are closing the school of civic virtues, where talent and valor have learned to defend the interests of citizens in courts." [39]

Gaudry and Le Berquier called these words prophetic. Such they were for France.

Those words turned out to be prophetic with regard to Russia as well. I hope to have the opportunity to relate elsewhere what happened in Russia in this respect after the October Revolution of 1917.

The organizations abrogated in Russia by Decree No. 1 tried to fight that decree. In a special decision, the Senate prohibited the application of the decree to judicial institutions. The General Assembly of the Petrograd Bar made a decision on November 26, 1917, in which it was said that Decree No. 1 cannot be recognized as a law, since it was issued by an incompetent agency. The Assembly directed its members to continue their previous activities in the old law courts.[40] The Moscow Bar concurred with the decisions of the Senate and the Petrograd Bar on December 3, 1917.[41] Similar decisions were made by assemblies of judges and lawyers in other cities.[42]

However, this fight was hopeless. The liquidation of all judicial organs was carried out in Petrograd by the Representative of the Investigation Commission of the Military-Revolutionary Committee on November 29, 1917. The activity of the Moscow judicial institutions was stopped with the help of armed Red Guards some weeks later. Such was the end of the Reform of 1864 and its institutions.

---

39 Jules Le Berquier, *Le barreau moderne,* pp. 26-27.
40 *Russkiye Vedomosti,* Nov. 27, 1917.
41 *Ibid.,* Dec. 5, 1917.
42 *Smolenskiye Vedomosti,* Dec. 30, 1917.

According to B. L. Gerschun, an eminent lawyer and a member of the last Council of the Bar in Petrograd, law practice became not only impossible but even dangerous for the members of the old bar. The quarters of the Council were occupied by the Bolsheviks in November 1918. This occasion was used by the new government to offer to the former lawyers[43] a mass transfer to the new organization of lawyers which was allegedly to be created in accordance with the old principles of the guild. The former Council of the Bar received permission to summon a General Assembly of the Bar in order to consider this proposition.

Before this last General Assembly of the Petrograd Bar, the Council of the Bar decided to stop the activities of the bar and of all its institutions. The Council entrusted to B. L. Gerschun the mission to make known this decision, and its reasons, to the General Assembly. This is how Gerschun describes the dramatic meeting: "When, in the General Assembly, which was attended by all the lawyers present in Petrograd at that time, I pronounced the words: 'the last hour of the guild has arrived' . . . I saw how many colleagues, especially the older ones, were sobbing silently. . . ." Gerschun said further: "We cannot commit an act of treason against the principles of the Russian guild of lawyers by giving up the most holy traditions of independence and freedom of the guild. . . . It is better to dissolve the guid; an honest death is preferable to a disgraceful life. . . ." [44] The General Assembly confirmed the decision of the Council.

The free Russian lawyer was dead.

---

[43] According to Ostrogorsky's Juridical Calendar for 1914, there were at that time 5,658 lawyers and 5,489 lawyers-in-training in Russia. M. Ostrogorsky, *Yuridichesky Kalendar'* (Petrograd, 1914), p. 501.

[44] B. Gerschun, *"Russland,"* in *Die Rechtsanwaltschaft*, Ed. By J. Magnus, pp. 229-230.

BIBLIOGRAPHY

OF

LITERATURE USED

Aksakov, I. S. *Sochineniya 1860-1886* (Works 1860-1886). Moscow, 1886-1887.

I. S. Aksakov v ego pis'makh (I. S. Aksakov in His Letters). Moscow, 1888.

Aldanov, M. A. "K 80-letiyu Maklakova" (On the Occasion of Maklakov's Eightieth Birthday), in V. A. Maklakov, *Rechi* (Speeches). Paris, 1949.

Andreyevsky, S. A. *Dramy zhizni. Zashchititel'nye rechi* (The Dramatic Events of Life. Speeches by the Defense). Petrograd, 1916.

Anisimov, S. *Kak eto bylo: Zapiski politicheskogo zashchitnika o sudakh Stolypina* (Thus It was. Notes on Stolypin's Courts by a Counsel in Political Trials). Moscow, 1931.

Annenkov, K. *Sistema russkago grazhdanskago prava* (System of Russian Civil Law). Vol. I. St. Petersburg, 1899.

Arsen'yev, K. K. *Glavnye deyateli i predshestvenniki sudebnoi reformy* (The Main Promoters and Predecessors of the Judicial Reform). St. Petersburg, 1904.

—— *Za chetvert' veka* (For a Quarter of a Century). Petrograd, 1915.

—— *Zametki o russkoi advokature* (Notes on the Russian Bar). St. Petersburg, 1875.

Bantysh-Kamensky, D. N. "Shemyakin sud v XIX stoletii" (Shemyakin's Justice in the 19th Century), *Russkaya Starina* (Russian Antiquity), VII (1873).

Barrot, Odilon. *De l'organisation judiciaire en France. Paris,* 1872.

Barshev, S. I. "O sude prisyazhnykh" (On the Court with Jury), *Russky Vestnik* (Russian Herald), 1857, No. 9.

—— "Ob ustnosti i glasnosti v ugolovnom protsesse" (On Oral Proceeding and Publicity in Criminal Procedure), *Yuridicheskiye zapiski, izdannye Petrom Redkinym* (Legal Notes published by Peter Redkin), II (1842).

Barsukov, N. P. *Zhizn' i trudy Pogodina* (The Life and Works of M. P. Pogodin). Vol XIX. St. Petersburg, 1905.

Bentham, Jeremy. *A Fragment on Government.* Oxford, 1891.

Berends, E. "Svyaz' sudebnoi reformy s drugimi reformami Imperatora Aleksandra II" (Relation Between the Judicial Reform and Other Reforms of Emperor Alexander II), in *S. U.* Vol II.

Berman, Harold. *Justice in Russia.* Cambridge, 1950.
Berman, Ya. L. "Deyatel'nost' voenno-okruzhnykh i polkovykh sudov" (Activity of Circuit and Regiment Courts-Martial), *Pravo* (Law), 1913, Nos. 36 and 37.
—— "Statistika advokatury" (Statistics of the Bar), in *Istoriya russkoi advokatury, 1864-1914* (History of the Russian Bar, 1864-1914). Vol. II. Moscow, 1916.
Berenstam, V. *V ogne zashchity* (In the Heat of Defense). St. Petersburg, 1909.
Blinov, I. "Sudebny stroi i sudebnye poryadki pered reformoi" (Judicial System and the Judicial Order before the Reform) in *S. U.* Vol. I.
Bobrishchev-Pushkin, A. M. *Empiricheskiye zakony deyatel'nosti russkago suda prisyazhnykh* (Empirical Laws of Activity of the Russian Court with Jury). Moscow, 1896.
Bochkarev, V. "Doreformenny sud" (The Court before the Reform), in *Sudebnaya Reforma* (The Judicial Reform). Edited by N. V. Davydov and N. N. Polyansky. Vol. I. Moscow, 1915.
Borodin, D. N. *Istorichesky ocherk russkoi advokatury* (Historical Sketch of the Russian Bar). Petrograd, 1915.
Borozdin, A. K. *Iz pisem i pokazany dekabristov* (From Letters and Testimonies of Decembrists). St. Petersburg, 1906.
Brazol', B. L. "Sledstvennaya chast'" (Preliminary Investigation), in *S. U.*, Vol. II.
Brunner, H. *Die Entstehung der Schwurgerichte.* Berlin, 1872.
Cardonne, C. de. *L'Empereur Alexandre II. Vingt-six ans de règne.* Paris, 1883.
Charykhov, Kh. M. "Pomoshchniki prisyazhnykh poverennykh. Ikh organizatsiya" (Lawyers-in-Training. Their Organization), in *Istoriya russkoi advokatury* (History of the Russian Bar), Vol. III. Moscow, 1916.
Chernomordik, E. Ya. "Uchrezhdeniya zamenyayushchiye sovet prisyazhnykh poverennykh" (Substitute Institutions for the Council of the Bar), in *Istoriya russkoi advokatury* (History of the Russian Bar). Vol. III. Moscow, 1916.
Chernov, V. M. "Tainye sovetniki i yavnye pogromshchiki" (Secret Councillors and Evident Pogrom Organizers), *Mysl'* (Thought). St. Petersburg, June 23, 1906.
Chubinsky, M. P. *Sovremennaya bor'ba vzglyadov za i protiv suda prisyazhnykh i reformatorskiya popytki v etoi oblasti* (The Contemporary Struggle of Viewpoints on Courts With Jury and Attempts at Reform in This Field). Kiev, 1897.
——"Sudebnaya reforma" (The Judicial Reform), in *Istoriya Rossii v XIX veke* (History of Russia in the 19th Century). St. Petersburg, 1907-1912. Vol. III.
Delo Beilisa. Stenografichesky otchet (The Beilis Case. Verbatim Report). 3 vols. Kiev, 1913.
Delo prisyazhnago poverennago A. D. Margolina (The Case of Lawyer A. D. Margolin). St. Petersburg, 1914.

Dmitriyev, F. M. *Istoriya sudebnykh instantsy i grazhdanskago appellyatsionnago sudoproizvodstva ot Sudebnika do Uchrezhdeniya o guberniyakh* (History of Judicial Institutions and of the Civil and Appellate Procedures from the *Sudebnik* to the Status of Provinces). Moscow, 1859.

Dohna, Graf A. zu. *Das Strafverfahren*. Berlin, 1913.

Dostoyevsky, F. M. *Dnevnik pisatelya za 1876 g.* (The Diary of a Writer for 1876) In his *Polnoye sobraniye sochineny* (Complete Works). 6th ed. Vol. XI. St. Petersburg, 1905.

Dovnar-Zapol'sky, M. V. *Memuary dekabristov* (Memoirs of Decembrists). Kiev, 1906.

Dubrovin, N. "Russkaya zhizn' v nachale XIX veka" (Russian Life in the Beginning of the 19th Century), *Russkaya Starina* (Russian Antiquity), XCVIII. (1899).

Dupin, A., aîné. *Profession d'avocat*. Vol. I. Paris, 1832.

Duvernois, N. L. *Kurs lektsy grazhdanskago prava* (Lectures on Civil Law). St. Petersburg, 1897.

Dzhanshiyev, G. *Epokha velikikh reform.* (The Epoch of the Great Reforms). Moscow, 1900.

—— *Osnovy sudebnoi reformy* (The Bases of the Judicial Reform). Moscow, 1891.

—— "S. I. Zarudny. Materialy dlya ego biografii" (S. I. Zarudny. Materials for His Biography), *Russkaya Starina* (Russian Antiquity), LVII (1888). No. 9.

—— *Vedeniye nepravykh del. Etyud advokatskoi etiki.* (Pleading of Morally Dubious Cases. Essay on Lawyers' Ethics). Moscow, 1886.

Eichenwald, Yu. *Siluety russkikh pisatelei* (Silhouettes of Russian Writers). Vol. II. Moscow, 1917.

Engels, F. *Anti-Dühring.* (In Russian) . Moscow, 1938.

Fedorov, M. "Iz vospominany po upravleniyu S.-Peterburgskim domom predvaritel'nago zaklyucheniya" (Reminiscences on the Administration of the St. Petersburg Pre-Trial Prison) . *Russkaya Starina* (Russian Antiquity) , CXXI (1905) , No. 1.

Ferri, Enrico. *Sociologia criminale.* Turin, 1892.

Filat'yev, G. V. "Dorevolyutsionnye voennye sudy v tsifrakh" (Pre-revolutionary Courts-Martial in Figures), *Katorga i ssylka* (Penal Servitude and Banishment), 1930, No. 7.

Foinitsky, I. Ya. "Ideya lichnosti v sudebnykh ustavakh i kodifikatsionnoye ikh znacheniye" (The Doctrine of the Individual in the Judicial Statutes of November 20, 1864, and Their Codificational Importance) , *Pravo* (Law) , 1899, pp. 2283-2298.

——*Kurs ugolovnago sudoproizvodstva* (A Course in Criminal Procedure). 2 vols. St. Petersburg, 1896.

—— *Na dosuge* (At Leisure). 2 vols. St. Petersburg, 1900.

—— *Zashchita v ugolovnom protsesse kak sluzheniye obshchestvennoye* (Defense in Criminal Cases as a Public Service). St. Petersburg, 1885.

Forsyth, William. *History of Trial by Jury.* London, 1852.

Franqueville, A. C. Comte de. *Le système judiciaire de la Grande Bretagne.* 2 vols. Paris, 1893.

Frydmann, Marcell. *Systematisches Handbuch der Verteidigung im Strafverfahren.* Vienna, 1878.

Fuks, V. *Sud i politsiya* (Court and Police). Moscow, 1889.

Gambarov, Yu. S. *Kurs grazhdanskago prava* (A Course in Civil Law). St. Petersburg, 1911.

Garofalo, R. *Criminologia.* Turin, 1891.

Gaudry, Joachim, *Histoire du barreau de Paris depuis son origine jusqu'à 1830.* 2 vols. Paris, 1864.

Gautier, Yu. "Otdeleniye vlasti sudebnoi ot administrativnoi" (Separation of the Judicial Power from the Administrative Power), in *Sudebnaya Reforma* (The Judicial Reform). Vol I. Moscow, 1915.

Gay, John. *Fables.* New York, 1883.

Gerschun, Boris. "Russland," in *Die Rechtsanwaltschaft.* Ed. by J. Magnus. Leipzig, 1929.

Gertsenstein, D. M. "Tridtstat' let tomu nazad" (Thirty Years Ago), *Byloye* (The Past), 1907, No. 6.

Glagol', S. "Protsess pervoi russkoi terroristki" (The Trial of the First Russian Women Terrorist), *Golos minuvshego* (Voice of the Past), 1918, No. 7-9.

Gneist, Rudolf von. *Die Bildung der Geschworenengerichte in Deutschland.* Berlin, 1849.

Gogol, N. V. *Tchitchikoff's Journeys; or, Dead Souls.* Translated from the Russian by Isabel F. Hapgood. 2 vols. New York, [1886].

Goldenweiser, A. A. "Perechityvaya rechi V. A. Maklakova" (Re-reading Maklakov's Speeches). *Novoye Russkoye Slovo,* New York, April 23, 1950.

Goldenweiser, A. S. *Crime a Punishment and Punishment a Crime;* leading thoughts in Tolstoi's "Resurrection," (with a letter from Leo Tolstoi). Translated from the Russian by E. A. Goldenweiser. Washington, 1909.

——————*Prestupleniye—kak nakazaniye, a nakazaniye—kak prestupleniye. Motivy Tolstovskago "Voskreseniya." Etyudy, lektsii i rechi na ugolovnye temy* (Crime a Punishment and Punishment a Crime; leading thoughts in Tolstoi's "Resurrection." Studies, Lectures and Speeches). Kiev, 1908.

Goldman, L. I., ed. *Politicheskiye protsessy v Rossii, 1901-1917* (Political Trials in Russia, 1901-1917). Moscow, 1932.

Goldstein, M. L. "Printsipy organizatsii advokatury" (Principles of Lawyers' Organization), *Vestnik Prava* (Law Herald), 1900, No. 1.

—————— *Rechi i stat'i.* (Speeches and Articles). Paris, 1929.

Gosudarstvennaya Duma. Pervyi sozyv 1906 g. (The First State Duma). *Stenografichesky otchet* (Verbatim Report). St. Petersburg, 1906.

—————— Vtoroi sozyv 1907 g. (The Second State Duma.) *Stenografichesky otchet* (Verbatim Report). St. Petersburg, 1907.

—————— Trety sozyv 1909 g. (The Third State Duma). *Stenografichesky otchet* (Verbatim Report). St. Petersburg, 1910.

Gradovsky, G. K. *Itogi 1862-1907* (Summing up, 1862-1907). Kiev, 1908.
Graham, Stephen. *Tsar of Freedom, the Life and Reign of Alexander II*. New Haven, 1935.
Gredinger, "Prokurorsky nadzor" (Prosecutor's Supervision), in *S. U.* Vol. II.
Grimm, D. D. "K voprosu o ponyatii i istochnike obyazatel'nosti yuridicheskikh norm (On the Question of the Concept and Source of Obligatoriness of Legal Norms), *Zhurnal ministerstva yustitsii* (Journal of the Ministry of Justice), 1896, No. 6.
Gruzenberg, O. O. "K voprosu o smertnoi kazni v Rossii" (On the Question of the Death Penalty in Russia), *Pravo* (Law), 1910, No. 23.
———— *Ocherki i rechi* (Sketches and Speeches). New York, 1944.
———— "Poruchik Pirogov" (Lieutenant Pirogov), *Sovremennye Zapiski* (Contemporary Notes). Vol XXI. Paris, 1924.
———— *Vchera* (Yesterday). Paris, 1938.
Gsovski, V. *Soviet Civil Law*. 2 vols. Ann Arbor, 1948-1949.
Hauriou, Maurice. *Principes de droit public*. Paris, 1910.
Heine, Wolfgang. "Wesen der Verteidigung," *Die Justiz*, No. 1 (1925).
Hélie, Faustin A. *Les constitutions de la France*. Paris 1880.
Herzen, A. I. *Byloye i dumy* (My Past and Thoughts). Leningrad, 1947.
Hessen, I. V. *Advokatura, obshchestvo i gosudarstvo* (The Bar, the Society and the State), Vol. I of *Istoriya russkoi advokatury 1864-1914* (History of the Russian Bar, 1864-1914). Moscow, 1914.
———— *Sudebnaya Reforma* (The Judicial Reform). St. Petersburg, 1905.
Hobson, John A. *Imperialism*. London, 1938.
Isayev, A. A. "Yuridicheskiya konferentsii v petrogradskoi advokature" (Juridical Conferences of the Petrograd Bar), in *Istoriya russkoi advokatury* (History of the Russian Bar). Vol. III. Moscow, 1916.
Istoriya russkoi advokatury 1864-1914 (History of the Russian Bar, 1864-1914). 3 vols. Moscow, 1914-16.
Jellinek, Georg. *Allgemeine Staatslehre*. Berlin, 1914.
Jhering, Rudolf von. *Der Zweck im Recht*. 2 vols. Berlin, 1893.
Karabchevsky, N. P. *Chto glaza moi videli* (What My Eyes Did See). Berlin, 1921.
———— *Delo Sazonova* (The Sazonov Case). St. Petersburg, 1906.
———— *Okolo pravosudiya* (Close to the Rendering of Justice). St. Petersburg 1902.
———— *Rechi 1882-1902.* (Speeches, 1882-1902). St. Petersburg, 1902.
———— *Rechi 1882-1914* (Speeches, 1882-1914) . 3d ed. Petrograd, 1916.
Karabegov, A. *Reforma sudebnykh ustavov* (The Reform of the Judicial Statutes of 1864) St. Petersburg, 1889.
Karamzin, N. "Zapiska o drevnei i novoi Rossii" (Memorandum on the Old and the New Russia), *Russky Arkhiv* (Russian Archives) 1870, p. 2225ff.
Karpovich, M. M. A review of Maklakov's speeches. *Novy Zhurnal* (The New Review). Vol. XXIV. New York, 1950.

Kelsen, Hans. "The Pure Theory of Law," *Law Quarterly Review*, L(1934) and LI(1935).

Kenigson, A. *Ocherk proiskhozhdeniya i istoricheskago razvitiya suda prisyazhnykh v delakh ugolovnykh*. (Essay on the Origin and Historical Development of Court with Jury in Criminal Procedure). Vitebsk, 1871.

Khomyakov, A. "O yuridicheskikh voprosakh" (On Juridical Questions), *Russkaya Beseda* (Russian Colloquy), 1858, No. 10.

Khrulev, S. "Sud prisyazhnykh" (Court with Jury), *Zhurnal grazhdanskago i ugolovnago prava* (Journal of Civil and Criminal Law), 1886, Nos. 8, 9 and 10.

Klyuchevsky, V. O. *Kurs russkoi istorii* (A Course in Russian History). Moscow, 1916.

—— *Lektsii po russkoi istorii* (Lectures on Russian History). Moscow, 1908.

Kohler, Josef. *Moderne Rechtsprobleme. Leipzig*, 1913.

Kolmakov, N. M. "Stary sud" (The Old Law Court), *Russkaya Starina* (Russian Antiquity), LII (1886), No. 12.

Koni, A. F. *Na zhiznennom puti* (On My Life's Path). Vols. I and II, Moscow, 1912-1913; Vol. III, Revel, 1922.

—— *Ocherki i vospominaniya* (Sketches and Reminiscences). St. Petersburg, 1906.

—— *Ottsy i deti sudebnoi reformy* (Fathers and Sons of the Judicial Reform). Moscow, 1914.

—— "Pamyati Nikolaya Ivanovicha Stoyanovskago" (In Memory of Nikolai Ivanovich Stoyanovsky), *Pravo*, (Law), 1901, No. 2.

—— "Sud prisyazhnykh" (Court with Jury), in *Entsiklopedichesky slovar' Brokgauza i Efrona* (Brockhaus and Efron Encyclopaedia). Vol LXIII. St. Petersburg, 1901.

—— "Sudebnye Ustavy 1864-1914" (Judicial Statutes 1864-1914), *Zhurnal ministerstva yustitsii* (Journal of the Ministry of Justice), 1914, No. 9.

—— *Vospominaniya o dele Very Zasulich* (Reminiscences of the Vera Zasulich Case). Edited and annotated by M. F. Feodorovich. Moscow, 1933.

—— *Za posledniye gody* (During the Last Years). St. Petersburg, 1898.

Korf, M. A. "Iz zapisok barona (vposledstvii grafa) M. A. Korfa" (From the Memoirs of Baron (later Count) M. A. Korf), *Russkaya Starina*, XCVIII-CI (1899).

Korkunov, N. M. *Lektsii po obshchei teorii prava* (Lectures on the General Theory of Law). St. Petersburg, 1909.

Kornilov, A. *Kurs istorii Rossii XIX veka* (A Course in Russian History in the 19th Century). Moscow, 1912.

—— *Modern Russian History*. Translated from the Russian by A.S. Kaun. New York, 1943.

Kotoshikhin, Grigory. *O Rossii v tsarstvovaniye Alekseya Mikhailovicha* (On Russia in the Reign of Aleksei Mikhailovich). St. Petersburg, 1906.

Kovalevsky, Maxim. *Russian Political Institutions*. Chicago, 1902.

Krylenko, N. V. *Za pyat' let. 1918-1922 g.g.; obvinitel'nye rechi . . .* (For Five Years. 1918-1922. Speeches for the Prosecution . . .). Moscow, 1923.

Kucherov, Samuel. "Administration of Justice Under Nicholas I of Russia," *The American Slavic and East European Review*, VII (1948), No. 2.

————— "The Jury as Part of the Russian Judicial Reform of 1864." *The American Slavic and East European Review*, IX (1950) No. 2.

————— "The Case of Vera Zasulich," *The Russian Review*, XI 1952) No. 2.

Kulischer, E. M. "Gruzenberg kak advokat" (Gruzenberg as a Lawyer), in Gruzenberg, *Ocherki i rechi* (Sketches and Speeches). New York, 1944.

Lavrinovich, Yu. *Kto ustroil pogromy v Rossii* (Those Who Organized Pogroms in Russia). Berlin, n. d.

Lazarenko, A. N. "Ocherk osnovnykh nachal sudoustroistv Rossii i glavneishikh zapadno-evropeiskikh gosudarstv (Survey of the Basic Features of the Judicial System in Russia and in the Main West European Countries), in *S. U.* Vol I.

Le Berquier, Jules. *Le barreau moderne*. Paris, 1869.

Lemke, *Politicheskiye protsessy* (Political Trials). Petrograd, 1923.

Lenin, Vl. *Sochineniya* (Works). 2d ed. Moscow, 1926-1932.

—————. ———— 4th ed. Vol IV. Moscow, 1946.

Leroy-Beaulieu, A. *L'Empire des tsars et les Russes*. 3 vols. Paris, 1881-1889.

Lesser, M. A. *The Historical Development of the Jury System*. Rochester, 1894.

Lippmann, Walter. *An Inquiry into the Principles of the Good Society*. Boston, 1937.

Lokhvitsky, A. V. "O nashikh khodatayakh po delam" (On Our Solicitors), *Russkoe Slovo* (Russian Word), Febr. 1860, p. 43-46.

Lyublinsky, P. I. *Na smenu starago prava* (In Place of the Old Law). Petrograd, 1915.

————— "Sud i prava lichnosti" (The Court and the Rights of the Individual), in *Sudebnaya Reforma* (The Judicial Reform). Vol. II. Moscow, 1915.

————— *Svoboda lichnosti v ugolovnom protsesse* (Freedom of the Individual in Criminal Procedure). St. Petersburg, 1906.

M. A. "Predely vedomstva distsiplinarnago suda v soslovii prisyaznnykh poverennykh" (The Limits of Competence of the Disciplinary Court in the Corporation of Lawyers), *Yuridichesky Vestnik* (Juridical Herald), 1891, No. 9.

Maciejowski, W. *Slavische Rechtsgeschichte*. Stuttgart, 1835-1839.

MacIver, R. M. *The Modern State*. Oxford, 1926.

Maikov, P. M. *Vtoroye Otdeleniye Sobstvennoi Ego Imperatorskago Velichestva Kantselyarii, 1826-1882* (The Second Department of His Imperial Majesty's Own Chancellery, 1826-1882). St. Petersburg, 1906.

Makalinsky, P. V. *Sanktpeterburgskaya prisyazhnaya advokatura, 1868-1888* (The St. Petersburg Bar, 1868-1888). St. Petersburg, 1889.

Maklakov, V. A. *Rechi* (Speeches). Paris, 1949.

—— "Spasitel'noye predosterezheniye. Smysl dela Beilisa" (A Salutary Warning. The Significance of the Beilis Case), *Russkaya Mysl'* (Russian Thought), November, 1913.

——. "Tolstoi i sud" (Tolstoi and the Court), *Russkaya Mysl'* (Russian Thought), March, 1914.

Mandelstam, M. L. *1905 god v politicheskikh protsessakh. Zapiski zashchitnika.* (The Year 1905 in Political Trials. Memoirs of a Counsel). Moscow, 1931.

Margolin, A. D. *The Jews of Eastern Europe.* New York, 1926.

——. *V polose likvidatsii* (In the Period of Liquidation). St. Petersburg, 1911.

Markov, A. N. *Pravila advokatskoi professii v Rossii* (Rules of the Lawyer's Profession in Russia). Moscow, 1913.

Marx, K. i. F. Engels. *Sochineniya* (Works). Ed. by D. Ryazanov. Moscow, 1928-1939.

Meshchersky, V. P. *Moi vospominaniya* (My Reminiscences). 2 vols. St. Petersburg, 1897-1898.

Mill, John Stuart. *On Liberty.* Boston, 1863.

Mittermaier, Carl J. *Erfahrungen über die Wirksamkeit der Schwurgerichte in Europa und Amerika, über ihre Vorzüge, Mängel und Abhülfe.* Erlangen, 1864.

Mokrinsky, S. P. "Sud prisyazhnykh" (Court with Jury) in *S. U.* Vol. II.

Mollot, F. E. *Règles sur la profession d'avocat.* Paris, 1842.

Molodaya advokatura (The Young Bar). St. Petersburg, 1908.

Montesquieu, Charles, Baron de. *The Spirit of Laws.* Translated from the French by Thomas Nugent. London, 1773.

Moskovskiye Vedomosti (Moscow Records), 1884, No. 316; 1866, Nos. 198, 263; 1867, No. 69.

Mukhanov, "O nedostatkakh nashego suda prisyazhnykh" (On the Defects of Our Court with Jury), *Zhurnal grazhdanskago i ugolovnago prava* (Journal of Civil and Criminal Law), 1882, No. 3.

Muromtsev, S. A. "Sud i zakon v grazhdanskom prave" (Court and Law in Civil Law), *Yuridichesky Vestnik* (Juridical Herald), 1880, No. 11.

Nabokov, V. D. "Obshchaya kharakteristika sudebnoi reformy" (General Characteristics of the Judicial Reform), in *Sudebnaya Reforma* (The Judicial Reform). Vol. I. Moscow, 1915.

Naryshkin-Kurakin, Elizabeth. *Under Three Tsars.* Ed. by René Fülöp-Miller. Translated from the German by Julia E. Loesser. New York, 1931.

Neklyudov, N. A. "Zaklyucheniye ober-prokurora ugolovnago kassatsionnago departamenta senata po delu Mel'nitskikh" (Report of the Chief Prosecutor of the Criminal Department of Cassation of the Senate on the Mel'nitsky Case, *Zhurnal grazhdanskago i ugolovnago prava* (Journal of Civil and Criminal Law), 1884, No. 5.

Neumann, Franz Leopold. *Behemoth; the Structure and Practice of National Socialism.* Toronto-New York, 1944.
Nevyadomsky, D. "A. V. Lokhvitsky," *Zhurnal grazhdanskago i ugolovnago prava* (Journal of Civil and Criminal Law), 1884, No. 6.
————. *Vechnye voprosy advokatury* (Eternal Problems of Lawyers). Moscow, 1886.
Nikitenko, A. A. *Zapiski i dnevnik* (Notes and Diary). 2 vols. St. Petersburg, 1904-1905.
Nolde, Baron A. E. "Otnosheniya mezhdu sudebnoi i administrativnoi vlastyami i sud'ba osnovnykh nachal Sudebnykh Ustavov v pozdneishem zakonodatel'stve" (Relation Between the Judicial and Administrative Powers and the Fate of the Basic Principles of the Judicial Statutes in Subsequent Legislation) in *S. U.* Vol. II.
Obninsky, P. N. *Sbornik statei* (Collected Articles). Moscow, 1914.
Ogarev, N. "Razbor osnovnykh polozheny preobrazovaniya sudebnoi chasti v Rossii" (Review of the Basic Principles of the Judicial Reform in Russia), *Kolokol* (The Bell), Nov. 15, 1862.
Orlovsky, P. "Znacheniye sudebnoi praktiki v razvitii sovetskogo grazhdanskogo prava" (Importance of Judicial Practice in the Development of Soviet Civil Law), *Sovetskoye gosudarstvo i pravo* (Soviet State and Law), 1940, No. 8-9.
Orlovsky, S. "Voenno-polevye sudy" (Field Courts-Martial), in *Bol'shaya Sovetskaya Entsiklopediya* (The Great Soviet Encyclopaedia). Vol 12. Moscow, 1928.
Ortloff, H. "Staat und Gesellschaft in der Strafrechtspflege," *Der Gerichtssaal, XLVII* (1892), No. 2-3.
Ostrogorsky, M. *Yuridichesky kalendar'* (Juridical Calendar). Petrograd, 1914.
Otchet Soveta prisyazhnykh poverennykh pri Kazanskoi Sudebnoi palate za 1908/1909 g. (Report of the Council of the Bar attached to the Kazan *Sudebnaya Palata* for the year 1908/1909).
Otchet Soveta prisyazhnykh poverennykh pri Khar'kovskoi Sudebnoi Palate za 1906/1907 g. (Report of the Council of the Bar attached to the Kharkov *Sudebnaya Palata* for the year 1906/1907.)
Otchet Soveta prisyazhnykh poverennykh pri Moskovskoi Sudebnoi Palate za 1885/86, 1887/88, 1892/93, 1896/97, 1899/1900, 1902/03, 1903/04 g. (Report of the Council of the Bar attached to the Moscow *Sudebnaya Palata* for the years . . .).
Otchet Soveta prisyazhnykh poverennykh pri Odesskoi Sudebnoi Palate za 1908 g. (Report of the Council of the Bar attached to the Odessa *Sudebnaya Palata* for the year 1908).
Otchet Soveta prisyazhnykh poverennykh pri S. Peterburgskoi Sudebnoi Palate za 1881/82, 1889/90, 1897/98, 1905/06 g. (Report of the Council of the Bar attached to the St. Petersburg *Sudebnaya Palata* for the years . . .).
Otchet o deyatel'nosti Gosudarstvennago Soveta za 1889 g. (Report on on the Activity of the State Council for 1889). St. Petersburg, 1891.

Pares, Bernard. *A History of Russia.* New York, 1941.

Pascal, Blaise. *The Thoughts, Letters, and Opuscules.* Translated from the French by O. W. Wight. New York, 1869.

Pennock, James Roland. *Administration and the Rule of Law.* New York, [1941].

Peretz, E. A. *Dnevnik* (Diary). Moscow, 1927.

Pergamaint, Joseph. "Le barreau russe," *Journal du droit international privé et de la jurisprudence comparée,* XXIX (1902).

Pergament, O. Ya. *Obshchestvennyya zadachi advokatury* (The Public Tasks of the Bar). Odessa, 1905.

"Peter the Great in England," *The Book of Days,* I. London, 1863.

Picard, Edmond. *Scènes de la vie judiciaire. Paradoxe sur l'avocat.* Bruxelles, 1893.

Platonov, S. F. "O russkoi advokature" (On the Russian Bar), *Zhurnal grazhdanskago i ugolovnago prava* (Journal of Civil and Criminal Law), 1875; Nos. 3, 4 and 5; 1877, No. 6.

Plekhanov, G. V. *Sochineniya* (Works). Vol. V. Moscow, 1924.

Pletnev, V. "Raboty po sostavleniyu proyektov sudebnykh preobrazovany do 1861" (The Work of Planning of Judicial Reforms as of 1861), in *Sudebnaya Reforma* (Judicial Reform) Vol. I. Moscow, 1915.

K. P. Pobedonostsev i ego korrespondenty (Pobedonostsev and His Correspondents). Preface by M. N. Pokrovsky. Moscow, 1923.

Pobedonostsev, K. P. *Moskovsky sbornik* (Moscow Collection). Moscow. 1896.

—— "O reformakh v grazhdanskom sudoproizvodstve" (On Reforms in the Civil Procedure), *Russky Vestnik* (Russian Herald), 1859, June and July.

Pokrovsky, M. N. *Brief History of Russia.* Translated by D. S. Mirsky, New York, 1933.

—— *Russkaya istoriya s drevneishikh vremen* (Russian History from the Oldest Times). Moscow, 1922-1923.

Polnoye sobraniye zakonov Rossiiskoi Imperii (Complete Collection of Laws of the Russian Empire). *Sobraniye pervoye* (First Collection), 1649–11 Dec. 1825. St. Petersburg, 1830-1839

—— *Sobraniye vtoroye* (Ssecond Collection), 2 Dec. 1825–28 Feb. 1881. St. Petersburg, 1830-1884.

—— *Sobraniye tret'e* (Third Collection), 1 March 1881–31 Dec. 1913. St. Petersburg, 1885-1916.

Polyansky, N. N. "Mirovoi sud" (The Court of Justices of the Peace), in *Sudebnaya Reforma* (Judicial Reform). Vol. II. Moscow, 1915.

—— "Zashchita i obvineniye v delakh o gosudarstvennykh prestupleniyakh" (Defense and Accusation in Cases of Crimes Against the State), *Pravo* (Law), 1910, No. 36.

Potekhin, P. A. "Otryvki iz vospominany advokata" (Excerpts from the Reminiscences of a Lawyer), *Pravo* (Law), 1900, pp. 2213 ff.

Pravo (Law), 1914, Nos. 23-30.

Proffatt, John. *A Treatise on Trial by Jury.* San Francisco, 1877.

Protsess A. I. Gillersona (Trial of A. I. Gillerson). St. Petersburg, 1910.
Protsess 1-go marta 1881 g. (The Trial of March 1st, 1881). St. Petersburg, 1906.
Ram, James. *A Treatise of Facts as Subjects of Inquiry by a Jury.* New York, 1890.
Reinke, N. M. "Kassatsionnaya instantsiya" (The Cassation Instance), in *S. U.* Vol. II.
Resheniya Grazhdanskago kassatsionnago departamenta Pravitel'stvuyushchago Senata (Decision of the Civil Department of Cassation of the Ruling Senate), 1866-1916.
Resheniya Obshchago Sobraniya kassatsionnykh s uchastiyem Pervago i Vtorogo departamentov Pravitel'stvuyushchago Senata (Decisions of the General Assembly of the Departments of Cassation of the Ruling Senate, with the participation of the First and Second Departments), 1869-1906.
Resheniya Ugolovnago kassatsionnago departmenta Pravitel'stvuyushchego Senata (Decisions of the Criminal Department of Cassation of the Ruling Senate), 1869-1916.
Rogovin, L. M. *Sistematichesky sbornik deistvuyushchikh zakonov o evreyakh* (Classified Collection of Operative Laws Concerning Jews). St. Petersburg, 1913.
Rozin, N. N. *O sude prisyazhnykh* (On the Courts With Jury). Tomsk, 1901.
S. R. See *Sudebnaya Reforma.*
S. U. See *Sudebnye Ustavy 20 noyabrya 1864 goda za pyat'desyat let.*
S-ov, P. "Ob advokature v grazhdanskom protsesse" (On Lawyers in Civil Procedure), *Russky Vestnik* (Russian Herald), March 1859, Book 2.
Saltykov, M. E. (N. Shchedrin). *Polnoye sobraniye sochineny* (Complete Works). Ed. by Kirpotin. Moscow, 1933-1941.
―――― *Poshekhonskaya Starina* (Poshekhonsky Olden Times). In his *Polnoye sobraniye sochineny* (Complete Works). Vol. 12. Moscow, 1906.
Sbornik Imperatorskago Istoricheskago Obshchestva (Collection of the Imperial Historical Society). Vol. 23. St. Petersburg, 1878.
Schilder, N. K. *Imperator Nikolai I* (Emperor Nicholas I). 2 vols. St. Petersburg, 1903.
Seredonin. S. M. *Istorichesky obzor deyatel'nosti Komiteta Ministrov* (Historical Review of the Activity of the Committee of Ministers). 5 vols. St. Petersburg, 1902.
Sergeich, P. *Iskusstvo rechi na sude* (The Art of Speaking in Court). St. Petersburg, 1910.
Shatrov, N. "K voprosu o zashchite soznavshikhsya podsudimykh" (On the Question of the Defense of Accused Who Pleaded Guilty), *Pravo* (Law), 1903, pp. 2329-2333.
Shcheglovitov, I. G. "Novye popytki izmenit' postanovku suda prisyazhnykh v Zapadnoi Evrope" (New Attempts to Change the Organization of the Court with Jury in Western Europe), in *S. U.* Vol. II.

————— "Sud prisyazhnykh" (Court With Jury), *Zhurnal ministerstva yustitsii* (Journal of the Ministry of Justice), Nov. 1913.

————— "Vliyaniye inostrannykh zakonodatel'stv na sostavleniye Sudebnykh Ustavov 20 noyabrya 1864 goda" (Influence of Foreign Legislation Upon the Formation of the Judicial Statutes of November 20, 1864), in *S. U.* Vol. I.

Shchegolev, P. E. *Dekabristy* (The Decembrists). Moscow, 1926.

Shelgunov "Iz proshlago i nastoyashchago" (From the Past and the Present), *Russkaya Mysl'*, 1885, No. 11.

Shershenevich, G. F. "Primeneniye norm prava" (Application of Norms of Law), *Zhurnal ministerstva yustitsii* (Journal of the Ministry of Justice), 1903, No. 1.

————— *Uchebnik russkago grazhdanskago prava* (A Textbook of Russian Civil Law). Moscow, 1914.

Shipov, S. P. "Kratkoye obozreniye istorii sudoproizvodstva i sudoustroistva v Rossii" (Brief Survey of the History of the Judicial System and Judicial Procedure in Russia), *Vremennik Obshchestva istorii i drevnostei rossiiskikh* (Herald of the Society of Russian History and Antiquities), XXII, Moscow, 1855.

Shirkov, V. P. "Ocherk obshchikh osnovany nashego ugolovnago protsessa po sravneniyu s inostrannymi zakonodatel'stvami" (Survey of the Basic Features of Our Criminal Procedure as Compared with Foreign Legislations), in *S. U.* Vol. I.

Sieyès, Emmanuel Joseph. *Qu'est-ce que le tiers état?* Paris, 1888.

Sliozberg, G. B. "Advokatura za 25 let" (Twenty Five Years of the Bar), *Zhurnal grazhdanskago i ugolovnago prava* (Journal of Civil and Criminal Law), 1899, No. 9.

————— *Dela minuvshikh dnei* (In the Days of Old). 3 vols. Paris, 1933-1934.

Sobraniye uzakoneny i rasporyazheny pravitel'stva (Collection of Laws and Decrees of the Government). St. Petersburg, 1863-1917.

Sobraniye uzakoneny i rasporyazheny RSFSR (Collection of Laws and Decrees of the RSFSR), 1917.

Spasovich, V. D. "Ob organizatsii advokatury" (On the Organization of the Bar), *Zhurnal ministerstva yustitsii* (Journal of the Ministry of Justice), 1896, No. 3.

————— "Proshedshee i budushchee Sudebnykh Ustavov" (The Past and the Future of the Judicial Statutes [of November 20, 1864], *Pravo* (Law), 1899, pp. 2272-2275.

————— *Sochineniya* (Works). Vol. III. St. Petersburg, 1890.

————— *Zastol'nyya rechi* (After-Dinner Speeches). Leipzig, 1903.

Spencer, Herbert. *Social Statics; or the Conditions Essential to Human Happiness Specified, and the First of Them Developed.* New York, 1875.

————— *The Man Versus the State.* Caldwell, 1940.

Speransky, M. M. *Vvedeniye k Ulozheniyu 1809 goda* (Introduction to the Code of 1809). Moscow, 1915.

Stein, Lorenz von. *Geschichte der socialen Bewegung in Frankreich von 1789 bis auf unsere Tage.* Leipzig, 1850-1855. 3 vols.

Stolkind, A. Ya. "Pamyati O. O. Gruzenberga" (In Memory of O. O. Gruzenberg), in O. O. Gruzenberg, *Ocherki i Rechi* (Essays and Speeches). New York, 1944.
Stoyanov, A. *Istoriya advokatury* (The History of the Bar), Kharkov, 1869.
Sudebnaya Gazeta (Court Gazette). St. Petersburg, 1896, No. 29.
Sudebnaya Reforma (The Judicial Reform). Ed. by N. V. Davydov and N. N. Polyansky. 2 vols. Moscow, 1915. [Referred to in the notes as *S. R.*]
Sudebnye Ustavy 20 noyabrya 1864 goda s izlozheniyem razsuzhdeny na koikh oni osnovany (Judicial Statutes of November 20, 1864, With the Motives on Which They Are Based). St. Petersburg, State Chancellery, 1867. Vol. I: Ustav grazhdanskago sudoproivodstva (Code of Civil Procedure). Vol. II: Ustav ugolovnago sudoproizvodstva (Code of Criminal Procedure). Vol. III: Uchrezhdeniye sudebnykh ustanovleny (Statutes of Judicial Institutions). Vol. IV: Ustav o nakazaniyakh, nalagaemykh mirovymi sud'yami (Code of Laws on Punishments to be Inflicted by Justices of the Peace).
Sudebnye Ustavy 20 noyabrya 1864 goda za pyat'desyat let (Fifty Years of the Judicial Statutes of November 20, 1864). 2 vols. Petrograd 1914. [Referred to in the notes as *S. U.*]
Sveshnikov, M. I. "Gosudarstvennoye znacheniye Sudebnykh Ustavov" (Public Importance of the Judicial Statutes [of November 20, 1864]). *Pravo* (Law), 1899, pp. 2283-2289.
Svod osnovnykh gosudarstvennykh zakonov. Izdaniye 1906 goda. (Code of Fundamental Laws. 1906 edition). *Svod zakanov Rossiiskoi Imperii* (Code of Laws of the Russian Empire), Vol. I.
Svod ustavov o preduprezhdenii i presechenii prestupleny. Izdaniye 1890 goda (Code of Laws on the Prevention and Suppression of Crimes). *Svod zakonov Rossiiskoi Imperii* (Code of Laws of the Russian Empire), Vol. XIV.
Svod voyennykh postanovleny (Military Code). Book XXIV. St. Petersburg, 1869.
Svod zakonov Rossiiskoi Imperii. Izdaniye 1857 goda (Code of Laws of the Russian Empire. 1857 edition). 15 vols. St. Petersburg, 1857.
Svod zakonov Rossiiskoi Imperii. Polnyi tekst vsekh 16 tomov, soglasovanny s poslednimi prodolzheniyami, postanovleniyami . . . (Code of Laws of the Russian Empire. Complete text of all the sixteen volumes in accordance with the last amendments and decisions . . .). Edited and annotated by I. D. Mordukhai-Boltovsky. 5 vols. St. Petersburg, 1912-[1914].
Syromyatnikov, B. I. "Ocherk istorii suda v drevneishei i novoi Rossii" (Historical Sketch of the Court in Old and Modern Russia), in *S. R.*, Vol. I. Moscow, 1915.
Tager, A. S. "Nadzor za organami soslovnago samoupravleniya" (Supervision Over the Organs of Self-Government), in *Istoriya*

russkoi advokatury (History of the Russian Bar). Vol. III. Moscow, 1916.

Tager, A. S. *Tsarskaya Rossiya i delo Beilisa* (The Tsarist Russia and the Beilis Case). Moscow, 1934.

Tager, P. S. "Administrativnaya deyatel'nost' soveta prisyazhnykh poverennykh" (Administrative Functions of the Council of the Bar), in *Istoriya russkoi advokatury* (History of the Russian Bar) Vol. II. Moscow, 1916.

―――― "Organizatsiya sovetov" (The Organization of the Councils), in *Istoriya russkoi advokatury* (History of the Russian Bar). Vol. II. Moscow, 1916.

Talberg, D. G. *Russkoye ugolovnoye sudoproizvodstvo* (Russian Criminal Procedure). St. Petersburg, 1889.

Tarde, Gabriel de. *La philosophie pénale*. Lyon, 1890.

Timofeyev, N. P. *Sud prisyazhnykh v Rossii* (The Court With Jury in Russia). Moscow, 1881.

Tocqueville, A. de. *Democracy in America*. Translated by Henry Reeve New York, 1851.

Trainin, A. N. "Distsiplinarnoye proizvodstvo v sovete prisyazhnykh poverennykh" (Disciplinary Proceedings of the Council of the Bar), in *Istoriya russkoi advokatury* (History of the Russian Bar) Vol. II. Moscow, 1916.

Tsarizm v bor'be s revolutsiei (Tsarism in the Fight Against Revolution). Ed. by A. K. Drezen. Moscow, 1936.

Tsitron, I. L. "Zhisnenny put' O. O. Gruzenberga" (O. O. Gruzenberg's Life), in O. O. Gruzenberg, *Ocherki i rechi* (Essays and Speeches). New York, 1944.

Uchrezhdeniye sudebnykh ustanovleny. Izdaniye 1892 goda. (Statutes of Judicial Institutions. 1892 edition). *Svod zakonov Rosiiskoi Imperii* (Code of Laws of the Russian Empire). Vol. XVI, Pt. I.

Ugolovnoye ulozheniye 22 marta 1903 goda (Criminal Code of March 22, 1903). Published and commented upon by N. S. Tagantsev. Edited by P. N. Yakobi. Riga, 1922.

Ulozheniye o nakazaniyakh ugolovnykh i ispravitel'nykh 1885 g. (Code of Laws on Criminal and Correctional Punishments). Commented upon by N. S. Tagantsev. St. Petersburg, 1895.

Unkovsky, A. M. "Novye osnovaniya sudoproizvodstva" (New Principles of Juridical Procedure), *Sovremennik* (The Contemporary), 1883, No. 1.

Usherovich, S. *Smertnye kazni v tsarskoi Rossii* (Executions in Tsarist Russia). Kharkov, 1933.

Ustav grazhdanskago sudoproizvodstva. Izdanie 1892 goda. (Code of Civil Procedure. 1892 edition). *Svod zakonov Rosiiskoi Imperii* (Code of Laws of the Russian Empire). Vol. XVI, Pt. I.

Ustav ugolovnago sudoproizvodstva. Izdaniye 1892 goda. (Code of Criminal Procedure. 1892 edition). *Svod zakonov Rossiiskoi Imperii* (Code of Laws of the Russian Empire). Vol. XVI, Pt. I.

Vas'kovsky, E. V. "Advokatura" (The Bar), in S. U. Vol. II.
—— Budushcheye russkoi advokatury (The Future of the Bar). St. Petersburg, 1893.
—— Kurs grazhdanskago protsessa (A Course in Civil Procedure). Vol. I. Moscow, 1913.
—— "O razborchivosti pri prinyatii del k zashchite" (On Scrupulousness When Accepting Defense Cases), Zhurnal yuridicheskago obshchestva (Journal of the Juridical Society), 1894, No. 6.
—— Organizatsiya advokatury (The Organization of the Bar). 2 vol. St. Petersburg, 1893.
—— "Znacheniye advokatury i zadachi eya organizatsii" (The Importance of the Bar and Problems of Its Organization), Zhurnal ministerstva yustitsii (Journal of the Ministry of Justice), 1895, No. 9.
Vernadsky, George. A History of Russia. New York, 1944.
Vladimirov, L. E. Psikhologicheskoye izsledovaniye v ugolovnom sude (Psychological Investigation in Criminal Court). Moscow, 1901.
—— Sud prisyazhnykh i metod razrabotki dokazatel'stv (Court With Jury). Kharkov, 1873.
—— Advocatus miles. St. Petersburg, 1911.
Vladimirsky-Budanov, M. F. Obzor istorii russkago prava (Review of the History of Russian Law). Kiev, 1905.
Vsepoddanneishy doklad ministra yustitsii N. V. Murav'yova o deyatel'nosti ministerstva yustitsii za 10 let 1894-1904 (Report on the Activities of the Ministry of Justice for 10 Years—1894-1904—submitted to His Majesty by Minister of Justice N. V. Murav'yov). St. Petersburg, 1904.
Vyshinsky, A. Ya. "Advokatura" (The Bar), in Entsiklopediya gosudarstva i prava (Encyclopedia of State and Law). Vol. I. Moscow, 1925.
—— Marksistsko-leninskoye ucheniye o sude i sovetskaya sudebnaya sistema (The Marxist-Leninist Doctrine of the Court and the Soviet Judicial System). Moscow, 1935.
—— Revolyutsionnaya zakonnost' i zadachi sovetskoi zashchity (Revolutionary Legality and Problems of the Defense in Soviet Courts). Moscow, 1934.
—— editor. Sovetskoye gosudarstvennoye pravo (Soviet Constitutional Law). Moscow, 1938.
—— Sud i prokuratura (The Court and the Prosecution). Moscow, 1937.
Vysochaishe uchrezhdennaya komissiya dlya peresmotra zakonopolozheny po sudebnoi chasti. Ob"yasnitel'naya zapiska (Commission on the Review of Legislation Concerning the Administration of Justice. Established by the Emperor. Explanatory note). 3 vols. St. Petersburg, 1900.
Wallace, Sir Donald Mackenzie. Russia. 2 vols. London, 1877.
Wasson, R. Gordon. Toward a Russian Policy. Stamford, 1951.

Winaver, M. M. *Advokatura i pravovoye gosudarstvo* (The Bar and the State Under the Rule of Law). St. Petersburg, 1905.

—— *Nedavneye* (Recent Times). Paris, 1926.

—— *Ocherki ob advokature* (Essays on the Bar). St. Petersburg, 1902.

M. M. *Winaver i russkaya obshchestvennost' v nachale XX veka* (M. M. Winaver and Russian Society at the Beginning of the 20th Century). Paris, 1937.

Wright, Benjamin F., Jr. "The Origin of the Separation of Powers in America," 13 *Economica,* 1933.

Yakimov, A. "Bol'shoi protsess ili protsess 193" (The Great Trial, or the Trial of 193 Persons), *Katorga i ssylka* (Forced Labor and Banishment), 1927, No. 8.

Zagorovsky, A. I. "Otzyv ob uchenykh trudakh privat-dotsenta E. V. Vas'kovskago" (Criticism of the Scientific Works of Assistant Professor V. E. Vas'kovsky), *Zapiski Imperatorskago Novorossiiskago Universiteta* (Notes of the Imperial Novorossiisk University), XCVII (1904).

Zaionchkovsky, A. M. *Vostochnaya voina, 1853-1856 (Eastern War, 1853-1856).* St. Petersburg, 1908.

Zakhar'in, I. N. "*Razskazy iz prezhnei sudebnoi praktiki*" (Stories from Past Juridical Activity), *Russkaya Starina* (Russian Antiquity), IX (1874).

Zasulich, V. I. "Vospominaniya" (Reminiscences), *Byloye* (The Past), 1919, No. 14.

Zavadsky, A. V. *Nesmenyaemost' sud'i i ego nezavisimost'* (Irremovability of the Judge and His Independence). Kazan, 1903.

Zhurnal Soyedinennago Departamenta Gosudarstvennago Soveta, (Journal of the Joint Department of the State Council), 1864.

INDEX

333